D1496900

THE POLITICS OF PUBLIC SPENDING IN CANADA

Ten people meet for the first time over lunch. They must decide whether they will share one check or ask for ten separate ones. In theory, if they decide on one shared check they will all choose the most expensive items. But if each were paying individually they would probably have chosen differently: nobody would want to miss the best food while paying for someone else to have it.

With this analogy, Donald Savoie tackles government's increased spending and our inability to cut back existing programs. He argues that they are rooted in the regional nature of Canada and in the fear that unless we all eat the best at the public banquet we will lose our share of public largesse. Savoie identifies the forces fuelling new government spending and also those that inhibit efforts to reduce it.

The regional factor is of first importance, but Savoie also looks at forces such as the role of the private sector and the pressures of special interest groups. Supporters of a new day-care program, for example, are likely to compare the cost of their proposal with other government measures in order to justify it. A regional minister in Newfoundland seeking support for construction of new wharfs is less likely to do a cost-benefit analysis of the project than to compare it with expenditures on an expansion of an airport in central Ontario.

Savoie has carried out extensive interviews with policy makers to find out how priorities are established within the federal government, how the planning process works, and how conflict develops between two groups in the budget process: the guardians and the spenders. Both increased spending and the inability to cut programs, Savoie argues, are the result of Canada's regional nature and the perception in various ministries that large budgets are a means for maintaining power and enhancing prestige. He concludes with suggestions for controlling spending, and makes a plea for important changes in the future.

DONALD J. SAVOIE is Executive Director, Institut canadien de recherche sur le développement régional and Professor of Public Administration, University of Moncton. He is the author of numerous books and articles including *Regional Economic Development: Canada's Search for Solutions*, and has published widely in journals of political science, public policy, and public administration.

Donald J. Savoie

THE POLITICS OF PUBLIC SPENDING IN CANADA

UNIVERSITY OF TORONTO PRESS
Toronto Buffalo London

© University of Toronto Press 1990
Toronto Buffalo London
Printed in Canada

ISBN 0-8020-5847-7 (cloth)
ISBN 0-8020-6755-7 (paper)

Printed on acid-free paper

Canadian Cataloguing in Publication Data

Savoie, Donald J., 1947–
    The politics of public spending in Canada

    Includes bibliographical references.
    ISBN 0-8020-5847-7 (bound). – ISBN 0-8020-6755-7 (pbk.)

    1. Government spending policy – Canada.
    2. Canada – Appropriations and expenditures.
    I. Title.

    HJ7660.S38 1990   336.3′9′0971   C89-094868-2

62,586

Dedicated to Julien Z. and Margaux C. Savoie

So two cheers for Democracy; one because it admits variety and two because it permits criticism. Two cheers are quite enough; there is no occasion to give three.

E.M. Forster

Contents

viii Contents

Preface

All writers are more in debt to others than is generally assumed. I owe a great deal to all those who travelled the territory before me and I acknowledge many intellectual debts in the notes. Others, however, are not so formally acknowledged. I must first thank the many present and former cabinet ministers, permanent federal officials, and representatives of the private sector, who gave so generously of their time and cheerfully dealt with all my questions. Several government officials also made important new data available. Interviews proved invaluable not simply as a source of information. They were an excellent opportunity to tap new ideas and test my own views on those who make the system work day after day.

I would like to single out Senator Lowell Murray and Gérard Veilleux, secretary of the Treasury Board. I met with Senator Murray on numerous occasions during the time I was researching this book. His insightful comments on Canadian politics and on the politics of governing led me to explore several avenues and issues that I had not – and would not have – identified. Mr Veilleux took a strong interest in my work, patiently answered all my questions on countless occasions, freely made his views known, and continually challenged my thinking. This is not to suggest that Senator Murray, Mr Veilleux, or any other official I consulted will agree with the findings of the study. Some are likely to disagree strongly with my conclusions. For this reason, I want to stress, with more than the usual emphasis, that the conclusions of this study are mine alone and I take full responsibility for them.

No doubt it would have been entertaining to attribute points and quotes directly to those I interviewed. It would also have been inappropriate to do so, because many specifically requested anonymity. They, however, know who they are and to what extent I am in their debt.

I am also indebted to John K. Galbraith. He was the first to suggest that I should write on government spending. I attended one of his lectures in 1986 where he expressed his deep concern about the inability of governments to do things right. I was taken aback that a leading liberal of the twentieth century and an influential advocate of increased government management of the economy would express concern over the presence of the state in society. We corresponded after the lecture, and in September 1986 I spent a delightful afternoon with him at his Cambridge home. He spoke at length about the growing 'ineptitude' of government and suggested that government bureaucracies had given the left a bad reputation. His view of the importance of a study on government spending also encouraged me. The major task now, he argued, was not to defend what government is doing or to suggest that new government activities be launched but rather to see to it that government does better what it is now doing. I would ask nothing more from the many hours I put into this work if in some small way it could be of benefit to students and practitioners of public administration in Canada.

The study will be of interest to students of public spending, in particular those who seek to understand the various forces fuelling spending in the federal government. These forces are both powerful and stubborn – they have consistently pushed back the most determined guardians of the public purse.

Sooner or later (and probably sooner), the book will also be of interest to even the most spendthrift cabinet ministers and officials. Eventually they will have to accept that we simply cannot keep on adding new costly government programs and initiatives without discarding some existing ones. The accumulated debt cannot continue growing at the rate it has since the early 1980s.

Ministers and officials in spending departments may well object to a study detailing their spending habits. They could claim that they are already subjected to close scrutiny through the work of the Public Accounts Committee, the auditor general, and the media, among others. Still, spending departments enjoy a monopoly position. They have a single source of income – public revenues – and there is no market mechanism to 'pressure' them to be efficient.

Several friends and colleagues have read parts or all of the manuscript of this book and have made important suggestions to improve the study.

I owe special thanks to John K. Galbraith, Robert A. Young, G. Bruce Doern, Gérard Veilleux, Nick Mulder, Benjamin Higgins, Jean Higgins, Cynthia Williams, Andy Stark, Peter Aucoin, and two reviewers selected by the University of Toronto Press. I greatly benefited from their comments and suggestions in revising the work. I owe a special debt to the reviewers of the University of Toronto for their forthright, perceptive, and constructive criticism of an earlier draft of this study. Their comments led me to undertake a substantial rewrite of several chapters. But all the defects of the book are mine.

I also owe a special thank you to Ginette Benoît and Colette Allain for typing and retyping the manuscript. Joan Harcourt and Mary McDougall Maude have made numerous editorial suggestions and the book is greatly improved as a result. I want to thank Christine Fisher, who delayed a trip to Britain to prepare my index.

As always, my family accepted with good cheer my decision to write this book. I can hardly overstate what their support has meant to me. I dedicate this book to our children, Julien and Margaux.

Acronyms of frequently employed phrases

A base	Resources required to continue existing programs into the next fiscal year at the same level of operation
ACOA	Atlantic Canada Opportunities Agency
B Budget	Amount of funds available for new program initiatives
BOGO	Bureau of Government Organization
CCDM	Committee of Co-ordinating Deputy Ministers
DREE	Department of Regional Economic Expansion
DRIE	Department of Regional Industrial Expansion
FAA	Financial Administration Act
FBDB	Federal Business Development Bank
FPRO	Federal-Provincial Relations Office
IMAA	Increased Ministerial Authority and Accountability
IMPAC	Improved Management Practices and Controls
IRDP	Industrial and Regional Development Program
MOUS	Memorandum of Understanding between the Treasury Board and line departments in implementing IMAA
MSERD	Ministry of State for Economic and Regional Development
MSSD	Ministry of State for Social Development
MTF	Nielsen 'Ministerial Task Force' Review
MYHRP	Multi-Year Human Resources Plan
MYOP	Multi-Year Operational Plan
OCG	Office of the Comptroller General
OPF	Operational Plan Framework
PAC	Public Accounts Committee
P & P	Cabinet Committee on Priorities and Planning
PCO	Privy Council Office
PEMS	Policy and Expenditure Management System

PMO	Prime Minister's Office
PPB	Planning, Programming and Budgeting System
TBS	Treasury Board Secretariat
UI	Unemployment Insurance Program

THE POLITICS OF PUBLIC SPENDING IN CANADA

1

Introduction

The expenditure budget states in dollars and cents – that is, in the most concrete of terms – who is to get what from government. This may well conjure up images of thick documents filled with numbers and obscure messages written in 'bureaucratese,' but in the end its importance can hardly be overemphasized. Two students of public administration, for example, have observed that 'budgeting is the most important annual ritual of government – the World Series of Government, or perhaps the Grey Cup of Government within the Canadian context.'[1]

The expenditure budget process is vitally important simply because it acts as the government's nervous system. It sends out signals to every department and agency and to all public servants about what is important to the government. The merits of new programs and new initiatives can be fully debated in public forum, in government departments, and even in cabinet, but they can never be pursued unless funds are made available. A senior official of the Treasury Board secretariat puts its this way: 'The budget process is about people competing for scarce resources, about the interplay of people, ideas, and goals and finally about decisions, real decisions, that lay down who won and who lost.'[2] Budgets, it has also been suggested, ' are the life blood of departments, supplying the transfusions of cash necessary for programs to operate, salaries to be paid, and public agencies to survive. Those cabinet ministers and public servants who do not recognize the crucial importance of the budget are destined to have short or low-profile careers.[3]

If the expenditure budget is about who wins and who loses, then on the face of it one can assume that there have been plenty of winners during the past fifty years. The dramatic growth in government spending has been well documented elsewhere, and there is no need to recapitulate it in detail. A brief look at the increasing scope in government spending, however, may provide a useful perspective.

Total federal government budgetary spending in 1920–1 was $476 million. This fell to $352 million in 1923–4. In 1939, total expenditure stood at $553 million and this figure included a special $25 million contribution for debt adjustment in drought area relief. In 1950–1 it amounted to $2.4 billion; in 1960–1, to $6.7 billion; in 1970–1, to $15.3 billion; in 1980–1, to $62 billion; in 1983–4, to $96.6 billion; and in 1987 – 8, to $122.5 billion. Total government spending as a percentage of the gross domestic product (GDP) represents a more accurate comparison of year-to-year increase in government spending, in the scope of government activity, and in assessing the size of government in relation to the size of the economy. The federal government expenditure budget represented 6.8 per cent of GDP in 1930–1, 16.0 per cent in 1940–1, 12.8 per cent in 1950–1, 17.6 per cent in 1960–1, 21.0 per cent in 1976–7, 23.6 per cent in 1982–3, and 23.0 per cent in 1986–7. In 1978–9 the net public debt stood at $60 billion compared with $85.7 billion in 1980–1, $160.8 billion in 1983–4, and $265 billion in 1986–7. Another useful comparison is the percentage of the total expenditure budget which is allocated to service the public debt. In 1960, 11.2 per cent of the total budget went to servicing the debt compared with 12.2 per cent in 1970, 16.2 per cent in 1980, and 23.0 per cent in 1987. In his first major economic statement as minister of finance, Michael Wilson declared: 'If we reach the point where we must start borrowing money just to pay the interest on our debts, we know we have a serious problem. But this is the situation in which the government of Canada finds itself today. This year almost 50 percent of government borrowing is required just to cover interest costs.'[4] By the time he tabled his fourth budget, well over 90 per cent of government borrowing was required to pay public debt charges.

SCOPE AND CONTRIBUTION OF STUDY

Several important questions will be addressed in this book. Why has allocation of resources never been able to replace addition of resources as the operating principle of the federal government's budgetary process? Does the decision-making process itself contribute to increased government spending? Has Canadian regionalism contributed to the growth in spending, and, if so, to what extent? When the costs of some programs increase, why are others not reduced to keep spending as a proportion of GDP constant? What roles do politicians play in expanding the scope of government activity and spending? What roles do permanent officials play? What forces will trigger a positive response inside government to spend on any given initiative? Given their different interests, how well do central agency and line department officials work together? Are some ministers and officials better than others at getting new money? This then is a study about the process involved.

The study's second objective is to demonstrate how decisions are made in government. In their widely read book on the British expenditure budget, Hugh Heclo and Aaron Wildavsky pointed out that one of the purposes of their book was to use the expenditure process 'as a spotlight for illuminating the characteristic practices of British government.'[5] This study has a similar purpose. Most important policy issues involve money. In Canada, as elsewhere, 'money talks.' And, as in Britain, the task of allocating money in the federal government 'is the most pervasive and informative operation of government.'[6] An examination of how spending decisions are made should reveal a great deal about the role of politicians and senior officials, and how they work together. It should also provide an 'immense window' on the administration of the federal government.

A great deal has been said of late about the increasing influence of permanent officials on policy and decision making in government. This is just one criticism of the federal public service. It stands accused of many other things, such as being 'large, cumbersome, expensive, and insensitive.'[7] Senior officials are well aware of this criticism. 'Bureaucrat bashing,' in the words of a highly respected federal senior official, 'is now in vogue.' He adds: 'It is not too much of an exaggeration to suggest that public administration in Canada today is at an historic juncture. Some very fundamental questions are being asked, more and more urgently, about the role of government in society, about how government is organized, and about public servants, their roles and relationships and the skills and values they need to do their job.'[8] I hope that a study on the struggle for money in government will shed some light on these questions. They are important questions, not simply for public administration but also for politics. So far, these questions have not attracted the kind of attention they deserve. As well, while exploring other important issues that affect public administration and politics, such as national unity, observers have often neglected the federal government expenditure budget.

The reason for this neglect is probably 'not because insiders will not

tell but because outsiders assume they already know.'[9] Nothing could
be further from reality. Compared to our knowledge of certain policy
sectors – such as the workings of federal-provincial relations and parliament – we know little about how the federal budget process works, and
we appreciate even less the kind of tensions it entails between ministers,
government departments, and regions.[10] I hope that this book will make
a useful contribution on this front.

In addition, the bulk of the literature dealing with public expenditure
attempts to explain the *total* levels of government spending only, to
deal with fiscal issues of federalism and to provide an assessment of
microeconomic performance and fiscal policy. Few attempt to explain
the allocation of resources between departments, or the impact a particular decision-making process can have on spending patterns. One would
be hard pressed to find more than a few studies on the politics of public
spending at the micro or agency level and accompanying decision-
making processes from the 'hundreds' of authors whose main field of
interest is public expenditure.[11] This study looks specifically at the
search for resources at the ministerial, departmental, and agency levels.

To do this I employ the 'guardian-spenders' framework, first
employed by Aaron Wildavsky in his analysis of the American budgetary
process and later with Hugh Heclo in their study of government spending in Britain.[12] Essentially, policy actors are viewed as a community, a
village if you like, with shared experiences and rules that govern their
behaviour. Spending departments act as advocates for their programs
and for increased spending while central agencies, such as (in Canada)
the Department of Finance and the Treasury Board secretariat try as
best they can to exert control on spending as guardians of the Treasury.
Wildavsky explains: 'Each expects the other to do its job; agencies can
advocate, knowing the centre will impose limits, and this centre can
exert control, knowing that agencies will push agencies as hard as they
can ... The interaction between spending and cutting roles makes up
the component elements of budgetary systems ... Every agency wants
more money; the urge to survive and expand is built in ... agencies are
advocates of their own expenditures, not guardians of the nation's
purse. And the job of the finance ministry ... is to see that they don't get
it.'[13] This is the first time that this approach has been applied to the
study of the expenditure budget process in Canada.

Though few are likely to put down this book thinking that it was too
short, some may think that some topics were not covered to the extent
that they would have liked. I do not, for example, deal extensively with

the revenue side of the budget. My interest is focussed on the spending side. Still, revenues are obviously important to the budget process and outcome and have an impact on the deficit. Accordingly, I outline briefly the more important developments on the revenue side of the budget since the early 1970s. These developments, as we will see, contributed to increases in the federal deficit.

THE LITERATURE

There is a growing body of literature that seeks to explain the growth in government spending. I do not propose in this study to present a detailed survey of the various theories. There are two excellent Canadian books that do this: Richard Bird's *The Growth of Government Spending*, and Doug Hartle's *A Theory of the Expenditure Budgetary Process*.[14] Although published in the 1970s, both books contain a thoughtful analysis and remain highly relevant today.

I recognize that those who toil away in government departments see little merit in attempting to define new theories of public spending or even to refine existing ones. The great majority of officials I consulted made this clear. They asked time and again why students of the expenditure budget process should attempt to run when they have yet to learn to walk. There is much work to be done, they insist, before students of public administration can realistically expect to produce general theories on spending. Theories depend on generalizations. Government officials directly involved in the expenditure budget process will invariably argue that to generalize is to oversimplify. To them the practice of budget making is much too untidy a business for generalizations. They consider that theories of public expenditure exude an aura of other-worldliness and hardly apply to the give and take of budget making.

Situations, they insist, are unique, each located in its own set of variables that cannot be scientifically explained. The problem of quantifying factors makes this impossible. They also argue that it is impossible to ignore variations of time and place if one seeks to understand the forces behind the development of the expenditure budget. A sudden monthly surge or drop in public opinion polls can lead the governing party, for example, to loosen the purse-strings. In addition, the role individual politicians and public servants play in the budget process is crucial and adds to the problem of establishing a definitive theory to explain all aspects of government spending. Some of the leading students of government spending agree with practitioners that an all-encompassing theory is impossible to achieve. Doug Hartle, for example, summed up the difficulty in this way: 'It is not possible to predict the precise outcome of the budgetary game, because there is so much room for strategic behaviour within complex sets of rules. The outcome depends largely on perceptions of perceptions rather than on facts. Personalities are important.[15] To be sure, all the theories that have been brought forward have strong critics, and even the most ardent supporter of one particular viewpoint will recognize that it contains shortcomings and is not complete. Two students of Canadian public administration explain that in Canada, as elsewhere, 'there is no single, widely accepted explanation for the growth of government ... Rather there are many explanations, some competing, and others complementary, each containing, no doubt, some element of truth.'[16]

Still, any author who sets out to push back the frontier of knowledge, even if his objectives are modest, has some theoretical obligations. Students of public policy and public administration also have a responsibility 'to probe current theories for weaknesses and develop new, more promising avenues of inquiry.'[17] This is after all the most promising avenue we have to develop new knowledge about how the 'real world works.'

My objectives on the theoretical front are modest. This study does not attempt to set out an all-encompassing theory to explain the growth in government spending. I outline briefly the most important theories and, in the concluding chapter, identify the theory that holds most promise, both for explaining the growth in spending and for further research and inquiry. It has not been possible in this study to give more than a superficial account of the relevant theories and literature; the reader is encouraged to consult the works of the students identified below to gain a full appreciation of the literature in the field.

There are both normative and positive theories of public expenditure. Normative theories are helpful in explaining 'past reality' but are of little assistance in telling us much about the future. They are also not concerned with government decision-making processes, about conflicting interests, about voters, politicians, and permanent officials. Indeed normative theories are 'based on assumptions that ... the decision-making process is irrelevant.'[18]

A well-known normative theory is Wagner's Law. Named after German economist, Adolph Wagner, it argues that growth in government spending is inevitable because of rising per capita incomes, urbanization, more complex communication requirements resulting from greater labour specializations, and so on. There are now a number of recent studies on the application of Wagner's Law and in particular on the influence of socio-economic factors, such as rising per capita income. They purport to show a direct link between increased government activity and the development of the modern economy. For example, the advent of the automobile and air travel meant that highways and airports had to be developed. Rules and regulations had to be devised to oversee the use of roads and air space. Moreover, new economic activities compelled governments to introduce consumer protection programs. Governments have also been drawn into new policy areas, such as energy, environment protection, and the sale of atomic power, which had been of no concern to past governments. Increased population also entails the expansion of government. The provision of public services to twenty-five million people in the 1980s requires larger expenditures than providing even similar services to ten million people in the 1930s. Rising income levels bring greater demand for government services, such as education and health care.

One of the most prolific students of government spending, Aaron Wildavsky, has suggested that incrementalism explains in large measure the growth in spending. He observes: 'The largest factor of the size of this year's budget is last year's budget. Most of the budget is a product of previous decisions.'[19] Politicians and officials, the argument goes, are incapable of stopping and starting programs quickly. Changes are simply incorporated into existing programs, but these relatively minor adjustments often only serve to extend the scope of the programs, and hence government spending continues to grow. Many other students of government support Wildavsky's conclusion. Henry Aaron, for example, insists that the one frequent explanation why some government programs are larger than others is that they were established earlier and had more time to grow.[20] In his study of the workings of the welfare state, Harold Wilensky concluded: 'Once a program is launched, precedent is the major determinant of who gets what the government has to give, and how much goes to the program or agency depends on what it got the last time around.'[21]

Wildavsky has in more recent years tried to go further and explain why incrementalism is essentially a one-way street or to determine 'what factors are operating in the environment of government ... apart from incremental processes that lead to selection of increases and rejection of decreases.'[22] He has come forward with some explanations. He presents a counter–Wagner law by suggesting that 'the size of spending in relation to the size of national product increases when economic growth declines not, as according to Wagner's law, when it rises.'[23] He looks to various forces to explain why this is so through a comparative study of budgeting in Britain, France, Japan, and the United States. He reports that the era of 'industrial maturity' has produced three spending trends: increased spending on social programs, a relative decrease in military spending, and an inability to increase revenues to keep pace with spending. He then develops what he labels a 'cultural theory of budgeting' maintaining that 'the size of the state today is a function of its political culture yesterday.'[24] Various countries, he asserts, have moved, albeit at different speeds, towards large government and redistributive measures, but prevailing economic and political conditions and ideology only tell part of the story. He insists that 'a cultural theory of government growth fits the facts better ... (so that) the size of government in any given society is a function (consequence, if you prefer) of its combination of political cultures.'[25] Wildavsky's brief contrast of Canadian and American political cultures is well worth quoting: 'The cultural difference is that the United States has had strong markets and weak hierarchies while both hierarchies and markets have been strong in Canada, though heirarchical norms do weaken as one travels west ... the consequences for legislation have been that Canadian public policy has been more egalitarian and redistributive than in the United States, while manifesting greater concern (due to market influence) for limiting total spending than is found in Europe.'[26]

One of the most important developments in the literature on government spending in recent years has been the emergence of self-interest theories of collective decision making or public choice theories. The works of James Buchanan, Anthony Downs, Gordon Tullock, William Niskanen, and Canadians Albert Breton and Doug Hartle should be consulted to gain a full appreciation of the public choice theories. The public choice school is of particular interest to this study because of its focus on the behaviour of policy and decision makers.

It is possible to trace the roots of public choice to Adam Smith and classical liberal economics. It owes its original inspiration to the application of the concept of economic man to the political and government arena. Public choice theorists suggest that politicians, permanent officials, and interest groups (albeit operating outside of government) continually seek to influence budgetary decisions. The behaviour of government decision makers is explained in terms of their own self-interest. In the case of politicians, their goal is to retain power, and the theory reports that in the budget process their behaviour is geared to ensuring the maximum number of votes come the next general election. Given that the poor in western democracies outnumber the rich and that politicians continually seek to maximize votes, new government programs will invariably be introduced and existing ones expanded. Anthony Downs, for example, explains that politicians 'act solely in order to attain the income, prestige and power which come from being in office. Thus politicians ... never seek office as a means of carrying out particular policies; their only goal is to reap the rewards of holding office.'[27]

James Buchanan and Gordon Tullock, among others, also argue that it is indeed possible to understand political decisions by understanding individual self-interest. The *Calculus of Consent* analyses the costs and benefits to the individual of government coercion. It asks several fundamental questions about the behaviour of individuals and interest groups and about the nature and degree of collectivization. They reject majority rule for the political arena, suggesting that as one goes further and further away from unanimity rule, it becomes increasingly difficult to determine whether decisions made are in the public interest. Interest groups can under majority rule arrange for discriminatory measures and by extension induce other interest groups to seek concessions or their own discriminatory measures. They conclude that an interest group will 'turn every effort toward improving its own position, within the limits of the prevailing rules.'[28]

Public servants, like politicians, are motivated by self-interest. The public servants' salaries and prestige invariably increase with larger budgets and more staff. Departments, as well as individual administrative units, therefore, always seek to maximize the size of their budgets and organizations. The strategies employed by public servants to increase their own budget allocations have been well documented. We are told that they overstate the benefits and underestimate the costs of proposed initiatives to make them more appealing to politicians, opt for policies that invariably require large organizations to administer, and prefer government action to the operation of the free market to resolve real or perceived problems.

William Niskanen has looked at how government departments and bureaux secure financial resources and concludes that bureaucrats are biased in favour of their own sector – the public sector – and that spending departments hold great advantage over anyone who would seek to limit increases. He attempts to show that the budgets are a direct outcome of the departmental 'maximizing behaviour of the sponsors and managers of bureaus.'[29] He argues that, given that government managers know how effective their programs are and that clients do not, the senior bureaucrats can function much like a monopoly supplier. As a result, even if they wanted to be demanding, the clients and those inside government who would want to restrict spending are not sufficiently aware of the costs and effectiveness to take the managers on. In short, bureaucrats invariably push the government decision-making process towards policies and programs that increase their own budgets. The result is that government spending grows, not because the population or even politicians wish it but because bureaucrats want it.

The application of the public choice theory to explain the behaviour of public servants has gained considerable popularity in recent years, and many social scientists believe it to be the most likely explanation for the growth in government spending. One, for example, recently went so far as to suggest that 'government bureaucrats, like any other bureaucrat (or indeed, any other people), are quick to seize on new program possibilities that promise general advancement – again, virtually without regard to likely results. Unless we try massive lobotomies, we are unlikely to change behaviour so rooted in human nature.'[30]

Two Canadians have also made substantial contributions to the public choice school. Albert Breton and Doug Hartle have both produced important works. Breton's widely read book, *The Economic Theory of Representative Government*, attempts to intergrate the work of several other public choice theorists.[31] He also seeks to identify the various forces that determine the demand for public policies and government programs. He compares the individual's demands for private and public goods and suggests that it is impossible, for example, for individuals to sell their access to public goods or to buy more of a public policy that they desire. Breton makes several points that are of special interest to this study. He argues that politicians in government trade with one another until a mutually acceptable coalition is struck. The purpose of the coalition is to ensure their government's re-election. Breton also looks at the behaviour of bureaucrats and concludes that they continually seek to expand the size of their bureax and the number of programs they administer. He argues: 'It is through maximization of this objective that bureaucrats are able to achieve the highest possible income and prestige consistent with the constraints to which they are subjected ... It also implies that bureaucrats are not responsive to the preferences of citizens, but are solely guided in their actions by the network of relationships linking them to politicians and other bureaucrats.' He adds that, other than through their relationships with politicians, 'bureaucrats have a professional life of their own and a pattern of life unrelated to the preferences of citizens.'[32]

Of particular interest to this study, however, is Doug Hartle's recent book *The Expenditure Budget Process of the Government of Canada: A Public Choice – Rent-Seeking Perspective*. It is of strong interest for several reasons. For one thing, he applies a public choice/rent-seeking perspective to the Canadian government expenditure budget. For another, he looks at some of the same forces I do, including the roles of political and bureaucratic actors in policy making, as well as the role of some key central agencies. Other than introducing the public choice/rent-seeking framework to the Canadian experience, Hartle makes important observations. He concludes that 'the most significant changes in the expenditure budget process are brought about when and only when the prevailing economic and political climate is propitious ... (and) the pervasive force of the status quo is surely a reflection of the endurance of well-entrenched rent-seeking groups.'[33] In the concluding chapter I will contrast and compare Hartle's conclusions with my own.

The public choice theorists, however, have been challenged on a number of fronts in Canada and elsewhere.[34] The Canadian political science literature, for example, has been broadly critical of them. Sandford Borins questions not only some of the findings public choice theorists have produced but also their research methods. He rejects, for example, the advice of public choice economists, such as Trebilcock, to avoid interviews with politicians and officials because they are always self-serving.[35] Borins points out that the files and the necessary data are not always readily available and that in some instances interviews are the only way to get at the information.[36]

Some political scientists, such as Samuel Beer and Alan Cairns (that is, the institutionalists), have looked to federal-state or provincial relations as an explanation for the growth in government spending. They argue that the pressure for increased spending in a federal country is substantially higher than in a unitary state. Alan Cairns explains: 'Eleven governments pursuing visions instead of one, 200 ministers building empires instead of 25, several hundred departmental heirarchies of civil servants seeking expansion of their activities instead of a tenth as many – all these provide an extensive supplementary impetus to the normal pressures for the expansion of the public service which are present in politics.'[37] It is, of course, well known that the federal and the provincial

governments continually compete to gain 'credit, status, and importance.' The constant jockeying for importance and visibility between the
'federalists' and the Quebec government in the late 1970s and early
1980s is an excellent case in point. But the competition for visibility
between the federal government and the provincial governments
extends well beyond Quebec. Such competition often involves the
spending of public money.

THE SETTING

There are of course a variety of reasons why government spending has
expanded on all cylinders during the past fifty years and particularly
over the past twenty-five. Robert B. Bryce, former deputy minister of
finance, has documented the heated debate the first 'Keynesian' budget
in Canada occasioned in cabinet.[38] Ever since, government has intervened to attenuate the lows in economic cycles and to soften the sting
of economic misfortune. It has not been nearly as successful, however,
in pulling back when the economy is performing well.

Keynesian logic provided a solid rationale for government to intervene in the economy. It gave a basis for countercyclical budgeting
and hence deficit budgeting. Government programs and measures to
stabilize the economy, to promote economic development and full
employment, became important. Formulated during the depth of the
Great Depression, Keynesian economics suggested that with latent
demand and no limit in factors of production, governments could create
the long-sought-after prosperous and rational societies. But Keynesian
economics also legitimized government deficits, and, in time, governments would spend more, tax more, and borrow more – a great deal
more.

The Keynesian revolution captured the Department of Finance and
the federal treasury of Canada as it did elsewhere. The Canadian government presented a major policy paper to parliament towards the end
of the Second World War which was clearly Keynesian in outlook. It
said that: 'The Government will be prepared, in periods where unemployment threatens, to incur deficits and increases in the national debt
resulting from its employment and income policy ... in periods of buoyant employment and income, budget plans will call for surpluses.'[39] Not
only the government, but Canadians in general willingly accepted the
new direction. They had emerged from the war determined never to
permit another depression of the kind witnessed in the 1930s. By war's

end, the public's belief in the ability of government to intervene and to manage the economy was high. Large latent demand and rapid population increase, combined with the realization that the government management of activity related to the war effort had been successful, gave governments carte blanche to expand. Canadians had learned during the war 'that governments were able, in moments of crisis, and when moved by an all-consuming goal, to lead the country to high levels of economic activity and employment.'[40] Not only did the allies win the war but the government had run the war economy well. Unemployment had fallen to zero, and yet prices had been held down. Growth of productivity and real GNP was accelerated, inequalities among social groups diminished, civilian consumption actually increased, there were no balance of payment crises, and foreign exchange rates remained stable. When the war ended, everyone was prepared for measures to avoid a return of the depression years. But the expected severe economic downturn did not materialize and the measures proved unnecessary. Still, governments (in particular, the federal government) were now convinced that they possessed 'a new arsenal of economic policy' to achieve high employment and generally manage the economy.[41]

In the pre-Keynesian days, however, the ideology of balanced budgets had prevailed in most political parties. In Victorian England, for instance, budget deficits were considered 'a great political, and above all, a great moral evil.'[42] British Prime Minister William Gladstone laid down, in simple terms, the budget process of the day: 'New wants are always coming forward, but where ... provision is made for those new wants (it) ought to be counterbalanced by new economies.'[43] Frugality in government spending was a matter of the most basic of principles and 'bubbles' of extravagance were not allowed to surface. The way to ensure this, in his view, was to 'estimate expenditures liberally, revenue carefully and make each year pay its own expense.'[44]

Even the depth of the Great Depression failed to shake the conviction that budgets should be balanced. One of the first priorities of Canadian Prime Minister R.B. Bennett in 1930 was to determine the precise financial position of the government, to institute tight controls on spending, and to seek ways to reduce the administrative costs of government. The result is that one can now easily trace the development of Treasury Board controls on spending and personnel matters back to the 1930s. Bennett clearly favoured a 'balanced budget' to restore the confidence of the private sector and 'rode the economy horse hard.'[45] The opposition Liberal party fully agreed with this approach.

The advent of the welfare state in Canada has been well documented. What is perhaps less known is that there are often strong forces pulling and pushing to expand government programs immediately after they are established. When a program is first established, it is frequently designed to meet a specific and relatively small target group. The resources, however, come from the general population. The target group itself will often seek to have the program expanded or non-designated groups will want to benefit from it as well.

The federal government's efforts in regional development provide an excellent example of this phenomenon. When the Department of Regional Economic Expansion (DREE) was established in 1969, its first minister, Jean Marchand, proclaimed that, if the department was to spend anything less than 80 per cent of its budget east of Trois Rivières, it should be viewed as a failure.[46] Atlantic Canada and the Gaspé were to be the department's prime beneficiaries.

By the time DREE was disbanded some thirteen years later, its programs covered all of Canada and its spending was about evenly split between the West, Quebec, and the Atlantic region. DREE's successor, the Department of Regional Industrial Expansion (DRIE), saw the bulk if its spending development program, Industrial and Regional Development Program (IRDP), go to Ontario and Quebec. These two provinces accounted for over 70 per cent of the total spending under IRDP in 1984–5.[47]

Regional development policy was only one of many redistributive policies the federal government introduced in both the economic and social fields in the 1960s, and its expenditure budget burgeoned during this period. Liberals had taken control of the political agenda of both major political parties, and few voices against big government were being heard. Those who dared to oppose government intervention to promote full employment and a more just and tolerant society had to couch their opposition in careful terms. The comments of a keen student of government in the United States about this period applies equally well to Canada. 'There was a time when Liberals lusted after federal expenditures to do good. If only there were billions for higher education or for mass transportation or for mental health, on and on, what wonders would be performed!'[48]

During this period even some socialists preferred increased public expenditures over nationalization of industry. British cabinet minister. Tony Crossland, for example, went so far as to suggest that it should replace nationalization as a central feature of socialism. Socialist policies, he argued, should be less concerned with the ownership of the means of production and place more emphasis on applying the gains of economic growth to greater equality through social development programs.[49]

And yet by the late 1970s one could easily discern a growing concern over the increasing presence of the state in society. This concern was not limited to reactionaries. Indeed, those who fear to tamper with existing government machinery have become today's conservatives.

Among the most distinguished and influential of these advocates of public spending and governmental management of the economy is John K. Galbraith. In a recent lecture, Galbraith said that neither he nor his colleagues of like mind had fully understood what they were doing in supporting the creation of vast economic and social programs. He went on to argue that 'It's more than the Liberal task now to defend the system. It is also the task that the system be better administered ... It is far more important now to improve the operation than enlarge and increase its scope. This must be the direction of our major effort.'[50]

Others have also sought to ring the alarm bell about government spending. A leading member of the Canadian business community recently observed that 'massive (federal) debt threatens our future prosperity as a nation. The total rises with every tick of the clock. Every 12 hours the public debt increases by another $40 million.'[51] This concern was echoed by the 1985 Royal Commission on the Economic Union and Development Prospects for Canada, which observed: 'The *reach* of the state has in many ways outrun both our administrative and technical capacities, and our capacity to ensure democratic accountability.'[52] Doug Hartle, however, has observed that 'for many years the forces pushing for more expenditures were overwhelmingly greater ... Now fiscal liberals are being forced into the defensive minority position once occupied by the fiscal conservatives.'[53]

By the early 1980s, politicians realized that less and less was big government held in high esteem. The need to control government spending and the deficit came to dominate the political agenda, perhaps as much as the need to expand economic and social programs had done in the 1960s. Now it is those who oppose cutting the deficit who must couch their views in careful terms. It is widely believed that there are many more forces than the modern economy and a growing population to explain the increasing scope of government activity and expenditures. Even the New Democratic Party, traditionally the most interventionist party, has addressed the importance of controlling the deficit.[54] The governing Liberal party made deficit reduction an important theme of its albeit unsuccessful 1984 election campaign. The Progressive Conservative party meanwhile made deficit reduction a high priority of the 'new' political agenda immediately after coming to power in 1984.

In his first major address as minister of finance, Michael Wilson made clear the government's commitment to reducing the deficit. He insisted that 'the growing public debt has become a severe handicap to economic progress and the most serious obstacle to economic growth.'[55] He went on to explain why it was important to control the deficit: 'Continued high deficits and growing debt will increasingly undermine confidence, put upward pressure on interest rates and reduce prospects for growth. Moreover, they increasingly constrain the federal government's ability to discharge its responsibilities for overall economic management and effective economic leadership.'[56] The task, however, would not be easy: Governments run deficits during recessions, which they recoup from increasing tax revenues during periods of economic expansion. Over the last decade, however, the federal government has run deficits not only in recession years, but in years of growth as well. Next year will mark the third year of recovery and the third year in which the deficit is continuing to rise.'[57] The solution, he argued, was to introduce important expenditure cuts, explaining that 'government has become too big. It intrudes too much ... (and) programs carry on long after the need for them has passed, and are only a fiscal drain.'[58] Wilson was not the first federal minister of finance or president of the Treasury Board to call for important cuts in federal spending. Such calls have been made time and again since the mid 1970s.[59]

We now know that political rhetoric is one thing but an actual cut in the expenditure budget is quite another. A look at the facts reveals that little in the way of spending cuts has actually been realized. Moreover, new spending programs for both economic and social development have been introduced since the early 1980s. All in all, the federal budget has shown remarkable resilience in the face of repeated calls for spending reductions, ministerial commitments to retrenchment, a change of government, and a broadly based consensus outside government that the expenditure budget should be better managed, if not reduced. This study attempts to understand why this is so.

ORGANIZATION

This book is divided into four parts. The first explains the federal government policy process. It is largely descriptive but provides useful background information for subsequent chapters. Part 1 begins with a brief review of parliament's role in the government expenditure budget. It describes where and how parliament, parliamentary committees, and the auditor general come into the budget process. It then goes on to explain how priorities are established within the federal government and how the planning process works.

The several attempts at revising the expenditure budget process are also reviewed in Part 1. The development of the federal government budget process is traced from line budgeting down to the more recent attempt to introduce the Policy and Expenditure and Management System (PEMS). I set out not only to describe how the various approaches worked, but also to answer why they were dropped or modified, how ministers and officials worked under each approach, and, finally, the impact each system has had on the expenditure budget.

Resource allocation decisions go considerably beyond the prescription of a particular policy-making process, however sophisticated it may be. One therefore has to look beyond the system to the deals, the trade-offs, and the end-runs to see how decisions are really arrived at. This is what the next two parts seek to do. As I noted earlier, I divide the actors in the budget process into two groups: guardians and spenders.

Both groups are of course easily identifiable: the guardians include the minister and Department of Finance and the president of the Treasury Board and its secretariat. Others can also play a guardian's role – notably, central agencies such as the Privy Council Office (PCO). The spenders are virtually everybody else, including ministers, departments, and agencies. I also include provincial governments, crown corporations, and various interest groups, either as spenders or on the side of the spenders.

The roles of both groups, the struggle for money, and the relative influence of each side are examined. I seek to answer the fundamental question: are the guardians too powerful or not powerful enough? I also examine the forces that motivate the government to spend.

In the last part of the study I argue that, while government spending and programs dominate thinking in government, decision makers are incapable of coming to grips with them. I argue that increased government spending and our inability to cut back existing programs are rooted in the regional nature of our country and in the belief that we must all eat the best at the banquet for fear of losing our share of public largesse. Let me provide an analogy. Ten people meet for the first time over lunch. A decision must be made as to whether they should share one check or have ten separate ones. The theory is that if they decide on one, shared check, they will all choose the more expensive items on the menu, which they would not have done if each was paying individually. Nobody wants to miss out on the best food while having to pay for someone else to eat it.

This study reveals that the same attitude is evident in government spending. Supporters of a new day-care centre, for example, in debating its merits, are likely to point out the cost of the proposal in relation to other government measures. Thus, the day-care proponents will invariably argue that the cost of their proposal is only a fraction of the cost of, say, purchasing new nuclear submarines. Or, when a regional minister for Newfoundland seeks support from selected colleagues for the construction of new wharfs in his province, he and his colleagues are not likely to spend much time studying a cost-benefit analysis of such a proposal. They are much more likely to argue that, it the government can spend money on expanding the Hamilton airport, which is only a short distance from the Toronto airport, it can afford to build new wharfs for the fishermen in Newfoundland. And so it goes with other ministers and other proposals.

THE DATA

Information for this study comes from a number of sources, including published and unpublished government documents. I also interviewed eighty government officials directly involved in, or close to, the federal government budget process. The interviews were conducted between October 1987 and July 1988. I also conducted seven interviews between February and May 1989 in light of changes to the budget process introduced in January 1989. Almost all the respondents were in the executive branch, although I did interview government backbenchers and two members of the opposition. The interviews were unstructured and each was tailored to the position of the respondents, some of whom were interviewed more than once. I made no attempt to draw a representative sample, which would have been impractical for the purpose of the study. I interviewed senior officials and ministers from both the Mulroney and Trudeau administrations. The interviews had four main goals. The first was to determine what goes on in the budget process. The second was to gain an understanding of the respondents' attitudes towards the process in general. The third was to find out what motivated them. The fourth was to determine from the perspective of the actors directly involved what are the forces behind decisions to spend. I also interviewed twenty representatives of the private sector between February and June 1988 to seek their views on the federal government expenditure budget and in particular on government programs for the private sector.[60]

PART I

The process

2

The machinery

Much has already been written about the role of parliament in reviewing the government's expenditure budget, about how priorities are established in the federal government, and about the elements of the central decision-making process.[1] It is important, however, to outline briefly the most important elements and recent changes to the process. This discussion is limited to features essential to a grasp of how the process works and how the expenditures budget relates to it.

In an organization as large and complex as is the federal government an elaborate policy- and decision-making process is necessary, if only to ensure that relevant policy actors can be heard. Such a process is now in place. Many officials in line departments and agencies, however, believe it is too constricting. One senior departmental official remarked: 'Since the late 1960s we have been processed to death. I no longer know what is more important – the process or the substance. We have now reached the point that, if I have to choose between a bright policy analyst with strong analytical skills and someone who knows his way around central agencies, I will opt for the one who can operate with ease in the system. I can get more mileage for my programs. Sad but true.'[2] To be sure, the decision-making process in the federal government is now elaborate and complex and involves countless committees of officials and politicians. There can also be no doubt that central agencies, for example, have grown in visible ways and have greatly extended their roles and influence. Anyone in government who does not know how the process as a whole works, where his or her organization fits in the scheme of things, and how to 'walk' a proposal through the various approval stages is severely handicapped. Yet few, if any, in central agencies take a particular delight in having such a complex and slow policy-making and decision-making process in place. But, they report, the demands of modern government and the nature of cabinet government itself require it. One senior central agency official explained:

The number of proposals coming from ministers and departments each year is great. Invariably each proposal impacts on several other departments. If there was no central process to sort all this out there would be complete chaos in government. In fact, there is now a fair amount of chaos even with the process in place. In addition, a government survives or falls as a collective body. One minister and his department cannot simply go off on a tangent with an idea. The prime minister and other ministers have to live with the collective and individual actions of all ministers. That is why we have an elaborate process in place. It is absolutely wrong for department officials, academics, and even politicians to say that the process is there because some powerful mandarins at the centre want it that way to increase their power and influence.[3]

Said another: 'Ministers themselves insist that there is a structure in place to ensure due process or to ensure that they can voice support or criticism of all proposals. Ministers have a responsibility to support their colleagues. The least they can expect in *no surprise* from colleagues.'[4]

PARLIAMENT: A REVIEW OF SPENDING PLANS

Notwithstanding recent and important changes to the process, there are some elements of the system that have remained basically constant. One such feature is parliament. The British North America Act made it clear that parliament alone has control over taxing and spending. It also established that the government is responsible for proposing a spending program before parliament. Several principles underpin parliament's role in the budget process. The first is that the government – or the executive – can have no revenue which is not sanctioned by parliament, and the second is that the government can make no expenditures except those approved by parliament. In addition, parliament does not grant a permanent right to spend, so that the government must submit a new budget every year. Thus funds allocated by parliament but not spent must lapse. Detailed spending plans are submitted annually in the form of spending 'estimates.' The government must also account to parliament for its management of public moneys, both revenues and expenditures.[5]

On the face of it, one may well assume that parliament plays a crucial role in the expenditure budget process. Constitutional niceties aside, however, it does not. Parliament does not exercise executive authority and, although spending estimates are tabled annually, parliament seldom even 'tampers with them.' They are invariably accepted as submitted. Parliament can only introduce motions to reduce the estimates, given the principle that spending must originate with the government. If a spending proposal is rejected, tradition requires that it must be taken as a vote of no confidence in the government and the government must resign – for to challenge the amounts of spending determined by the government would bring into question the confidence of the House of Commons in the cabinet. This is the single most important reason why parliament, particularly with a majority government in place, merely 'rubber stamps' the expenditure budget. One Progressive Conservative backbencher recently explained: 'If we could change spending plans without bringing down our government, you can safely assume that some departments, agencies, and crown corporations would never get what they receive every year. CBC jumps to mind as an excellent case in point. But believe me there would be others. And I have no doubt whatsoever that I reflect the majority view of the government caucus.'[6] Said another: 'There are many areas of government activity where we have virtually no say. The budget is the best example. We see the spending estimates at the same time as everybody else. And by the time we see the government's spending plans – they are signed, sealed, delivered, and above all not to be changed in any way.'[7] However, as we shall see later in this study, this does not prevent government backbenchers from exerting pressure on the government either individually or in groups, such as a regional caucus, to spend more or to support special projects.

The role of parliament in the expenditure budget process is thus largely restricted to 'legitimizing' the government's spending plans. As an institution, it does not directly influence one way or another the outcome of the budget process, and it does not control government spending by determining expenditure levels either for the government as a whole or for specific departments or functions. In theory, parliament is central to the budget process but 'in practice it is a marginal actor ... Spending continues to be looked at as piecemeal and on a short-term basis by the House of Commons.'[8] As is well known, parliament does not set priorities – it merely reviews those of the government in full public view.

Still parliament plays an important 'watchdog' role and no doubt prevents ministers and departments from redirecting funds for purposes other than those for which they were approved through the estimates. Parliament must appropriate funds for a specific purpose before the expenditure occurs. Its authority to spend is obtained through the passage of appropriation acts, which are based on the main and supplementary estimates.

The president of the Treasury Board initiates the process in late January or February of each year by tabling the main estimates. The estimates are tabled simultaneously in the House of Commons and in the Senate, where they are referred to its Standing Committee on National Finance. When the estimates become law they are known as the appropriation act for the year. These estimates list the spending plans of each department for the forthcoming fiscal year (1 April–31 March) and provide some information on all federal government programs. There are now established deadlines for approving the estimates so that departments know that their spending plans cannot be delayed indefinitely. The rules of the House of Commons provide that, if the expenditure budget has not been approved before 30 June, it is voted upon on that date. Interim supply, a special legislative instrument, provides for the operation of the government for the period 1 April to 30 June by appropriating a percentage of the total expenditure budget requested. Since the government cannot shift funds from one program to another without parliamentary approval or spend more than was approved by parliament in the original appropriation act, and since the government cannot possibly provide resources for all unforeseen circumstances, a process is in place by which the government may seek parliamentary approval for new resources throughout the fiscal year. The government can and does present at various times throughout the year 'supplementary estimates.' The president of the Treasury Board usually presents the first such estimates in November.

After the estimates have been tabled, they are sent to the relevant standing committees which evaluate the policies and programs of all the departments. These committees carry out a detailed examination of departmental estimates, so that the Department of Agriculture's estimates are reviewed by the Standing Committee of Agriculture, those of External Affairs and Defence by the Standing Committee on External Affairs and Defence, and so forth (see table 1). The chairperson of the committee is always a government member and the membership, which is about twenty, reflects the proportion of seats each party holds.

TABLE 1
Parliamentary standing committees and departments reviewed

Standing committees	Departments
Aboriginal Affairs and Northern Development	Department of Indian Affairs and Northern Development
Agriculture	Department of Agriculture
Communications and Culture	Department of Communications
Consumer and Corporate Affairs	Department of Consumer and Corporate Affairs
Energy, Mines and Resources	Department of Energy, Mines and Resources
Environment	Department of Environment
External Affairs and International Trade	Department of External Affairs
Finance and Economic Affairs	Department of Finance Department of National Revenue
Fisheries and Oceans	Department of Fisheries and Oceans
Government Operations	Privy Council Office Department of Public Works Department of Supply and Services Treasury Board
Justice and Solicitor General	Department of Justice Solicitor General
Labour, Employment and Immigration	Employment and Immigration Canada Department of Labour
National Defence	National Defence
National Health and Welfare	Department of National Health and Welfare
Regional Industrial Expansion	Department of Industry, Science and Technology Atlantic Canada Opportunities Agency Western Diversification Office.
Secretary of State	Secretary of State
Transport	Ministry of Transport
Veterans Affairs	Veterans Affairs Canada
Elections, Privileges and Procedure	
Human Rights	
Management and Member's Services	
Public Accounts	
Research, Science and Technology	

When a department's estimates are reviewed by a particular committee, the minister is called to defend the estimated expenditures. This process often also involves the officials of his or her department, who, if the minister so desires, may be called upon to explain or defend the estimates for the department. In addition to considering departmental estimates, standing committees may on occasion examine the various policy proposals for which the government is seeking legislation.

The main estimates are presented to parliament in three distinct parts, all at the same time. Part I provides an overview of the government's spending estimates, and presents a historical trend in total spending and a breakdown of the spending in terms of policy sectors and envelopes. Part II outlines spending according to departments, agencies, and programs. Part III provides still more information on each department and the programs. All in all, the main estimates consist of over 15,000 pages of information and stacked on top of each other the documents are about three feet thick. Appendix 1 illustrates a page from Part II of the main estimates, and Appendix 2, a page from part III, both from 1987–8 fiscal year.

Once the committees report back to the House of Commons, a vote on the total estimates is taken. The committee reports in fact consist of nothing more than a motion to approve the estimates. The parliamentary calendar, thus, is as follows:

mid-February	The main estimates are submitted to parliament by the president of the Treasury Board; standing committees of the House begin considering them.
end of March	Parliament votes on interim supply – providing authority to the government to spend some funds from the beginning of the fiscal year, 1 April, until the end of June, when full supply for main estimates is voted.
end of May	The standing committees report to parliament.
end of June	Parliament votes on the main estimates.
mid-November	First supplementary estimates submitted to parliament.
mid-December	Parliament votes on the first supplementary estimates.
early March	Final supplementary estimates submitted to parliament.
late March	Final supplementary estimates voted on by parliament.

Most observers consider that parliament generally, and standing committees in particular, do not play a significant role in the expenditure budget, and this for a host of reasons. There is, of course, the politics of the House of Commons to be reckoned with. Committees dominated by government members will be reluctant to raise questions that may serve to embarrass cabinet or individual ministers. In addition, it should also be remembered that most members of parliament have little interest in reviewing the 'effectiveness' and 'efficiency' of the administration of continuing programs. Members have very little positive visibility back in their ridings for having thoroughly reviewed existing programs. The result is that few work 'full time' with the committee system. One explained. 'I tend to avoid these committee meetings. There is nothing in them for my constituents and therefore for me. Simply put, nobody there ever votes for me. Besides I never worry about spending insufficient time in parliament and parliamentary committees. Whether I am there or not or members are there or not in the end changes nothing in the scheme of things.'[9] But there are other reasons. Two keen observers of government correctly point out that 'not only procedural and partisan factors account for Parliament's limited influence on government spending.'[10] The estimates and the accompanying information on programs are far too complex and written in such obscure bureaucratese that most MPs cannot grasp them sufficiently well to engage in a meaningful debate on the merits of government programs. 'Through thousands of pages the Blue Book (looks) ... every bit like a major metropolitan telephone directory and probably less fun to read. The Blue Book can be a gold mine of useful information but only when in the hands of someone highly experienced in finding his or her way through its numerous rows and columns.'[11] It must also be remembered that committees pit members of parliament (who often have more pressing needs to look after in their ridings than looking at pages and pages of information in the estimates book) against ministers and officials, who have a thorough knowledge of the departmental programs and budgets.

Officials, in particular, regard appearances before standing committees to explain departmental estimates as anything but productive. 'The whole thing,' remarked one, 'lacks seriousness. I have never once been properly challenged at these committee meetings. I always come away feeling that MPs couldn't care less. And this is true of MPs from all three parties.'[12] It would appear that even members of parliament would agree with this assessment. There have been consistent problems in having a quorum at committee meetings and on average 'only a small group (6 to 7 members ...) usually attend more than half of a given committee's meetings.'[13] Moreover, the 1979 Royal Commission on Financial Management and Accountability (Lambert Commission) concluded that 'the large number of substitutions (one member replacing another for a committee meeting) suggests a lack of seriousness on the part of committee members in developing any expertise in the subject-matter dealt with by committees of which they are members.'[14] More recently, a leading journalist in Ottawa wrote that 'some committees are exercises in irrelevance ... others are exercises in grandstanding ... One committee meets less than once a month – one meeting lasted exactly a minute.'[15]

Recent changes proposed by the special all-party McGrath committee and designed to strengthen the role of parliamentary committees appear to have had no impact on the expenditure budget process. 'Departmental estimates are waved through on an uninformed vote, as they were in pre-McGrath days.'[16] Government officials do not disagree with this observation. They contend, however, that the changes brought about by the McGrath committee have strengthened parliamentary committees in that they can now commission studies and propose new policy initiatives. The government is obligated to respond to the proposals within a set of period of time. Proposals, government officials report, rarely involve cutting back programs. Members want to be able to report to their constituents back home that they proposed bold new initiatives. These initiatives inevitably involve the spending of public funds. In this sense, recent changes to the working of parliamentary committees have added to and strengthened the spending forces on Parliament Hill. One senior government official suggests that parliamentary committees 'since they have staff resources appear to be in competition to see which one can come up with the most costly and grandiose scheme. They never add up the total cost of what all of them would like to propose.'[17]

THE AUDITOR GENERAL: THE INHIBITOR

There is one committee of parliament – the Public Accounts Committee (PAC) – that is highly visible and perhaps more effective than the others. This is because it is chaired by an opposition member and also because the committee reviews the auditor general's report on a section-by-section basis. Committee members are assisted in their work by the staff of the auditor general. This not only ensures visibility, it also ensures that the government is always on the defensive. It also means, however, that the Office of the Auditor General dominates the Public Accounts Committee's agenda.

The Standing Committee on Public Accounts dates back to 1867. The committee functions as the audit committee of parliament and, by its own admission, does not deal with policy matters.[18] Its task is to examine the consistency between the proposed and actual expenditures. Accordingly, its main role is to pursue and investigate the financial shortcomings of departments, which it accomplishes through an examination of the public accounts and the auditor general's report. After its review, the committee makes a series of recommendations to parliament on ways to improve the government's financial management. For instance, the committee in its 1987 report urged that improvements be made in the quality of the tax expenditure information and in the way such information is presented to parliament.[19] This recommendation was first made in the 1986 auditor general's report.

The committee's report, however, is never debated in parliament, and it is often noted that the government rarely implements the committee's recommendations. The committee's effectiveness clearly does not lie in its ability to change government policies or even existing administrative and financial practices. Rather, it is effective simply by 'being there' and by being able to call on officials to explain their departmental 'financial shortcomings.' 'Public Accounts,' explains one experienced federal official, 'is a great check against doing foolish things. If a minister pressures us to do something that is clearly not on, we can point out that if we were to go ahead we could be hauled before Public Accounts to explain our actions. Sometimes this is all that is required to kill a project.'[20]

Outside government, the auditor general is the most visible scrutinizer of government accounts and, inside government, he is the most widely feared. The office of the Auditor General reports directly to parliament annually on whether funds have been spent as authorized and whether proper financial records have been kept. The office has long enjoyed considerable autonomy from the government and, since 1977, its mandate and scope have been substantially strengthened.[21] Beginning that year, the office was granted the power to report whether departments have adequate means to measure the effectiveness of their programs, in addition to determining whether government spent its funds legally and efficiently. The 1977 changes removed the office from the Financial Administration Act and granted it its own legislation.

The changes also led to a new, more comprehensive approach to auditing. No longer would the office undertake a post-audit of the activities of every department. Instead, a broader approach would be employed, one which would carry out a systematic review of a limited number of programs. The search for 'horror stories,' it was reported, would give way to an audit that would place emphasis on the three 'e's – economy, efficiency, and effectiveness – and thus 'value for money.' The auditor general's mandate now requires that the office report to the House of Commons 'instances where accounts have not been faithfully and properly maintained and where rules and procedures have been insufficient and when money has been expended other than for purposes for which it was appropriated or without due regard for economy and efficiency.'[22]

To be sure, although there have been changes in the Office of the Auditor General in recent years, its principal product remains the annual report which still 'places an emphasis on the negative.'[23] The news media continue to give wide coverage to the report and remain primarily concerned with horror stories. The auditor general readily admits this and recently observed: 'I have become increasingly troubled that it is taken for granted that the appearance of the annual Report of the Auditor General is primarily an occasion that allows the media and the opposition parties in Parliament to embarrass the government of the day.'[24]

It is true, of course, that the media delight in giving the auditor general's report a full airing for a day or two each year. Said one journalist: 'There is one figure in Ottawa who triggers pure, unadultered adulation in the media. The Great Canadian Hero is the Auditor General ... We love this guy ... (his) operation saves news organizations thousands of dollars a year to allow him to go hunting for the smoking guns and the foul ups and the scams that any government with a large civil service is going to entangle itself in.'[25] And so, every year in December when the auditor general tables his report, we continue to learn, from the media, of its 'juiciest' stories. We hear, for instance, about the Department of Defence spending $12 million on bullets that do not 'shoot straight' or a $4–5 million grant to the theme park at the West Edmonton Mall after government officials had recommended that it be turned down.[26] There is little doubt that (even more so than in the case of the Public Accounts Committee) the media attention to the auditor general's report has prevented ministers and officials from pushing ahead with proposals that could be fingered as candidates for the report.

The auditor general's report, however, contains a great deal more than horror stories. It is replete with detailed cases of management and financial shortcomings in government. In the 1987 report, for instance, the auditor general commented on productivity problems in the Department of Supply and Services, on an inadequate financial reporting system in the Department of Transport, and on inadequate information to parliament on remission programs on the part of Revenue Canada. Much more often than not, however, departments simply pay lip-service to these findings, generally viewing such criticism as naive and short-sighted. The issues, they are likely to insist, are never as straightforward as the auditor general would like everyone to believe. They also regard the auditor general as someone 'hovering over the action to swoop down on the wounded after the battle.'[27] That is, the staff of the auditor general is never there when actual decisions have to be made, bearing in mind the political and administrative circumstances of the day.

The auditor general is feared in government if only because of the publicity given the annual report. This is not to suggest for a moment that the office is widely approved of or even respected. Many are convinced that the auditor general's mandate has been extended far beyond any reasonable limit. One senior official no doubt voiced the opinion of others when he observed: 'The Auditor General in the last 10 years has moved *light years beyond* the role of auditor, towards a broad assessment of government management and decision making.'[28]

Many outside observers have also questioned the increasing scope of the auditor general's mandate and the wisdom of carrying out 'value-for-money' audits. Audits based on the three 'e's and the consequent value for money would, the auditor general of the day insisted when it was introduced in the late 1970s, provide administrative and financial discipline and become the government's 'bottom line.' A number of sceptics, however, doubt whether accountants have the capacity to carry out such tasks, since many government programs result from political judgment alone.[29] Still others question whether it is appropriate for accountants to undertake value-for-money audits in government.[30] Certainly the auditor general has made some sweeping statements that serve to raise the eyebrows of many in government, as in a recently expressed doubt as to whether the Department of Defence could successfully engage in a war effort. Defence specialists openly wonder how the auditor general and the 'hordes' of accountants are in a position to make such an assertion and in any event question whether it is the proper role of an auditor to make such a judgment.

Regardless of whether one agrees that the auditor general should carry out comprehensive value-for-money audits, there is no convincing evidence anywhere to suggest that the office has had much of a positive impact on the expenditure budget. The office is now costly to operate, with an annual budget of $50 million a year, and the auditor general's principal product and virtually *sole* contribution to government and society is the annual report. Some have suggested that the auditor general's budget would fail its own cost-effectiveness test.[31] It has certainly witnessed strong growth over the years. In 1970–3, the Office of the Auditor General had a budget of $4.4 million and 298 person-years. By 1988–9, its budget had jumped to over $48 million and 619 person-years.

The auditor general, through the annual report, has urged government to launch major initiatives over the past ten years. Some of the proposals were widely debated, both in political circles and in the media, which no doubt explains why they were in the end adopted. These included the establishment of the Office of the Comptroller General (ocg), widespread evaluation of programs, and Improved Management Practices and Controls (impac). While costly, it would be extremely difficult to argue that any of these initiatives have met with any degree of success. Both program evaluation and ocg will be discussed later in this study.

impac generated a great deal of paperwork and countless meetings between departments and central agencies, as well as within departments, with the goal of improving management in government. Several years later, however, there is precious little evidence to suggest that the exercise has had any appreciable influence on the day-to-day operations of government. impac's objective was to promote the establishment of sound management practices for planning, financial administration, management information, program evaluation, and internal audit. Officials in line departments insist that the limited improvements that were forthcoming would have been made in any event, albeit perhaps a little later. Though impac was first introduced in 1979, it did not prevent some departments, notably drie, from seriously overspending their budget several years later. One official insists, however, that the exercise 'no doubt cost much more than it saved. But don't count on the Auditor General to report this in one of his annual reports.'[32] A central agency official directly involved agrees, pointing out that 'one would have to have a truly well-developed imagination to suggest that the IMPAC initiative was much of a success.'[33] The IMPAC program was finally terminated on 31 March 1988.

The Office of the Auditor General, then, has had little direct impact on the expenditure budget, other than probably increasing the overhead cost of government in the belief that it would contribute to more effective evaluation of ongoing programs. It is true that the office inhibits the spenders in government from supporting initiatives that do not hold the test of public scrunity, but it is difficult to argue that it has had any influence on the total size of the expenditure budget. Projects that cannot meet the test of public scrunity are often merely replaced by others that do.

Similarly, parliament does not control spending in the sense of determining the levels of expenditures for particular departments, functions, and levels. It reviews government spending plans but rarely influences them. MPs by and large see little merit in developing an expertise in the program requirements of departments. Government members, not wishing to embarrass one of their own ministers, avoid raising substantive issues on departmental spending in the House. Opposition members meanwhile limit their participation to calling for increased spending on a particular program or specific problem and take little interest in pursuing more substantive issues related to the budget, either in the House or in standing committees.

In any event, members are not privy to decisions made in preparing the expenditure budget. They see the final product, the estimates books, only when they are tabled in parliament and thus publicly released for the first time. To see the real forces shaping the expenditure budget we have to look inside government to see how spending policies and programs are defined.

SETTING PRIORITIES – THE MACHINERY

The Trudeau government completely overhauled the cabinet committee system.[34] Trudeau made the changes to promote policy coordination between departments and to strengthen the decision-making influence of ministers. To be sure, full cabinet would continue to bear collective responsibility for all policy, but now ministers would have an opportunity to study the several hundred issues submitted annually by their colleagues for decision and to express their points of view. It was felt that, since cabinet could no longer possibly deal adequately with all or even a majority of the issues, much of this review would now be delegated to cabinet committees. Cabinet and its committees certainly have a heavy workload. Typically, in the course of one year, there are over 300 meetings of cabinet and cabinet committees (50 cabinet meetings alone), at which ministers review well over 800 memoranda and produce over 700 records of decision, approve around 70 bills to submit to parliament, and over 4000 orders in council. Treasury Board alone will make over 5000 decisions in a single year.

Decisions of cabinet, unlike Treasury Board minutes and orders in council, carry no legal authority. Accordingly, there are no statutes or clear rules to decide which issues need to go through the cabinet committee system and which do not. To the experienced officials, however, it is clear when a proposal should be put through the cabinet system. It is necessary 'if it (i.e., a proposal) requires new financial resources, if it requires new legislation, if it has direct effects on the mandates of other ministers, or if Cabinet solidarity would require other ministers to defend a decision on a controversial proposal.'[35] The decision as to whether or not a proposal should be submitted to Treasury Board is more straightforward. There are statutes which require that specific transactions obtain Treasury Board approval.

Since Trudeau introduced his major changes in the late 1960s, numerous other changes, albeit less significant, have been made to the cabinet committee system. Throughout these changes the Priorities and Planning Committee (P & P) has remained the pre-eminent cabinet committee – so much so that it is often referred to as the inner cabinet or the executive committee of the government. Membership in P & P is certainly a coveted prize among ministers. The committee is chaired by the prime minister and membership includes the minister of finance, the president of the Treasury Board, the chairpersons of other cabinet committees, and a handful of senior ministers. The latter are usually selected for regional reasons or because of their great personal and political influence, which often go hand in hand. P & P is the only cabinet committee other than that on security and intelligence which only members may attend. Non-members may only attend if they have a special invitation from the prime minister. Though there have been some attempts to adopt the same policy in some other cabinet committees of late (for example, Treasury Board), any minister may attend any other committee meeting, whether or not he or she is a member. And, like cabinet, the P & P agenda is relatively loose, permitting a freer, more wide-ranging discussion and an eye for emerging issues. P & P recommendations coming before full cabinet are rarely, if ever, challenged. In fact, P & P frequently ratifies other cabinet committee decisions on behalf of cabinet. The choice as to whether cabinet or P & P should undertake this responsibility depends on the number of ministers having an interest in the proposal – issues of broad political interest will likely go to full cabinet – and in the timing. If there is some urgency, a proposal is likely to go before the first meeting to take place.

P & P sets the government's broad political agenda, deals with the major planning elements of government, such as the fiscal framework, 'politically manages' major issues for the government, and, like full cabinet, acts as court of last resort for ministers wishing to overturn or amend a cabinet committee decision. It also acts as a 'super' coordinating committee of cabinet.

Prime Minister Mulroney introduced yet another coordinating committee of cabinet, called the Operations Committee. It has become commonly known as the 'Maz committee' because of its chairman, Deputy Prime Minister Don Mazankowski. The committee is not in a strict sense a decision-making body. It merely reviews issues and prepares proposals for full cabinet. In the words of one senior official, 'the Maz committee clears the underbrush on a number of issues and proposals. Its role is one of facilitator. It is true that it is not a decision-making body, but once you have walked a proposal or an issue past that committee you are pretty well home free.'[36] The reason for this is quite simply that the chairman is one of the most powerful ministers in his own right, and because the prime minister relies a great deal on the committee for advice and to give 'operational directions' to the government. Membership on the Maz committee is restricted to the deputy prime minister, the minister of finance, the president of the Treasury Board, and the chairpersons of the cabinet committees on economic and social development, foreign affairs, and defence.

There are four sectoral policy committees which form the first tier in the cabinet committee system. They are the Cabinet Committee on Economic and Regional Development (CCERD), Social Development (CCSD), Foreign and Defence Policy (CCFDP), and Privatization and Regulatory Affairs and Government Operations (CCPRAO). Each of these committees with the exception of CCPRAO oversees the spending 'envelopes' and deals with the great majority of policy issues in their respective sectors. The result is that their agendas consist 'of detailed proposals from ministers, many of which have expenditure implications which must be compared with other proposals competing for the committee's envelope resources.'[37] Their role in managing their spending envelopes will be examined more closely in subsequent chapters.

Cabinet committees relate to ministers, departments, and full cabinet in the following fashion. A minister and his or her department will identify a problem, decide on a preferred course of action, and then consult with relevant departments and their ministers to enlist their support or at least attenuate their opposition. A memorandum to cabinet is prepared which defines the problem, the issues, and alternatives and concludes with a recommended course of action. Once signed by the minister, the document is forwarded to the relevant cabinet committee. After the committee considers the document, it is sent along with a recommendation to cabinet or P & P for final approval. The committee's recommendations are appended to the cabinet agenda. Any ministers may reopen any issue listed in the appendix, although in practice it is rarely done. Cabinet decisions are recorded in a formal document known as 'records of decision' which are circulated to ministers and relevant officials.

There are other cabinet committees. The Treasury Board is the oldest and it is reviewed in considerable detail later in this study. Other committees include Communications, Legislation and House Planning, Security and Intelligence, Public Service, and Special Committee of Council. With the exception of the latter, which handles all routine issues requiring governor in council approval or those which by statute require that the government rather than one minister make the decision, these cabinet committees meet less frequently. Their functions are made clear by their names. Thus, the committee on Communications develops general policies in support of government communications objectives; the Committee on Legislation and House Planning sets legislative priorities for the government; and so on. They are of less concern here because they do not have spending envelopes. Tables 2 and 3 illustrate the cabinet committee system under the Trudeau and Mulroney administrations, respectively.

SUPPORTING THE MACHINERY

There are several important agencies whose principal function is to support the cabinet and its committees. Labelled central agencies, they include the Prime Minister's Office (PMO), the Privy Council Office (PCO), and the Federal-Provincial Relations Office (FPRO).

The Prime Minister's Office is described as 'partisan, politically ori-

TABLE 2
Cabinet committees under the Trudeau government, 1983

	Priorities and Planning
Public Service	Communications
Security and Intelligence	Legislation and House Planning
Special Committee of Council	Foreign Affairs and Defence
Western Affairs	Government Operations
Social Development	Economic and Regional Development
Treasury Board	Labour Relations

TABLE 3
Cabinet committees under the Mulroney government, 1988

Priorities and Planning	Operations (Ops) Committee
Public Service	Legislation and House Planning
Security and Intelligence	Foreign Affairs and Defence
Special Committee of Council	Privatization and Regulatory Affairs and Government Operations
Social Development	Economic and Regional Development
Treasury Board	Labour Relations
Communications	

ented, yet operationally sensitive.' Its role is to connect the political party in power with the government, bringing to the attention of the prime minister partisan considerations to proposals coming from departments or issues facing the government. It does this through face-to-face briefing of the prime minister, as well as through short briefing notes attached to documents, including cabinet documents.

The office exerts power in other ways. A former head of the Prime Minister's Office remarked that 'the most valuable resource in Ottawa is the time of the Prime Minister. To work on four or five problems requires saying no to hundreds of other requests.'[38] It is the job of the Prime Minister's Office to determine who has access to the prime minister. If the office, for example, allows one minister to see the prime minister with a spending proposal, then clearly that minister will have an advantage over others, who may well also have proposals but who are unable to gain similar access.

The PCO, unlike PMO, is staffed by career public servants. Its pre-eminent status in the government is made clear by the fact that the clerk of the Privy Council Office and secretary to the cabinet is the most senior federal public servant. It is also largely on his advice that the prime minister appoints deputy ministers.

For the purpose of this study, it is important to underline that an important part of the PCO responsibility is to act as the 'Cabinet Office,' in the sense of facilitating the movement of material and proposals through cabinet committee and full cabinet. The PCO provides secretariat support to cabinet and to all of the cabinet committees except Treasury Board. It would be wrong to assume, however, that PCO is entirely concerned with pushing paper back and forth between cabinet and departments. The agency also does a great deal more. It organizes, coordinates, and communicates the results of cabinet and cabinet committee meetings, and it is hardly possible to overstate the importance of these functions to the government's decision-making process.

PCO is organized to assist the cabinet committee system. Each cabinet committee is supported by a secretariat headed by a senior level PCO official, with a staff ranging from three to about twelve. These officials manage the system on behalf of the prime minister and cabinet and thus it 'gives them considerable responsibility and influence. PCO staff advise departmental officials about the preparation of Memoranda to Cabinet, establish agendas for Cabinet committee meetings, brief the Prime Minister and committee chairmen, draft decisions ... (and) more generally maintain an overview of government policies and programs and, in particular, a continuing sense of the *cutting edge* of issues and problems ...'[39]

These functions carry important responsibilities. Let us assume, for example, that a minister and his or her department have been able to convince the majority of ministers and the system of the importance of a particular proposal. A PCO official, however, considers the proposal to have important shortcomings from a government-wide perspective. Perhaps this is because of a particularly strong and valid objection from a single department; perhaps it is because the prime minister is contemplating future initiatives that are not yet known to departments. If the PCO official fails to convince the committee chairperson of the perceived shortcomings, he or she can still brief the prime minister when the matter comes before full cabinet or P & P. Although this has occurred in the past, it is only done in exceptional cases.[40]

The prime minister is thoroughly briefed by PMO, PCO, and FPRO before attending any cabinet or cabinet committee meeting. 'The Prime Minister's briefing book,' it has been reported, 'usually consists of a three-inch thick black binder with all Cabinet documents (e.g. memoranda to Cabinet from sponsoring ministers, committee reports, relevant records of decision from previous Cabinet deliberations), a briefing note (of 1–10 pages) on each item from one or both PCO and the FPRO and a briefing note from PMO'[41]

PCO staff assume yet another important task after a cabinet or cabinet committee meeting. They prepare committee reports and the records of decision. Cabinet decisions are not always straightforward. It is well known in government that most ministers will talk about anything and everything in cabinet and cabinet committee meetings and that the deliberations themselves 'meander from issue to issue ... without any formal specifications of the resolution of the matters under discussion.'[42] It is left to the committee chairpersons to sum up the discussion and to define the decisions and to PCO staff to draft the decisions. These records of decision are then circulated to ministers and departments and constitute government policy.

The FPRO became a separate agency in 1975. It had been before a secretariat inside PCO and reporting through the clerk of the Privy Council. It is now headed by a deputy minister who, since 1980, reports directly to the prime minister. This, in particular, gives the agency clout in Ottawa.

Officials in FPRO explain their principal role as one of 'managing' federal-provincial relations on behalf of the prime minister and the cabinet. PCO, they explain, 'manages' the government operations in the same way FPRO manages federal-provincial relations. And, like the clerk of the Privy Council, the secretary to the cabinet for FPRO attends all sessions of the prime minister's committees, such as P & P and cabinet meetings. Because federal-provincial relations are so central to policy making in Ottawa, they add, the prime minister and cabinet must continually have two streams of advice: one about government operations from PCO and the other about federal-provincial relations from FPRO.

FPRO then provides the prime minister with a capacity to bring together federal-provincial issues and to give some guidance to his ministers. Managing federal-provincial relations has essentially come to mean managing federal-provincial tensions. There are only so many such conflicts the federal government can properly deal with over a period of time and there is only a degree of such tensions the general public can tolerate. To contain federal-provincial tensions, it is important to know when to 'give in' or when to 'hold the line' with the provinces. The prime minister clearly will want to hold the line on high-priority issues to him and his government. The best ways to manage this is to have someone at the centre who can take a broad view across spending envelopes, sectors, and departments to establish which issues are important to achieve key federal objectives. Ministers and departments on their own are not likely to be able to do so, simply because they do not have the capacity to step back and take a government-wide look. It may well be that, for a minister and his or her department, one federal-provincial issue may be considered vital to departmental objectives. However, when viewed from a government-wide perspective, several other issues may enjoy higher priority. This is where FPRO comes in. In short, it does for federal-provincial relations what PCO does for the federal government.

That said, FPRO does not enjoy the same prestige and the same influence over the expenditure budget as does PCO. FPRO does not have a spending envelope and does not provide secretariat support to cabinet and cabinet committees. Thus, it is not nearly as effective as PCO or the Treasury Board in playing a 'financial gatekeeper' role in government.[43] There is as a result not much incentive for departments to abide by the coordinating efforts of FPRO. Still, the office has direct access to the prime minister, participates directly in the briefing process when spending proposals come forward in the cabinet system, and can play the 'prime minister's card' to support or oppose a particular spending proposal. Experience has shown that it is willing to do so.

GOVERNMENT PLANNING PROCESSES

There are basically three levels of planning in the federal government: government- or cabinet-level planning, policy planning, and departmental planning. Each level is concerned with identifying policy objectives and choosing appropriate means to achieve them.

Government-level planning is the responsibility of cabinet and, more specifically, of P & P. It is an ongoing process but there are four notable types of planning 'events': the election campaign, cabinet and P & P retreats, the speech from the throne, and the budget.

Election campaigns provide golden opportunities to take planning out of the hands of the government machinery and put it into those of party strategists and party leaders. Members of parliament may well participate in planning new policies and government measures in readying their party for an election campaign, but permanent government officials generally do not. The hurdles of PCO, FPRO, and the Treasury Board are completely irrelevant here, and new commitments are made without the machinery of government undertaking any analysis or scrutiny.

Once in power, however, election campaign commitments come under close scrutiny and are put through the hurdles of the government machinery. Ministers certainly do not lose sight of their campaign commitments. From time to time they want to step back to see what progress has been made and to look ahead to determine how best to plan their future efforts. Cabinet and P & P retreats provide such opportunities. These retreats have now become part of the federal government's decision-making landscape.

Cabinet retreats at Meech Lake and P & P meetings in St John's and Lake Louise, among several other locations, have been the site of major decisions on government priorities for the upcoming year, as well as for laying down legislative plans. These retreats – commonly referred to in government as the 'lakes and lodges exercise' – always entail a great deal of official preparation and background documents, and they provide ministers with an ideal occasion for raising basic political issues and for injecting a new political direction to the government planning process. The most important of these retreats is the September P & P meeting, held either at Meech Lake or, if the PMO decides that the government would benefit from the visibility such a meeting always entails, outside Ottawa. Senior ministers are just back from their summer holidays and fully rested. The retreat provides the opportunity to take stock of the past twelve months and to discuss the government's overall priorities for the coming year.

The speech from the throne is a high-profile document that lays out the plans of the government for the upcoming legislative session. The prime minister is the lead actor in this exercise and so the document is prepared in the Prime Minister's Office. Ministers are, however, given an opportunity to contribute ideas and suggestions. All ministers and departments are always eager to see their fields – or, even better, their departmental programs – singled out in the speech from the throne. This constitutes an important cue for them to develop new spending proposals. They will invariably highlight the relevant quote in the speech in support of their programs as they submit their proposals through the approval process.

The budget is also, of course, an important government-wide planning event. For one thing, it affects the resource side of the government planning process. For another, it addresses specific policy areas, ranging from federal-provincial fiscal arrangements and social policy issues, to economic development and tax expenditure policy. As we shall see later, final budget preparation is tightly held in the Department of Finance. A number of ministers, however, do raise issues or proposals in advance with the minister and the department for possible inclusion in the budget.

There are also several other government-wide planning events, although they are not held on a regular or annual basis. They include major studies, task forces, royal commissions, and the preparation of white papers.

Responsibility for policy planning or second-tier planning is focused in the cabinet policy committees. The purpose of linking them to cabinet committees is to integrate departmental policies and instil a longer-term planning process across departments. When the PEMS approach was first introduced, it was believed that this in turn would give rise not only to new spending proposals, but also to the phasing out or redirecting of low-priority programs. Policy-level planning, then, was designed to cut across departmental plans and provide the basis for comprehensive economic or social development plans.

The third planning level is the department. Notwithstanding the central agencies and the cabinet decision-making process, there are still a large number of spending decisions that are taken by ministers and officials at the department. A survey revealed that over 4000 spending decisions were taken in DRIE before it was disbanded without its having to refer to central agencies.

Departments have an elaborate internal monitoring and evaluation system to review existing policies and programs. Some programs can be adjusted internally and funds can be freed up or shifted from one to another. These new measures again result from an internal planning process. Departments also plan spending proposals to compete with other departments for new funding. They consider various options, lay out human and financial resources required to undertake the proposed measures, and consider organizational options to deliver the proposals, if approved.

Quite apart from the competition for new funding, departments must also respond to Treasury Board requirements to report annually on the cost of operating existing programs. This they do by submitting Multi-Year Operational Plans (MYOPS), of which more will be said later in this study.

It is important to stress, however, that planning at whatever level is directly tied to the government's expenditure budget. The federal government's budget process and the way it is put together have undergone important changes over the past twenty-five years. The next chapter traces the development of the expenditure budget over this period.

3

The expenditure budget process

The main functions of the expenditure budget process in the federal government – control, management, and policy planning – have not altered significantly over time, yet the process itself has undergone major changes. Numerous attempts have been made over the years to improve the flow and quality of information going to decision makers and to strengthen the ability of the government to assess the success of its activities. This in turn has required new techniques and new approaches so that the process has, particularly over the past twenty-five years, been in a continuous state of evolution. This chapter traces this evolution.

LINE BUDGETING

In Canada, as elsewhere, line-item budgeting was the first style of budgeting employed. It is remarkably simple to operate. It concentrates on costs and control and is little concerned with output or with determining what is being accomplished by the expenditures.[1] In line-item budgeting, which lasted from Confederation to the 1960s, departments and agencies requested funding for objects of expenditure, and funds were allocated on this basis. The process operated on a year-to-year basis and little attempt was made to undertake long-range planning. It began with each department preparing a request for funds which was then submitted to decision makers for approval. The request outlined in detail the requirements for staff, travel expenses, and program funding for the coming year. Table 4 provides an example of how, in the 1962–3 estimates, Vote 25 on the administration, operation, and maintenance of 'National Parks and Historic Sites and Monuments' was presented

TABLE 4
Vote 25 – Department of Northern Affairs: National Parks and Historic Sites and Monuments, 1962-3*
Illustration of standard objects of expenditure

		1962-3	1961-2
Salaries and wages	(1)	6,343,038	5,891,907
Overtime	(1)	133,453	128,496
Allowances	(2)	14,895	18,580
Professional and special services	(4)	121,330	78,982
Travelling and removal expenses	(5)	103,883	82,478
Freight, express, and cartage	(6)	27,809	25,499
Postage	(7)	9,080	7,880
Telephones and telegrams	(8)	39,753	33,966
Publication of departmental reports and other material	(9)	53,040	49,890
Exhibits, advertising, films, broadcasting, and displays	(10)	18,400	13,800
Office stationery, supplies, and equipment	(11)	61,275	60,184
Materials and supplies	(12)	629,908	602,346
Repairs and upkeep of buildings and works	(14)	242,718	242,718
Repairs and upkeep of roads, bridges, streets, sidewalks, and trails	(14)	293,282	295,228
Rental of land, buildings and works	(15)	1,482	2,008
Repairs and upkeep of equipment	(17)	482,204	468,439
Rental of Equipment	(18)	2,300	
Municipal or public utility services	(19)	172,484	135,498
Payments to individuals or groups in respect to agreements entered into by the minister pursuant to the Historic Sites and Monuments Act for the preservation and commemoration of historic sites	(20)	106,000	49,000
Unemployment insurance contributions	(21)	40,474	31,310
Sundries	(22)	34,592	32,705
		$8,931,400	$8,248,914

*The criteria to determine what constitutes a vote is explained in Canada, Treasury Board, *Policy and Expenditure Management System Manual*, chapter 8. Broadly speaking, there is now one vote per program.

for approval to the Treasury Board by the Department of Northern Affairs and National Resources.

When the departments had finalized their expenditure estimates, they would submit them to Treasury Board analysts who would review them in detail and initiate discussions with departmental staff. Some changes to the estimates could be agreed to at this level. Disagreements were referred to higher-level Treasury Board and departmental officials. Remaining disagreements were presented to the board itself, where ministers would make the final decisions. Often ministers were invited to attend board meetings when their departmental estimates were being considered.

We now know that the Treasury Board review of estimates followed no clear-cut pattern. Often the confidence that existed between the Treasury Board analysts and departmental staff had an impact on final budgetary figures for a department. Certainly little evaluation of the purpose of public spending and departmental programs took place. This was true throughout the period that line budgeting was in place in the federal government. The estimates, or the expenditure budget, were regarded simply as a means through which departments obtained 'sustenance.'[2]

Some advances, however, were made in the preparation of estimates. Prior to 1937, for example, the estimates had no basic principle of organization.[3] Some votes covered a whole program, others only selected activities, still others covered capital projects in a region, and some covered the purchase of specific items, such as books and magazines. In addition, there was a list of all permanent positions in government in the estimates.

The government adopted a new format for its estimates in 1938. Treasury Board officials later explained that the changes were necessary because 'only an experienced accounting officer, with ample time at his disposal, can compute the real cost of most services.'[4] Several major revisions were introduced. For one thing, all the votes under the control of a particular minister would now be displayed together in one place. This, it was felt, would encourage greater accountability to parliament. For another, items of a general character were to be eliminated, and all expenditure items were to be assembled under responsible departments. The result was that the government now knew far better than at any time in the past the actual cost of individual programs.

The 1930s also saw important steps made to acquire some degree of central control of spending. For instance, the Office of the Comptroller of the Treasury was established in 1931 by the Bennett government to set up an elaborate system of 'commitment control,' designed to ensure that funds were spent only for the purposes for which they had been voted and that departments would not overspend their budgets.

The coming of the Great Depression reinforced the view that austerity and a balanced budget would restore business confidence in the economy. This, it was believed, was the key to shake the country out of its economic doldrums. But the Bennett government soon realized that it was ill-equipped to reduce the cost of government. 'Much to Bennett's horror,' it is reported, 'it appeared that the economic and social chaos in the country at large was hardly any worse than the administrative chaos which had reigned in the federal bureaucracy for years, insofar as financial control was concerned.'[5] Line-item budgeting was effective in controlling input costs and limits on spending, but was seriously lacking in controlling the use of funds once the budget had been struck.

In establishing the Office of the Comptroller of the Treasury, Bennett also centralized administration and removed most accounting functions from departments. The Office of the Comptroller had, at its peak, close to 5000 officers scattered in all departments, in all regions, and abroad.[6] These officers were responsible for examining all expenditures prior to payment. They were instructed to withhold approval and refer to Treasury Board any expenses which, in their view, were not lawful charges against appropriations and to report when any department had overcommitted a vote. To carry out these responsibilities, the office kept elaborate records of all outstanding commitments and expenditures.

At the beginning of each fiscal year, the office established a breakdown of each vote approved by parliament. These breakdowns were known as allotments and usually corresponded to the standard objects of expenditures as set forth in the details of the estimates that departments presented to Treasury Board for approval. Accounts were then set up in the books and the amount approved entered in each account. When expenditures were submitted for certification, the amount was deducted from the account. In this manner, the comptroller always had a running balance for each vote and each account and knew the uncommitted balance, the portion committed but unspent, and total expenditures to date. Departments had a duplicate accounting system in place to monitor their spending. Whenever proposed expenditures exceeded the amount in the account, only the Treasury Board could authorize new funding or, as much more frequently happened, a transfer of funds from one account to another could be effected by increasing one account and decreasing the other. Figure 1 summarizes the expenditure process under line-item budgeting. As the figure indicates, after the establishment of the Office of Comptroller of the Treasury, line-item budgeting placed strong emphasis on the control of spending even after expenditure levels had been established. Conversely, this style of budgeting placed little emphasis on policy planning and management. Even in 1960 the estimates still broke down expenditures into thirty-four standard objects. Expenditures were also still presented to parliament in two forms. The first section presented departmental expenditures classified

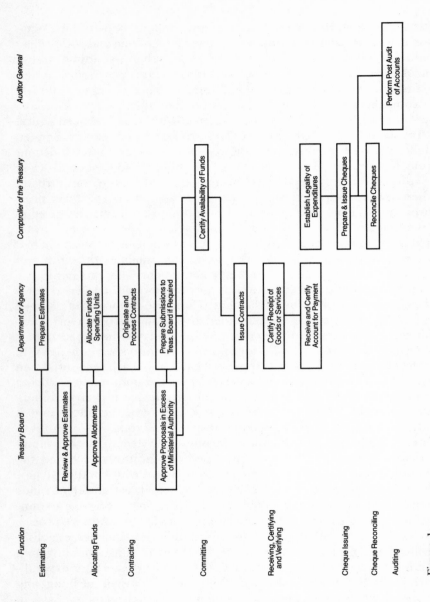

Figure 1
Summary of the expenditure process in government in line-item budgeting

according to broadly defined operations and services. The second section classified the expenditures in each vote and department into the standard objects. The standard objects codified spending based on the item the money was to be spent on and accordingly were designed more to fit traditional accounting principles than a comprehensive approach to budgetary review.

By the late 1950s, however, the government began to ask fundamental questions about financial and personnel management, as well as government organization. The budget process in particular was viewed by many as unsatisfactory. For example, critics suggested that the form of the estimates did not permit intelligent scrutiny of spending in parliament since the classification used did not refer to programs. This made it difficult to assess the need for continuing, modifying, or enlarging specific programs.

Senior ministers, including the prime minister, were increasingly concerned about the growth of government, in particular that of the public service. As well, representatives of the business community were urging the government to examine its efficiency, as had happened in the United Stated under President Hoover.[7] The Diefenbaker government responded by establishing the Royal Commission on Government Organization (commonly known as the Glassco Commission). The commissioners were directed 'to inquire into and report upon the organization and methods of operation of the departments and agencies of the Government of Canada and to recommend the changes therein which they consider would best promote efficiency, economy and improved service in the despatch of public business.'[8]

THE GLASSCO COMMISSION'S RECOMMENDATIONS
ON BUDGETING

The Glassco Commission came forward in 1962 with a series of recommendations designed to improve the government's budgeting process and to integrate expenditure management with policy analysis and decision making. Essentially, it urged the government to do away with line-item budgeting and adopt a program approach to budgeting. The commission suggested that the traditional concern with audits to ensure parliamentary control over resources was no longer sufficient. An approach was needed to determine whether the purposes and results of programs were consistent both with their legislated intents and with their objectives. The commission also proposed that expenditure and revenue projections be made for a five-year period, with departments and agencies required to submit long-term forecasts.

The commission's argument was that '[the] ponderous system, virtually unchanged in the past thirty years, is regarded by many as the price that must be paid under democracy in order to hold public servants properly accountable.'[9] However, the commission was quick to add that 'the system in place no longer did the job.' 'What was a relatively simple government organization in 1939,' it reported, 'had become today a complicated system of departments, boards and commissions engaged in a multitude of different tasks. Obviously, the methods found effective for the management of the relatively compact organization of the prewar days cannot control without extensive alteration, the vast complex which has come into being in the past twenty years.' The commission went on to insist that the government's financial controls were too cumbersome in that there was a wide variety of 'checks, counterchecks and duplication and blind adherence to regulations.'[10]

It then recommended sweeping changes to the existing process, arguing that it was necessary to get at existing programs and their funding, rather than concentrating exclusively on proposed increases, as in the past. It put it this way: 'If a vote currently provides for an establishment of 100 and the proposed establishment is 105, the emphasis is on justifying the need for the additional five positions rather than on making an objective review of the continuing requirement for all positions previously authorized.'[11] Even the Treasury Board itself and its staff, the commissioners insisted, were primarily concerned with the details and controlling of proposed expenditures, rather than with whether the need that initially gave rise to them still existed.

The commission presented a series of recommendations on a variety of issues. Its main recommendations on the expenditure budget process were as follows:

1 Votes should be reduced in number and more clearly describe the purposes of expenditure.
2 All cost elements of individual programs should be consolidated within one vote.
3 Estimates should be prepared on the basis of programs of activity rather than by standard objects of expenditure.
4 The costs of major common services should be charged to user departments.
5 Where appropriate, revenue should be offset against related expen-

diture, and votes should be displayed, voted, and controlled on a net basis.

6 All fees charged for services should be reviewed periodically to relate revenues and expenditures.

7 The Establishment Review Procedure should be undertaken as part of the overall estimates review and not as a separate exercise.

8 Overall forecasts of government expenditures and projected revenues should be prepared annually, covering a five-year period.

9 More objective standards for the analysis of estimates should be developed and employed, both by senior departmental management and by Treasury Board during the review process.

10 Departments and agencies should be given the necessary financial authority and be held accountable for the effective management of the financial resources placed at their disposal.

11 Departments and agencies should adopt modern management reporting techniques.

The Government accepted the great majority of the Glassco Commission recommendations. In fact, the commission staff had worked closely with Treasury Board officials and some of the recommendations had already been approved before the commission issued its final report. For example, in 1961 the Treasury Board began to reduce the number of votes with a view to associating each one with a major program and undertook to forecast expenditures beyond the next fiscal year. In 1962, the Treasury Board asked departments to submit five-year forecasts of expenditures associated with maximum and minimum levels of activities. Shortly after the release of the Glassco report, the government established the Bureau of Government Organization (BOGO) to coordinate the implementation of many Glassco recommendations. The bureau was headed by a senior deputy minister and a close working relationship between BOGO and the Treasury Board secretariat was established.[12] In time, a joint appointment was even made to head both BOGO and the Treasury Board secretariat. In addition, numerous joint committees and study groups were established.

The Treasury Board secretariat undertook an intensive examination of the estimates process and vote workings in presenting the expenditure budget to parliament. Four pilot departments were selected to reform the presentation of their estimates for 1966–7. Though the estimates were tabled in their traditional form that year, the exercise gave the board and the departments an appreciation of the work involved in presenting the estimates to parliament in both program format and vote structure and to project expenditures on a multi-year basis. With lessons learned from the pilot departments, the Treasury Board issued new guidelines for a trial run for the 1967–8 estimates and for proper presentation thereafter. By the end of the 1960s, the estimates had undergone major revisions so that public spending could be examined by parliament with more precision. The estimates were broken down by departments, then by votes (which were increasingly defined along program lines), and finally by standard object of expenditures within votes or according to the types and services on which money was spent.[13] As early as 1964–5, the number of votes had been reduced from 550 to 220, vote wording was revised to express program objectives, and capital and operating votes were separated. These changes were made to ease the introduction of the Program Planning Budgeting System (PPB) in government.

The commission's greatest impact on the expenditure budget process, however, was 'that it created a climate for change.'[14] There was now a willingness in government to do away with long-established procedures. After Glassco tabled its report, it becomes widely accepted and even fashionable in some quarters in government to argue that the line-item budgeting style had outlived its usefulness. That approach to budgeting, it was believed, simply assumed that most of 'what is, is good and should remain.'[15] The government, even cabinet ministers, had been much too preoccupied with evaluating administrative costs, such as salaries, travel expenses, or the procurement of material. In addition, the scrutiny of departmental transactions by central agencies, notably Treasury Board and the Office of the Comptroller General, had been far too detailed. Not only did this inevitably sap the initiative of public servants, but no one could be held responsible for any failure. In any event, virtually no thought had been given to whether or not there was still a need for the various programs or if they were achieving their goals. The result was that 'it was forgotten that one bad policy decision or one ineffective program could cost the country more than the Treasury Board could possibly save in a hundred years by saving pencil stubs.'[16]

Thus, the stage was set for a new approach to budgeting, one which would break from the past, and, in the 1960s, the federal government embraced PPB, a new concept to budgeting that was initially introduced in the United States.[17]

THE WAX AND WANE OF PPB IN CANADA

A keen student of the federal government expenditure process describes

PPB as a 'grandiose concept' that 'seeks to determine the package of policy instruments which simultaneously achieves the optimum realization of the government's objectives over time.'[18] A leading practitioner was even more enthusiastic, explaining that 'PPB seeks almost by definition to bring under review all that has been, as well as all that might be, to query the conventional wisdom, and to advance if necessary unconventional alternatives.'[19] To most practitioners and observers at the time, PPB held great promise, and few dissident voices were heard. Shortly after the federal government declared its intention to introduce PPB, several provincial governments, including some of the smaller ones whose expenditure budgets were relatively easy to manage, announced that they would do so as well. The government of New Brunswick, for example, announced with considerable fanfare the introduction of PPB to the province in 1970.[20]

PPB was seen as the instrument that would enable departments to define objectives and assess the full cost of programs. It was also seen as the means by which the cost-benefits of alternative programs could be evaluated, as well as providing a capacity to ascertain the costs of future programs and spending proposals. This would leave ministers free to consider larger issues and broader questions. The thinking was that if ministers are given information on administrative details they will make decisions on details, but if they are given information on policies and programs they will make policy decisions. In short, PPB was an appealing alternative to incrementalism. The extent to which it was regarded in Ottawa as a dramatic and effective new approach to budgeting is best exemplified by the minister of finance's statement at the time the approach was introduced. 'PPB,' he boldly declared, 'is a major budget breakthrough.'[21] The approach was considered to be such a powerful instrument that many believed it would actually remove politics from the budgeting process – it would provide such clear and rational answers that ministers would be compelled to embrace them. This was so widely believed that senior officials felt the need to reassure ministers that they would continue to make the key decisions and that politics would still weigh heavily in the decision-making process. Al Johnson wrote, for example, 'PPB must not seek to substitute science for politics in the decision-making process.'[22]

In 1968 the president of the Treasury Board issued a guide to departments and agencies on how to implement PPB. The guide explained that the approach was designed to reveal the most feasible way of attaining an objective and to determine the best way to achieve the greatest benefit for a given cost. It outlined the key concepts of PPB: (a) the setting of specific objectives; (b) the systematic analysis to clarify objectives and to assess alternative ways of meeting them; (c) the framing of budgetary programs in terms of programs directed towards the achievement of objectives; (d) the future projections of the cost of these programs; (e) the formulation of plans of achievement year by year for each program; and (f) an information system for each program to supply data for the monitoring of achievement of program goals and for the reassessment of the program objectives and the appropriateness of the program itself. A separate chapter of the guide was devoted to cost-benefit analysis. This chapter urged managers to state clearly their program objectives and then to list and describe alternative ways of achieving them. Finally, they were to construct mathematical models for experimenting with the proposed alternatives before determining their costs.[23]

All departments plunged headlong into implementing PPB, and by 1970 all departmental expenditure budgets were submitted along PPB lines. Budgets were broken down into programs and multi-year forecasts were prepared for each program. This tactic, it was believed, would prevent departments from launching programs with limited resources and expanding them considerably in future years. In addition, departments were asked to define goals for all their programs and activities and to come up with objective criteria to determine whether the goals were being met. Major changes were also introduced from 1969 to 1971 in the way the estimates were put together and presented to parliament. Specifically:

1 expenditures were presented by departments in terms of programs with a statement of objectives;
2 each program was broken down into activities (the various alternative means by which program objectives were to be reached) and total costs displayed according to standard objects of expenditures;
3 non-budgetary items (loans, investments, and advances) were shown in conjuction with the appropriate program;
4 estimates for the coming year were compared to the forecast of expenditures for the year just coming to an end and to the actual expenditures of the previous year for each program;
5 grants or capital expenditures that exceeded $5 million were segregated into separate votes;
6 salary range data were replaced by data on authorized and planned person-years;
7 the number of standard objects was reduced to twelve.

In 1969, a revised form of expenditure control was also introduced which gave more freedom to departments in moving money around within programs. Thus the Treasury Board was relieved of excess involvement in day-to-day departmental administration to concentrate on evaluating departmental programs and activities. In 1970, the Treasury Board introduced the concept of A-B-X budgets to take effect in fiscal year 1971–2. The A budget consists of those expenditures necessary to finance ongoing programs in the new year at their existing level of service, while the x budget focuses on low-priority program elements that could be discontinued. The margin between revenue and the A budget, plus savings through the x budget, provides 'new money' for the B budget to finance expansion of existing or new programs. This was done in the hope that it would enhance PPB's program review process.

At the time the federal government introduced PPB, it also put in place major changes in the machinery of government. By definition, PPB requires a strong capacity at the centre, as well as trade-offs to respond to the information coming from the various rational economic tools put in place. As we saw in the previous chapter, a powerful Priorities and Planning Committee of cabinet was established. Central agencies were also established (Treasury board secretariat) or expanded (the Plans Division in the Privy Council Office). The role of the Plans Division was to prepare or have departments prepare papers on broad social and economic trends or on specific wide-ranging problems. These agencies were intended to integrate a number of disparate processes, including the evaluation of existing programs, the identification of new priority areas, and planning new legislative proposals. In brief, rational economic planning would now drive decision making in government, and planning was to be integrated with the budgetary process, with planning as the master and budgeting as the servant.[24]

Within a few years, however, it became apparent that PPB had serious shortcomings. By the mid-1970s, it was pronounced dead in the United States and in some provincial governments. Two observers now report that 'anyone who did a cost-benefit analysis on the introduction of PPB ... would be forced to conclude that it was not worth the effort.'[25] Certainly PPB entailed considerable paper work, countless meetings, and the hiring of a great number of systems analysts and operation research specialists in Ottawa. Yet looking back we now know that it led to 'very few program terminations or dramatic shifts in expenditure patterns.'[26] If anything, PPB led to increased spending in the administrative costs of

government. Numerous new positions were also established to implement PPB, particularly in the areas of planning, evaluation, and policy
and program coordination. Moreover, in moving away from line budgeting, the Treasury Board loosened its control over costs such as travel,
consultant contracts, and the like. Some senior officials now report that,
as a result, departmental budgets for these items mushroomed in the
late 1960s and 1970s. 'It became too easy,' said one, 'for departments
to get money for travel, for consultants, for staff, for new equipment
and the like. We lost control over spending and we got little in the way
of program reduction. PPB became the problem and no longer the
solution.'[27] To be sure, expectations for PPB were high. This led two
students of public administration to observe: 'It might well be that PPB
has not failed, but rather that some people expected – and others
promised – more than PPB could ever deliver.'[28]

Nevertheless, it quickly became obvious that to bring quantitative
analysis into the expenditure budget process was no easy task. For one
thing, defining specific objectives for programs and activities proved
difficult. There was often more than one objective for any given program
and virtually every program impinged directly or indirectly on the goals
of others. Thus, in defining its program objectives, a department had to
contend with those of another, which could be in conflict. For example,
grants to encourage labour mobility out of Atlantic Canada may have
increased national economic efficiency and the total number of new jobs
created at the national level, but might be in direct conflict with the
regional development goals of another department.

Thus, program objectives, if ever defined at all, were more often than
not vague and of little value even as a checklist to evaluate the program's
effectiveness. In turn, it became virtually impossible to develop a set of
criteria to determine the success of the programs. There was little in the
way of experience to draw from. To be sure, ministers and officials had
looked at objectives when budgeting by standard objects was the norm,
but only in a superficial manner. PPB was also largely ineffective in
bringing together the total picture of the expenditure budget and in
showing unequivocally that a particular program had failed. However,
in instances where PPB techniques could show that a program was meeting its objectives and that a strong need still existed for it, the sponsoring
department was sure to parade the findings in front of Treasury Board
and other cabinet committees.

From the Treasury Board perspective, PPB had important shortcomings. It was felt that many program enrichments, valid as they were
within a narrow program perspective of PPB evaluation criteria, were

implemented in the absence of a clear overall expenditure framework. Much as in the past, the government plan reflected the incremental costs of ongoing programs. PPB techniques were trotted out in instances where they could justify enriching a particular program, but were never heard from in other circumstances. Ministers became increasingly concerned that the expenditure budget did not reflect changing government priorities.

Yet PPB had been introduced because it promised to contribute greatly to the policy-planning function of the expenditure budget. The other two functions of the modern budgetary system – control and management – would, it was assumed, fall into place under the direction of PPB's strong policy-planning capacity. After a few years, however, there were few in the federal government who believed that PPB was having any positive impact on the policy-planning function, let alone the other two. The search was on once again for a new approach.

Of the three factors that led the federal government to search for new solutions, two had been instrumental in the introduction of PPB in the first place: the inability of the government to control the growth of its total expenditures, or to assess the effectiveness of the expenditures in meeting their objectives. The first point was brought home by the auditor general in 1976 when he wrote that 'Parliament – and indeed the government – had lost or was close to losing effective control of the public purse.'[29] The third factor was a desire to strengthen the policy-making role of ministers and cabinet, who felt that in doing away with line-item budgeting they had lost control of the policy-making process. In any event, by the late 1970s, the federal government had defined a new approach: the Policy and Expenditure Management System (PEMS) or the envelope system. Though the government believed that PEMS would accomplish what PPB could not, it was careful this time not to raise the kind of expectations it had in introducing PPB. This time senior officials simply announced that PEMS would improve the capacity of the government to integrate policy making and expenditure management and also ensure greater ministerial controls over these functions.[30]

PEMS: THE ACRONYM FOR THE 1980s

Why PEMS: To be sure, the PPB shortcomings noted above forced the government to look for new solutions. But there was also widespread concern over the continued growth of the expenditure base resulting from increased spending in statutory expenditure programs. This growth was squeezing out money to support new initiatives. What, it was asked, if the government had to deal suddenly with new emergencies? It also had become clear that if reductions were to be made it would be far easier to reduce discretionary expenditure programs, regardless of their high priority in relation to a number of statutory programs. It is in this environment that PEMS was introduced in 1979. It was considered a rational expenditure budgeting system that would specify reserves over a medium-term period that would be made available to finance new initiatives and help to identify programs of relatively low priority for possible reduction or termination.

PEMS was designed, therefore, to provide ministers with information about the effects of their decisions on the growth of approved and continuing programs. The growth in the expenditure base, together with the fiscal framework which specifies desired total outlays, would provide both a clear indication of the funds (that is, policy reserves) available for expected new initiatives and provide room for manoeuvre in the face of unexpected developments. PEMS also provides the framework by which the government can make decisions to enrich or reduce programs, given the priorities attached to them.

How does PEMS work?[31] First, contrary to what is widely assumed outside government (and even among some federal public servants), PEMS does not constitute a complete break with the past. The transition from PPB to PEMS was much less dramatic than was that from line-item budgeting to PPB. A number of important characteristics of PPB were incorporated into PEMS. In fact, for officials directly involved, in both the Treasury Board secretariat and various departments, PEMS represented an opportunity to improve upon PPB and the traditional resource allocation process. PEMS, like PPB, calls for specific program objectives, the definition of program benefits, the development of a comprehensive framework for classifying programs, information systems to evaluate the effectiveness of individual programs, and the ability to project cost over several years. PEMS, however, differs from PPB in several ways. First, it seeks to forge a link between operational planning and the broader government-wide strategic planning process. Secondly, it was conceived as a collective top-down decision-making process. Under PEMS, cabinet and cabinet committees set expenditure ceilings and establish priorities. Programs are then developed within these constraints. Thirdly, PEMS concentrates more on planned results as a basis for allocating resources within established expenditure limits than it does on program objectives, as did PPB. The multi-year operational plans (MYOPS) under PEMS seek to define planned results.

The first clear manifestation of the emerging system was the establish-

ment in November 1978 of the Board of Economic Development Ministers.[32] This 'board' was given spending authority over a set amount of
funds earmarked for economic development. The practice was institu-
tionalized by the short-lived Conservative government under Joe Clark
and by the subsequent Liberal government through the creation of
specific policy 'envelopes.'

PEMS, it was hoped, would integrate policy and expenditure decision
making more fully than PPB ever did. Under PPB, cabinet committees
approved policy proposals and left the spending issue to Finance or
Treasury Board, with the result that new commitments were easily made
by the committees. They simply did not have to reconcile their policy
decisions with the government's spending plans. A Treasury Board
official explained the difference between PPB and PEMS in this fashion:
'You can compare policy and expenditure decisions to a pair of scissors.
The two blades must meet for the process to be effective. Under PPB they
would never meet. Cabinet committees would make policy decisions and
leave it to someone else to make resources available. PEMS has changed
this. Now cabinet committees have to make both policy and spending
decisions or see to it that both blades meet at the same time. They have
expenditure limits or envelopes consistent with the government's fiscal
plan.'[33] In short, the envelope accounting system would face the cabinet
committees with the fiscal consequence of their decision (the envelopes
are shown in table 5). In the past, the cabinet committee, if it wanted to
approve new spending proposals beyond what was available in the
budget, simply reviewed existing policies and programs and their
resource levels and then brought about the necessary changes in funding levels to reflect their changing priorities. Now, under PEMS, ministers
would have to make tough decisions if they wanted to approve new
spending proposals. In short, the intent was to place responsibility for
saving squarely on the shoulders of those who spent and turn all ministers into at least part-time guardians. PEMS would also 'put first things
first' by establishing priorities and fiscal *limits* before developing expenditure plans.

The policy areas and the new policy reserves had to be managed. The
cabinet committees managing the policy areas in turn required support
'in the making of trade-offs necessary to stay within limits of the budget
envelopes and in ensuring the integration of policy and spending
plans.'[34] Given that the bulk of the work was on the economic development and social policy scenes, two new central agencies were established
in 1979: the Ministry of State for Economic Development (which
replaced the Board of Economic Development Ministers and which later

TABLE 5
Expenditure plan by envelope ($ million)

	1984–5	1985–6	1986–7	1987–8
Economic and regional development	14,851	11,823	11,750	11,955
Social development	50,538	51,812	54,785	57,200
Fiscal arrangements	5,985	5,941	6,005	6,200
External affairs and aid	2,639	2,479	2,970	3,370
Defence	8,762	9,094	9,765	10,200
Parliament	196	198	205	220
Services to government	3,789	4,439	3,805	3,985
Public debt	22,455	25,441	27,275	23,200
Total envelopes	109,215	111,227	116,560	121,330
Reserves not allocated by envelope*			1,081	2,380
Lapse			–1,006	–1,160
Budgetary expenditures	109,215	111,227	116,635	122,550

*Includes Treasury Board Vote 5: Government Contingencies

became known as the Ministry of State for Economic and Regional Development) and the Ministry of State for Social Development.

These ministries gained their influence by acting as gatekeepers to the policy reserves. Richard Van Loon summed up their role this way:

Before proposals go to the appropriate Cabinet committee they are normally widely discussed with ministry officials and considered by a committee of deputy ministers (i.e., mirror committees) chaired by the Deputy Minister of State. The Cabinet committee is provided with written advice on the basis of these deliberations and in addition the ministry briefs the chairman of the Cabinet committee and can use that occasion to forward any objections it may have to a proposal. Coordination and integration within the sector are to be achieved through the overview functions of these agencies and because of the fact that proposals will not normally proceed to Cabinet committees before a thorough examination by the ministries.[35]

One determinant of envelope size – indeed the major one – is the activities already under way and included within the envelope. The content of each was largely decided when PEMS was adopted in 1979, though this initial allocation has been added to and slightly modified by the ongoing funding decisions taken by governments since that time. The total cost of funding all the accepted activities in an envelope is the product of discussions between each department included in the policy sector (or envelope) and the Treasury Board through the MYOP process.

Another determinant of envelope size is the forecast for both the total amount of government revenues and the level of expenditures the government should be seeking in relation to this revenue forecast. This information is provided in the fiscal framework supplied by the minister of finance. In addition to the views of the minister are the sectoral overviews, provided by the sectoral cabinet committees. These overviews, developed by the respective secretariats to the policy committees, are supposed to provide reflections on the priorities and outstanding commitments in each of the policy areas. To a degree, they reflected the concerns and agendas put forward by the individual departments/ ministers in their own 'strategic overviews.'

It is necessary to digress briefly to explain the various reserves under PEMS. There are five major reserves. First, there are the policy reserves or top-up funds for which departments can apply to a policy committee (such as the economic and regional development committee or social development committee). Secondly, there is the operational reserve. Proposed cost adjustments to approved departmental operational plans that do not arise from policy decisions can be funded from this reserve. These adjustments may result from cost overruns on approved projects, unanticipated workload increases, rescheduling of multi-year expenditure commitments, and so on. All funding from the operating reserve must be approved by the Treasury Board, and we will return to the reserve again when we look at the operation of the Treasury Board. Thirdly, the federal government is obligated to meet certain commitments of statutory or quasi-statutory nature. These commitments are in some instances tied to certain economic variables such as the rates of unemployment and inflation. Funding from the statutory reserve is available only to cover cost overruns resulting from changes such as revisions in the underlying economic or demographic assumptions in these statutory programs. Fourthly, earmarked funds are set aside in the expenditure framework to meet known requirements for which any number of technical or other arrangements have yet to be resolved. When these arrangements are resolved, the items are incorporated into departmental reference levels on A base. For example, the government may well unveil a major funding decision for space research and science and technology. Until such time as cash flow issues can be resolved, or which department will be doing what determined, it is not possible to incorporate all the necessary funding in reference levels of departments. Fifthly, there is now a centrally held reserve managed by the minister of finance. It has come to represent a significant source of funds set aside to meet large pressures in the framework. When it is not sufficient, the government can break the fiscal framework or increase the total level of the expenditure budget to provide for new funds.

Decisions on new spending, new programs, or improvements in the quality of existing programs under PEMS are to be taken by the policy committees and are funded from the policy reserves whose resources are determined by subtracting the amount of the A budgets, or the funds required for continuing programs, from the total expenditure allocation. What is left over is what is available for policy reserves. In the event that the A budget takes most, all, or perhaps even more than the total expenditure allocation available, then cabinet must still engage in an x budget exercise. It should be noted, however, that under PEMS there ought not be an x budget exercise. PEMS was designed to avoid centrally directed x budget exercises by having sectorally directed exercises that would enrich policy reserves.

Underpinning the PEMS top-down fiscal planning and policy direction is the bottom-up expenditure management process whose main instrument is the MYOP. The MYOPs are the main means of ensuring a review of the resources needed to deliver approved and ongoing programs over a three-year planning period. The basis for developing the MYOPs is the departmental Operational Plan Framework (OPF). All departments have defined their own OPFs. OPFs provide the rationale behind the MYOPs in that they detail the departmental goals, the internal management structure and decision-making process, and program objectives.

Departmental MYOPs are reviewed by the Treasury Board secretariat before they are approved by Treasury Board. These status quo planning documents provide forecasts of the financial and personnel resources needed to operate approved programs and, therefore, of the baseline estimates of program costs in future years. Individual MYOPs enable the Treasury Board to determine the levels of resources to be allocated to departments and agencies and to identify resource allocation and program management issues that emerge from the analysis of trends in resource utilization. Moreover, the cost of ongoing programs, as approved by the Treasury Board, provides a necessary important input into the fiscal planning exercise and the determination of resources to be allocated to the various policy sector envelopes. The top-down fiscal planning and bottom-up expenditure management are thus developed hand-in-hand, each providing information that leads to adjustments in the other. Each fall, the Department of Finance produces a status quo fiscal plan, and suggests broad alternative approaches to deal with the

TABLE 6
Major steps in expenditure planning cycle

Calendar year	Stage of expenditure planning	Responsibilty
Spring 1988	Submission of Annual Management Report* detailing, inter alia, results for 1987–8, updating OPF/results, linkages, etc., and problem areas for the planning period	Deputy minister
	Analysis of report with highlights on resouce pressures, results achieved relative to targets, and updates on OPF results	Program branch (TBS)
June 1988	Report to Treasury Board on resource pressures for current and future fiscal years	Program branch (TBS)
June 1988	Strategic direction to departments and TBS on approach to multi-year budget update	Treasury Board
Summer 1988	Preparation of multi-year budget update for 1989–90, 1990–1, and 1991–2 in accordance with TB direction	Departments
Fall 1988	Report to P & P on expenditure pressures	President of Treasury Board
Fall 1988	Analysis of multi-year budget update and report to Treasury Board on main estimates for 1989–90 and reference levels for 1990–1 and 1991–2	Program branch (TBS)
Winter 1988	Participation in fiscal framework and priority-setting exercise	President of Treasury Board
Winter 1988	Revision of multi-year budget update and preparation of 1989–90 main estimates	Departments/ program branch (TBS)
February 1989	Tabling of 1989–90 main estimates	President of Treasury Board)

*Submitted pursuant to an IMAA MOU

economic and fiscal environment. The minister of finance then sets out multi-year fiscal situations with respect to government priorities, advises on the fiscal plan based on economic fiscal and expenditure projections, and makes recommendations on envelope levels and policy reserves. Meanwhile, expenditure planning figures for a given fiscal year are developed and refined through the multi-year planning process and become firmly established in the winter prior to the start of a fiscal year. Table 6 describes the operation of the expenditure planning cycle, highlighting its major events.

The Treasury Board secretariat stands at the centre of the ongoing MYOP exercise. The process entails sustained contact between Treasury Board analysts and departmental officials. It offers the Treasury Board a more intimate knowledge of the operations and the resources required for government programs. A major component of the expenditure budget is the person-year complement and the MYOPS give the Treasury Board the mean of controlling person-years. They also give the board, other cabinet committees, and full cabinet their only window on the government's overall spending budget.

Shortly after PEMS was introduced, the government made still more changes in the way it presents its estimates to parliament.[36] As part of the 1981–2 estimates, it introduced a new document, entitled the Government Expenditure Plans. Now known as Part I of the estimates, the document, as we have already seen, provides an overview of total spending, while describing the plans for each of the broad policy areas and highlighting significant changes in spending patterns from year to year.

The next year, the government introduced another document, labelled Part II, which contains information on each program of government for which funding is requested. It includes a summary of appropriations, a general statement of objectives of the programs and proposed spending, and the required number of person-years for the various activities in which the program is engaged. The most significant change in the estimates is Part III. This part presents a separate expenditure plan for each department and outlines in considerable detail each of the department's programs.

THE ACRONYM FOR THE 1980S IS IN DIFFICULTY

PEMS, it has been suggested, was the result of the 'continuing attempts within the federal government to impose financial and qualitative discipline and a notion of collective responsibility on what was hitherto a rather undisciplined policy process.'[37] However, towards the end of the Trudeau government's last mandate, it became increasingly clear that such discipline as had been instilled into the policy process was being seen as counter-productive by some. Reforms were clearly required. It was just a case of what and when.

Ministers found the process much too bureaucratic. Many of them also felt that PEMS increased the influence of permanent officials over policy at their expense. They objected, in particular, to the mirror committees of deputy ministers meeting to consider spending proposals before they did. Ministers also became convinced that the system had become far too cumbersome – that, in their efforts to impose collective decision making, the central agencies had gone too far in restricting the actions of ministers and departments, Some ministers were convinced that PEMS gave unelected officials in central agencies too much control over policy processes and outcomes and, in so doing, had usurped the minister's role in determining government policy. For the system to function in the interests of good government, they insisted, individual ministers and departments had to be allowed to exercise their judgment and use their initiative. This was not happening with PEMS, and it was widely believed among ministers that the approach had failed to give them the critical policy role it had promised.[38]

Even senior officials began to acknowledge the problems as early as 1983. The then deputy secretary to the cabinet (plans) in the Privy Council Office asked in a widely circulated paper: 'Is the system too heavy and burdensome on ministers and officials? Is there too much paper in the system and are there too many rules? Do we have the right balance of the kinds of decisions ministers are being asked to take collectively rather than individually?'[39] He simply asked the questions and did not attempt to provide answers.

John Turner, however, did, during his brief stay as Liberal prime minister. The first thing he did, when he came to office, was to 'stream-line' decision making in government. He explained that the policy process had become 'too elaborate, too complex, too slow, and too expensive.'[40] He disbanded the two central agencies that were playing a key role in PEMS: the Ministers of State for Social Development and for Economic and Regional Development. The mirror committees of deputy ministers were also abolished. Departmental strategic overviews were no longer requested by the cabinet committees, and departments simply stopped preparing them. Mulroney continued with the changes Turner introduced and did not attempt to re-create the ministries of state. The Mulroney government did seek to introduce a new management style in government which gives greater decision-making authority to individual ministers. This change, however, would further reduce the degree of cabinet collegiality which is crucial to the operations of PEMS. We will return to this later in our review of the work of the Treasury Board.

There were other problems identified with PEMS. Some departments began to bypass policy committees and go directly to the Department of Finance with their spending problems. Many inside government regarded this as a breakdown in the discipline required to make PEMS work effectively. We will also return to this point in the next chapter.

Once again it is ironic that one of PEMS' major shortcomings was precisely the thing it was designed to resolve. The purpose of PEMS, it will be recalled, was to strengthen the role of ministers in the policy process. Yet only a few years after its introduction, ministers had become some of its most strident critics. They were convinced that they had lost some of their traditional influence and that their capacity to make decisions had been hobbled. PPB, it will also be recalled, had been introduced to control the growth in spending. It had been expected to show clearly which programs were no longer responding to the need for which they were first designed and also uncover programs that were not meeting their stated goals. Yet several years after PPB was introduced, the government was told that it had lost or was close to losing effective control of the public purse.

What this suggests is that no new policy process or new government machinery, however well defined, can in itself provide the 'financial and qualitative discipline' to shape the government's expenditure budget. The first part of this study suggests that the failure to cut government spending is not for want of a policy-making process and the machinery of government. The actual policy actors, their personalities, the capacity of ministers to work with their officials, the ability of some ministers to do 'end-runs' on the system, and other such factors have a far greater impact on the government's expenditure plans than any well-reasoned policy process ever can. This study also argues that the growth in government spending cannot be explained, let alone curtailed, by such a process. Thus, as we suggested in the first chapter, one has to look beyond the process to what motivates key policy actors to explain the growth in government spending.

PART II

The guardians

4

Finance: Keeper of the public purse

The minister and Department of Finance still occupy a position of some pre-eminence and influence in Ottawa.[1] This is communicated to everyone in the federal government in both subtle and not so subtle ways.

The department has a long history and remains the most important economic portfolio in the ministry. One senior finance official explained: 'Our department is a child of Confederation. We are as old as the country. We have a long history and a strong corporate culture. There is never any doubt about who we are or what is our mandate. We are, after all, the keeper of the public purse.'[2] An outside observer recently commented that 'the Department's monopoly rights as the sole supplier of some of the government's most important policies (tax and stabilization policies) and its guardian right to advise and influence the policy output of virtually every other government agency, confer upon the Department and its Minister a mantle of influence and prestige that is unparalleled within the structure of government.'[3]

Even the most casual observer of the federal government is aware of the long line of distinguished public servants who have served in the department. They include Clifford Clark, John Deutsch, and Robert Bryce. Similarly, the minister of finance is traditionally one of the government's most senior, sure-footed, and trusted ministers. The political damage incurred by the sudden departure or firing of virtually any minister in Ottawa can usually be contained. Not so in the case of the minister of finance, for he (to date only men have held the office) is the government's leading spokesman on economic policy. He must take the lead in rebutting the opposition on economic issues in the daily question period in the House. No minister of finance has ever been fired and the sudden departure of John Turner as finance minister in the mid-1970s caused, in the view of many, irreparable political damage to the Trudeau government, which went down to defeat in the next general election.[4]

The minister of finance always sits on the most important cabinet committees. His position on Priorities and Planning is, of course, assured, and he traditionally plays a leading role in its deliberations. He also usually sits to the immediate right of the prime minister in cabinet and he is expected to speak on most issues. Although the finance minister is always appointed vice-chairman of the Treasury Board, he never attends its meetings, for to do so would be to suggest that he accepts a subordinate position to the president of the Treasury Board[5] – clearly an untenable admission.

Finance officials themselves also enjoy considerable status in government. For one thing, their position commands a higher classification than comparable positions in other departments and the significance of this can hardly be overemphasized in such a hierarchical organization as the federal government. The position of deputy minister of finance rates a DM–3 classification, the highest possible in the federal government and one that is restricted to only a handful of positions, including that of the clerk of the Privy Council and secretary to the cabinet and the deputy ministers of the most senior, largest, and prestigious departments, such as External Affairs. The deputy minister of finance is also a member of the powerful Committee of Co-ordinating Deputy Ministers (CCDMs).[6] Finance is also often the only department to have two associate deputy ministers. And so it goes down the line. Most of the assistant deputy minister (ADM) positions in Finance command an EX–5 classification, while the great majority of ADMs in other departments rate an EX–4. General directors and directors in Finance meanwhile are classified at the EX–4 and EX–3 levels, which is unheard of in line departments.

Finance officials also cover the entire range of governmental activity. They are concerned with fiscal policy, federal-provincial relations, government expenditures, tax policy, international trade and finance, as well as social and economic policy and programs. They pride themselves on having the largest department of economics and the best pool of economic intelligence in the country.

Still many would argue that Finance has, since the 1960s, lost some of its prestige and influence and that it no longer dominates economic policy to the extent it once did. There are several reasons for this. The introduction of PPB and later PEMS, the establishment of the Treasury Board secretariat as a separate agency, the cabinet committee structure (including the powerful P & P), have all diffused the making of economic policy. Until the mid-sixties, few voices inside government offered alternative views on economic policy to those of the Department of Finance. Trudeau sought to introduce a more collegial and rational approach by making more extensive use of cabinet committees, by expanding the mandate of the Privy Council and of his own office, and by establishing a host of new economic departments. This opening up of economic policy making was not unintended. When told that his changes would upset the minister of finance and his officials, Trudeau is reported to have responded that Finance *had* to be upset: 'Otherwise the minister there would be as powerful as I am.'[7]

In addition, the Bank of Canada, by embracing monetarism in the mid-seventies, served notice to the Department of Finance that its monetary policy would no longer play an 'accommodation role.' Targets for the money supply would now be firmly established while 'adjustment to shocks in the economy would occur through exchange rate flexibility ... The Department of Finance was left with a relatively reduced role.'[8]

It will also be recalled that when both John Turner, the minister of finance, and his deputy minister, Simon Riesman, resigned in the mid-seventies, they did so in protest that the department had been downgraded because the government no longer relied on it for economic advice. Mr Riesman 'found himself unable to control the economic policy advice being tendered the government: sometimes he didn't even know what the advice was.'[9]

The Department of Finance also suffered a setback with the November 1981 budget, introduced by Allan MacEachen, which called for significant tax increases resulting from the closing of tax loopholes on the assumption that the economy would continue to expand rapidly, despite high interest rates. But by the time the budget was tabled, economic growth had come to a stop. Those who lost the tax loopholes joined others – such as representatives of western interests who were still reeling from the National Energy Program (NEP) introduced the year before – who felt the budget should be expansionary and hurled accusations of ineptitude and arrogance at the government. Ian Stewart, a highly respected career public servant, resigned as deputy minister of finance. In his letter of resignation to the prime minister, Stewart acknowledged that 'the Department of Finance and many of those who inhabit it have come under considerable public attack.'[10] Shortly afterward, Marc Lalonde, Trudeau's trusted Quebec lieutenant, replaced Allan MacEachen as minister of finance.

The 1981 MacEachen budget left strong lingering doubts among senior ministers concerning the Department of Finance's competence: they sensed that Finance lacked the necessary political and analytical skills to protect the government's political interests in preparing the budget, some joining government backbenchers in questioning the competence of the department. One P & P member at the time now reports that he only saw the budget one hour before MacEachen rose in the House to deliver it. 'Yet we were expected to defend it. That proved difficult not only because I had no say whatsoever in any part of it but also because I profoundly disagreed with it. I made it clear later at P & P that the government could no longer blindly place its political fortunes in the hands of the Department of Finance.'[11] Donald Johnston, president of the Treasury Board, wrote: 'Who had been consulted [on the 1981 budget]? Certainly not Cabinet ministers. I can vouch for that. The budget documents had been preserved from the eyes of all except key officials in the Department of Finance and, I presume, the Prime Minister himself. I was both offended and amazed that, as the Treasury Board President ... I had not been consulted ... We had shot ourselves in the foot with the infamous MacEachen budget.'[12]

Today, the ancient power of the Finance fiefdom is no longer; now all departments and agencies whose mandate affects the economy have their own expertise and are quite prepared, through their ministers, to tender advice on economic policy to the prime minister and the ministry. The present Department of Finance is thus different from the one that operated from Confederation to the early 1970s. An indication of this is the fact that Finance has had as many changes in deputy ministers since the early 1970s as it had from Confederation to 1970.[13] It is against this backdrop that we will consider the role of the department in the government's expenditure budget process. Finance officials themselves of course recognize this change, and attempts have been made under Marc Lalonde and Michael Wilson to restore the department's pre-eminent position in Ottawa. Such efforts invariably have an impact on the guardian role the department seeks to play.

FINANCE AND THE EXPENDITURE BUDGET

The roles and responsibilities of the Finance Department have been examined elsewhere. For this study, we shall only present a brief review of its role in the preparation of the government's expenditure budget. While no one doubts it is central to the process, few outside government and even inside it (other than some central agency and senior departmental officials) have a full appreciation of the department's role. Briefly stated, the Department of Finance has the following responsibilities in the expenditure budget process: (1) the minister of finance establishes the fiscal plan and prepares and presents the budget; (2) the minister and department evaluate the departmental proposals in both economic and social policy fields and advise the government on their appropriateness; and (3) the minister and department approve the capital budgets of crown corporations.[14]

It is hardly possible to exaggerate the importance of the fiscal plan to the expenditure budget. It gives Finance considerable influence on expenditure planning because it enables the department to determine, with limited outside interference, spending ceilings. The current expenditure budget process (or PEMS) permits Finance not only to formulate the fiscal plan, but also to determine the composition of individual spending envelopes. Before PEMS, it was Treasury Board that was responsible for allocating financial resources between departments.

There are various considerations that make up the government's fiscal plan.[15] The most important is the previous year's fiscal plan. Sudden changes in direction are not normally foreseen, especially on the spending side, so that last year's fiscal plan provides a clear indication of what next year's is likely to look like.

Finance officials then prepare a series of 'base case' economic and fiscal forecasts. The department reviews a wide range of economic indicators, such as the health of the labour market, production, foreign trade, and their implications for the economic outlook. It also undertakes a continuous assessment of the economic conditions of the United States and other countries. A policy error in Washington or a crop failure in the USSR can have an important impact on the Canadian economy. From these considerations and projected revenues and expenditures, the department then studies the impact of possible fiscal measures on the economy and prepares macroeconomic policy recommendations. These forecasts, together with political priorities as outlined by cabinet committees – in particular, those of Priorities and Planning – provide the basis for the minister's fiscal plan.

The preparation of the fiscal plan is now a continuing process. As David Good writes: 'The morning following the budget speech the government is already preparing for its next budget.'[16] Initially, the minister sets out to P & P, in multi-year terms, a 'no-policy change' in the fiscal situation. He also outlines the economic environment, with its underlying strengths and weaknesses, and presents broad alternatives to deal with the fiscal and economic situation, giving an appreciation of the impact of the alternatives. In turn, P & P members make their views known to the minister. Later the minister gives an indication of room available for policy reserves within the recommended fiscal plan, and again P & P members have an opportunity to express their views on the situation. Next, the minister reports again to P & P with a firm set of fiscal and economic projections, advises on the fiscal plan and reports on any possible changes to the tax policy, and makes final recommendations on the overall level of envelopes, including policy reserves. Finally, P & P can endorse the recommendations and may provide general direction to the minister in the allocation of reserves. P & P may also direct that an x budget process be initiated – requiring departments to cut a specific amount in their spending.

As mentioned above, the fiscal planning process is an ongoing one. The most important period, however, is the fall of the year. We saw in the previous chapter that P & P meets outside of Ottawa in early autumn (the lakes and lodges meetings) to map out its political and legislative agenda for the next twelve months. In preparation for this session and for several more during the next few months, the minister of finance reviews and updates the government's fiscal plan. This review is crucial not only for the upcoming budget but also for the government's spending plans.

There are three basic aspects to this review. (1) For the fiscal year in progress, the plan might be adjusted, by total or by function of expenditure, in light of the most recent economic developments and changing priorities. If this review reveals that revenues are down, then it can place pressure on proposed new spending. (2) Total outlay levels and their distribution by policy sector, or envelope, are revised for the upcoming fiscal year on the basis of the economic environment and the desired fiscal stance, the estimates provided by the Treasury Board of the current dollar costs of approved programs, and priorities for policy initiatives for each resource envelope. (3) Initial preliminary projections of total outlay levels and their distribution by resource envelope are made for the third planning year (the fifth year in the fiscal planning process). The timetable that follows locates the Department of Finance in the budget cycle.

Spring and summer	Finance produces status quo fiscal plan, suggests broad alternative approaches to deal with economic and fiscal environment. Prime minister may request individual ministers to set out their priorities which could then be reviewed by policy committees of cabinet. This has come to replace departmental strategic overviews first introduced with PEMS.
Late summer and fall	P & P considers overall directions and priorities. Minister of finance sets out multi-year fiscal situation with respect to government priorities; finance ministers' meetings; first ministers' conferences on the economy; consultations with business and labour.
December	Minister of finance advises P & P on fiscal plan based on fully developed economic and fiscal projections, makes recommendations on envelope levels and policy reserves. P & P determines fiscal framework and allocations by envelope, and defines overall priorities and major policy initiatives.
February	The minister of finance presents his budget.

The public, the opposition, and indeed government members of parliament get their first glimpse of the fiscal framework when the minister of finance makes his budget speech and tables a series of budget papers in the House. The budget is in theory, of course, designed to accomplish a great deal more than report on what the federal government will be spending in the upcoming fiscal year. The department's involvement in stabilization policy is widely known and it could rightly be labelled the 'Department of Economic Policy.' The budget is Finance's most visible output and provides an authoritative review of past, current, and future economic factors that have an impact on the country's economic performance. Finance claims to employ the budget to unveil its arsenal of measures, either to stimulate a sagging economy or to slow it down. Fine tuning the economy can be done through new taxes, new spending measures, wage and price controls, and so on.

Finance has an evaluative impact on departmental proposals in both the economic and social policy fields. The minister is expected to speak to all spending proposals coming before P & P and cabinet, and the department is intricately involved in the appraisal of spending proposals by all departments and agencies. Richard Phidd and Bruce Doern explain that 'the Minister of Finance reacts to policy initiatives from other departments since he has an important responsibility for financial management.'[17] The reactions of the minister and his department to spending proposals are easily predictable: they are anti-interventionist on most matters and traditionally oppose all proposals for new spending. Finance is in the business of saving public money, not spending it.

R.B. Bryce, a former deputy minister of finance, explained that 'much of the work of the Department of Finance is of the nature of a critical appraisal of the proposals of others.'[18] Another finance official reported that 'departments are constantly coming up here with ill-conceived ideas which would either screw-up the economy and/or employ an economic instrument like taxation, for a social or cultural goal. I find it satisfying and exciting to see these policy proposals shot down by our boys purely on the grounds of economics.'[19] This anti-interventionist bias is driven home to new finance employees early on. One former finance official recounted his early experience in the department. 'Shortly after I went to the Department, I was asked to prepare a briefing for the Minister on a proposal from the Department of Health and Welfare. I concluded that the proposal was a good one and I recommended that our Minister support it. I sent the note up the line but a few days later I was called into the Deputy Minister's office. He made it very clear that I had prepared a *stupid* note. 'What if the note had gone ahead and the Minister would have supported the proposal before his colleagues?' he asked. He then explained that there were many departments and agencies and thousands and thousands of officials whose job is to prepare spending proposals. Our job is to oppose them. We are the internal opposition in goverment. He concluded by asking, "if we don't protect the Treasury, who do you think will?" '[20]

Finance plays its opposition role to spending proposals in various ways. Officials will oppose new proposals at interdepartmental committee meetings or in bilateral meetings or exchange of correspondence with departments. You can always count on finance officials, reported one senior departmental official, to pour cold water on proposals. The minister, after having been properly briefed by his officials, will also voice his views at cabinet and cabinet committee meetings. These norms have shaped the department to be constantly reactive.

One observer concludes that Finance's strong anti-interventionist bias and its concern for the integrity of the fiscal framework inhibit its adopting a take-charge attitude and from establishing new critieria for economic policy. 'Finance,' he argues, 'has failed to come forward with anything more sophisticated than a reflex anti-spending posture.'[21] Expenditure policies have now become an end in themselves rather than a means to new economic policies. The efforts of the minister of finance and his department are less and less to sort out when to inflate, when to deflate, when to do nothing, when to cut spending, or when to increase it. Increasingly, they are directed to controlling the growth in total spending. The result is that now the work of the Department of Finance is not so much what economic policies they would like to advocate to 'manage' the economy but rather to determine how far they have to back away from these policies to accommodate the spending demands of the ministry. If one looks at it from another perspective, however, one could argue that the department, far from taking the lead in defining new approaches to regional or industrial development, energy policy, and so on, simply sits back and, in the words of one departmental official, 'shoots holes in proposals to stop things from happening.' Looked at from this view, Finance is a typical central agency, and the central agencies, as is well known, are noted for their ability to stop policy or program initiatives rather than for their ability to come forward with them.[22]

To be sure, spending ministers expect little in the way of direction or support from the minister and the Department of Finance for their spending proposals. Conversely, they are not likely to support Finance. Ministers, much like the media, are prone to label budgets according to who the minister of finance is, so that we have a Wilson, Lalonde, MacEachen, Crosbie, or Chrétien budget. Some spending ministers are convinced that it takes little time for the Department of Finance to capture any newly appointed minister and turn him into a non-interventionist, nay-sayer politician. One senior minister in the Trudeau cabinet explained:

Finance can turn any politician into a right-wing crusader. Look at Lalonde, a free-spender in Health and Welfare in the 1970s. Yet once in Finance he could not see the merit of new spending proposals like he once did. Look at

MacEachen, the most liberal and interventionist of liberals, going back to Saint Laurent. Once in Finance, he consistently opposed government intervention except when it came to Cape Breton. His position on the Kirby Fisheries Task Force is a case in point. Look at Chrétien. He was once proud to boast that he had established more new national parks than any other minister in Canadian history. Even the Treasury Board could not stop his spending ways. As President of the Treasury Board, he launched a costly and ambitious government decentralization program. Trudeau appointed him in Finance and that was the end of him.[23]

The minister and the Department of Finance know full well that their work seldom is popular. They also know that they must always keep an eye on taxation since, while they alone get the credit for reducing taxes, they also get most of the blame for any increase in taxation. Spending ministers, in contrast, only get credit for increases in spending. The threat of possible tax increases or a big jump in the deficit remain the most potent instrument the minister of finance has in holding back new spending. But clearly this is not enough. He cannot play the role of guardian alone and unassisted. He needs the support of others.

FINANCE AND FRIENDS

The most important ally of the minister of finance is the prime minister. In the words of one former senior finance officer, 'the Minister of Finance can only be effective to the extent the prime minister wants him to be. With his support, he can do a great dealing pushing back spending proposals. Without it he will largely be ineffective.'[24] There are constant pressures on the minister of finance to break open the fiscal framework to fund new spending proposals in P & P and cabinet meetings. The prime minister (as reported by a senior central agency official who regularly attended P & P meetings) 'must not sway, or appear to sway in favour of the spenders. If he does, the Minister of Finance, is, well, cooked.'[25]

The support a prime minister is prepared to give to his minister of finance appears to depend on a host of factors. There are the obvious ones, such as the timing of the next general election – the closer it is, the less likely is the minister of finance to get his all-out support. The general state of the economy is another. If revenues are down, then the prime minister could well agree with his finance minister in P & P that spending must be controlled. If revenues are buoyant, then he is likely to side with the spenders. All this suggests, as one finance official put it, 'that at times one wonders how we manage to get the purpose of our fiscal policy backwards. The deficit and politics now dictate how much the government will spend. Very little else seems to matter.'[26]

To be sure, these factors are important, but senior central agency officials insist that the personal relationship a minister of finance is able to strike with the prime minister, and the management style of both, are more important. In Canada, much as in Britain, 'the PM must appear impartial but broadly backing the Minister of Finance. The spending ministers always outnumber the Minister of Finance and unless the PM backs him, he'll always lose.'[27] Two former ministers of finance, Allan MacEachen and Marc Lalonde, were close to former Prime Minister Trudeau, and both enjoyed his complete support while they held the Finance portfolio. MacEachen was credited with having orchestrated Trudeau's return to the party leadership with the caucus in 1979. On his return to power, Trudeau named MacEachen both deputy prime minister and minister of finance, leaving no doubt in cabinet, P & P, and caucus that MacEachen had his full support. 'Ministers,' according to one former finance official, 'quickly took note.' 'Even after MacEachen presented his disastrous budget,' he explained, 'Trudeau stood by him.'[28] Marc Lalonde had always been a key Trudeau ally and, when the prime minister needed someone to pick up the pieces after MacEachen, it was he who was chosen. Lalonde, it was widely known in the ministry, also had Trudeau's complete backing throughout his stay in Finance.

Other ministers of finance, however, did not have so close a relationship with the prime minister, and their roles as guardians were affected. While Jean Chrétien, for example, held the portfolio, Prime Minister Trudeau announced a series of spending cuts without consulting him. This led cabinet ministers and senior officials in Ottawa to conclude that Trudeau had seriously undermined his minister of finance. Chrétien, indeed, considered resigning the portfolio, but decided against it because of the message it would send to Quebec which had just elected the separatist Parti Québécois to power. (Chrétien, it will be recalled, was the first French-Canadian finance minister in Canadian history.) Although Trudeau is reported to have explained to Chrétien that he merely accepted what the Finance Department had urged him to do ever since he came to power – that is, to cut spending – some ministers assumed that Chrétien had lost the confidence of the prime minister and, as a result, that Finance had lost some of its clout. A weakened

Finance Department of course meant better chances for spending ministers to get their proposals through cabinet. Chrétien explained: 'It's a survival game ... So even if those who weren't happy with me in Finance didn't create the situation, I knew they would try to take advantage of it.'[29] He secured a promise that no one would interfere with his preparation of the next budget and this served to reassure finance officials that he had not lost control in the cabinet. He later observed, 'I could see them [i.e., Finance officials] smiling at the thought of going into a big fight and winning the budget.'[30] The next budget was an election year budget and many observers assumed that it would contain a series of 'political goodies.'[31] It did not. Chrétien's budget was highly 'conservative': the promise he had extracted from Trudeau, according to Chrétien, enabled him and his officials to play their guardian role and present a non-expansionist budget.

Michael Wilson, many senior officials in Ottawa report, never has enjoyed the same level of support from Prime Minister Mulroney that MacEachen and Lalonde had from Trudeau. Three reasons are given for this. First is Mulroney's tendency to strike bilateral spending deals with premiers and some ministers. For example, he agreed to Premier Devine's special request to provide funds to Saskatchewan wheat farmers and to that by Elmer MacKay, minister of revenue, to fund a special reserve for laid-off Trenton rail car workers. The minister of finance in such situations has two choices – to quit or pick up the pieces. Invariably, he picks up the pieces. Secondly, Michael Wilson's close association with Bay Street is a tempting target for spending ministers from virtually every region of the country. They tend to dismiss Wilson's political sensitivity and his ability to understand disadvantaged regions and people. One senior official suggested that Mulroney himself also had strong reservations regarding Wilson's political judgment. 'The boy from Baie Comeau,' he reported, 'somehow never feels at home with what he hears from Finance. One always suspects that he believes that the finance message can only be sold on Bay Street, the *Financial Post*, and the *Globe*'s *Report on Business*.'[32] Thirdly, though a senior minister, Wilson has never been made deputy prime minister.

The minister and Department of Finance, as we have already seen, face two crucial tests in playing out their guardian roles. First is the annual budget exercise. Second is their review of proposals put forward by departments and agencies and their participation in cabinet and cabinet committee meetings.

In planning the fiscal framework, the minister of finance in late summer attends P & P where the chairpersons of the policy committees outline their priorities for the coming year. The minister's participation in the deliberations at this stage is limited. On the basis of what he hears and of the economic outlook and projected revenues, he returns to P & P some time later with a proposed fiscal framework. It is here that he lays out what will be available in the policy reserves. No vote is taken at such meetings. Clearly, however, the minister cannot put aside completely what he has heard earlier from the chairpersons of cabinet committees. One member of P & P explained: 'The minister of finance knows full well that he can't come back with empty hands – or worse, with only spending cuts – when he has been told by senior ministers that funds are required to undertake new measures. He is never formally voted down but a consensus can easily be reached suggesting that he and his officials should go back and look at the numbers all over again.'[33] The minister also knows full well that he cannot take a strong position which is absolutely hopeless to defend. Douglas Hartle explains that 'it must not be forgotten that his credibility hinges to a considerable degree on seldom going to war without a victory: this can be achieved only by a careful selection of the battlegrounds on which to fight.'[34] This is why every finance minister seeks to bring the prime minister on side. At critical points in the budget process and in establishing the fiscal framework, he will have lunch or private chats with the prime minister to ensure his support at P & P and cabinet meetings. It is important to remember that on fiscal matters a majority of two in cabinet – the prime minister and the minister of finance – can usually carry the day.[35]

The negotiating style of the minister of finance depends on both his abilities and his personality. Michael Wilson, for example, is viewed as hard-working, solid, and competent but not as possessing a particularly strong personality. He, in the words of one finance official, 'avoids confrontations whenever he can. He does not like a good scrap like say Crosbie, Chrétien, or Lalonde did.'[36] Accordingly, Wilson prefers to present his case full of 'facts and figures' before cabinet and P & P meetings. Chrétien, for his part, was particularly adroit at face-to-face negotiations and personal meetings. Ministers tended to avoid such confrontations with him and instead tried to take him on in cabinet or P & P. Lalonde had a forceful personality but was also in full command of the 'facts and figures' and, according to one former P & P member, 'very few would take him on anywhere. Rather they would try to go around him to the PM or Treasury Board, but invariably with very little success.'[37] No matter the personality or negotiating style, the task remains the same for spending ministers: get as much as you can from Finance, knowing it will be difficult. Any finance minister knows full well that giving in to one minister will result in a rush from others with equally valid spending proposals. As a result, he will always want to negotiate on his own turf and not on theirs. He will rely on his departmental brief – that is, on the state of the Canadian economy and the country's finances – and not on the political merits of individual proposals or departmental policies.

Finance's guardian role, however, has been made somewhat more difficult in recent years because the department is no longer in a monopoly position in terms of projecting government revenues and economic forecasting. Albert Breton argues that the Department of Finance, because of its monopoly position, would knowingly undermine its revenue forecasts to maximize its power.[38] Thus the department would forecast revenues for the coming year to be less than actually measured in order to lower expectations among spending ministers. With this tactic, the finance minister could paint a particularly gloomy fiscal picture, with large requirements. When the projected levels of economic activity turn out to be incorrect, the minister can then loosen the purse-strings and dispense new funds to departments. This in turn enhances Finance's bureaucratic power.

Few inside government, even in departments and agencies, now subscribe to this theory. We saw earlier that a number of federal departments built up in the 1970s policy-planning capacities of their own. The collegiality of the Trudeau cabinet committee system also led to the 'emergence of other central agencies with ambitious roles in the fiscal and economic areas ... the Treasury Board Secretariat, (and) the expansion of the Privy Council Office to serve an elaborate Cabinet committee system.'[39] Independent economic think-tanks, such as the C.D. Howe Institute, can also now challenge Finance's 'economic numbers' and ministers now quite happily report to their colleagues findings of their departments or of outside research institutes if they wish to challenge those of Finance. Richard Van Loon explains: 'Where once the Department of Finance had a near monopoly, a host of well-publicized competitors sprang up and ministers or officials who might want to disagree with the official forecast could shop around among projections from the Conference Board, the C.D. Howe Institute, Informetrica, Data Resources and various banks and investment dealers until they found a set of projections they liked better. That none of these sources was necessarily any better than the Department of Finance was not crucial: what counted was the existence of apparently equally credible alternatives;'[40] For this reason and perhaps for others, finance officials now present realistic numbers to P & P in establishing the fiscal framework, also claiming (quite correctly) that their economic forecasts have consistently been slightly more optimistic over the past five years than those of independent or private sector research groups. The one exception was Wilson's 1988 election-year budget which many considered to be overly optimistic, particularly in regard to its multi-year forecast of projected revenues.

Our discussion thus far should not suggest that the minister and Department of Finance are alone in playing a guardian role. The PMO, the PCO, the FPRO, and the Treasury Board secretariat – and for some time after the introduction of PEMS, the Ministry of State for Economic and Regional Development (MSERD) and the Ministry of State for Social Development (MSSD) – all 'analyzed, appraised and tested' spending proposals from their own perspectives to ensure that they were reconciled with the government's overall policy framework, budget, and desired federal-provincial relations. We have already seen that these central agencies are concerned that 'due process' is respected and that they are particularly adroit at stopping things. They are, in the words of one senior departmental official, 'great goaltenders, but they can't score – they simply can't make things happen.'[41]

FINANCE AND THE NEW PEMS

PEMS, it will be recalled was expected to establish fiscal limits before developing spending plans. It would place 'responsibility for saving with those who spend.' The fiscal plan would encompass total revenues and expenditure and so provide a clear picture of the government's role in the economy. Overall spending limits, as well as specific limits to each budgetary envelope, were to be established. Each spending item and program was assigned to an envelope which, in turn, was assigned to a cabinet committee that had the responsibility for allocating resources within the policy area or the envelope. Policy reserves would be set aside for new spending but, if this was not sufficient, the cabinet committees would be forced to cut or curtail some programs to meet established spending limits.

Briefly stated, that is how PEMS was designed to work. What happens, however, when ministers want to approve new spending proposals but are not prepared to cut or curtail programs to respect aggregate spending limitations within the envelopes? What happens when those who spend want to continue spending but do not want to assume the responsibility for saving? There is no other choice available but to break the fiscal framework.

The fiscal position of the government since the introduction of PEMS has resulted in a string of small policy reserves for allocation by the policy committees. The architects of PEMS did not focus so much on what would be available each year in the policy reserve as on the level of discipline which the system would impose on ministers. Spending ministers, of course, have a different point of view. Those with large spending departments, such as Employment and Immigration, can bypass the committees, and reallocate their departmental budgets to finance their own proposals. Similarly, ministers with strong political clout can also bypass cabinet committees and establish new special envelopes to finance new programs, as Marc Lalonde did when he was minister of energy, mines and resources.[42] This situation, of course, has made matters worse for the vast majority of ministers who have neither clout nor large departmental budgets. They must, as former Treasury Board president Don Johnston graphically phrased it, 'waste valuable time in Cabinet committees haggling over a piece of the pie – like so many fish wives.'[43]

Out of frustration, most ministers with spending proposals soon began to bypass the near-penniless cabinet committees and go directly to the minister of finance or P & P. There they met with some success. The practice first began under Trudeau, and has continued, if not expanded, under Mulroney. Their success has meant, however, that the fiscal framework has become far more flexible than was hoped. Since 1981, there has been a long list of special spending proposals supported by special allocations. From the Trudeau administration, these include nearly $1 billion for housing over two years, approximately $1 billion for special job creation efforts, and $100 million for a renegotiated Adult Occupational Training Act. Under the Mulroney administration, they include over $1 billion for western grain farmers, new funds for a new child-care policy, and over $1 billion each for the new regional agencies for Atlantic and western Canada.

Special allocations are made by P & P, supposedly on the advice of the minister of finance. In many cases this is what happens. The fact that it happens, however, does not mean that either the minister or his department was in full agreement with the sponsoring minister. For example, Michael Wilson and Finance were strongly opposed to the first billion handed out to grain farmers. But one senior central agency official explains: 'Wise (i.e., John Wise, the minister of agriculture) played that file beautifully. He had all his ducks lined up when the proposal came before P & P. Caucus had voiced strong support a few weeks before. He saw to it that other western ministers made strong representations in cabinet committees and even in cabinet. He played the Devine-Mulroney connection to perfection in presenting his case. Wilson simply didn't have a chance. I have been around government a long time and I have seen many ministers with a knack to get funding when none is available. John Wise ranks among the best of them.'[44]

There are other instances where it is highly unlikely Finance would have willingly agreed to open the fiscal framework to fund new initiatives. For example, the department has long been opposed to special federal regional development efforts. The conventional view in Finance is that regional disparities are best left to market forces and that government intervention only makes matters worse. Only a few years after DREE was established, for instance, Finance put it on top of its list in recommending to cabinet four policy areas that should be reviewed for possible cutbacks. It remained there until the department was finally disbanded in 1982. Wilson himself declared in his first major statement as minister that 'more attention needs to be given ... to the *economic* impact of regionally-oriented interventions, including the costs to some regions, and to the national economy, of policies favouring specific regions.' He added that 'a substantial element of current federal spending on economic development may be doing more to hinder than to promote private sector growth.'[45]

Yet by 1987 Prime Minister Mulroney announced two new regional development agencies with over $2 billion of new money. Both agencies were developed under the watchful eyes of Mulroney himself and the deputy prime minister. To have opposed funding the agencies in P & P would clearly have been a war that Finance could not possibly have won and so the fiscal framework was broken.

Some observers suggest, however, that these special allocations strengthen the role of Finance in the allocation of resources. The breakdown in discipline under PEMS is the result of Finance striking deals with spenders. The strength of PEMS, the argument goes, would come from Finance denying rather than approving countless spending proposals. Practitioners in government agree, stating that there are now three places where spending ministers and departments can go for funding. Ministers in large departments can still reallocate their expenditure budget, though this is the court of last resort, even for the largest of departments. If their proposals are relatively modest – say, less than

$50 million – they can go to the policy reserve attached to the relevant cabinet committee. Proposals requiring large sums are sent to Finance and P & P and are funded from special provisions.

Richard Van Loon has speculated on why Finance has assumed such a role. He contends that the minister may be in a better position to turn down proposals than the chairpersons of cabinet committees. He also speculates that a large central special allocation fund could get lost in the various policy reserves, so that special allocations when made would lose their political impact. Yet another possible reason is that the chairpersons of policy committees may not be able to sort out how to allocate a large central special allocation fund between the cabinet committees.[46] Whatever the actual reason, he insists that 'this feature of the system has further buttressed the power of the Minister of Finance.'[47] Certainly, special allocations provide him with opportunities to dish out largesse and have ministers come to him to strike deals. Not only can they obtain new funding from him but spending ministers can also avoid the struggle through the laborious policy committee process.

This may well serve to buttress the power of Finance, and no doubt this fact has not been lost on finance officials who have seen the influence of their department wane since the late 1960s. The department, however, has regained some of its influence, although at a cost. The use of special allocations also means that the keeper of the public purse is prepared to see its fiscal framework compromised from time to time. The position of keeper of the public purse is always easier when it is clear to everyone that the expenditure lid is clamped on tight. If one spending minister is able to pry open the lid even only once, it invites others to try to do the same.

Neither the special allocations nor the centrally held reserve, as already noted, began or ended with one minister of finance. They started with MacEachen, continued with Lalonde, and their use has expanded with Wilson. Mulroney's management style is responsible for the growing flexibility in the fiscal framework. 'Mulroney's philosophy,' it has been suggested, 'assumes that political leadership is about the accommodation of interests and not the interplay of ideas.'[48] It has been observed that Mulroney's leadership style 'is transactional rather than collegial. His preference is to deal with individuals on a one-to-one basis rather than on a collective basis.'[49] The discipline required under PEMS does not lend itself to this style of leadership, and one can appreciate the increasing use of special allocations under Mulroney.

Finance itself has also seen important changes. A new deputy minister,

Stanley Hartt, was appointed. He had never before worked in the federal government, let alone in the Department of Finance. Apart from Grant Reuber's brief stay as deputy minister in 1979, Hartt's appointment marked the first time in the history of the Finance Department that someone from outside government was catapulted directly to the post.[50] Although an outsider can obviously bring fresh thinking to government policy and continuing programs, he is unlikely to appreciate fully the traditions and the requirements of a long-established corporate culture found in a department such as Finance. A long-time employee of the Finance Department, for example, is far more likely to appreciate the importance of keeping spending ministers at bay than someone who has never worked there. 'An outsider coming into the system,' one senior official remarked, 'will invariably attach more importance to what ministers say they want individually than collectively. The result is that the outsider recently brought in is often seen going around the system pushing a project of one kind or another.'[51]

Some senior federal officials readily admit that Hartt was much more open to striking bilateral deals with ministers and their departments than his predecessors, Marshall Cohen or Ian Stewart, ever were. They are quick to add, however, that this could be the result of his frequent consultations and his long and close association with the prime minister. One senior official remarked: 'No question Stanley understood very well the power games involved in spending. He fully appreciated that you can only push so far and that ministers would lose credibility if they always came up empty. And so yes, he would strike deals and would not let himself get tripped up with the mandate and responsibilities of Finance.'[52]

The position of deputy minister of finance traditionally is one of the most senior, visible, and demanding of all such positions in Ottawa. Permanent officials in spending departments quickly learn to appreciate his style and where and how he may be vulnerable to new spending proposals. One former deputy minister of a line department commented: 'Finance has always had the strongest Deputy Ministers. They lecture the Cabinet as if they were ministers themselves.'[53] Traditionally, few have been receptive to special pleading for new spending outside of the normal expenditure process and have often defined their role as a supporting one in turning down requests from spending ministers. Said one former deputy minister of finance: 'People who look at the process from the outside tend to think there is a sharp line between the Minister and his Deputy: well that isn't the case at all. The Finance

Minister is frequently against his colleagues in the Cabinet and he needs as many arguments as can be mustered.'[54]

The important point here is not so much whether a seasoned federal public servant should be picked over an outsider to be deputy minister of finance. Rather, it is that personalities can have an important impact on government spending. This is true both of politicians and of senior permanent officials. Lalonde could not be moved off the fiscal framework easily. Conversely, Wilson is reported to be 'much too civilized' to take on the best of the spending ministers at their game, and one of his deputy ministers (perhaps at the direction of the prime minister) showed an openness to strike individual deals.

FINANCE: THE SPENDING DEPARTMENT

When asked how he saw Finance playing its role as guardian of the public purse, a senior departmental official shot back, 'some public purse, some guardian. Take a close look and you will see Finance is a spending department like the rest of us. The difference is that they don't care to admit it.'[55] Finance indeed has spending programs and is ultimately responsible for the government's tax expenditure account. Finance has direct responsibility for a number of federal-provincial fiscal arrangements. The department provides funds in its annual expenditure budget which are paid to the provinces under a number of statutory authorities. For example, it transferred in 1987–8 some $5.6 billion to designated provinces under its fiscal equalization program.

Finance officials, however, contend that their role in federal-provincial relations is more a government-wide one than a departmental one. Their policy advice extends to the allocation of fiscal resources between levels of government, intergovernmental transfers, tax harmonization, fiscal and economic harmonization with the provinces, intergovernmental aspects of fiscal and economic stabilization, and intergovernmental taxation. Finance has had the responsibility for fiscal federalism, they insist, ever since federal-provincial financial agreements first surfaced.

A more recent development for Finance, at least in the public's view, is its involvement in tax expenditure or spending by not taxing. Every policy analyst in the federal government recognizes Finance's predominant role in forming tax policy. In any event, few spending departments took any interest in tax expenditures until the late 1970s. David A. Good writes that 'cabinet ministers and their departments do not have high tax consciousness. When it comes to money, ministers and their departments are mostly interested in their expenditure budgets. They view money in terms of what they are allocated to spend and not in terms of the tax concessions which their clients might receive.' He goes on to point out that 'many departments are reluctant to propose tax changes which could benefit their constituents by large dollar amounts, because they feel that they will be unable to control the specific design of the tax subsidy. Once in the hands of the Department of Finance, spending departments believe that it is hard to negotiate the specific design of the tax subsidy.'[56]

By the late 1970s, however, interest in tax expenditure among ministers, departments, and their client groups picked up considerably. With less new money available for spending programs, tax money was regarded as 'free-money' and 'more easily accessible.'[57] The government's commitment to limit growth in spending to less than the growth rate in GNP also made tax expenditures more popular since they are not counted in the total expenditure budget. Finance has been reporting increasing pressure from spending ministers to change the tax system, one official observing that 'we are now getting inquiries and even recommendations on changing tax policies from all sides, from ministers, departments, interest groups, and for all kinds of reasons from housing, child care, and regional development.'[58] Yet the minister of finance has even more say on tax policy than on expenditure changes and this for a host of reasons. For one thing, few spending ministers and departments purport to be experts on taxation policy. Departments may have economic analyses and planning units, but none has a taxation policy unit. As a result, everyone recognizes the expertise of Finance in this area, and few are prepared to challenge it. In addition, the minister of finance need not consult as widely on tax policy as he needs to on the fiscal framework, for instance. The budget speech is his occasion to announce important tax changes and, given the requirements of budget secrecy, he can dictate most tax changes without consultating his colleagues.

Despite the fact that Finance has the upper hand in establishing tax policies, we now have an array of tax expenditure accounts, described by Finance as 'a provision in the tax system that provides preferential treatment to certain taxpayers in comparison to a norm or benchmark tax structure.'[59] Others describe it simply as 'giving by not taking.' Some have lamented the fact that considerable time and effort is spent analysing budgetary expenditures but that tax expenditures 'almost entirely escape any form of governmental or public scrutiny.'[60] We do know, however, that by 1980 some 200 tax expenditure items had been identified, of which Finance could cost only about half and that by 1985 over 300 such items were identified, approximately 200 of which were designed for the business community. There is still no breakdown of the total cost of tax expenditures, and senior finance officials argue that to determine it would be virtually impossible.[61] In his 1986 annual report, however, the auditor general estimated the cost to be 'about $28 billion annually for 1983' and suggested that if all tax expenditures were eliminated, the annual deficit would be wiped clean.[62] Finance officials insist that 'the Auditor General was grandstanding because there is no way he can arrive at that figure.'[63] Finance officials are correct. One cannot obtain a total figure for tax expenditures as conventionally calculated. The auditor general himself wrote in a separate report in 1986 that his tables on tax expenditures could not be added up to give a total figure because 'removal of provisions would cause interactions of effects, with unpredictable total net effect, and because estimates are lacking for some individual tax expenditures.'[64]

Though it is not possible to get a precise total figure, it is widely accepted that tax expenditures are costing taxpayers at least $30 billion annually. It is also now possible to arrive at a precise figure on selected tax expenditures. Revenue Canada officials, for example, report that the scientific research tax credit cost the federal Treasury $2.6 billion before it was shelved.[65] This lucrative, 50 per cent tax credit was introduced in the early 1980s to encourage investment in research and development. The measure came under harsh criticism because of the cost and because it did not deliver what it promised. A leading media representative dismissed the tax credit as 'an ill-conceived scheme, contrived by the Minister of Finance and his deputy (minister).'[66] That the incentive had failed did not go unnoticed inside the federal government. Line departments and their ministers could now point the finger at Finance, not only for behaving as a spending department, but for achieving limited success. That said, it is important to recognize that the pressure for new tax expenditures comes largely from spending ministers and their departments. If it were up to only the Department of Finance to decide if there ought to be tax expenditures, there would be few of them indeed.

Finance took on another costly initiative in the mid-1980s. Two banks in western Canada (the Commercial and the Northland) experienced severe difficulties in 1984 as a result of a sharp downturn in the real estate market in western Canada and the weakness of the oil industry.

The federal government first attempted to prop up the Commercial Bank and later moved to liquidate both banks. In doing so, the minister of finance announced that the government would protect uninsured deposits at both banks.

Subsequently the government established a judicial inquiry to investigate the collapse of the two banks. The Estey Inquiry blamed the banks' management but also singled out the inspector general of banks in the Department of Finance for the failure of the bail-out. The inquiry report outlined in some detail how the thinking in Finance evolved during the crisis.[67] The department had considered a series of counterbalancing factors in reviewing the situations of both banks. However, it had only one precedent to guide it: the Home Bank case in 1924. In that case two ministers of finance had been warned that the bank was in difficulty and both had refused to intervene.[68] To do so would have involved the department's investing government funds in a business enterprise – a financial institution, no less. Yet, Finance reasoned that the Home Bank failure had occurred some sixty years earlier. It was deeply concerned with maintaining discipline in the country's economic and financial system and also with the international implications of the situation. Mickey Cohen, deputy minister of finance at the time, explained the department's position: 'I think I would describe it by saying to you, on a scale of zero to ten, if zero meant let the bank fail and ten meant save it, some of us were at four and some of us were at six. Nobody was at zero; nobody was at ten. By the time it all finished, we had all kind of come to an essential consensus at, what I would qualify, as five and a half to six; that is to say we had all reluctantly agreed that we should save this bank.'[69] Later, in an interview, a senior official explained that 'the integrity of the country's banking system was involved here. Finance simply had to do something. One billion dollars is a lot of money, no question. Frankly, however, I have seen the government spend a billion on worse things.'[70]

In announcing the rescue package, Finance declared that it would leave the banks 'in a strong position of solvency.'[71] The Estey Inquiry, however, described the rescue plan as 'a desperately contrived creation,' 'half-baked,' 'ill-starred from the outset,' and 'having no chance of success.'[72] The inquiry, as mentioned above, pinned much of the blame for this on Finance's inspector general for banks. When the Commercial Bank folded, the government 'decided it had a moral responsibility to compensate fully all depositors and creditors of the CCB (and later) extended compensation to Northlands depositors.'[73] The total cost to the government amounted to $1 billion and the inspector general resigned over the matter.

The minister of finance sponsored the proposal in government and secured the funding. Clearly, the policy envelope did not have the necessary reserve and he initiated a series of spending cuts and 'expenditure containment measures' to finance the initiative.

The bank rescue did, however, in the eyes of spending ministers and departments, compromise Finance's role as guardian of the public purse. How can a guardian, they would ask, have two sets of rules – one for themselves and one for other departments? Certainly, spending ministers could argue that they had been given little opportunity to debate the merits of the bank rescue or the many tax expenditure schemes introduced by Finance in relation to their own spending proposals. While it is true that pressure and proposals for new tax expenditures rarely, if ever, comes out of the Department of Finance per se, it is the department that puts together tax expenditure packages, including the eligibility criteria. All in all it would make it difficult for Finance to espouse restraint, to argue against special compensation to wheat farmers, or government intervention in the economy, after bailing out one bank and compensating the depositors of two.

5

The Treasury Board:
Keeper of the expenditure budget

The Treasury Board is the oldest committee of cabinet. It was established on 2 July 1867 and made a statutory committee in 1869. Unlike for most other cabinet committees, its responsibilities are specified in legislation under the Financial Administration Act. They include acting for the government on matters relating to general administrative policy, financial management, personnel management, and 'such other matters as may be referred to it by the Governor in Council.'[1] Treasury Board is also the only cabinet committee that does not rely on the Privy Council Office for secretariat support. It is served by two secretariats: those of the Treasury Board and the office of the Comptroller General.

Most Treasury Board decisions relate to the board's statutory authorities under the Financial Administration Act and, where they do not involve issues of general policy, are not referred to cabinet but are reflected in a 'letter of decision' from the Treasury Board secretariat to the deputy minister of the department concerned. On matters of more general concern to the ministry (such as annual estimates, person-year controls, and certain general administrative policy directives), the Treasury Board produces committee reports for confirmation by full cabinet or the Committee on Priorities and Planning.

The modus operandi of Treasury Board differs from that of other cabinet committees: its president and his ministerial colleagues sit on one side of the table while the officials of the Treasury Board secretariat sit opposite and present the cases to be considered. Only in exceptional circumstances are ministers and officials from the department under review invited to elaborate on the case, but they are usually asked to leave before the Treasury Board ministers make their decision. In the case of other cabinet committees, ministers present their own cases and, accompanied by selected departmental officials, they sit around the table in no particular order.

Before considering the guardian role played by the Treasury Board, it is important to distinguish at the outset the roles played by the Treasury Board itself, its president, and its secretariat (see appendix 3). The Treasury Board consists of its president, who chairs board meetings, the minister of finance, and four other cabinet ministers. The board decides on submissions put forward by ministers. The president directs the work of the secretariat and the Office of the Comptroller General (OCG) – both of which are headed by deputy ministers – which is to develop policies and programs. The secretariat is responsible for advising the president and the board on policies, directives, regulations, and program expenditures in respect of the government's financial, human, and material resources. The OCG develops policies for financial and management accounting and reporting, program evaluation, and internal audit. More is said about these responsibilities later in this chapter.

MANAGING THE EXPENDITURE BUDGET

The responsibilities of the Treasury Board in the expenditure budget have evolved over time. Chapter three traced the evolution of the budget process and one could see the changing role of the Treasury Board in the various phases of this evolution. There are many who believe that the Treasury Board lost a great deal of its influence with the introduction of PEMS, one having remarked that 'those who have looked at [the] pre-PEMS period see the development in 1978 of the Board of Economic Development Ministers as representing a failure of the Treasury Board.'[2]

The role of the Treasury Board and the secretariat under PEMS has been described as 'the bookkeeper for the system and also [responsible] for the A base.'[3] The Privy Council Office, in describing how PEMS would work, wrote that the Treasury Board is responsible 'for the overall integrity of the financial and other resource systems, the accuracy of costing of present and proposed policies put before ministers and Parliament, as well as timely advice to ministers on the efficient management of public resources generally.'[4] Thus the Treasury Board's current role in the expenditure budget extends both to the allocation of new money (that is, funds from the policy reserves), and to the A base, or the administration of ongoing programs. The board is also responsible for ensuring that the programs are appropriate to the policy objectives and that the resource levels are right. In addition, it retains the only legal authority to approve departmental resource requirements and program management aspects of policy committee decisions.

That said, the Treasury Board secretariat no longer determines what programs will be expanded or cut in the budget. This responsibility now belongs to the policy committees, while the secretariat has become 'a kind of expert scorekeeper to ensure that the ignorance or self-interest of certain actors [do] not cause inadvertent overcommitment of resources.'[5] As a result, when a spending minister seeks new money from a policy reserve, the department must work with the secretariat's program branch to determine the proposed initial costs as well as those for subsequent years. In fact, a department is expected to consult the Treasury Board secretariat or the Department of Finance for an assessment of its capacity to absorb the cost of a proposal. The secretariat's assessment of the department's capacity is often noted in the memorandum to cabinet prepared by the department in its attempt to secure new funding from the policy reserve.

The secretariat's program branch also reports to cabinet from time to time on the government's expenditure plans, including the resource implications of all cabinet decisions and the status of commitments on a multi-year basis. The branch also conducts multi-year forecasts of spending requirements and reports to P & P. It cooperates with the Department of Finance in preparing the government's fiscal plan by providing the multi-year expenditure component.

The Treasury Board president, along with the minister of finance, is an ex-officio member of all policy committees of cabinet. The program branch briefs the president on any or all spending proposals coming before cabinet committees or cabinet. All of these are analysed with respect to resource requirements, program design, planning, implementation, and evaluation. A program branch representative attends policy committees of cabinet where he or she acts as a technical adviser on questions of person-years and cost. A report is also prepared periodically on total and envelope expenditures.

The bulk of the work of the program branch, however, is with continuing programs or with managing the A base. Once the estimates are approved in parliament, departments are not completely free to spend their allocated resources in that the Treasury Board sets regulations and policies which must be met before funds can be spent. If these cannot be met or if the proposed initiative entails spending beyond an established level, further Treasury Board approval must be secured.

There is thus a continuing flow of departmental submissions to the board throughout the year. Some are simply submissions for board approval to proceed with initiatives for which funding has already been secured. These can cover a wide range of activities, from requests for approving terms and conditions for payments of grants, to approval of major capital projects and of various types of allotment controls. These submissions in themselves do not entail the allocation of additional funds beyond those approved in the estimates. They do, however, require a great deal of preparation on the part of departments and the secretariat before being presented to the board. The program branch presents nearly 2000 such cases in a year.

There is, however, one reserve at Treasury Board that departments can tap for new funding. Each year a special operating reserve is provided for in the estimates. In 1988–9, for example, $360 million was placed in reserve to fund expenditures of a miscellaneous character which could not have been foreseen when the estimates were drawn up.[6] Like the policy reserves which are allocated throughout the year by the relevant cabinet committees, the operating reserve is allocated to departments at various times in the year by the board. Cases that could qualify for funding from the operating reserve include unanticipated increases in workload, emergency situations that threaten health and safety, and so on. Thus, the board will consider allocating funds from the operating reserve to meet adjustments to the cost of operating the government's approved policies and programs, and departments will seek funding from the operating reserve when approved funding levels cannot keep pace with the costs of running the program. Once approved they, together with transfers between votes, are tabled in parliament as supplementary estimates. Policy committees do not have access to the operating reserve to finance new or enriched programs. However, the Treasury Board may refer such proposed cost adjustments to the policy committees for review if they are substantial or if they give rise to policy issues.

The operating reserve represents potential new funding. Some ministers and departments may turn to it after they have been denied funding by the policy reserve or even before going to the policy committee, thinking that they would have a better chance of success with the operating reserves. At times, the line between the policy and operating reserves is blurred, at least in the eyes of departments. In the words of one program branch official, 'some ministers and departments at times try to expand their programs through the operating reserve, particularly when they are shopping around for small ticket items, say, around $5 million. If they succeed, then the new funding becomes part of their A base so that they would have expanded their program without policy approval. I can honestly say, however, that we have been quite successful over the years in keeping this under control. Whenever we have failed, it was a result of special deals struck at the political level.'[7]

The Treasury Board is also the keeper of the government's person-year complement – a responsibility largely overlooked by the literature on the subject. Yet, to those inside government, the person-year complement is of vital importance to their organizations. Its cost is also an important part of the expenditure budget. In the 1988–9 main estimates, some $14.5 billion was put aside for salaries and wages and another $1.6 billion for such things as travel and removal expenses, out of a total $110 billion. There are several costly items in the expenditure budget that require little or no person-years to manage. Public debt charges, for example, total over $30 billion. Other expenses, such as federal contributions to equalization payments, and health care and social services under various federal-provincial agreements ($18 billion for 1988–9), require little in the way of person-years because the actual delivery of these services is done through the provinces. If one removed debt charges and certain transfer payments to the provinces from the expenditure budgets, the administrative overhead cost of government would easily represent over 30 per cent of the total expenditure budget. Some have put the figure much higher. A senior official of the Office of the Comptroller General, for example, suggested it could be as high as 75 per cent.[8] Here, however, one has to go further and isolate various federal transfer payments – such as old age security payments and family allowance ($18 billion for 1988–9) – together with the person-years required to operate the program (2763 person-years).

Officials of the Treasury Board secretariat not only acknowledge the importance of the person-year complement in the expenditure budget, they also recognize that the board is the government's only guardian of person-years. They are quick to add, however, that the person-year complement is directly linked to new policy and program approvals. 'It is difficult, to say the least,' said one official, 'to control person-years on the one hand when other cabinet committees are approving new initiatives on the other. Not always but in many instances new spending requires new person-years to deliver the product.'[9] Thus, when spending proposals are approved by policy committees, the sponsoring department meets with Treasury Board officials to determine new person-year requirements. Traditionally, the departments will state fully (if not overstate) the necessary person-year requirements, while Treasury Board officials will try to bring down the numbers being requested.

Secretariat officials, however, readily admit that they have two handicaps in this exercise. First, the program branch's total staff complement is only 158. They must not only oversee the government's expenditure budget, including the preparation of the estimates, but advise the president and cabinet committees on the 'overall integrity of the financial system,' on new initiatives, on the review of MYOPS, and on the government's person-year complement. The result is that they can easily be overwhelmed by 'facts, figures and people from departments.' Secondly, in only a few instances are there objective and clear-cut criteria to determine productivity and person-year requirements (for example, the number of people required to process x old age security payments). In most instances, requests for new person-years are based on comparable activities in the department or elsewhere. An example will illustrate the point. A new regional development agency – the Atlantic Canada Opportunities Agency (ACOA) – was established in 1987. Programs that originally came under DRIE were transferred to the new agency. DRIE's person-year requirements for these programs had been about 200, so that when ACOA officials met with the Treasury Board secretariat to work out its new organization, the starting point for discussion was 200, because this is what DRIE had in its A base for the programs. ACOA officials simply refused to consider anything less as a starting point for discussion. In the end, ACOA won over 300 person-years, to deliver the programs and staff a new head office.

There are reasons to believe, however, that 200 person-years as a starting point was a high figure. DRIE, it will be recalled, was an amalgamation of the old Department of Regional Economic Expansion and Industry, Trade and Commerce. When former Prime Minister Trudeau announced the new department, he assured all employees of both disbanded departments that no one would be laid off.[10] The result is that there were offices of between 70 and 35 people in New Brunswick and Prince Edward Island. Some provincial DRIE offices, such as that in PEI, had only three or four applications before them at the time DRIE was disbanded. The unnecessarily large number of both federal and provincial officials engaged in industrial development in Atlantic Canada had been made clear in the consultations with area residents and businesses and the consultant's report to the prime minister on the establishment of ACOA.[11] Still, agency officials, with the support of their minister, insisted on employing DRIE's A base to determine their person-year requirements. It was difficult for a mere handful of Treasury Board secretariat officials with only a limited – if any – knowledge of regional development programs to challenge their view.

Once the secretariat has completed its review of any submission for new person-years, it prepares a presentation to the board outlining the requirements, together with a recommendation. Once approved, the new person-years become a part of the department's A base. In only exceptional cases will the board itself engage in any discussion on the issue. If program branch officials are not always in a position to challenge the numbers being requested, then, obviously, a handful of ministers gathered for a two-hour weekly meeting (bearing in mind all the other pressures and demands that come with being a minister) are in no better position to do so. The result is that well over 95 per cent of the cases submitted to the board are approved as recommended.

Treasury Board secretariat officials have an opportunity to review a department's A base during the annual MYOP exercise. In fact, the documents required of departments to prepare the main estimates on what funding departments will actually get for the coming year are forwarded to the Treasury Board secretariat after the MYOP review in the fall and the results of that review are forwarded to departments. The Treasury Board describes MYOPS as 'the primary means by which departments and agencies develop sound estimates of the resources, both financial and person-year, required to implement approved policies, programs and strategies in order to accomplish agreed results in a given fiscal year.'[12]

The secretariat initiates the process with a 'call letter' to the departments which lays out what information is required for the MYOPS. They are asked to report on a wide array of issues about their spending plans, as well as all workload and program changes resulting from the budget speech or from cabinet approvals that have not been already incorporated in the reference level. The latter is essentially last year's budget and allowance for increased costs, such as salary increases. A series of forms are provided to facilitate the preparation of the MYOPS.

The secretariat then reviews all departmental and agency MYOPS. Like the departments themselves, the secretariat begins with the reference level approved a year earlier. It then incorporates cabinet and Treasury Board approvals since the last main estimates review, allows for cost adjustments for salaries, and revises forecasts for statutory program costs as a result of demographic and economic changes and essential workload or technical adjustments. After the review, the secretariat submits a report to the president and subsequently to the board itself. The report highlights issues that secretariat officials feel should be brought to the attention of ministers for resolution. These issues vary greatly. They can range from new resources requested as a result of significant workload adjustments to how to close down the trade negotiations office after the conclusion of the free trade negotiations with the United States, to the most appropriate means of meeting strong pressures for common needs such as translation services, and so on. Recommendations are also made to the president and the board regarding the identified issues. After the board has dealt with them, the president seeks cabinet approval to prepare the main estimates to present to parliament.

The MYOPS, as we saw earlier, do not give rise to sudden or sharp turns in the government's expenditure plan. One secretariat official explained: 'The MYOPS and the main estimates assume a no policy change or a status quo environment. These are simply not the instruments to introduce new policies or to eliminate programs. That is now the responsibility of policy committees of cabinet and P & P.'[13] Another official suggested that the 'MYOPS generate an incredible amount of paper. Yet sometimes, I think we should simply provide a 4 per cent increase to last year's reference level and do away with all the paperwork. I am not sure that much would be lost.'[14] Still other secretariat officials, however, insist that the MYOPS provide an important window for central agency officials on the operations and programs of line departments. When cost-cutting exercises are undertaken to replenish the policy reserves or to cut back spending, the Treasury Board analysts invariably turn to the MYOPS as a key information source to help cabinet make its decisions.[15]

MANAGING HUMAN RESOURCES

The federal public service is by far the largest institution, public or private, in Canada. It employs over 238,000 people for whom the Treasury Board represents the employer. This responsibility, together with a host of other changes in personnel management, including collective bargaining, was introduced in 1967. Nearly 50 per cent of the Treasury Board secretariat's staff currently works on human resource management. The Treasury Board is now responsible for the development of personnel policies, the classification of positions, the application of the Official Languages Act, the coordination of the government's human resources planning process, and for conducting negotiations and consultations with the unions.

The challenge facing the government's personnel manager is immense. Consider the following. The Treasury Board is the 'employer' for about eighty departments and agencies which vary considerably in size. There are seventy-eight occupational groups in the federal public service, including medical doctors, plumbers, air traffic controllers, and secretaries. Thirty per cent of the employees work in the National Capital Region; the remaining 70 per cent are spread out over 7000 kilometres across Canada or serve abroad. The great majority of the employees belong to a union; in fact, they belong to fourteen unions and seventy-eight bargaining units.[16]

The secretariat's staff relations branch represents the employer in all negotiations with the unions and attempts to strike the best possible deal for the government. It is a specialized function, and traditionally few officials from outside get involved in the branch's work. Officials in the branch prefer it that way. They report that their ability to negotiate the best possible deal can be compromised when someone from outside is drawn into the negotiations.

It is well known that labour leaders will try to lobby ministers, particularly the Treasury Board president, in the hope of getting concessions. 'Some ministers,' reveals an official, 'completely stay out of the process, either as a matter of principle or because they are too busy elsewhere. But other ministers tend to get involved and meet with labour leaders privately. It can be difficult for us when ministers get involved. There have been times, for example, when we heard from the unions themselves that our minister had agreed to a demand. One thing is certain: whenever ministers get involved directly in the process, there is a cost to taxpayers because they rarely ever win anything from the unions – they always give in.'[17]

The role of the Treasury Board and the secretariat in personnel management issues extends far beyond collective bargaining. The personnel policy branch in the secretariat develops the policies and systems for managing the public service work force. It is now widely accepted that employment practices in the federal government should serve as a role model and a standard setter for other sectors of the economy.[18] They are, of course, subject to a degree of public scrutiny shared by few other organizations. Personnel practices must adhere to the government's own social policies and demonstrate their compatibility in their day-to-day application.

This and court rulings have led the federal government to introduce a number of progressive policies. For example, section 11 of the Canadian Human Rights Act prohibits differences in wages between male and female employees who perform work of equal value. Between 1978 and 1984, the Treasury Board resolved a series of complaints resulting in 4000 employees in female-dominated occupations sharing $39.1 million in equal pay adjustments. In July 1987 a settlement was reached with hospital sevices workers. costing $20 million, including retroactive pay.[19] The president of the Treasury Board also invited all bargaining agents to participate in a joint union-management initiative to oversee the implementation of a comprehensive plan to achieve equal pay within the federal public service. Estimates of the cost of achieving this amount to over $200 million annually and over $1 billion in retroactive payments.[20]

The Treasury Board has also launched a series of special recruitment initiatives to bring more women, aboriginals, visible minorities, and the handicapped into the federal public service and into management. The Treasury Board sends out specific directives to departments and agencies to assist in meeting government-wide objectives. For example, it decided to double the number of women in management over a five-year period, to hire 2700 disabled persons over three years, and to increase the number of visible minorities in both permanent and term positions.[21] The Treasury Board takes the lead in promoting special employment equity action, and some of these initiatives require a number of new person-years and increased financial resources. Wearing this hat, the board obviously puts aside its guardian role and becomes a spender – a fact that does not go unnoticed by spending ministers and their departments.

The board, however, does play a clear guardian role in the classifying of position levels. It retains the authority with respect to management positions and delegates authority to those in middle and lower levels, while setting out the guidelines to be employed by departments to determine classification levels. Still, secretariat officials report that whenever authority for classifying positions is delegated to departments, there is invariably a 'creeping up' in classification levels. As well, there is always pressure from departments to classify senior management positions upwards. Particularly in recent years, with less chance for advancement than in the 1960s and 1970s, there has been a constant flow of requests for reclassification to the point where, in the words of one secretariat offical, 'about one-third of all executive level positions are in for possible reclassification, with something like over 90 per cent of them upwards. It is one tough grind for us; we have to say no a lot more often than we can say yes.' He also reported that an audit of position classifications carried out in 1983 revealed that over 20 per cent of the postions audited were 'misclassified.' Virtually all of these commanded a higher classification (and hence a higher salary) than the responsibilities warranted.[22]

It is also important to note that the board's most important instrument for managing the government's human resources policies is the Multi-Year Human Resources Plan. The MYHRPS are an integral part of the budget expenditure process and support departmental Multi-Year Operational Plans – the MYOPS. They consist of two parts: overview and plans, issues and concerns. The first part deals with human resource requirements to support departmental goals. The second part offers departments and agencies an opportunity to communicate specific concerns to Treasury Board, such as new policy direction or central agency reporting requirements.

The MYHRPS sent by departments and agencies to Treasury Board and to the Public Service Commission report on human resource problems that are beyond the capacity of individual departments to resolve or that have implications for the government as a whole. They also represent an opportunity for departments to outline the human resource plans they intend to pursue and serve as achievement reports on the previous year's activities. For the Treasury Board and other central agencies, the MYHRPS provide key information on a host of government-wide human resource issues which the board can use to develop its objectives and policies.

MANAGING PRUDENCE AND PROBITY

Two students of public administration recently observed that, in an organization as large and complex as the government of Canada, 'it is necessary to have some organization to ensure that all of the diverse and centralized units in the organization are conducting their administrative activities in an appropriate and reasonably uniform manner.'[23] There must be certain administrative and financial rules, they argue, that should be binding on all departments and agencies to ensure common practice, prudence, and probity in the business of government. This is true, not simply because the government is a large and complex entity to administer, but also because it is expected that the ethical standards of those who conduct 'business' in government should be very high. Since the 1970s, in particular, there has been strong concern and anxiety among the general public about the integrity and administrative efficiency of government procurement, including its contracting practices. In June 1970, it will be recalled, the House of Commons held a special debate on the government's failure to protect the public treasury in refitting the aircraft carrier, *Bonaventure*. The opening motion included accusations of 'waste, extravagance, and other abuses in the spending of government money.' During the debate, opposition members from all parties hurled accusations at the government and concluded with pleas to introduce 'administrative integrity.' Specific cases were identified, such as the awarding of two separate contracts – for different amounts – to remove fifty-two chairs from the *Bonaventure*'s briefing room.[24] The concept of 'let the manager manage,' introduced only a few years earlier by the Glassco Commission, was now being put severely to the test, at least in the political arena.

In response, the then Treasury Board president unveiled new measures to improve 'efficiency' in government. One of the most important of these was the establishment of a special administrative policy branch in the Treasury Board secretariat. The branch was designed to draw up administrative norms for departments, covering fields like accommodation, construction contracts, travel, material acquisitions, and an accounting system for these expenditures. In a circular, Treasury Board made it clear to all departments that the work of the branch would be directed towards ensuring 'qualities of probity and prudence' in government. The new branch quickly identified two types of administrative activities: those dealing with the quantity and quality of goods and services (such as accommodation and furnishings) and those dealing with acquiring them (contract regulations). The branch uses three instruments: legislation (such as the Financial Administration Act or Access to Information Act, regulations (mandatory instructions approved by the governor in council), and directives (mandatory instructions approved by the Treasury Board that are normally to be followed).[25]

There are now some sixty-six active policies, virtually all of which are built on the principle that transactions beyond the prescribed threshold conducted by individual ministers may only be concluded with the approval of the governor in council or the Treasury Board. The mechanism through which departments seek that authority is typically a submission to the Treasury Board.

In the fiscal year 1986–7, the administrative policy branch processed a total of 1469 such submissions, distributed as follows: property, 556; material, 210; services, 427; information, 127; and others (mainly tax remission orders), 149. A good number of the administrative policies have a direct impact on spending. Some restrict the numbers of persons and permitted spending on consulting contracts, others concern government purchasing, some limit the use of public funds that can be spent on conferences and hospitality, and still others outline in detail what can be claimed as expenses when travelling on government business. Some policies are designed to place restrictions on departmental spending during the last months of the government's budget year to ensure that departments do not go on a spending binge to use up their allocated budgets. For example, a Treasury Board policy restricts the purchase of telecommunications and electronic office equipment during the last three months of the fiscal year.

The Treasury Board also recently introduced new measures to improve the management of federal real property holdings. The government of Canada now owns real property – airports, national parks, office buildings, and military bases – valued at more than $50 billion. Over the years, assorted pieces of legislation have assigned the mangement and control of these properties to various ministers and crown corporations, so that the custody, control, and maintenance of real property has been exercised by forty-six different government departments, agencies, and crown corporations at an annual cost of $5 billion and 34,000 person-years.[26] The federal government has come under criticism in recent years – notably from Erik Nielsen's 1984 Task Force on Program Review – for the way it manages its real property. To deal with this criticism, a branch was set up in 1986, the bureau of real property management, 'to ensure more effective management of the government's property holdings.'[27]

THE OFFICE OF THE COMPTROLLER GENERAL

Shortly after assuming the position of auditor general in 1973, J.J. Macdonell was reported to have expressed shock and dismay on hearing that the federal government did not have a 'chief financial officer.'[28] Worse still, he discovered that the Treasury Board secretariat did not have a financial administration division. The position of comptroller of the Treasury had been abolished in the 1960s after the Glassco Commission had recommended the decentralization of financial administration to departments.

In the fall of 1974, Macdonell launched an ambitious financial management and control study. The twelve-month study brought together thirty-four chartered accountants from sixteen firms. With the cream of the nation's accounting profession on his side, he met cabinet ministers and senior deputy ministers to sell them on the idea that a chief financial officer for the government, a comptroller general, was required. The suggestion met with strong resistance and Macdonell decided to hold off for a while and omit it from his annual report. He did say to the Public Accounts Committee, however, that he could not even find financial administration on the Treasury Board's organization chart, and he went on to express the hope that a deputy minister level appointment would be made to oversee how money was being spent in government. The president of the Treasury Board, Jean Chrétien, was quick to resist the suggestion. He did not want two deputy ministers reporting to him, he said, because 'I do not want to be caught between two men.'[29] In addition, permanent officials were firmly of the view that the study team of 'leading accountants' from across the country had simply fallen 'prey to ... the mythology that the public sector is the same as the private sector.'[30]

By 1976, Macdonell had lost patience with his discussions with senior officials, and his annual report made public his widely reported warning that 'Parliament and indeed the Government – has lost, or is close to losing, effective control of the public purse.'[31] He went on to propose a fundamental restructuring of the Treasury Board secretariat. The secretary of the Treasury Board would keep all his current responsibilities except those relating to financial management and control. These would be turned over to the new position of comptroller general. The incumbent would hold the same rank as the secretary to the Treasury Board and would also report directly to the president of the Treasury Board. Specifically, he wrote that the comptroller general should be responsible for the 'design, development, implementation and monitoring of adequate systems and procedures to ensure ... that public moneys and assets are under effective custody and control at all times, that accounting procedures and financial reports throughout government ... conform to acceptable accounting principles and standards ... that expenditures of public moneys are made with due regard for economy and efficiency and that satisfactory procedures measure the effectiveness of programs.'[32] The auditor general's report was tabled on 22 November 1976. That same afternoon the then Treasury Board president, Robert Andras, rose in the House to announce the setting up of a royal commission on financial management and accountability with a mandate 'to ensure that financial departments and agencies meet the highest attainable standards.'[33]

The press expressed deep concern that the appointment of a royal commission was simply an attempt to delay for a few years at least Macdonell's suggestion that a comptroller general be appointed.[34] Pressure on Andras mounted. Many government members of parliament reported in caucus that their constituents were even more concerned with the issue of financial control than with the newly elected nationalist government in Quebec. Andras requested a meeting with the auditor general to review his report and to consider the establishment of a new Office of the Comptroller General. A series of one-on-one meetings followed, with Andras trying to get the auditor general to agree that the comptroller general should report to the secretary of the Treasury Board as an associate secretary. He was unsuccessful. It was, however, agreed that, although there would be two separate deputy ministers, there would be only one department with the staffs of the office and the secretariat working closely together. Andras sought approval for the new office from P & P. He met considerable resistance there and from senior officials, particularly those in the Treasury Board secretariat. He reported to P & P, however, that he had *negotiated* a deal with the auditor general and that, unless he could deliver it, the government would be subjected to a new round of criticism from the media, the Public Accounts Committee, and Macdonell himself. With the support of the prime minister, Andras was finally able to get his proposal through. The agreement he concluded with the auditor general suggested that the comptroller general would be responsible for:

1 designing and guiding the implementation of systems of financial reporting, financial management, and financial control to provide assurance that public moneys and assets are expended with probity, economy, and efficiency and that public moneys and assets are under effective custody and control; and assessing the adequacy of such systems in departments and agencies;
2 the preparation and signing of the public accounts and certain other financial statements of Canada;
3 the accounting principles and practices for the accounts of Canada;

4 the structure of accounts to be used by departments and agencies for the preparation of financial reports;

5 recommendations on the form of the public accounts;

6 reform of the estimates;

7 review and approval of all accounting systems and procedures supporting the financial information and statements included in the public accounts;

8 recommendations as to how capital budgets might be changed to improve expenditure control and financial reporting;

9 reporting to the president of the Treasury Board on the adequacy of departmental systems and procedures for evaluating effectiveness, and of systems for measuring efficiency;

10 working with the Public Service Commission and the Treasury Board secretariat to recruit, train, and deploy financial officers;

11 providing guidance to chief financial officers of departments; ·

12 reporting to the president of the Treasury Board on significant variances between financial and operational plans and projected actual results;

13 assisting departments, agencies, and corporations to design and develop or improve financial managment, control, and reporting systems;

14 liaison with the auditor general;

15 development, maintenance, and evaluation of detailed policies and guidelines on the internal audit function of the government;

16 the provision of a cental advisory service to departments and agencies concerning financial administration policy, principles, and standards of the government, and the provision of authoritative interpretations of legislation, regulations, and policies relating to financial administration.

The auditor general took great care to explain that, despite the similarity in titles, he did not wish to see the re-establishment of the comptroller of Treasury. That position had been abolished, he noted, in the 1960s and it should not be resurrected. The new comptroller, he reported, would design policies and would not be present in departments, checking specific expenditure items.

Notwithstanding the agreement reached between Andras and the auditor general and agreed to by the prime minister and P & P , there was still considerable opposition to the new office in Ottawa. In fact, it took the government nearly a year to appoint the first comptroller general, and many outside government felt that officials were deliberately dragging their feet in the hope that the idea would eventually die. Officials from the Privy Council Office feared that two strong deputy ministers with similar responsibilities for different but interrelated areas of management policy would soon be at each other's throats, with only the political level to arbitrate disputes. Their fears would prove to be well founded.

Treasury Board secretariat officials felt that many of the comptroller general's responsibilities overlapped with their own. Specifically, they felt that, at a minimum, items 6, 8, 9, 10, 12, 15, and 16 were their responsibilities. How could they be split into two organizations, they asked, both headed by deputy ministers and both reporting directly to a minister? Surely, they argued, the secretariat's program branch which is responsible for resource allocation and utilization should be the centre responsible for financial management and administration. They also felt that the Treasury Board could not afford to have dual points of contact with spending departments. There would be confusion as to the lead agency and plenty of opportunities for the spenders to divide and conquer, to circumvent the system by exploiting the growing confusion and rivalries. Attempts to resolve who does what would only lead to a byzantine and cumbersome partnership that would dilute responsibility and accountability.

Worse still, the Office of the Comptroller General, over time, would assume the role of management consultant to departments and in numerous instances attempt to become an intermediary between departments and central agencies. It had launched, as noted in an earlier chapter, new management initiatives such as IMPAC which had proved costly but which achieved precious little in terms of concrete results. The Treasury Board secretariat, as guardians of the expenditure budget, looked on with deep concern as the Office of the Comptroller General generated new demands on departments which, in turn, led them to request new resources for corporate management systems and the like. There have also been numerous other irritants between the secretariat and the Office of the Comptroller General, and their working relationship has been less than engaging since the office was first established.

To Treasury Board officials, the establishment of the Office of the Comptroller General was a purely political move to placate the media, the auditor general, and the Public Accounts Committee. 'The problem they wanted resolved,' one insists, 'was a political one; their intention was not to institute greater financial controls in government or to improve public administration generally. The consideration that went into all this was – we've got a political problem. Now, how do we get out of it? The answer was if we do appoint a comptroller general – we will make a good number of people happy, so let's do it – and to hell with the rest.' He went on to argue: 'We knew right from the start that his office would not do much. Now the verdict is in and now we know for sure that it didn't do much.'[35]

In terms of the expenditure budget, the office's most important short-coming has been in evaluating programs. It assumed full responsibility for the coordination of evaluation planning, for policy guidance, and for assessing the quality of evaluation findings in studies carried out by departments. And shortly after the office was set up, it served notice that it would urge departments to establish program evaluation and that it would conduct studies on issues of interdepartmental or government-wide concern. It would also take the lead in developing the appropriate methodology and procedures for such evalutations. A keen student and practitioner of public administration predicted shortly after the office was established that the growing concern over increased government spending would lead to 'a new industry, *the Evaluation Industry*.'[36] We now know, ten years later, that program evaluations did indeed develop into a growth industry and that it grew around the Office of the Comptroller General.

By 1980 there were seven program evaluations in the government which were declared to be compatible with OCG guidelines in terms of corporate organization, internal policy, and long-term planning. There were also thirty-four evaluation studies carried out in the federal government in 1980–1. By 1984–5 there were program evaluations in thirty-seven departments and over one hundred studies being carried out. By 1986–7, departmental evaluation plans covered 'virtually all expenditure programs' in government.[37] The cost has now become substantial. It involves over 300 person-years and numerous outside consultants. The total cost of program evaluation is now reported to amount to about $50 million a year.

There are few supporters in Ottawa of program evaluations. It is often suggested in departments that 'someone should evaluate the eva-lutators.' The evaluators did evaluate themselves in 1984 and concluded that 'there [was] scope for further improvement in the quality of studies and a need to elaborate the policy for evaluation of interde-partmental and broad policy areas.'[38] Some officials consider this conclusion to have been much too positive. What the review should have looked at was the ultimate benefits of program change resulting from evaluation and the procedures for cabinet reconsideration of programs based on evaluation studies. The OCG and program evaluation, the argument goes, seem to be concerned only with methodologies and how many programs have been evaluated. Put more bluntly, evaluators seem to be kept busy turning cranks not connected to anything. The result is that one would be hard pressed to point to even a handful of programs that have been reduced or eliminated as a result of an evaluation study. The Nielsen Task Force concluded that 'government program evaluations were generally useless and inadequate. Yet, guided and inspired by the Office of the Comptroller General, departments have put in place significant evaluation groups over the past years.'[39] Outside observers have also urged program evaluators in government to emphasize more 'realism' in their work, with some bluntly saying that their work has no impact on the expenditure budget.[40]

One important problem is that evaluation studies are piled on top of one another, even though there does not appear to be a 'market' for them. If, for example, a study suggests that a program is functioning well and that there is a strong need for it, departmental officials will circulate it widely and simply add 'we knew all along and we have been saying so.' If, however, an evaluation study is critical of a particular program, officials will be far more reluctant to share it. In fact, a senior official in the program branch at TBS reveals that the branch has received less than half of the last 250 program evaluation studies which have been carried out.[41] We need not test our imagination too much to conclude that the evaluation studies that have not been received are unlikely to endorse the programs fully. The Nielsen Task Force explained the difficulty: 'routine evaluations conducted by departmental officials are undertaken for the department's deputy minister. By definition, therefore, they tend to be self-serving.... The fact that evaluation results are now subject to disclosure under Access to Information legislation tends to make them even less frank.'[42]

An equally important consideration is that the program branch in TBS and not the OCG could make better use of the program evaluation function and would be better suited to direct priority areas for evaluation. The branch, which is charged with providing 'advice to the Treasury Board on the allocation of resources and [communicating] to departments and agencies the policies, directives and decisions of Treasury Board which affect the use and level of resources,' should also be evaluating programs. As it is, there are two central agencies singing from 'different hymn books' about program effectiveness and efficiency. One can make recommendations on resource allocation to ministers and the other is responsible for evaluating program effectiveness. The one with clout makes only limited use of program evaluation results, not simply because they are largely 'useless and inadequate,' but also because the responsibility for program evaluation lies with the Office of the Comptroller General and not with the Treasury Board program branch. The program branch also has little opportunity to reorient the program evaluation function to the requirements of the expenditure budget. Spending departments are, of course, well aware of this and so are not forthcoming in sending copies of evaluation studies that might report negatively on their programs. None of the ministers and officials from spending departments I consulted expressed any degree of satisfaction with the government's program evaluation. Even officials in central agencies, including some directly involved, readily admit that the program has shortcomings. One official in a large spending department commented: 'We went along with it because there is no mileage in not doing so. But it is just that much more paperwork we have to do to satisfy paper-hungry central agencies. I have no illusion whatsoever – it is a bit of a charade which has no impact on what we do and how we do it.'[43] Another was even more critical. 'I get a chuckle whenever I hear central agency officials suggesting that we can't get our act together. If anyone can't get their act together it is them, not us. The OCG and the Treasury Board secretariat is really a tough act to follow in terms of working at cross purposes.'[44]

More moderate observers suggest that program evaluation has taken OCG away from financial management into broader program issues. The result is that the comptroller general has never succeeded as the government's chief financial officer. The auditor general recommended the establishment of a position of comptroller general because the financial management and control systems of departments and agencies were thought to be below acceptable standards of quality and effectiveness. Several years after a comptroller general was appointed, there were still departments overspending their budgets – as, for example, DRIE in 1987. The Department of Indian Affairs and Northern Development also had difficulty controlling some of its spending programs. Separate audits had suggested that there was a need to strengthen financial controls and guidelines in both departments.[45]

INCREASED MINISTERIAL AUTHORITY AND ACCOUNTABILITY –
ANOTHER ATTEMPT AT LETTING MANAGERS MANAGE

In a major policy statement during the 1984 election campaign, Brian
Mulroney pledged that his government would make 'productive
management ... a top political priority ... [and introduce] a philosophy
based on accountability, appropriate delegation of authority and the
encouragement of creative and efficient management within the civil
service.' He went on to add that his government would 'shift from
reliance on regulations, controls, and detailed procedures towards
greater reliance on managers' competence and their achievement of
results. Our goal is to simply to govern – and to let managers manage.'[46]
The call by Mulroney to let the managers manage could hardly be
described as a bold new concept in public administration. The Glassco
Commission had made it its principal theme over twenty years before.
But, as Peter Aucoin and Herman Bakvis have observed, by the mid-
1980s, nonetheless, deregulation of management and decentralization
could still be put forward as reform proposals and initiatives.'[47]

Mulroney made good on his election campaign pledge and, shortly
after his party came to power, the president of the Treasury Board,
Robert R. de Cotret, introduced a new approach to management in the
federal government – Increased Ministerial Authority and Accountability (IMAA).[48] This last attempt to let managers manage could have important implications for the Treasury Board as keeper of the expenditure
budget.

The constant push and pull between centralized control and 'letting
the managers manage' has meant that one viewpoint is in the ascendant
for a while, followed by a swing back to the other. One can easily
trace, from the 1930s on, how and when the pendulum has swung. As
mentioned in an earlier chapter, the Glassco Commission had recommended that ministers concentrate on larger policy issues and not on
administrative or management concerns. It was highly critical of the
overcentralization that burdened departments, and the Treasury Board
was identified as one of those perpetuating this situation. Subsequently,
departments were given wider latitude in awarding contracts, in reallo-
cating funds within programs, and so on. By the late 1970s, however,
the auditor general, the media, and outside observers were expressing
deep concern that the government had lost the ability to control spending. New measures were introduced to tighten financial and administrative control.

Yet, in the mid-1980s, the minister of finance announced in his budget speech new measures to give 'individual ministers and their departmental managers ... more latitude and more direct responsiblity to manage the resources entrusted to them so that they can react quickly and effectively to the changing environment.'[49] Treasury Board President de Cotret summed up the objective of the new approach by pointing out: 'We will be more concerned with what departments do both in program results and in meeting service-wide policy objectives and less concerned with how well procedural rules are followed.'[50] However, he was quick to add: 'I want to make it clear that Treasury Board remains responsible for the *Financial Administration Act* and other statutes. What we are talking about is changing the way in which we fulfil our responsibilities.'[51]

IMAA's central purpose is to increase, over time, departmental authority and accountability and change the way Treasury Board fulfils its mandate. IMAA is being implemented through two complementary initiatives – a general review of Treasury Board policies, and the development of individual memoranda of understanding between departments and the Treasury Board.

The policy review is designed to identify the potential for greater flexibility, deregulation and delegation, to reduce reporting requirements to the board, and generally to simplify policy. The review has prompted changes. Among other things, departments can now sponsor conferences without having to secure Treasury Board approval, the ceiling on competitive contracts for construction and consulting without reference to the board has been doubled, departments can classify positions, except in the management category, and approve organizational changes. The information required in both the MYOPS and MYHRPS has also been reduced and simplified, and the Treasury Board's approval process in several areas has been streamlined. For example, the number of reports required under various administrative policies has been reduced by 65 per cent and the delegation of authority in certain areas of human resource management has reduced departmental requests to the secretariat by about 1000 a year. Moreover, departments can now carry into the next fiscal year 5 per cent of their capital budget, to a maximum of $25 million in 1988–9, rising to $75 million in 1990–1. These changes, among others, have reduced Treasury Board's involvement in the day-to-day operations of departments. The result is that Treasury Board submissions have declined by almost a third, from 5100 in 1983–4 to 3500 in 1986–7. A further 10 per cent reduction is expected as approved increases in departmental authority are implemented fully.[52]

The second major activity in implementing IMAA is the negotiating of memoranda of understanding (MOUS) with departments and agencies. To date, three departments have signed MOUS with the Treasury Board – Labour, Customs and Excise, and Employment and Immigration – and several other departments and agencies have initiated discussions with the secretariat. The memorandum of understanding outlines the department's increased authority and flexibility in delivering programs and establishes an accountability framework against which performance can be assessed. The MOU covers the responsibilities of all the branches in the secretariat and the OCG; it spells out in one place the levels of authority delegated to deal with all Treasury Board policies. The Treasury Board secretariat is also suggesting that any savings realized by departments as a result of more efficient operations under IMAA will be left in departments for reallocation to priority initiatives.

IMAA is having an important impact, among other branches and areas at the board, on the program branch, and on the expenditure budget process. As already noted, there are three main functions of a budgeting system – control, management, and policy planning. IMAA aims at emphasizing greater individual authority and accountability over the use of public resources. It does so by reducing and relaxing controls on many activities that previously required prior Treasury Board review and approval so that ministers and departments can exercise greater flexibility in allocating approved resources. This is accompanied by a revised accountability regime to protect the integrity of the expenditure management process and the application of stricter cash limits to departmental expenditures. In terms of the three main functions of the budgeting system, IMAA thus represents a shift in emphasis towards management and policy planning and away from micro detailed controls.

Statutory responsibility and authority for a broad range of financial and expenditure management practices are contained in the Financial Administration Act. The exercise of many of these responsibilities is covered by regulation and in detailed Treasury Board controls. Under this control system, specific authorities are sought and justified by ministers and their departments before the fact, but there is relatively little subsequent reporting of performance and results, and little capacity at the centre to hold accountable those who ignore or evade policies and standards. Treasury Board ministers are given a good perspective on what departments plan to do and the resource levels needed to carry out these plans, but they have little firm evidence about whether they have been effectively implemented and whether resources have been allocated efficiently and economically.

Under IMAA, the program branch retains its primary responsibility of advising the government on the least cost to operate ongoing programs and of assessing detailed departmental expenditure plans needed to prepare the estimates. The secretariat's program branch can also expect to be called upon to advise the government on resource allocation issues, because the reduction in transactions is expected to give Treasury Board ministers more time to consider the broader issues of resource allocation and the quality of management in the public service.

ACTORS

It is important to highlight the role of some actors in managing the expenditure budget. It is now widely accepted that the emergence of other cabinet committees and later PEMS – in particular Priorities and Planning – has weakened the power and the prestige of the Treasury Board in the budget process. Members of the board itself, with the exception of the president, are junior and command only limited weight in cabinet. For example, custom has it that only the president is a member of P & P. The minister of finance is also a member of both P & P and Treasury Board, but never atttends Treasury Board meetings. Few ministers – especially junior ones – take any satisfaction in playing watchdog on spending ministers and departments. Junior ministers require the support of more powerful colleagues for their own projects or spending initiatives so that they usually do not want to be seen frustrating the spending proposals of senior ministers.

The guardian role is often left to the president and the secretariat staff. The president not only has the prestige to lead other Treasury Board ministers to the kind of decision he wishes to see, he is also expected to assume an important guardian role in other cabinet committees and in cabinet. As a Treasury Board analyst explained, 'if he is not on the side of the angels in the spending game, who is?'[53]

As is the case with the finance minister, the personality of the president of the Treasury Board and his standing among cabinet colleagues have a strong influence on how he plays the guardian role. The most successful Treasury Board presidents, according to secretariat officials, have been 'those that have a strong enough personality to be able to say no to the toughest of ministers and take them on in cabinet committees and full cabinet.'[54] But personality is not enough. The president of the Treasury Board also needs some political clout. It is important that he or she is considered to have sound political judgment. Spending ministers will quickly rally against a Treasury Board president who is simply a nay sayer and who is unwilling 'to save a colleague's hide from time to time.'[55] In short, an effective president must know when to give in or when to strike a deal, for political reasons. Otherwise, ministers 'will send messages in many varied, subtle and not so subtle ways to the PM and PMO that he will get the government in a heap of political problems.'[56] Thus an effective Treasury Board president must continually walk a thin line between holding back spenders and giving in from time to time.

Some spending ministers have devised schemes to 'get by' Treasury Board. The most common one is to announce an initiative publicly and seek to attract as much visibility as possible before submitting the proposal for approval to the board. It is true that, since PEMS, departments no longer come to the Treasury Board for new money to finance their initiatives except from the operating reserve. Still, ministers need to secure Treasury Board approval to proceed with major projects even though they have the required funding in their departments. Some ministers on occasion will simply ignore this requirement and unveil the initiatives. Treasury Board has then two options: it can either approve the project when it is finally submitted or, in the words of a secretariat official, 'leave the offending minister out to dry and simply not approve the project.'[57] There is obviously a great deal of reluctance among Treasury Board ministers, particularly so now since they are more junior ministers, to embarrass one of their own. It is usually left to the president to 'reel spending ministers back in. But first or second time offenders are rarely left out to dry. Repeated offenders will be warned by the president to stop the practice or the next time he could well be on his own hook.'[58]

There is a view fairly widely held among officials that the most effective president is one who has no other responsibility than playing a guardian role. Treasury Board presidents who combine this role with another responsibility either lose sight of their primary guardian role or compromise it over time. Examples will illustrate the point. Herb Gray held two important responsibilities in the last Trudeau government: he was president of the Treasury Board, and 'political' or 'regional' minister for Ontario. Regional ministers not only oversee the dispensing of whatever political patronage is available for their region, such as orders in council appointments, but they are also charged with looking after the government's political interest in their region. Other ministers from the region, but particularly government MPs, will often turn to their regional ministers to support an initiative in their riding. In wearing two hats – one as guardian and one as spender for Ontario, the country's largest and wealthiest region – Gray saw his guardian role compromised. Spending ministers from other regions simply dismissed his pleas for tighter control of the purse-strings when he himself was lobbying ministers and departments to support projects earmarked for Ontario.

Don Mazankowski provides a more recent example. He combined several roles, including deputy prime minister, house leader, president of the Treasury Board, chairman of the operations committee of cabinet, and regional minister for Alberta. In his capacity as deputy prime minister and chairman of the operations committee, Mazankowski assumed the role of 'political fixer' in government. Again, ministers and governments would turn to him to resolve particular issues and he would orchestrate particular deals on their behalf. But, as one secretariat official observed, 'there has to be consistency if you want to be effective in limiting the spending appetites of ministers. You simply cannot flip back and forth between guardian and spender to suit the moment.'[59]

Robert de Cotret is reported to have had more success as Treasury Board president than Gray or Mazankowski. He played his guardian role fully until he started to promote economic development in Montreal. In his first year, however, he served as 'full-time' president of the Treasury Board. He played an important role in launching the 1984 cuts in spending, in promoting IMAA, and in speaking strongly in favour of spending restraint. According to one secretariat official, 'de Cotret was a full-time minister who played the 'schoolteacher' and 'police officer' role well. He laid out the rules and then acted as a police officer among his colleagues to ensure that all rules and allocations were followed.'[60]

Spending ministers and departments, of course, are quick to 'size up' both the minister of finance and the president of Treasury Board to see where they may be vulnerable. In the case of the Treasury Board president, they obviously prefer a minister who is open to striking 'political deals' or who is a 'deal maker' rather than one who always plays by the rules and the process. No matter who the president is, however, spending departments generally view the Treasury Board secretariat and other central agencies with a degree of cynicism. 'A necessary evil – necessary and evil' said one departmental official.[61] 'Largely unnecessary and largely evil,' said another.[62]

To be sure, conflicts between the Treasury Board and line departments, as elsewhere, are rooted in the fact that both sides have different criteria to measure success. The Treasury Board secretariat measures success in terms of its ability to keep spending within reasonable limits, while spending departments view success in terms of funding and accomplishments. In the federal government, however, the conflict extends further. There is in the departments a deep sense of frustration over central agency control and interference in their day-to-day operations. A group of senior government executives summed up the situation in this fashion: 'The power of central agencies is so overwhelming that ministry executives do not feel they have adequate authority to do the jobs they are asked to undertake. We spend more and more time trying to manage the overhead imposed by central agencies (Treasury Board, Finance) which want to control even minor financial and administrative decisions. The staff organizations impede line decisions instead of facilitating them, and yet we are the ones held responsible when things go wrong. It is as if we are not trusted to do the jobs we were hired to do. This is so demoralizing and energy-sapping.'[63] The problem was also summed up thus: 'Treasury Board determines how departments budget, classify positions and organize functions. The Public Service Commission prescribes how managers will hire and promote staff. The comptroller general sets guidelines for internal audit and evaluation. The Department of Supply and Services establishes procedures for making purchases. Public Works has responsibility for the acquisition and maintenance of accommodation.... Each of these groups has some authority to prescribe how managers should act, yet assumes little or no responsibility for the results of managers' actions, should they turn out to be unsatisfactory because of conflicting demands.'[64]

IMAA is designed to overcome some of these constraints. There is, however, a great deal of cynicism in departments about the government's latest attempt to let managers manage. 'Here we go again,' said one senior departmental manager. 'I have seen it so many times. I doubt very much if this version will work any better.'[65] The reason for the cynicism, it appears, is twofold. First, and on this both central agency and line department officials agree, there is a political problem. Support for removing rules and regulations from the centre exists until such time as a minister or a department 'blows it.' 'One high-profile incident

like the Bonaventure case, the Coté affair, or even senior officials doing
something improper always makes ministers, especially Treasury Board
ministers, want to tighten up to avoid further embarrassments.'[66] Secondly, departments insist that by their very nature central agencies want
to control and interfere, and ministerial declarations like the one on
IMAA have in the end little impact. 'Central agencies,' explained one
departmental official, 'always want to make themselves relevant. How
do they become relevant? By second guessing what we do. Certainly
not by assisting us or by coming forward with new ideas to do things
differently. They simply sit in judgment.'[67] Another agreed that central
agency officials in their desire to be relevant interfere through countless
demands for information and data. He insists that they often then turn
around and 'use the information we provided against us.'[68] Yet another,
speaking about the need for central agency officials to be relevant,
argued: 'How else could they justify their existence? The worst thing,
however, is that the whole central agency apparatus is very expensive to
maintain. Finance, Treasury Board secretariat, the comptroller general,
Federal-Provincial Relations Office, Privy Council Office, Public Service
Commission, and so on, must require at least 5000 person-years
to operate [the exact figure is 4736]. That makes for a lot of people
walking around trying to be relevant.' He added, 'If they are really
serious about cutting spending, why don't they start in their own
backyard?'[69]

For central agencies, however, 'letting the managers manage' and
IMAA are not as simple and straightforward as line department officials
would like everyone to believe. Some insist that at times line officials
welcome central agency rules, regulations, and procedures, even though
they do no care to admit it. Central agencies can be convenient for
departments when confronted with a difficult proposal from one of
their important client groups. A department can always blame it on
the Treasury Board in explaining to clients why it cannot support a
particular proposal. 'I heard time and again from acquaintances, said
one Treasury Board secretariat official, 'that a particular group was not
able to get funding because it was turned down at the Board. When I
checked, I very often discovered that the matter was never even submitted to us.'[70] Another stated that at times departments submit proposals
for, say, reclassifying positions, knowing full well that they can never be
approved. It is 'far easier to blame it on the board or pass the buck' she
explained, 'than [tell] your own people that it doesn't make sense.'[71] Yet
another official insisted that 'IMAA will be more of a difficult adjustment

for departments than the Treasury Board secretariat.' 'The problem,' he stated, 'is not so much to let managers manage as it is to make managers manage.'[72] We will return to this point later in the study.

6

From Glassco to Nielsen:
Inquisitors from the private sector

From time to time, ministers or senior officials see a need to subject the government's operations to an independent review. Invariably, the private sector is asked to participate, frequently because the media and public pressure had forced an independent inquiry. The establishment of the Lambert Commission in the late 1970s, for example, resulted from widely reported concerns that the government was close to losing control of its spending. The Glassco Commission had been set up in 1960 by the Diefenbaker government because the prime minister and senior ministers were deeply worried about their inability to control the growth in government spending. The Nielsen Task Force on program review was established by Prime Minister Mulroney one day after he came to power on the advice of the then clerk of the Privy Council and secretary of the cabinet because 'he and senior officials in central agencies had observed the inability of government over the years to control the proliferation of programs and to get rid of ones that should be terminated.'[1] The thinking is always that an outside review will either bring new insights to old problems or bring an objective and detached assessment of ongoing activities and their delivery. The implicit assumption is that the private sector does not have a vested interest in ongoing government programs and that they are also better managers.[2]

Outside reviews in Canada have looked either at management practices, as did the Lambert Commission, or at programs, as did the Nielsen Task Force. This chapter looks at these reviews and considers their impact on government spending. Much has already been said in this study on the Glassco Commission and to a lesser extent on the Lambert Commission; accordingly, this chapter concentrates more on the efforts of the Nielsen Task Force.

GLASSCO: GOING DOWN AN UNTRAVELLED ROAD

We know that the Glassco report called for sweeping changes to central agency management functions. We also know that it advocated a program approach to budgeting – that is, that any program which no longer served a need or which was not being administered properly would be identified. More important, however, by 'letting the managers manage' the Glassco Commission was convinced that government operations would be managed more efficiently and this over time would bring important savings for the Canadian taxpayers. Tight financial controls introduced some thirty years before were abolished, and decision-making authority was delegated to departments.

These changes had a profound impact. Central agencies sought more and more to concentrate on the long-term issues, on assessing the viability of ongoing programs, and less on day-to-day operations. The previously strict control exercised by central agencies over administrative matters, such as salaries, travel, office equipment, was removed. One senior official explained: 'Those who were not in the federal government before Glassco can't begin to imagine what it was like. We were constantly nickled and dimed to death. Ordering office supplies and planning a trip were no easy matter. All that changed after Glassco.' He added: 'We all had to change the way we did things and for nearly all of us it was a trip down uncharted waters.'[3]

Another result was numerous appointments of private sector representatives, many of whom had worked in the Glassco Commission, to senior positions in government. Moreover, 'in the years that followed, large numbers of officials with private sector financial and personnel background were also brought in to the public sector to implement the radical reforms.'[4] All in all, the reforms were such that a keen and long-time student of government observed that the Glassco report brought 'a sort of managerial revolution in the bureaucracy.'[5]

Within a few years, however, Glassco's dream of letting the manager manage was in difficulty. For one thing, PPB, a child of the Glassco Commission, was not performing to the standard expected. One observer remarked that, after several years, 'the government still seems to be paying the high cost of establishing new management concepts while it has not yet reaped the benefit.'[6] Another suggested that Glassco 'failed to address itself to the operation of Cabinet and Parliament.'[7] In other words, Glassco saw the need to delegate authority to departments but did not provide a clear direction for how managers would be accountable within government and from government to parliament. In addition, PPB did not lead to a fundamental review of existing programs, and after several years one could 'count on the fingers of one hand programs which had been cut.'[8] It was not long before the auditor general, the opposition, and the media again began to ring alarm bells over the growth in government spending and the lack of accountability. Less than twenty years after the Glassco Commission was established, the federal government called for another study of government operations that would again bring in the private sector. In announcing the Royal Commission on Financial Management and Accountability, Robert Andras, Treasury Board president, stated that the Glassco report had recommended 'the need to delegate responsibility and authority to managers' but it was beyond its mandate to identify an 'accountability safeguard.'[9] He went on to explain that 'the difficulties that have been encountered in attempting to develop, in the post-Glassco era, the concept of managerial accountability in the government environment are accordingly one of the factors which have prompted the initiative I just announced.'[10]

The auditor general's call for the establishment of the Office of the Comptroller General, segregated from the Treasury Board secretariat and reporting directly to the president of the Treasury Board, had also placed the government in a difficult position. The appointment of a comptroller general, Andras pointed out, 'as a sort of *umpire*, to quote the Auditor General himself, calls into question not only fundamental aspects of government organization but also some basic tenets of our parliamentary system of government ... this is quite straightforward and will be easily grasped by all Parliamentarians.'[11] The government firmly believed that ultimate responsibility for financial control 'rests with Parliament and Parliament alone and this can only be exercised if the principle of collective and individual responsibility of Ministers to Parliament is upheld.'[12] Given the auditor general's recommendation, 'Parliament, the Government and the citizenry,' Andras declared, 'was in a quandary.'[13] The government believed that a thorough review of issues and problems was urgently required and hence the appointment of a royal commission.

THE LAMBERT COMMISSION: A ROAD NOT TRAVELLED

The commission's mandate was twofold: 'to ensure that financial management and control exercised at all levels ... meet the highest attainable standards (and) to establish effective administrative accountability of deputy ministers and heads of Crown agencies to the Government, and, where appropriate, to Parliament.'[14] Allan Lambert, president and chairman of the board of the Toronto Dominion Bank, was appointed to chair the commission.

Shortly after the Lambert Commission was established, the Trudeau cabinet, as we have already seen, bowed to public pressure and announced that it would establish the Office of the Comptroller General along the lines suggested by the auditor general. One of the important reasons for establishing the Lambert Commission suddenly evaporated. The commission and staff quickly concluded that the appointment of a comptroller general would not in any way interfere with their work, and Lambert said this publicly. The commission pushed ahead with its work plan and hired several well-known people in the private sector as advisers and consultants. The commission also interviewed over one hundred representatives of the private and public sectors and the academic community before preparing its final report.[15] The commission saw two problems that needed to be resolved. First, it expressed the urgent need 'to avoid waste' in government. It declared that 'in the context of today's fiscal situation and the pervasiveness of government activity, managers in the public service are being challenged to rediscover a sense of frugality and a commitment to the careful husbanding of resouces.'[16] Secondly, it argued that the serious malaise in management in government stemmed from 'an almost total breakdown in the chain of accountability.'[17] It then sought to repair this situation and to restore a sense of frugality and good management to government operations. It presented over 150 recommendations, ranging from a restructuring of the Treasury Board secretariat and the Public Service Commission to the transfer of the government's day-to-day cash management to the Department of Finance from the Department of Supply and Services. To strengthen accountability in government, the commission urged, among other things, that deputy ministers be appointed for three to five years and that goals be set for all managers in government. Moreover, it recommended the goals should provide 'an objective basis for measuring the manager's performance.'

The commission noted with great concern that ministers, deputy ministers, and senior managers were far more interested in policy issues than management ones.[18] Deputy ministers, the commission concluded, were largely deficient in management skills. It then argued that central agencies should take the lead in evaluating the performance of deputy ministers and that importance be attached to their management functions.

To ensure a proper evaluation of senior managers and to ensure that increased emphasis would be placed on management rather than policy, the commission recommended a complete overhaul of the central agencies. It reported:

The deficiencies in the central management of government today relate in no small measure to a failure to plan thoroughly at the top. Accepted, instead, is a planning process too often dependent on trying to marry unco-ordinated proposals coming up from the bottom. There is a consequent failure to budget rationally, and a confusion of responsibility for control and evaluation. The follow-up by central management to see if commitments have been met or indicated levels of performance attained has been lacking. The shortcomings of the existing system stem as well from a failure to define precisely and distinctly the tasks and responsibilities of the central agencies. Accountability of the central agencies themselves for the way in which they have performed their own roles is incomplete.[19]

The commission recommended that the Department of Finance be strengthened and that it take the lead in planning both the revenue and expenditure budgets. It also recommended that the management of governmental functions be 'consolidated.'[20] Specifically, it called on the government to rename the Treasury Board the Board of Management, and recommended that it assume new responsibilities for overseeing all aspects of management in government. The Board of Management would be supported by two secretaries of the board, one the secretary for personnel management and the other the comptroller general. The former would assume responsibilities for 'government-wide policies on manpower planning, appraisal of senior management personnel ... collective bargaining, classification and official languages.'[21] The role of the Public Service Commission would, in turn, be substantially reduced, with most of its responsibilities transferred to the Board of Management. The commission recommended that the Public Service Commission be reconstituted as a 'Parliamentary Department with the duty of ensuring that selection and appointment to the public service are made on the basis of merit.'[22] The Office of the Comptroller General would be renamed the Financial Management Secretariat, but its deputy head would continue to carry the title of comptroller general. The commission felt it was important to 'augment ... the authority and responsibility of the Comptroller General if he is to pursue his role as chief financial officer.'[23] The comptroller general would now have the mandate to assess the overall performance of departments and agencies and to screen the allocation of resources to departments and agencies. As a result, the program branch of the Treasury Board secretariat would be transferred to the Comptroller General's Office. The commission concluded that 'The Board of Management would provide a single focus for the central management of government, consolidating the responsibilities for personnel and financial management. This consolidation would enable the establishment of clear lines of accountability for all facets of management from departments and agencies, through the Board of Management, to Parliament.'[24]

The government in the end rejected this view of accountability and many of the commission's recommendations. To many senior officials, the Lambert Commission 'had a very naive view of how government operates. It had a strong private sector bias in its work. What works in the private sector does not necessarily work in government and no doubt what works in government would not apply in the private sector.'[25] One senior official reported that, when the Lambert report was released, 'we [i.e., senior departmental officials] went away for a day and a half session to study the report. We were able to finish the review after only just a few hours. The report did not measure up in any way and it was far removed from the quality and substance of the Glassco Commission. The Lambert report was simply fluff, pure fluff with no practical application.'[26] A keen student of the federal government also observed that the Lambert report was 'insufficiently sensitive to the fact that government is essentially a political operation — rational management is never enough.'[27]

Many senior government officials felt that the commission even lacked a basic grasp of how parliamentary government works. They argue that, in describing a process in which departments are accountable 'through the Board of Management to Parliament,' the commission confused the roles of the executive and legislative branches of government and the manner in which individual ministers are directly answerable to parliament for the exercise of their responsibilities. They point out that the president of the Treasury Board answers to parliament for the exercise of *his* responsibilities, including that to develop good management practices and standards. Other ministers, however, are not, and cannot be, responsible *through him*, or through the Treasury Board which he chairs, to parliament. The president of the Treasury Board, in addition, should not report to parliament on the performance of individual ministers, deputy ministers, or departments.[28]

Given the strong misgivings senior officials had about many of the Lambert recommendations, the report never enjoyed much support inside government. One observer predicted at the time that the Lambert Commission report was released that the recommendations were not 'likely to be accepted ... as an integrated whole. Some of their recommendations will be acted upon: others will not.'[29] This is precisely what occurred. When the recommendations could be acted upon without 'upsetting the system,' or when the government had already moved along the lines suggested in the report, a press release was issued reporting that another recommendation from the Lambert report had been accepted. It is extremely difficult to find much evidence, however, 'that Lambert led to many fundamental changes to the way the federal government operates, to a rediscovery of a sense of frugality and a commitment to the careful husbanding of resouces' in government, or any reduction in government spending. The Treasury Board secretariat, the Office of the Comptroller General, the Public Service Commission, and the Department of Finance continued to function pretty well as they had in the past. Certainly no consolidation of the management function of government took place. Deputy ministers continued to be rotated far more frequently than the three to five-year period recommended. The list goes on. The Lambert Commission was also soon to be overshadowed by another major development in the setting of government priorities and in the expenditure budget process – the introduction of PEMS.

THE NIELSEN TASK FORCE: ANOTHER ROAD NOT TAKEN

The day after coming to power, Prime Minister Mulroney announced the establishment of a ministerial task force (MTF) to review existing programs with a view to eliminating those that no longer served a purpose and consolidating others in the hope that not only savings, but also better government, would result. The prime minister explained, in making the announcement, that he was asking the task force to review government programs to make them 'simple, more understandable and more accessible to their clientele' and that decision making be 'decentralized as far as possible to those in direct contact with client groups.'[30] The clerk of the Privy Council and the secretary to the cabinet, as we have seen, had recommended such an exercise to the incoming prime minister. The Conservatives had campaigned not only against government waste and inefficient programs but also on the need to redefine the role of government in the economy. It was hardly a surprise to anyone then that the new government would welcome an invitation for a fresh look at all government programs, particularly one that came from the most senior public servants. Still, the recommendation contained an important signal – PEMS had not succeeded in leading to a reordering of government priorities in the past and there was obviously little confidence among senior officials that it would do so in future.

In announcing the establishment of a ministerial task force, the prime minister also announced that it would be chaired by Erik Nielsen, the then deputy prime minister, and that it would consist of three additional senior ministers – the minister of finance, the president of the Treasury Board, and the minister of justice. Nielsen was thought to be particularly well suited to the task: he was a senior minister, at the time he had no departmental responsibility, he was widely considered to be tough-minded, and he was a veteran of many parliamentary wars. Shortly after Mulroney's announcement, Nielsen declared that a private sector advisory committee, drawn from various business groups as well as professional and labour organizations, was being established to assist the task force. Philip Aspinall, a partner in Coopers and Lybrand, and Darcy McKeough, a former senior cabinet minister in Ontario and a leading business spokesman, were asked to lead the private sector participation and a senior official of the Treasury Board secretariat, Peter Meyboom, was appointed to lead the public sector participation.[31]

The task force was asked to review government programs with the responsible ministers. It was thought to be important to establish a 'challenge' function at the centre immediately because line ministers would soon be 'captured' by their departments and by program beneficiaries. Still, it was agreed early on that the task force would not constitute a committee of cabinet so that it could carry out its work in a more informal fashion than could a cabinet committee. Its recommendations would be submitted directly to Priorities and Planning (or one of its subcommittees).

One of the first initiatives the task force undertook was to prepare an inventory of existing programs. The inventory encompassed both spending programs and tax expenditures and divided the programs into 'nineteen program families.' Only a few of these 'families' were limited to single departments, with the others crossing departmental lines. The inventory revealed well over one thousand federal government programs and brought home to the new government the enormous task confronting it. Nielsen described the problem in this fashion:

The inventory has shown us the extraordinary complexity of our task. Each program in its own way is a monument to some problem of the past. Programs are often designed on an ad hoc basis, and targeted to a single problem without much reference to other programs that may address similar problems. From the client's viewpoint, this can result in a confusing hodgepodge of sometimes conflicting programs. We must, therefore, ask ourselves to what extent the orginal problems still exist and to what extent the original solution is still valid. For instance, through Agriculture Canada, the federal government still manages pastures and livestock in western Canada. Is there still a need, I must ask, to have bulls (or sacred cows) in federal pastures?[32]

Once the inventory was completed, the task force established nineteen study teams to review the nineteen program families. This approach was favoured over a department-by-department review because it would avoid duplication and also because it would avoid a portfolio-by-portfolio review with the responsible minister. This, it was felt, would reduce the influence of spending ministers. Given that the task force was carrying out a program, and not a management review, the central agencies were also excluded from participation. The task force decided to concentrate on programs with an outside clientele. Excluded from the review were defence, foreign aid, and public debt charges. The task force finally selected 989 federal programs and services for review, 'reflecting annual federal expenditures of more than $92 billion, including tax expenditures' in 1984–5.[33]

The study teams, made up of both public servants and private sector representatives, usually consisted of about 15 members. Some were led by public servants and others by private sector people, but in all instances the teams were about equally divided. All in all, 102 representatives of the private sector served on the various study teams, compared with 99 federal public servants. Some 20 provincial public servants were also invited to participate on selected study teams.

Early on, the task force decided to complete the study in one year. The teams were asked to report sequentially, but each was given about three months to complete its work. All were able to meet the three-month deadline. Once this phase was over, the study teams would discuss their reports with their private sector advisory committee and subsequently submit them to the MTF. Darcy McKeough provided the liaison between the study teams and MTF, which reviewed in considerable detail most of the reports, although changing very little in them. There was a great deal of concern throughout this exercise, particularly on the part of government officials, that the private sector people on the teams were 'walking around with a slashing mentality.' It was important for the task force ministers to take a 'political look at the report before they went too far.' Once the reports had been through MTF they were to be submitted directly to P & P or to a special subcommittee of P & P.

Given that many of the recommendations called for program cuts, it was originally envisaged in central agencies (notably PMO and PCO) that MTF ministers would be unanimous in their proposals to P & P. It would then be left to P & P to consider the 'politics' of study team reports and to 'orchestrate' the implementation of the various recommendations. We now know that ministers on the task force were often split on the study team reports. Erik Nielsen, the minister of finance, and the president of the Treasury Board consistently supported the findings of the study teams, but the minister of justice, the one spending minister, consistently opposed them. The result was that the study team reports and recommendations were simply submitted to P & P or special P & P meetings in essentially the same manner that they were originally presented to the MTF. P & P ministers expressed concern that the recommendations should have been reviewed for 'political' and 'professional' considerations before being submitted. Some felt that more than four ministers should have reviewed the proposals, particularly since three of those involved were not spending ministers, and that officials from central agencies or selected departments should have gone over the reports as well. In the end, they were hesitant to take a position on the reports without a more thorough political and bureaucratic review.

All the reports have now been made public and there is no need to discuss them here. Suffice it to note that all of them sought to reduce the scope of some programs or to eliminate others. None recommended that programs be expanded or that new ones be introduced. All study teams asked questions such as 'Why is the federal government in this field?' and 'What should be its role?' All teams were well aware of the new government's desire to 'downsize' government and to reduce its spending. They sought to respond by pointing to programs that could be cut back or by looking at possibilities for devolution to the provinces, privatization, and contracting out.

The nineteen study group reports were tabled on 11 March 1986.[34] The review recommended one-time expenditure and tax reductions of between $7 to $8 billion. The study groups recommended substantial reductions in subsidies to agriculture, fisheries, transportation, and business. One report urged that the government rationalize sales tax exemptions, terminate what it labelled obsolete programs (for example, credit reinsurance and management excellence), and cut back various direct subsidies (such as ferry subsidies). It also urged important cuts in regional development programming and the abolition of the Federal Business Development Bank (FBDB). Another recommended that virtually all major agricultural subsidies, including those earmarked for dairy, feed freight, and feed tax rebate, be eliminated or substantially modified. Another reported that the government was overinvesting in training and suggested reductions in and termination of some programs. The report on culture and communications recommended the elimination or reduction of subsidies to the arts. Yet another recommended sweeping changes to the government procurement policy and urged that the government adopt a comprehensive 'make-or-buy' (that is, contracting out) policy. Some members of the private sector advisory committee stated that they viewed the make-or-buy recommendation as the single most important recommendation of the program review. There were numerous other recommendations covering all policy fields and the great majority of programs surveyed.

The government did not act on many of the MTF recommendations. With a few exceptions, it rejected major program cuts or substantive reductions in either direct subsidies or tax expenditures. There are, in the words of one federal official directly involved in the Nielsen Task Force, 'still bulls and sacred cows in federal pastures three years after Nielsen. Virtually all the programs reviewed are still in place and virtually intact. In fact, since 1984 we have added many more new programs than we have done away with.'[35] The government instituted $280 million in direct ongoing expenditure reductions and $215 million in tax expenditure which can be attributed to the Nielsen Task Force. It cut the credit reinsurance and the management excellence programs, adjusted the investment tax credit scheme, and issued guidelines on the 'stacking' of business subsidies and tax credits. It also reduced direct training expenditures and sold some of its surplus land. Moreover, the government established a new unit in the Treasury Board secretariat to manage government property more effectively and approved a make-or-buy policy in September 1986. However, only limited progress has been realized in its implementation.

It is important to underline the fact that the task force was set up by the Mulroney government and provided its guardians early on with detailed recommendations on how to reduce spending. We should also remember that the recommendations were presented to a party that had campaigned on cutting back the scope of government during the election and that had repeated time and again during its first eighteen months in office the need for 'downsizing' the federal government.

Why did the Nielsen Task Force recommendations have such a limited impact on the government agenda? There are a host of reasons. Many officials involved at the time report that the structure of the task force itself posed a problem. As already noted, only one of the four ministers had a spending department so that most ministers felt that the task force lacked balance. Many permanent officials in line departments were dismayed when they learned that, since it was a program review and not a management review, the central agencies were to be excluded from the exercise. 'Some officials had hoped that agencies such as the Public Service Commission and the Treasury Board secretariat – their persecutors – would get a rough going-over, and were not only disappointed when that didn't happen but considered it unfair and inappropriate.'[36]

It is also widely argued in the federal government, particularly in central agencies, that the Nielsen Task Force took too long to complete its work to be effective. Study teams did report within three months. The review, however, took over a year, in part because of the time it took to have the reports examined by task force ministers and P & P. As months went by with little indication of what the review would recommend, there was growing disquiet among departments and, after some time, also among ministers. Some reports were leaked to the media, which served to heighten the concern line ministers and officials were already showing. The report (which was leaked) on Indians and Natives, for example, called for savings of $280 million and a reduction in the department's person-year complement. The prime minister quickly assured the native community that there 'would not be any expenditure reductions in native programming and that there would be consultations on all proposed changes.'[37] Still, the leak confirmed that, as the review dragged on, secrecy became much more difficult to maintain.

After several months, the government lost momentum and, according to some observers, public support for its program review. The conventional wisdom is that a government must make tough decisions early in its mandate. Not only does a long review extend uncertainty for clients of various programs, but it also increases problems of coordination inside government. Some ministers, after a few months in office, quite naturally want to take charge of their departments and advance new initiatives. A program review puts everything on hold, even if a minister would like to propose spending cuts for the department. And when you extend a program review for a year, 'you are,' in the opinion of a central agency official, 'really testing the tolerance level of most ministers.'[38]

Added to the above is the kind of relationship a minister establishes with his or her department. Many members of the Mulroney government, including virtually all of the key advisers, had welcomed the program review immediately upon assuming office. Decisions to cut back programs, they asserted, must be made before ministers are captured by their departmental officials. Central agency officials are well aware of this view. One senior official explained: 'There are distinct phases most ministers go through when they are first named to the cabinet. The first phase is that nearly all officials are not to be trusted. The second phase, which usually comes fairly quickly, is that my officials and my deputy minister can be trusted but not the rest. The third phase is the realization that officials are there to assist ministers. Well before the Nielsen Task Force finished its work most ministers were well into the second phase.'[39] Many had already established strong working relationships with their deputy ministers and departments and, as they became more comfortable with their portfolios, they wanted to 'call the shots.' In addition, when leaks from the task force occurred, it was left to the relevant ministers – not to Nielsen – to defend their departmental interests and programs in the House.

Ministers and departments essentially felt left out of the Nielsen Task Force. Departments and even central agencies played a passive role – one largely restricted to responding to requests for information. Some study teams, however, did try to cooperate more fully with departments, and in some instances they were able to strike a good working relationship with them. Nielsen himself would hold a 'bilateral' meeting with the relevant ministers when a study team had completed its report. But this did not always bring ministers on side. Junior ministers were too intimidated by Nielsen – he was the deputy prime minister, after all – to put their case forward as effectively as they should have, and senior ministers simply walked away from the meeting as if nothing had happened. Deputy ministers saw the study team reports, but only after the task force had carefully gone over them. Meanwhile memoranda to cabinet on the task force that went to P & P or to its subcommittee were for 'Ministers' Eyes Only.' The result was that deputy ministers and other departmental officials never felt a part of the deliberations. Departments were never given the opportunity to challenge the work and findings of the task force studies. By the time Nielsen tabled all the reports and their findings, there was little commitment or even desire in departments to support the recommendations.

In some isolated instances, departments and agencies did recommend to their ministers program cuts that had been identified by Nielsen. A former senior official of the Canadian Mortgage and Housing Corporation (CMHC) reported that the agency had been trying, for some time, to rationalize some of its programs. When Nielsen looked at housing programs, CMHC sent information on their programs to the study team that highlighted weaknesses in their social housing programs. Nielsen subsequently recommended that social housing assistance be directed solely to households in need and that too much emphasis was placed on new construction rather than on the rehabilitation of existing housing. CMHC quickly sought a cabinet decision to implement these recommendations, which it obtained.[40]

Another similar example was the Katimavik program which the Department of the Secretary of State had been trying to end for some time. Katimavik was regarded by departmental officials as a highly 'political' program, in that it had not been conceived in the department itself, but had high-profile support from Prime Minister Trudeau and his long-time friend, Senator Jacques Hébert. The department had commissioned an evaluation of the program in the early 1980s which suggested that it should be terminated and had subsequently recommended to cabinet that the program be cut. It is now widely known in Ottawa that Trudeau intervened at the last minute, against the wishes of a majority of his ministers, to save the program. When the Nielsen Task Force was established, the department quickly pointed to Katimavik as one program that could easily be cut. Nielsen made it one of his recommendations, and the department jumped at the opportunity and obtained P & P approval to end the program.

But such instances were rare. Generally, departments sought to downplay the Nielsen recommendations. As noted earlier, they were not included in the exercise, and it was certainly not in their interest to promote the findings of the task force. One senior department official characterized the Nielsen Task Force as a 'we and they' exercise, with Nielsen, the minister of finance, the Treasury Board president, and private sector representatives brought in for the review ranged on one side of the debate and the departments on the other.[41] Ministers also did not rush in to support the task force recommendations. Nielsen himself left cabinet after he was termed a 'political liability' for the Mulroney government. He was widely criticized in the media for being overly secretive (thus earning the nickname 'velcro lips') and for mishandling the resignation of a cabinet colleague, Sinclair Stevens. However, with Nielsen gone, no other minister came forward to champion the task force findings in cabinet. Responsibility for overseeing its reports was turned over to the Treasury Board president. But that proved difficult, if only because the task force had been so closely identified with Nielsen, both in government and in the media. Gordon Osbaldeston, the clerk of the Privy Council, who had recommended the program review, also left government. Over time, the Privy Council Office became less and less helpful to the review, coming to regard it as a sort of rival central agency. Moreover, PCO's tolerance for an aberration of the regular decision-making process, which Nielsen represented, waned over time.

The Nielsen Task Force findings thus became an exercise in search of support in government. Many decisions were taken immediately after the reports were tabled, but most were minor. It was estimated that at least 700 decisions were required to deal with the task force recommendations. Major decisions were deferred or rejected. Over 200 recommendations were immediately turned over to policy committees for further review and labelled 'call-backs.' Another 40 were not acted upon at P & P becasue they required Treasury Board decsions. Some three years after Nielsen tabled the reports, few of these 'call-backs' have been acted upon.[42]

The most damaging criticism of the Nielsen Task Force, however, was that its work was inherently biased. Line departments and, later, their ministers criticized the task force time and time again because it did not review the work of central agencies. One senior departmental official explained: 'If Nielsen was really serious about cutting back spending, eliminating waste in government and improving program delivery, then the first place you should look at is central agencies.'[43] The fact that three of the four ministers on the task force did not have any departmental responsibilities confirmed the worst fears. As already mentioned, the minister of justice was the only person on the task force to speak for spending ministers and consequently it was never possible for a unanimous recommendation to go to P & P and cabinet.

The task force was also accused of having a regional bias in its work. The proposed cuts in programs and tax expenditures would have had a disporportionate impact on the Atlantic provinces, the Prairies, and, to a lesser extent, Quebec. While recommending substantial cuts in subsidies in fisheries, agriculture, and transportation, the study groups ignored the attendant economic and social consequences. This was not lost on ministers, MPS, economic and regional associations, or the media. They were all quick to question how programs and tax expenditures were selected for review. Why, they asked, did the task force not look at textiles and automobile quotas, oil and gas pricing policies, other tariffs, certain tax expenditures or incentives to promote development in the high-tech sector? Had these programs been selected, they insist, then Ontario and southern Quebec would have borne the brunt of spending cuts – which, being much stronger economically, they could have done more easily. One senior minister from Atlantic Canada reports that he intervened time and againt to 'bury' the task force review. He explained why. 'The dice were loaded against us in the whole Nielsen Task Force. First, central agencies were excluded. The Ottawa bureaucracy always knows how to protect itself, we never have to worry about that. Then recommendations on the National Capital Commission were quickly canned. Ottawa knows how to protect itself. Tariffs, quotas, and programs largely designed for the industrial heartland were excluded. No worry, the industrial heartland always knows how to protect itself. What were we left with – the peripheral regions. We simply couldn't let that happen.' He added: 'Clearly we were not playing on a level playing field. I was quite prepared to look at cutting programs but not when you start with the poorest regions.'[44]

The Nielsen Task Force's recommendation to do away with the Federal Business Development Bank was also tossed aside because of its regional implications.[45] The study group concluded that Canadian financial markets and institutions were no longer as immature as when FBDB had been established. The group also pointed out that every provincial government now had in place measures supporting small business, including loan guarantees. It concluded that FBDB's loan portfolio should be privatized or sold to provincal institutions. Taking away its main line of business led to the inevitable conclusion that FBDB should be abolished.

When ministers from the Montreal area discovered this, they rallied to the defence of FBDB, whose head office is in Montreal. Montreal, they argued, could ill afford to lose the head office of a national financial institution. Robert R. de Cotret, the then Treasury Board president and member of the Nielsen Task Force, argued strongly on behalf of retaining FBDB. By the time the task force completed its work, it was unsure what to recommend. It reported that 'further work was necessary' on the work and future of the bank.[46] No further work was initiated, and FBDB is still operating much as it did before the Nielsen review. But the FBDB case reveals that in the Nielsen exercise, as in the day-to-day operations of government, 'guardians are not always playing the guardian role.' If the Treasury Board president could jump to the defence of Montreal, then there was even more reason for the regional ministers of, say, Newfoundland or Manitoba to defend their own regions which were lagging economically far behind Montreal.

FORGET FORGET

Canada's unemployment insurance (UI) program is considered by many to be vitally important to the country's social security. It is also a controversial program. Many private sector representatives have long denounced it.[47] Not only is it expensive, there are charges that it weakens the country's work ethic. Less than a year after the Mulroney government came to office, it established a commission of inquiry 'to review all demands of the Unemployment Insurance Program – the extent of coverage, the criteria for eligibility, the amount and duration of benefits, and the financing of the program.'[48] At the time the commission was set up, the total annual cost of operating the UI program was $11.5 billion. The government appointed Claude Forget, an economic consultant, to head the commission. He was assisted by five members, including two from the private sector, one from academe, and two from organized labour. The commission held a number of public consulations, commissioned a series of background papers, and produced its report in November 1986.

The commission recommended sweeping changes to the UI program and called for a $3 billion cut. The recommendations were aimed at cutting back benefits for two categories of workers, seasonal workers and the so-called 'ten and forty syndrome' workers. The latter, it has been argued, are those who work for only enough weeks to qualify for insurance and then go back on UI – those who work for ten weeks and collect UI for forty, year in and year out. The report also recommended major changes to the way self-employed fishermen benefit from the UI program. Fishermen are entitled to benefits that are paid out according to special rules and largely funded from general revenue. The commission suggested that these benefits should be phased out over five years and that fishermen be treated like other workers under the UI program. The commission also recommended that 'regionally extended benefits' under UI be 'progressively abolished.' It concluded that government should 'sweep away the present variations that plague the system and produce both inequity and complexity.' It recommended that there should be only 'one entrance requirement, one benefit phase, and one maximum duration of regular benefits.'[49]

Regionally adjusted UI benefits were introduced in the mid-1970s as a transitional measure to ease the effect of tightened job entry conditons. They were to have expired in December 1980 but were extended to mid-1982, pending the report of a federal task force on unemployment insurance. The measure has since been renewed several times. Benefits became linked explicitly to national and regional unemployment rates because it is more difficult to find work in regions with high unemployment. Thus, people there need added protection. The right to UI benefits has a variable entrance requirement of ten to fourteen weeks which is determined regionally on the basis of the national unemployment rate. In 1988, for example, regions with over 9 per cent unemployment required only ten weeks of insurable employment; over 8 per cent required eleven weeks; over 7 per cent, twelve weeks; less than 6 per cent, fourteen weeks. Unemployment insurance benefits arising from local unemployment rates were to be financed from general government revenues rather than the premiums of employers and employees. But Forget argued that regionally extended benefits did not constitute 'social insurance.' They were rather 'income support' and as a result did not belong in an unemployment insurance program. In short, as Forget reported, there were 'variations that plagued the system.'

Forget submitted his report to the government amid a storm of controversy. He was hardly able to secure a unanimous agreement even from his own commissioners for his recommendations. In fact, all six commissioners – including Forget himself – added supplementary statements to the report. The labour representatives had disagreed fundamentally with the suggestion that 'variations plagued the system.'

The reception of the Forget report in some political circles was scarcely positive. As could be expected, cabinet ministers, MPS, and provincial governments from regions which stood to lose the most from the proposed changes were quick to voice their opposition. Business groups from Atlantic Canada also jumped in the debate to register their opposition.[50] The federal government was soon on the defensive and senior federal cabinet ministers from slow-growth regions and representing areas dependent on the fishery sought to reassure their constituents. John Crosbie, the federal cabinet minister from Newfoundland and a member of P & P , cut short the controversy when he went to his home province shortly after the report was released and was widely reported to have said: 'Forget in English spells forget, so let us all forget Forget.'[51] Other ministers from Atlantic Canada, eastern Quebec, and other regions where a high proportion of employment is seasonal, such as parts of British Columbia, applauded Crosbie. One government MP explained why.

The cost of maintaining regionally adjusted benefits and special benefits for fishermen is about 500 million dollars a year. Why should we cut these benefits back? If it is to save money, then I could point to many other areas where half a billion could be saved with much less hardship to Canadians. I would start with Ottawa. Just stand on Parliament Hill and look around at all the government buildings well populated by high paid civil servants. You want to save money, start there – don't start with fishermen or the unemployed. I can tell you that if the government had gone ahead with the Forget report it would have lost some of its members of parliament and a few cabinet ministers.[52]

Crosbie and the other 'dissenters' bring to mind former senior Trudeau cabinet ministers, such as Allan MacEachen and Roméo LeBlanc, and other Liberal members of parliament, who had also argued that if the objective was to save money, the government should look elsewhere. If the guardians in government could not convince an important segment of their own caucus, there was little hope that it could rebuff the opposition in parliament and convince the country. The Forget report was quietly shelved and the unemployment insurance program operates basically as it has since the 1970s. The minor changes that have been introduced recently have only extended benefits. The program, for example, has been amended to enable natural fathers to receive maternity benefits should the mother die or become disabled. In addition, on 14 October 1987, the government decided to extend once again the variable entrance requirements beyond 1 January 1988, when it had been scheduled to expire, explaining that it would be continued until improvements in regional disparities had been achieved. This is precisely the same explanation given by the previous government.

We have seen that private sector representatives have from time to time been brought in to look at government management practices and programs in the hope that they would pinpoint areas where spending cuts could be made and management improved. To be sure, they have identified programs which could be cut or reduced and suggested numerous management reforms to improve efficiency in the administration of government. By and large, however, these imported guardians have had limited impact on the actual operations of government or on government programs.

In the case of the Glassco Commission, their recommendations did lead to far-reaching changes in administration. Several years later, however, when the Lambert Commission was established (also with strong private sector representation) it sought, depending on who one consults, either to rectify or complete the work of the Glassco Commission. Regardless of what it actually tried to do, it is now clear that it had virtually no impact on the structure, program delivery, or management practices in government.

Private sector representatives have also been asked to review the viability of government programs. Here, too, their recommendations have had limited impact. The Forget report was shelved. The Nielsen Task Force study groups presented hundreds of recommendations to cut or reduce programs. With a few exceptions, they have also been rejected or simply not acted upon.

Government officials are not surprised at the inability of private sector people to bring about change in government operations and programs, since they believe that the private sector has a naive view of how government works. 'They come in looking for a bottom line, for a definitive answer to real or perceived problems and they come forward with the most hare-brained of solutions,' said one official.[53] Another explained that 'business people don't realize that in government if you push one button or if you pull one lever it invariably rebounds elsewhere in government on another program or agency. Things are never as simple as they think they are.'[54] Yet another argued: 'You want to see how out of touch the business community is about government, just take a look at what the Lambert Commission recommended about accountability.'

Had the government implemented those recommendations we would be in an unholy mess.'[55] Business people, they add, never have to deal with conflicting goals, with constantly changing political direction, with close scrutiny from the media, the auditor general, or parliamentary committees, and so have little appreciation how complex government decision making is and has to be. Many of the detailed restrictions imposed on government managers are there to control a process rather than to provide direction.

They also insist that private sector representatives are often ill-equipped to carry out program reviews. They point to the Nielsen Task Force study teams as evidence. Many government officials suggest that most of its private sector representatives had 'a cut and slash' mentality. One explained that 'everything was so simple for them. Simply cut programs and everything will be okay. Government people on the study teams were finally able to bring some sense to the exercise. Otherwise it would have been a total fiasco.'[56] Some politicians also have reservations about the capacity of business people to review government programs. After the Nielsen and Forget reports, the Mulroney government proved reluctant to involve the private sector again in the review of programs. For their part, the Liberals appointed only one of the four commissions reviewed in this chapter, although they held power for over twenty of the past twenty-five years, and that was the Lambert Commission. The Trudeau government established it in part because of strong media and public pressure to do something about improving financial management in government and also in an attempt to forestall setting up the Office of the Comptroller General. The problem, according to one senior cabinet minister,

is that business people take great liberty in suggesting cuts. But that is the easy part. The tough part is to sit down and implement them. We have to live with those suggestions, business people don't. They simply go back to their businesses. I, for one, learned something from the Nielsen and Forget exercises. When you set up a commission to review programs – you send out a message to clients that you are thinking of cutting back the program. After all, you don't set up a commission to make a program more generous. When the commission tours the country you get people worked up because they expect the worst. Then the commission tables the report. This usually confirms their worst fears. As a result, we scared people three times and have yet to cut or reduce the program. Then we have to come in to repair the political damage. There must be a better way to cut spending.[57]

He went on to argue that proposed spending cuts should never be 'telegraphed' outside of government before they are acted upon.

The next chapter looks at that approach. Governments, over the past several years, have had some success in cutting programs and administration. The cuts, however, were not recommended by outside 'inquisitors' or identified as a part of a PPB or PEMS-based program review. As we will see, they were inspired at the highest political level, and they were pieced together in haste.

7

Cuts from above: On the road from Bonn and Toronto

Spending cuts in government do not occur from the bottom up. It is rare indeed for a program director to recommend that his or her program or the organization itself be eliminated or even reduced. It is simply not in the interests of spending departments to identify potential expenditure cuts. PPBS and PEMS, despite their promise and techniques, made little headway in introducing such a discipline in government or in identifying programs which should be reduced. The Nielsen Task Force acknowledged this fact and reported on the 'pervasive force of the status quo ... [as] the most intractable issue of all ... Even where a given program is proven demonstrably useless, perverse or excessively expensive, abrupt termination often proves to be impossible.'[1]

Experience in the federal government reveals that, when important spending cuts have been achieved, the prime minister's hand has been present and highly visible. 'When all is said and done,' observed one senior central agency official, 'the prime minister is the one person with the clout to cut spending.'[2] In short, the prime minister is the one guardian with the power to jolt the status quo and indeed has been the driving force behind most major attempts at cutting or checking spending since the early 1970s. Such instances include: the Trudeau government's commitment, made on Thanksgiving Day, 1975, to hold spending to the growth trend in GNP; Trudeau's announcement immediately on his return from the Bonn economic summit in 1978 of a cut of $2 billion; and, finally, Prime Minister Mulroney's commitment to cut spending immediately on assuming office in 1984. This chapter reports on these cuts, how they were realized, and the extent of their success.

ATTACKING INFLATION

In October 1975, Donald S. Macdonald, Trudeau's minister of finance, tabled a policy statement that 'Canada [was] in the grip of serious inflation.' He went on to warn that if inflation continued or became worse there was 'a grave danger that ... the nation [would] be subjected to mounting stresses and strains.'[3] His department had identified increasing government spending and the growing deficit as one of the leading causes of inflation. To be sure, government spending was growing rapidly in the early 1970s. On a national accounts basis, federal spending in 1973–4 jumped 22.6 per cent over the previous year, by 28.3 per cent in 1974–5, and by 18.5 per cent in 1975–6. In his statement, Macdonald pledged to hold future increases in spending to no more than increases in the gross national product and to cut spending where possible. The statement warned, however, that 'there is little scope for government to reduce expenditures – or the growth in expenditures – without affecting one or more of the following: transfer payments, programs, and the quality or quantity of service to the public.'[4]

Jean Chrétien, then Treasury Board president, was asked to identify spending cuts and to define measures to check the growth in government spending. He reported to parliament on his efforts on 18 December 1975. After speaking at length about the difficulty in reducing expenditures, Chrétien observed that 'when you carry out ... a review, you come to a conclusion ... [that] cannot be described too often – particularly to those who talk glibly about cutting expenditures as if it were an easy thing to do. That conclusion is that there is very little, almost nothing, that can be cut without hurting someone.'[5] He spoke from experience, since some six months earlier Chrétien had, in effect, 'negotiated' with his colleagues a cut of nearly $1 billion. This, it will be recalled, was in pre-PEMS days when the Treasury Board played a key role not simply in managing the government's A base but also in allocating financial resources for new initiatives. When Chrétien's officials identified possible cuts, he simply turned to his colleagues and said 'we either go with this or you come with other cuts from your department that come to the same amount.'[6] Some accepted the Treasury Board cuts, but the majority either tried to negotiate them down or point to less politically difficult cuts. Chrétien unveiled the results of the exercise on 2 July 1975 which called for spending cuts of $963 million. Some $100 million was cut from proposed capital spending, including $10 million from public works and $15.7 from the airport security program.

Another $254.9 million was cut from a host of organizations, including research granting councils, the Canadian International Development Agency (CIDA), and voluntary organizations. Several programs in health and welfare were cut by another $299.7 million. However, the largest cut – $357.4 million – was made in non-budgetary items, such as crown corporations.[7] In announcing the cuts, Chrétien once again gave ministers the option to accept them or 'choose other items that come to the same totals.'[8] Chrétien's job was made much easier than expected because he had secured the prime minister's full support. In fact, much of the anti-inflation initiatives, of which cuts in government spending was an important feature, came from Mr Trudeau's closest advisers in the Prime Minister's Office and the Privy Council Office.

Chrétien once again had Trudeau's full support in the fall when he undertook a second round of cuts. This time, however, he sought more to limit future growth in spending than to cut programs. He announced that salaries of members of the House of Commons and Senate and senior officials would be frozen for fifteen months; new directives would be issued to reduce spending for travel, motor vehicles, furniture, and conferences; proposed capital spending for accommodation for the public service, in fisheries and environment, was also cut back, as were proposed budgetary increases for DREE, External Affairs, and Environment, among others. Research funds for granting institutions, such as the Canada Council and the Medical Research Council, were frozen for two years. Person-years for higher-salaried positions were also frozen at the 1975–6 level. A few program cuts were made; Information Canada, for example, was cut, and others were reduced, including manpower and training programs.[9]

The Trudeau government remained anxious to show that it was in firm control of the treasury after it had pledged to hold spending to growth in GNP, and it called on the provinces and the private sector to show similar restraint.[10] In addition, the new Treasury Board president, Robert Andras, reported to parliament in early 1977 that he had directed his officials to go over departmental spending plans time and again to see if savings could be realized before finalizing the estimates. He compared his order 'to put spending plans once again through the grinder' to Nicolas Boileau's 'Vingt fois sur le métier remettez votre ouvrage.'[11]

Andras reported that he had teamed up with Jean Chrétien to turn away 'a great number of highly commendable proposals to expand and improve federal programs.'[12] Their biggest accomplishment, Andras reported, was to break 'the notion that the Treasury Board is somehow obligated to find additional funds for every worthwhile program expansion or new program and the notion that all that is needed to get these funds is to join the spending queue.'[13] He also reported: 'We have cut the fat.' Growth in the public service had been restricted to less than 1 per cent per year for both the 1976–7 and 1977–8 fiscal years.[14] In addition, several restraint measures were introduced. There was a ban on first-class air travel, restrictions on the use of taxis, and a call for the purchase of small vehicles and for energy conservation in government. Parking spaces for government employees were to be limited and those who got a parking space would have to pay. Yet another measure restricted the use of outside consultants.[15] Few programs, however, were eliminated or even reduced. Chrétien put forward the reasons: 'An indiscriminate slashing of programs would have disruptive effects on the economy, bear harshly on many people and impair the efficiency of government in providing essential services to the public.'[16]

Important changes were also made to federal-provincial financial arrangements. Beginning in 1977–8, federal contributions to such federal-provincial programs as medicare, hospital insurance, post-secondary education were made under a new financing formula. The contributions were no longer tied to provincial expenditures but rather to a combination of tax points and per capita cash payments. The changes reduced 'federal outlays in 1977–8 by close to one billion.' In addition, the government decided to suspend for one year the indexing of family allowance payments for 1976–7. In terms of federal programs, the Local Initiatives Program (LIP) was confined to high unemployment areas, the Company of Young Canadians was terminated, and foreign aid was capped.[17]

These changes and others slowed down growth in spending. By early 1978, Andras was able to report that the government, as promised, had restricted the growth in federal government expenditure to the general trend of increase in GNP. The growth in spending was limited to 7.1 and 10.4 per cent, respectively, between 1976–7, and 1979–80 and was less than growth in GNP.

Still, by mid-1978 the government had not been able to 'wrestle inflation' to the ground, as Prime Minister Trudeau had said he would. When Trudeau left for an economic summit meeting in Bonn that summer, Canada's inflation rate was still hovering around 10 per cent, despite four years of government restraint. Inflation was the principal item on the agenda at the Bonn summit where the consensus was that growth in government spending was fuelling inflation everywhere. Helmut Schmidt, the West German chancellor, with whom Trudeau had a close working relationship, also pressed this point to Trudeau in private meetings.

On his return to Ottawa, Trudeau met with his closest advisers who told him that the government would be unable to keep the growth in spending in line with increases in GNP unless further spending cuts were made. Public opinion polls were also less than encouraging, and the economic policies of the government were held to be its Achilles heel. The problem, it was concluded, was that the prime minister was widely perceived to have only a limited interest in economic policies.[18] His advisers agreed that something had to be done urgently and suggested that Trudeau should deliver a speech on the economy on national television. This time Trudeau did not limit himself to generalities, or even to yet another pledge to limit further the growth in spending. He announced that $2 billion would be *cut* from federal expenditures. He reported that the federal government was spending far too much money and spending it inefficiently. He concluded that 'we must have a major re-ordering of Government priorities. We must reduce the size of Government.' He added that it was not possible to sustain a $7 billion annual deficit for any length of time and that unless government spending was checked, 'Canadians within several years would almost certainly be faced with a fiscal crisis.'[19] He did not, however, provide any details on where the cuts would be made. He simply stated that the details would be announced shortly and that he was asking several ministers to return from their holidays to implement the new expenditure reduction policy. He did commit his government to turn the post office into a crown corporation and to hold the line on growth in the public service. Trudeau had consulted no one from his cabinet before making the announcement – not even the guardians, the minister of finance and the Treasury Board president.[20] Chrétien and Andras were, however, the first to be called back to identify where cuts could be made. The prime minister in his speech had promised that Andras would announce the cuts within a month. This time, however, the guardians' job would be relatively easy. Spending ministers were well aware that *le mot d'ordre* for the cuts had come from the top and, if they could not deliver, their leader, and hence the government, would be in great difficulty with the electorate. A general election was expected shortly.

THE BONN CUTS

'Finance and Treasury Board had a field day after Trudeau's Bonn speech,' reports a senior departmental official.[21] Chrétien had been able to secure Trudeau's complete support for the 'conservative' budget he would table in November 1978.[22] Andras was asked to report as quickly as possible to Priorities and Planning on possible cuts. Both guardians delivered. In his budget speech, Chrétien reported that the country's unemployment rate was on the rise but said that his budget 'should create an atmosphere of stability in the country and that it should aim at lowering costs, including the costs of government.'[23] Barely two weeks after the prime minister's speech, Robert Andras unveiled $1.5 billion in spending cuts. Of this amount, he explained, $1.25 billion constituted specific cuts in programs for the current fiscal year and the next. Another $250 million would be cut in administrative costs. He also revealed that further spending cuts would be made in the coming months, totalling another $1 billion.[24] Thus, Trudeau, without having consulted any of his most senior ministers, including the finance minister, had set the stage for cuts of $2.5 billion.

A few days after Trudeau's speech, the p & p began an intensive schedule of meetings. To get the process going, Andras submitted a list of possible cuts to programs that did not contribute to the government's current priorities. He also tried to keep across-the-board cuts to a minimum; he asked, for example, for a 1 per cent cut in all departments and agencies. Andras specified, however, that every department and agency contribute to some extent.

The Treasury Board secretariat was particularly well placed to suggest cuts in spending, having just completed a detailed program review. In addition, p & p had, in the spring, commissioned special studies on selected programs, originally to be completed by September. Secretariat officials were also intimately involved in this process. Immediately after Trudeau's televised speech, p & p directed that the studies be submitted a month early.

Armed with a series of fairly detailed recommendations from his officials, Andras was able to come before p & p with a menu of possible cuts, totalling more than 7 per cent of the federal expenditure budget.[25] This menu was based on the special studies and the program review secretariat officials had carried out. In selecting from this list, P & P was able to determine within two weeks the size of the cuts for all but a few departments and was also able quickly to approve in principle many specific program cuts. There was an important caveat – in the majority of cases, the total of the identified cuts was to represent an assigned quota for the department but the minister was given the option of changing or modifying them within the assigned quota. The trade-offs proved particularly difficult for certain ministers. When a minister rejected a proposed cut and replaced it with another, it was often because there was an interdepartmental issue to clear up. These were usually resolved through the president of the Treasury Board, subject to P & P ratification. Even these cases, however, were virtually settled by early September.

The cuts were unveiled in two phases. The Treasury Board president, as noted earlier, made public a series of cuts on 16 August 1978, totalling $1.5 billion towards the $2.5 billion target set by the prime minister. Andras also announced that 5000 federal public service jobs would be eliminated and that over 100 programs would be affected. By way of example, the Defence Department was asked to reduce 'committed expenditures' by $100 million. The budgets for CIDA and the CBC were frozen at their 1978 levels, which added over $200 million to the cuts. Some programs, such as Canfarm, an agricultural services agency, were eliminated, saving $6 million annually. The bilingual bonus for public servants was also eliminated, at a saving of $35 million a year. It was also decided to 'mothball' the LaPrade Heavy Water Plant and save $150 million.[26]

On 8 September Chrétien and Andras announced another $1 billion cut.[27] This brought the total expenditure reduction to $2.5 billion. This last round of cuts concentrated on capital building programs, grants of all types, and research. A number of regulatory agencies also saw their expenditure budgets grow less than they would have under normal circumstances. Some budgets were also 'shaved': the Canadian Radio-Television and Telecommunciations Commission (CRTC) was instructed to reduce its budget by $500,000 over two years, the Foreign Investment Review Agency (FIRA) lost $400,000, and the Department of Consumer and Corporate Affairs was asked to cut by $7.6 million.

The minister of finance added that still more cuts were possible. The next round, however, would be made in federal-provincial programs. Chrétien revealed that the prime minister had sent a telegram in late August to open discussions 'to curb growth' in federal payments to the provinces. The goal, he reported, was to cut another $500 million.[28] He also announced a major reform of the government's child benefits system. For the first time ever, a refundable tax credit was introduced into the federal tax system in order to make social security more selective. Chrétien declared that benefits would be reduced for those who are better off but increased for lower- and middle-income families. The basic federal family allowance was reduced to $20 per month in January 1979, the tax credit of $50 per child was eliminated, and the tax exemption for children aged 16 and 17 was reduced to $460. In turn, a new child credit for middle- and lower-income families of $200 per year for each child eligible for family allowance was introduced.[29]

In announcing this last round of cuts, Chrétien and Andras again said that some of the cuts could still be altered by departments. What was important, they insisted, was that departments accept the size of the cuts to be realized. They were free to identify better alternatives than those suggested by Treasury Board within the amounts attached to departments.

A number of departments felt that the program review and the special studies had armed the Treasury Board with information for the government to extract more than a fair share of cuts. Treasury Board officials would encounter resistance in the years to come from departments over their participation in program or special review studies. Andras himself admitted that 'the spending cuts were handled in a "ham-handed way." ' He acknowledged that the way they had been made and announced could well lead one to conclude that the government was 'in a state of crisis management.' He added, however, that 'if you stayed with the orderly sort of process ... the thing is that you will build up such a resistance and such a justification not to do it.'[30]

Still, most departments took full advantage of proposing options within an expenditure reduction 'quota.' In some instances, they welcomed the opportunity. The Council on Rural Development was associated with DREE but reported directly to the minister. The council's purpose was to 'advise the minister on the scope, direction and continuity of the federal government's policies and programs for rural development.'[31] From time to time it was critical of DREE's policies and the department's lack of concern for rural development. When the department was asked to cut, it quickly pointed to the council. There were other similar examples. In addition, some suggested cuts in their capital budgets rather than in their operations. The Public Works accommodation program was cut by almost $100 million and some reductions were instituted in the purchases of 'fine art.' These cuts, however, would be only temporary.

The Trudeau government's willingness to continue with spending cuts waned as the 1979 general election approached. In fact, the government started to announce new spending for job creation and industrial development. In the fall of 1978, for example, the government set aside $300 million from the cuts to support new measures 'to assist industry to exploit new markets, to develop new technology and to reorganize to meet (new) challenges.'[32]

The Trudeau government went down to defeat in May 1979. The newly elected Progressive Conservative government, under Prime Minister Joe Clark, quickly made clear its intention to cut spending. Clark's minister of finance, John Crosbie, and his Treasury Board president, Sinclair Stevens, issued a joint statement in July on government spending. The statement read: 'Our government feels we cannot tolerate the spending level inherent in past actions, and we intend to face up to the problem of taking some hard decisions which are necessary to get government spending in this country under control.'[33] Stevens suggested, for example, that 60,000 jobs in government could be eliminated. Crosbie, in his first budget, declared that one of the government's most important goals was to reduce the size of the deficit. He reported that the annual growth in government spending would be limited to 10 per cent and he raised a number of taxes, including an excise tax of 25 cents a gallon on gasoline.[34] Within six months, the Clark government fell on the issue of the budget.

Returned to power in 1980, Trudeau had a new set of priorities – constitutional reform, energy, and the assertion of the presence of the federal government. The goal of the finance minister, however, remained the same as it had been in the last Trudeau administration – to keep government expenditures within GNP growth, to cut spending, and to reduce the deficit. However, by late 1981 and early 1982, Canada was plunged into the second sharpest decline in economic activity in the twentieth century. In 1982, GNP fell by 4.4 per cent and employment by 3.3 per cent. Unemployment reached 12.8 per cent – a level unprecedented in the post-war period. The Trudeau government was in no mood to pursue spending cuts or stick to its objective of limiting growth in spending to the increase in GNP. It did introduce a program designed to limit growth in spending in a number of government programs to 6 per cent in 1983 and 5 per cent in 1984. Pay increases for federal government employees were also limited to 6 and 5 per cent.[35] The government, however, announced a string of new spending measures, including $500 million for job creation, $500 million for small businesses, and $400 million for housing. Later, a $4.8 billion special recovery program was unveiled. It combined new spending with a 'reprofile' of existing programs to support private sector investment, to upgrade public facilities such as harbours, wharfs, roads, tourist attractions, and agricultural facilities. The bulk of the new spending was made in the last year of Trudeau's mandate. These initiatives were to be financed through savings realized from wage restraint and indexation. Spending cuts between 1980 and 1984 were mostly plowed back in the policy reserves to permit new spending by cabinet policy committees. They did not reduce either overall government spending or the deficit.

In April 1980, for example, P & P directed the cabinet Committee for Economic Development to review low-priority programs with the objective of finding funds to replenish the economic development envelope's policy reserve. This exercise simply represented a redeployment of resources allocated to the envelope to keep the total within the levels established by the fiscal framework. Cabinet was unwilling to redirect resources from other policy fields to provide extra resources for economic development nor was cabinet willing to increase total spending to do so. The secretariat of the cabinet Committee on Economic Development was then directed to work with the Treasury Board secretariat to formulate details providing for $500 million of possible cuts in the A base for the 1981–2, 1982–3, and 1983–4 fiscal years. Departments in turn were asked to identify their lowest-priority programs, which accounted for 20 per cent of the department's expenditure base. The exercise turned up $454 million in cuts. Program reductions accounted for one-third of the total and deferrals for nearly one-half. The Treasury Board secretariat, however, was concerned over the probable lack of permanent reductions that would eventually be realized from these deferrals. The concern of TBS officials proved valid. Although some forty-two programs were reduced or deferred, most of these modifications resulted only in one-time savings. They had little lasting impact in reducing the expenditure budget.

In January 1981, another A base review was conducted of the economic development envelope. The review concentrated on grants and contributions which accounted for about one-half of the expenditures of the envelope. This review did not lead to many cuts, although a decision was taken to reduce the least profitable services of Via Rail. In August, yet another A base review focused on subsidies and cost-recovery. The secretariat was directed to work with officials of the relevant line departments to prepare lists of possible reductions. The result of this exercise led to adjustments to nineteen programs. However, cost recovery items accounted for over 40 per cent of the $430 million freed up to replenish policy reserves over the period from 1981–2 to 1984–5. It is important to stress once again that the cuts and cost-recovery items did not result in permanent net expenditure reductions. They simply freed up resources for new spending commitments.

REVISITING THE TRUDEAU CUTS

The Trudeau government, as noted above, had declared on Thanksgiving Day 1975 that the trend of increase in its spending would not rise more quickly than that in the GNP. It made the same commitment in its first budget after returning to power in 1980. Figure 2 shows that, on the face of it, it was successful between 1975 and 1979. Figure 3 later in this chapter shows that it was unsuccessful during its 1980–4 mandate. To be sure, the increase in spending in 1982 and 1983 was due in part to cyclical factors. Changes in spending arise from three sources: cuts in spending, new initiatives and new spending, and cyclical conditions. A sudden downturn in the economy of the kind which occurred in the early 1980s has obvious impact, for example, on the unemployment insurance program on the expenditure side and on corporate and personal income taxes on the revenue side.

The period 1975–9 provides a better test of the ability of the Trudeau government to meet its goal. From 1976 to 1980 growth in government spending was lower than that in GNP. As figure 2 shows, this was in sharp contrast to fiscal years 1973–4, 1974–5, and 1975–6. Thus, one could conclude that the government was successful in meeting its objective.

That said, several points should be noted. The basis for control of government spending was defined in terms of total *outlays*, that is, both expenditures and balance sheet accounts. To the end of 1979, non-budgetary expenditure reductions – such as loans, investments, and advances to crown corporations – bore the brunt of the restraint policy, accounting for *36.2 per cent* of total reductions. The bulk of the reductions here were the result of policy decisions to have crown corporations borrow in private capital markets rather than draw on the consolidated revenue fund.[36]

Cuts in planned expenditures in each fiscal year from 1975–6 to 1980–1 are shown in table 7. The cuts are divided in terms of operations and capital, transfer payments, and non-budgetary items.

Table 8 breaks down the cuts into several categories to determine

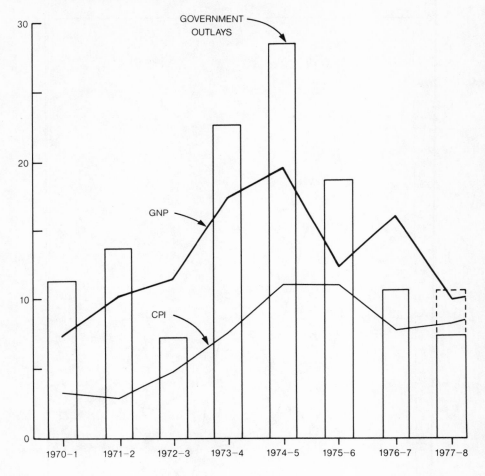

Figure 2
Growth of government outlays, GNP, and CPI, 1970–1 to 1977–8
Source: Canada, Treasury Board
Note: Dotted lines reflect 1977–8 EPF tax transfers and 1979–80 changes in child
tax benefits.

which led to permanent decreases in spending, which represented only
temporary decreases, and which constituted transfers to other
jurisdictions.

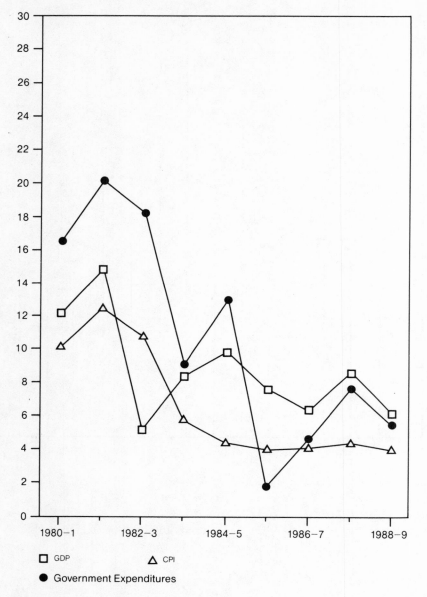

Figure 3
Growth of budgetary expenses, GDP, and CPI

TABLE 7
Planned expenditure reductions by type of expenditure, 1975–6 to 1980–1 ($ millions)

Type of reduction	Fiscal year					
	1975–6	1976–7	1977–8	1978–9	1979–80	1980–1
Operations and capital	280	280	250	698	1026	394
Transfer payments	232	697	–	449	541	651
Total – budgetary	512	977	250	1147	1567	1045
Non-budgetary	286	768	–	1125	433	501
Total reductions	798	1745	250	2272	2000	1546

SOURCE: Canada, Treasury Board
*Changes in loans, investments, and advances

TABLE 8
Expenditure reductions by category of reductions, 1975–6 to 1980–1 ($ millions)

Category of reduction	Fiscal year					
	1975–6	1976–7	1977–8	1978–9	1979–80	1980–1
Permanent decrease	182	1091	250	1229	937	513
Temporary decrease	383	409	–	226	355	54
Transfer to other jurisdictions	25	–	–	48	15	719
Reduction applied to fund otherwise lapsed	2	28	–	90	81	131
Miscellaneous	206	217	–	679	612	57
Total reductions	798	1745	250	2272	2000	1546

SOURCE: Canada, Treasury Board

The $719 million identified in table 8 as a transfer to other jurisdictions is a change in the unemployment insurance program. The change shifted a larger share of its financing to the private sector through increased premiums. This did not constitute a cut in the program or a reduction in the level of service, but merely a change in the source of financing. There were other such instances. For example, Central Mortgage and Housing Corporation (CMHC) sold $450 millions in assets in 1978–9. This was considered a permanent reduction in total outlays since it was viewed as a program decision to reduce levels of service.[37]

Employing total outlays as the determining criteria to see if the government was able to limit growth in spending below growth in GNP overlooks the cost to the federal treasury of transferring tax points to the provinces and tax expenditures. Two examples illustrate the point. The federal government introduced the Established Programs Financing (EPF) arrangements in 1977–8. In doing so, it transferred new revenues to the provinces in the form of tax points, instead of as direct transfer payments. Federal revenues were reduced by $1.274 million in 1977–8. If that funding had been provided in the form of transfer payments, the growth in federal government spending for that year would have been 10.2 per cent rather than 7.1 per cent. This alone would have meant that the annual growth in spending that year would have been higher than the growth in GNP. The revised way of financing the child care system offers a similar example. Direct spending for family allowance was decreased while the program was enriched through a child care tax credit. The estimated net impact on federal revenue was a reduction of $650 million. Had this been provided in direct spending rather than revenue loss, combined with changes in financing federal-provincial programs through EPF it would have increased 1978–80 spending by $2.1 billion and increased the growth rate from 8.9 per cent to 10.2 per cent.[38]

A retrospective analysis of the cuts left a large *miscellaneous* category, consisting of both across-the-board reductions in departmental operating budgets and a series of small program reductions. It was not possible to determine precisely if the cuts led to permanent decreases in departmental budgets.[39]

It is possible, however, to discern a marked increase in tax expenditures from 1975–6 on. These are not counted in determining total government outlays and so they became 'the preferred subsidy route during the last decade.'[40] For example, measures were announced in the November 1978 budget to encourage fixed investment, including an increase in the investment tax credit basic rate from 5 to 7 per cent, and from 10 to 20 per cent in slow-growing regions. The tax credit was also expanded to include transportation equipment. There were also many other similar measures introduced in earlier and subsequent budgets but which were never totalled as part of the 'total' expenditure budget.

The finance minister and Treasury Board president announced in the summer of 1978 that 5000 positions would be cut in the public service. At the time they made the announcement there were 242,414 person-years in the federal government. One year later the number stood at 237,503. Thus the government was able to make the 5000 person-year cut stick. However, it did not stick for long. By the time Trudeau stepped from power in 1984, the number had climbed back to 241,534.[41]

ON THE ROAD TO TORONTO

The press wrote at length about Brian Mulroney's lack of specific policy objectives when he became prime minister in 1984. It was not clear, the press reported, what his Conservative government would do on the environment, on natives issues, on regional development, and so on. What was clear, however, was that Mulroney favoured 'restraint in government and a greater dependency on the private sector to generate economic growth.'[42] In a major campaign speech in Toronto, Mulroney had pledged that his government would 'spend smarter' and would employ the most advanced techniques to 'eliminate program duplication and overlap.' He also said that since 'coming to Ottawa from the private sector, I have been appalled by the waste of time and talent (in government)' and pledged, if elected, to 'challenge on-going programs.'[43]

Within weeks of coming to power, the Mulroney government reported its firm intention to honour the 'Toronto' commitment. If anything, the government would go further and slash spending. The prime minister, Michael Wilson, the minister of finance, and Robert R. de Cotret, the Treasury Board president, all soon reported that 'the cupboard was bare.' The fiscal position of the federal government was in a 'precarious' situation. 'Canadians,' de Cotret wrote, 'may be surprised by the depth of the financial disarray into which the Government of Canada has fallen ... The origins of the problem (however) are clear – for too long the government has been spending money which it did not have.'[44] The solution, he explained, was also clear. 'In a pragmatic, considered, fair way, the government must review and reduce its expenditures.'[45]

The Mulroney government was sworn to office on 17 September 1984 and, one week later, de Cotret announced a temporary freeze on staffing and on discretionary spending to give ministers time to review programs and activities to ensure they were consistent with the new government's policies.[46] Mulroney immediately wrote to all his ministers and asked them to report in writing as soon as possible not only on their priorities for their departments but also on possibilities for expenditure cuts. He also spoke at length in cabinet and P & P meetings on the importance of expenditure reduction. Michael Wilson happily took the cue and made this the centrepiece of his first major economic statement in parliament. Wilson said: 'In each of the past ten years the expenditures of the federal government have exceeded its revenues ... unless we begin now to put our fiscal house in order, the burden of debt will continue to mount rapidly.'[47] The government, he reported, had no choice but to move quickly to reduce spending. 'Our goal,' he stated, 'is to reduce the projected level of annual expenditure by 1990 by $10 to $15 billion.'[48] A few months later, in his 1985 budget speech, Wilson firmly set the goal at $15 billion by 1990–1.[49] With the prime minister's firm support, the two guardians at Finance and Treasury Board set out to identify areas where spending cuts could be made. Mulroney had initiated the process, it will be recalled, by asking ministers to put down on paper where spending cuts could be realized in their departments. He also, as we have already seen, established the Nielsen Task Force and Forget Commission on the unemployment insurance program.

Mulroney then asked de Cotret to lead 'an intensive ministerial review of all programs' and to identify on an urgent basis areas where expenditures could be reduced.[50] He and all ministers were directed to consider all avenues for cutting spending, including the reduction of general overhead costs, cost recovery, the cutting back or elimination of programs, and the reduction of loans and investments to crown corporations. The review examined all programs and 'fundamental questions [were] asked about all expenditures.'[51] That said, the review did not deal with large, complex policy issues or seek to restructure programs such as subsidies to industry. This was left to the Nielsen Task Force, the Forget Commission, and more internal government studies.

The review ignored the formal decision-making processes, such as PEMS. To have gone through the policy committees would have been far too time consuming, and the newly elected government was anxious to get on with the job. And, in response to the prime minister's instructions, ministers on their own identified some areas where cuts could be made. Meanwhile, de Cotret was briefed by Treasury Board secretariat officials on potential cuts in all departments and agencies. He then held bilateral meetings with spending ministers and attempted to reconcile both lists. From there de Cotret went to P & P with his recommendations. Less than two months after coming to office, cabinet approved a package to reduce budgetary expenditures and increase revenues by a total of $3.619 billion. It also agreed to reduce non-budgetary expenditures (loans and investments) by $625 million. Moreover, Wilson secured cabinet support for a host of reviews, ranging from pension reform for MPs to old age security.

The November 1984 spending cuts were detailed in a thirty-page appendix to a report de Cotret tabled in parliament. Some of the cuts were predictable, given that the Conservatives had either fought for them while in opposition or campaigned for them in the 1984 election campaign. Thus Canagrex, a crown corporation to promote the export of agricultural products, and Canertech, a subsidiary of Petro-Canada investing in a renewable energy project, were wound up, at a saving of nearly $40 million. Other programs which had never been held in high esteem by the party were cut back. The operating budget of the CBC was reduced by $75million and its capital budget by $10 million. The Petroleum Incentives Program (PIP) was reduced by $250 million and DRIE was cut back $200 million. A new foreign post of ambassador to the United Nations Food and Agriculture Organization in Rome, to be filled by Eugene Whelan, former agriculture minister in the Trudeau government, was cancelled. Numerous capital projects were cancelled or deferred. A freeze on the development of national parks saved nearly $227.8 million and several cost-recovery measures were introduced or increased, bringing in nearly $200 million in new revenues. There were also a number of non-program cuts. About $700 million of the total cuts came from overhead reductions and general restraint measures.[52]

The guardians had little time to congratulate themselves on the November cuts before they initiated a new round. Wilson was busy laying the groundwork for his first budget to be tabled in May 1985. He decided to up the ante from his November statement and, as we saw, state firmly that the government would 'achieve *net* expenditure reductions of $15 billion in 1990–91.'[53] More cuts in spending were now necessary. Both Wilson and de Cotret quickly accepted, however, that the next round would not be as easy as the first one. Areas such as Energy and DRIE programming could provide for large and relatively painless reductions, but they had been taken in the first round and were no longer available. Spending ministers had also become much more familiar with their departments by now and would resist further spending cuts more energetically. Still, Wilson and de Cotret rejected a general freeze or across-the-board spending cuts, fearing that high-priority programs might be affected, and programs which ought to be pruned, ignored. The thinking was that they should not simply cut back all the programs inherited from the Trudeau administration but rather eliminate or substantially reduce those that were at variance with the philosophy and approach of the new government.

Wilson also insisted that substantial cuts should be made to create room to finance new spending initiatives to implement campaign commitments. He made it clear that funding for new spending – including campaign commitments – could only come from cuts in the expenditure budgets. The guardians quickly identified several likely candidates. Finance, it was agreed, would take the lead in reviewing major social, federal-provincial, and energy programs. The Treasury Board secretariat would review, among others, major transportation programs, subsidies to business, and privatization initiatives.

The secretariat quickly put together a list of potential spending cuts. Its officials have a good knowledge of the programs of the departments and agencies for which they are responsible and usually can put together a list of possible cuts in short order. They had done so for the November cuts and they would do so again in preparation for the May budget.

Some potential cuts could be identified easily. AECL had two plants in Cape Breton producing heavy water that was clearly surplus to Canada's requirements. In any event, Ontario Hydro could produce heavy water at less cost. In addition, AECL's board of directors had been recommending closure of the plants since the early 1980s. Allan J. MacEachen, a Maritimer and powerful minister in the Trudeau cabinet, had resisted all suggestions that the plants be closed, even from his own officials when he was finance minister. Secretariat officials also held that cuts could be made in agriculture, in 'unproductive' transportation subsidies, and in DRIE programs. Unlike other departments, a good part of DRIE's budget is largely uncommitted for two to three years down the road. The department can always turn down businesses applying for assistance even though their proposals may meet the eligibility criteria. The same cannot be said for family allowance, the old age security program, and so on.

The guardians, Wilson and de Cotret, put together a long list of cuts for consideration by P & P.[54] Spending ministers, however, were now beginning to voice strong objections. The then DRIE minister, Sinclair Stevens, urged that cuts in his department be put off until he completed his own program review. Similarly, the minister of transport strongly objected to cuts in subsidies to Via Rail, and the agriculture minister warned that there would be a 'political' price to pay in cutting back agricultural programs. The list of potential cuts was pared down as budget day approached. Still, Wilson was able to announce program cuts totalling $455 million in 1985–6, rising to $1.4 billion in 1986–7, and to over $1.9 billion in 1990–1.[55]

Wilson and his advisers were convinced that, to be effective, expenditure reductions had to go beyond cutting back selected federal programs. The federal government transfers billions in cash annually to provincial governments in support of a host of federal-provincial programs. In fiscal year 1985–6, for example, the federal government was going to transfer to the provinces well over $20 billion in cash and tax transfers. Wilson was able to secure the approval of the prime minister and of P & P to limit the rate of growth of transfers to the provinces, amounting to savings of about $2 billion for the federal treasury by 1990–1. With this adjustment, transfers to the provinces were expected to grow by about 5 per cent per year until 1990–1.[56]

The guardians also took aim both at universality in social development programs and the indexation of selected programs designed to protect individuals against inflation. The government, however, was in no mood to tackle the universality issue. Mulroney, his PMO advisers, and some key ministers felt that they were as yet ill-prepared to 'tamper' with the principles of universality in social programs. In any event, 'consultation papers' were being released on child care and elderly benefits in January 1985, and several ministers insisted that it would be poor politics to overhaul social programs before people had an opportunity to react to these papers.[57]

Indexation was a different matter. The guardians argued strongly in favour of cutting back on full indexation on selected programs. If the government was serious about cutting back spending, they insisted, indexation had to be part of the package. Everyone, they argued, should 'bite the bullet' and participate in reducing federal expenditures: not just federal programs and federal-provincial programs should be affected, but individuals as well. Again, they met resistance from several key spending ministers who argued that it was too early to move on the indexation issue. For one thing, they reminded their colleagues that during the election campaign the party had pledged a return to full indexation in the post '6 and 5' era. Moreover, the consultation papers released in January made no mention of cutting back on indexation.[58] Still, the guardians carried the day and Wilson was able to announce in his budget that family allowances and old age security would increase by the annual change in the consumer price index (CPI) in excess of three percentage points. This measure would save the federal treasury another $2 billion by 1990–1.

The guardians put forward another suggestion that met with little resistance. It was quickly agreed that 15,000 positions would be cut from the federal public service. Mulroney himself had talked about giving public servants pink slips when he ran for the leadership of his party and while in opposition. 'I'd cut everywhere and under every circumstance,' he had boasted. Mulroney was not alone in holding this view in the new government. 'Conservatives' had often pointed to the public service 'as a highly visible example of the Trudeau government's legacy of waste, inefficiency and patronage.'[59] And so, when the option of cutting 15,000 public servants was put forward, few voices were heard in P & P against it.

Why 15,000? 'Why not?' answered a P & P member.[60] Certainly the number was not based on any in-depth study or assessment of what could be eliminated. One senior central agency official contends that the 15,000 was picked because 'it was a good round figure. It meant that to cut 15,000 positions over five years you had to cut 2 per cent of the positions in the federal public service in the first year and 1 per cent in each of the remaining four years. It made for nice and tidy targets.'[61]

It was also agreed early on to sell crown corporations. Several were immediately put up for sale, including Canadian Arsenals, Canadair, de Havilland, and Eldorado Nuclear. This, it was reported, would reduce the government's cash requirements by about $675 million and the federal deficit by approximately $350 million in 1985–6. De Cotret was also asked to head up a ministerial task force to develop a plan to ensure that privatization remained high on the government's agenda. It is important to stress that senior members of the Progressive Conservative party pointed to privatization while in opposition and in the early months of Mulroney's first mandate as a deficit reduction measure. They no longer speak of privatization in this manner. The rationale now for privatization is that it is no longer appropriate for the treasury to own at least some crown corporations and that the private sector should be encouraged to take a more active and dominant role in the economy.

Lastly, a number of 'better management measures' were introduced. The government served notice that it would end full indexation of pensions for MPs and public servants. The May 1985 budget also eliminated automatic adjustments to departmental budgets to compensate for inflation. Specifically, the Treasury Board secretariat would not allow for adjustments to operating costs and for automatic adjustments to grants and contributions in departmental MYOPs. There was also a one-time 4 per cent reduction in non-defence capital budgets. In addition, cash management initiatives were introduced designed to bring well-established business practices into the federal government. For instance, electronic banking would speed the transfer of deposits of public money through financial institutions to the credit of the receiver general, departmental bank accounts would be reduced from 1000 to 22, efforts would be made to reduce the level of outstanding amounts owed to the government.[62]

Some six months after he tabled his first budget, Wilson sought a new round of spending cuts. Pressure on the expenditure ceiling of $105.4 billion set in his May budget was coming from a number of sources. Revenues were believed to be lower than projected, and some finance officials were concerned that the new 'soft' approach in Revenue Canada would erode income tax collections. The biggest pressure, however, came from the requirements associated with the bank failures in western Canada. Wilson strongly felt that the government had to stay within the expenditure ceiling established in his budget. Otherwise a signal would be sent to the public and to the public service that the government was less committed to fiscal restraint than it claimed to be. In his opinion, to waver on deficit reduction as the economy was improving would severely damage the government's credibility. Wilson and de Cotret developed a package of 'expenditure containment' measures totalling $1.2 billion. This new round of cuts, however, did not involve the participation of any spending ministers to the same extent that previous cuts had. To ensure the package's approval, however, Wilson decided to obtain the prime minister's support at a private meeting and subsequently present the package to P & P as a fait accompli. Both Wilson and de Cotret were convinced that without Mulroney's firm support and unless he himself instructed both P & P and his ministers to pursue the 'expenditure containment' there was little chance of success. The package was in fact approved by P & P on the prime minister's insistence and was implemented. The package involved: the deferring of various initiatives into the 1986–7 fiscal year; a freeze on unspent policy and operating reserves; a 3 per cent cut in the departmental operating budgets; the deferral of uncommitted DRIE and CIDA program funds; and reduced funding levels for selected programs. A few months later, in February 1986, the Treasury Board president froze all discretionary spending to reduce year-end spending.

When Wilson rose in the House on 26 February 1986 to deliver his budget speech, he could state that the government had checked government spending. He said, 'This government [has] moved decisively to bring spending under control ... And none too soon.' 'Spending restraints were necessary,' he added, 'to halt the upward spiral in our deficit.'[63] For good measure, he announced 'a $500 million special reduction in non-statutory government programs' from the very budget he was presenting on that day. He reported that the Treasury Board president would shortly announce the plan to implement the cuts. He also asked all MPs to accept a $1,000 cut in pay and reported that senior government official should not receive their regular annual increase in salaries.[64]

In planning another $500 million cut, Treasury Board had to put aside Defence and Official Development Assistance (ODA) spending because the government had committed itself to a prescribed growth rate in spending for both areas. For this round of cuts, de Cotret sought to provide ministers with considerable flexibility to identify how their departments should reduce their spending. Departments were given expenditure reduction targets, established so that spending cuts would be directed more towards departments with relatively large, discretionary spending in overhead costs and subsidy payments. Every effort would be made to minimize cuts in activities related to health, safety, and security and services to the public. Low-income groups would also be protected. In addition, the Treasury Board secretariat asked all departments to avoid layoffs. In turn, the secretariat pledged to reduce the 'paper burden' it imposes on departments. For example, it would continue the practice, introduced the year before, of reviewing departmental spending plans – the MYOPS – only once a year rather than twice. The clerk of the Privy Council and the Treasury Board secretary cosigned a memorandum to all deputy ministers, heads of agencies, and senior executives on 'Tighter Resource Management: A New Corporate Culture.'[65]

Still, the Treasury Board would soon find that implementing the new round of cuts would be difficult. Some secretariat officials were increasingly concerned with Finance's 'off-the-wall' proposals to cut spending.[66] They were being consulted in a superficial fashion only, but were left to pick up the pieces to implement them. The stress and strain of continually going back to departments for more spending reductions was starting to show. Certainly, spending ministers and their departments were sending out all kinds of signals that enough was enough. The Nielsen Task Force was one thing but spending cuts every six months was another. The more senior ministers were now also telling the prime minister to intervene on their behalf and to get Finance and Treasury Board 'under control.'

The Treasury Board found implementing the new cuts difficult. It had hoped to develop an implementation plan quickly, if only looking ahead to the 1986–7 fiscal year. Accordingly, secretariat officials requested departments to come forward with suggested spending cuts as soon as possible. However, it was only nine months after Wilson's budget speech that de Cotret unveiled the details of the $500 million cut. He reported that it would not result in further layoffs of public servants and, as stated above, that programs targeted 'to people in need,' and to 'programs in areas of health, safety, security, [and] service to the public,' would not be compromised. The $500 million cut was spread over twenty-six departments and agencies, with Employment and Immigration and DRIE taking the largest reductions – $76 and $50 millions, respectively.[67]

Spending cuts, however, were now out of favour. The guardians could hardly work up any interest outside their own departments to launch another round. In fact, it became increasingly clear after Wilson's 1986 budget that spenders were beginning to turn the tide and win some major battles with the guardians. There were a series of new spending announcements for the Special Canadian Grains Program, for Defence, for relocating laboratories out of Ottawa to Winnipeg, and so on. In his February 1988 budget speech, for example, Wilson reported on a series of new spending initiatives rather than further cuts. The government had announced in the previous months new funding for child care, for economic development in the Atlantic and the West, for agriculture, and for science and technology. Wilson did announce another round of spending cuts; however, it would amount to only $300 million, would be carried out in a similar way to the $500 million cut announced in his 1986 budget, but would only be made in the 1989–90 fiscal year.[68] By that time, the expected general election would have been won or lost.

REVISITING THE MULRONEY CUTS

The minister of finance, it will be recalled, had pledged in his first budget speech to cut *net* expenditure by $15 billion by 1990–1. This means that any new spending measures introduced by the government between 1984–5 and 1990–1 would have to be offset by further spending cuts, in addition to a $15 billion cut. In short, the goal was to reduce the projected level of annual expenditures by 1990–1 by $15 billion.

The government has not been successful in meeting this goal. To be sure, expenditure cuts were made and important restraint measures were introduced. It can be argued that, if the growth in government spending had been left unchecked from 1984–5 levels, the main estimates for 1990–1 would be considerably higher. Some government representatives may well argue that the five-year *cumulative* impact of restraint measures could have been as high as $60 billion. They can also argue that the annual growth in the deficit has been reversed: from $38.2 billion in 1984–5, to $32.3 billion in 1986–7 and $29.3 billion in 1987–8. But these figures tell only part of the story. Many policy decisions involving new spending and public debt charges have largely offset the impact of the various spending cuts.

In addition, some of the early cuts were in reality spending deferrals and they have had no impact on the goal of cutting back net expenditure by $15 billion by 1990–1. For example, the halting of construction of a new embassy in Washington at a cost of $63 million was included in the November 1984 spending cuts. In reality the project was only deferred. The November 1984 spending cuts also called for a reduction of $180 million to official development assistance (External Affairs). The cut was made, but at the same time the government reaffirmed its commitment to allocate 0.6 per cent of GNP by 1990 and 0.7 per cent by 1995 for official development assistance. Thus, CIDA's budget went from $1.36 billion in spending and $365.2 million in loans and advances in 1985–6 to $2.2 billion in spending and $25.1 million in loans and advances in 1988–9.

CN Marine and Via Rail are two other examples. In the November 1984 cuts, the government announced savings of $21.5 million in the CN Marine's administrative costs because a new separate crown corporation was being established and savings of $93 million because of cutbacks in subsidies to Via Rail. In tabling the 1988–9 main estimates, however, the Treasury Board president reported an increase of $28 million in subsidies to Marine Atlantic to cover operating costs. In the case of Via Rail, the government declared shortly after it came to power that Canadians had to 'Use it [Via Rail] or lose it.' The 1987–8 appropriation for Via Rail, however, was increased by $111.9 million through supplementary estimates, or from $500 to $611.9 million. An important reason for the increase, it was explained, was that the forecast increase in revenues did not materialize because of a decline in the number of passengers taking Via Rail.

DRIE also provides an excellent example where cuts were announced but were not completely realized. The Mulroney government included cuts in DRIE programming every time it unveiled expenditure reductions or spending containment measures. Comparatively speaking, as we said above, DRIE programs could be cut back easily. The tap, however, was left open when it should have been shut. By fiscal year 1986-7, DRIE had overcommitted its grants and contributions by $80 million. On 30 July and 25 August 1987, Treasury Board approved special funding for the department. By early 1987-8, it became clear that DRIE had seriously overcommitted its approved expenditure levels, and in the summer of 1987 the government injected $350 million in the DRIE budget to permit the department to honour its commitments.[69]

The finance minister had announced in his 1985 budget a partial de-indexation of old age pensions. The government was quickly on the defensive. Opposition to de-indexation came from a variety of groups, notably organizations representing senior citizens. The deficit, they argued, should not be fought on their backs and spending cuts should be made elsewhere. Wilson restored full indexation of pensions on 27 June 1985.[70] The Mulroney government pledged to end full indexation of pensions for MPS and public servants. It never did so.

There are areas where the federal government has been able to make the cuts stick. It did, for instance, go ahead with its plans to cut $2 billion from projected increases in transfers to provincial governments. The government said in 1986 that it would strive to improve its cash management and it has. Since 1985, it has introduced a series of measures that have saved $539 million, with further expected savings of $700 million between 1988 and 1991. Among other things, the government has adopted payment of suppliers of goods and services on due date, paid large grants in instalments, better-managed cash balances to avoid non-interest earnings, accelerated remittances of taxes and other payroll deductions, and so on.[71]

The government was also successful in restricting the growth in spending in the operating cost of government. Cuts in operating costs were announced in the early part of the Mulroney government mandate and these have been implemented. It was possible for Don Mazankowski, the deputy prime minister, to claim in April 1988 that 'the cost of running the government has gone down. Wages and operating costs – excluding Defence – have fallen to 11.8 percent of budgetary expenditures. Compare that to 13.8 percent in 1984-85.'[72]

The government has also made solid progress on its commitment to cut 15,000 person-years from the pubic service between 1986-7 and 1990-1. By the time the Treasury Board president tabled the

1988–9 main estimates, a total reduction of 10,524 person-years had been achieved. If the reference levels provided to departments for 1989–90 and 1990–1 are respected, the government will have achieved its goal. It also appears that the person-year reduction is being carried out with a minimum of dislocation to public servants. As of 25 March 1988, only 634 employees had been laid off. Of these, nearly 300 still had priority rights for reappointment to a federal government position for new job openings for one year following layoff. It is also reported that some quite willingly accepted being laid off because of the attractive severance pay.[73]

It is necessary, however, to qualify the success of the government's person-year reduction initiative. For one thing, well over 1000 of the positions shown as cut were in fact only transferred or devolved to provincial governments, territorial governments, Indian bands, and the private sector. In devolving the positions to other governments, the federal government also transferred the required funds to pay their salaries. For example, in 1988–9 the Department of Indian Affairs and Northern Development (DIAND) transferred 175 person-years as a result of the implementation of the comprehensive devolution plan for the transfer of programs and responsibilities to Indian control, and in 1987–8, Correctional Services reported a decrease of 236 person-years, largely because it devolved some of its responsibilities to provincial governments. In both cases, the federal government signed an agreement to transfer the necessary funds to pay the salaries. The cost of the function obviously is still paid by the federal government, although it does not carry the person-years on its books.

In addition, it appears that cutting the remaining 4476 positions will be much more difficult than cutting the first 10,524. The largest cut occurred in the first year and was relatively painless. Departments do not always 'burn' all their person-years. For example, a department may have 20,000 person-years, but not all positions are likely to be filled for twelve months because it is not possible to plan for all promotions, retirements, and transfers to make full use of the person-year allotments. In the first and second year of a person-year cutback, departments can manage the cuts by not staffing all vacant positions. Treasury Board officials report that departments are now burning much more of their person-year allocations than in past years.[74] As further cuts are required, it will be increasingly difficult for departments to accommodate them.

Departments are also putting strong pressure on the Treasury Board for new person-years. In particular, departments and agencies with major policy initiatives to implement are coming forward with requests for more personnel. National Revenue, for example, is concerned that the tax reform package entails numerous new activities for them to implement. Departments like Fisheries and Oceans and National Health and Welfare are also well aware of the government's commitment to enhance food inspection and are requesting new personnel. New regional development agencies in the West and Atlantic Canada are in turn reporting that they will need still more staff because of the government's decision to have them deliver programs rather than provincial governments. And the list goes on.

The Mulroney government, but particularly the Trudeau government, it will be recalled, had pointed to government travel as another area of operations where spending cuts could be made. The Trudeau government met with some success early on, but after a few years spending on travel went back up. Figure 4 traces spending on travel in both current and constant dollars for a ten-year period from 1978 to 1987.

Still the Mulroney government has been successful in cutting the growth in spending in the operations of government and services to government. Spending in this category has grown less than growth in GDP and inflation. It was also successful in limiting the growth in spending in energy, transportation, recreation, culture and communications, and employment and training.

The impact of restraint, however, has been uneven. Some areas have grown faster than the GDP during the five-year period from 1984–5 to 1989–90. Based on status quo projections, aboriginal programs, agriculture, fisheries and oceans, foreign aid, and external affairs have grown faster than growth in GDP. Public debt charges, however, lead all areas with an increase of 55.5 per cent between 1984–5 and 1989–90, compared with a growth of 38.2 per cent in GDP. In short, the major impact of restraint has taken the form of squeezing operating and capital spending in departments and increasing cost recovery.[75]

Little program restructuring has occurred. Moreover, a number of programs that were cut back or frozen when the Mulroney government first came to power in 1984 have since been injected with new funds. For example, the government announced in 1984 that it would cut back its small-craft harbour programs. In 1988, it announced measures to revitalize the small-craft harbour programs. It plans to inject $85 million of new funds over three years and is also committed to maintaining an

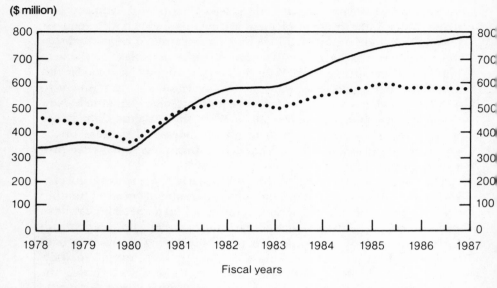

($ million)

Fiscal years

Solid line represents actual dollars
Broken line shows constant dollars
Based on CPI excluding energy

Figure 4
Travel expenditures for ten years, ending 31 March 1987
Source: Office of the Comptroller General

annual funding level of $70 million, an increase of 44 per cent over the existing level. In 1984, the government also froze all proposals for developing new national parks. A few years later, it announced plans to develop a new South Moresby National Park at a cost of $106 million to the federal Treasury. In November 1984 and May 1985, the government announced cuts in agricultural programs. Later, it announced a string of measures to assist farmers, particularly grain and oilseed producers. In 1986–7, $1 billion was allocated to the special grains program under the Western Grain Stabilization Act (WGSA). The following year another $1.1 billion was made available and it appears that special payments to WGSA to assist farmers in dealing with depressed grain prices will continue to be provided.[76]

After a few years of spending restraint, the Mulroney government also announced a series of costly new spending plans. In June 1987, it announced that $1.05 billion of new money would be available for the establishment of the Atlantic Canada Opportunities Agency. A few months later, $1.2 billion of new money was allocated to the Western Diversification Office (WDO). A year later it agreed to share the cost of a $1 billion special regional economic development initiative with Quebec. The government also announced a new seven-year National Strategy on Child Care, costing over $3 billion. The cost has since been revised upwards on several occasions. In early 1988, Prime Minister Mulroney stated that the government would be spending $1.3 billion on science and technology over five years. He also announced major new funding for space activities, following the 1986 speech from the throne reporting that a new Canadian space agency would be created. The government also approved a white paper on defence that guaranteed 2 per cent real growth in defence spending for a fifteen-year planning period.

The cost of some of these measures, including promised spending on child care, space activities, and science and technology, has yet to be built into the government's expenditure plans or the main estimates. Nevertheless spending has already started to shoot up after two years of restraint. Government spending in 1985–6 increased only 1.8 per cent over the previous year and 4.6 per cent in 1986–7 over 1985–6. However, by 1987–8, spending had climbed by 7.7 per cent over the previous year. Spending for 1988–9 is projected to increase by 5.5 per cent over 1987–8, but there are indications that actual spending for 1988–9 will be higher still. In 1985–6, the annual growth in spending was lower than the annual increase in inflation. However, the opposite is true for 1986–7, 1987–8, and 1988–9. Figure 4 compares annual growth in spending, gross domestic product, and inflation from 1980–1 to 1988–9.

The Mulroney government can argue, as it has on many occasions, that it reversed the annual growth in the deficit. However, apart from its first two years in office when spending cuts and restraint measures were actually implemented, a robust economy and increased taxation and revenues have contributed largely to the decline in the annual rate of growth in the deficit. Several new taxes have been introduced, and others have been increased. The minister of finance explained that some of these were specifically designed to bring down the deficit.[77] We will return to this point later in the study.

All in all, the guardians in the Mulroney government, after a strong start, were hardly any more successful in checking the growth in government spending, in challenging the status quo, and in restructuring government programs than were the guardians in the Trudeau government. The chapters that follow explain why spenders consistently have had the upper hand. They look not only at the spenders, their thinking and strategies, but also at the forces that fuel new spending.

PART III

The spenders

8

Ministers: Nothing succeeds like excess

Cabinet ministers sit at the apex of power in government. Especially when a majority government is in place, their collective authority to change existing policies, enact new programs, and abolish existing ones is virtually unrestricted. They can decide at a single cabinet meeting to abolish any number of programs and, if the prime minister so wishes, they can eliminate one or even several departments. In 1984 the short-lived Liberal government of John Turner, for example, abolished two ministries of state with the stroke of a pen. With non-statutory programs, cabinet also has effectively limitless power to increase or cut spending to whatever level it wishes. Even in the case of statutory programs, ministers can announce their decision to reduce spending and make their decisions stick.

However, before taking any such decisions, ministers must look in several directions at once. First, they must look to their own constituencies, their lifeline to cabinet and parliament. They must look to their party militants who provide some of the resources to fight elections. They must look to the government caucus to ensure that their own backbenchers will support them. They must look to provincial governments, for there are now few policy fields the federal government can occupy unilaterally. They must even look to other nations on certain issues to ensure that their actions do not bring strong objections from abroad. They must always look to the media and the polls to see if they still command public support. And they must look to their own departments to secure advice and support for their plans.

Little wonder then that many in Ottawa regard cabinet as a kind of blender where numerous political and economic considerations go in and policies and decisions somehow come out. To ensure that the blender works, ministers regularly put in sixteen-hour days. Long hours, however, do not deter members of parliament from wanting a place in cabinet. It is for most of them a prized possession and the reason they entered politics in the first place. If they are appointed to cabinet, there is every chance that they will be spenders rather than guardians – since virtually all ministers (even the finance minister) head departments that spend public funds.

But before they can make it to cabinet, they must usually first get elected to parliament. This chapter looks briefly at the politics of getting elected, the role ministers play in their departments, and how ministers influence government spending.

GETTING THERE

One former federal cabinet minister observed that 'in Canada, we have elections and commitments but no politics.'[1] By 'politics,' he meant policy debates – and many others have come to the same conclusion. Harold Clarke et al. have observed that 'a class-based definition of economic problems [has been] discouraged, partly because the political culture [is] attuned more to questions of national and cultural integration.'[2] For their part, political parties, 'rather than dividing the electorate among themselves along clear and stable lines of social cleavage, constantly compete for the same policy space and the same votes ... Voters are rarely presented with a clear choice between world views and the political projects that follow from them, but more commonly with appeals to narrow interests and proposals that amount to little more than short-term tinkering.'[3] As a result, party candidates at general elections and party members 'organize around leaders rather than around political principles and ideologies, and expect the leader to work out the multitude of compromises required for [the] party to enjoy electoral success.'[4] There is now a growing body of observers who argue that, on policy matters, political parties have – particularly in recent years – not performed well or even adequately.[5]

Though they have weak ideological roots, Canadian political parties do serve an important purpose. They 'act as giant personnel agencies for the recruitment and election of individuals to public office.'[6] It is rare indeed for someone to be elected to parliament as an independent or without being the official candidate of one of the three major political parties. The first step in winning a seat in the House of Commons, then, is securing a nomination. As the party's official candidate, one has the party's financial and human resources to assist in winning the constituency. The candidate must, however, promote the party's electoral platform in the constituency. Often, this poses little problem for candidates. Typically, the electoral platforms of all three parties avoid taking clear policy choices and all seek to win the 'same votes' by 'straddling' the political centre without losing their 'core supporters.' In Canada, it is as important for parties to appeal to non-committed voters as to their own core supporters, if the objective is to win the election. About two-thirds of Canadian voters have been described as 'flexible partisans' having limited 'durable' ties to any political party.[7]

New spending commitments are invariably made in all national campaigns since it is the spenders rather than the guardians who dominate strategy meetings where electoral platforms are put together. The guardians will have some influence only in an election campaign when the government is seeking a new mandate. But in the few instances where electoral campaign themes have been influenced by the guardians, their political parties have had limited success. For instance, the Clark government fell on a vote of no confidence after the minister of finance introduced his first budget calling for an 18 cent tax increase on gasoline and asking Canadians to accept 'short-term pain for long-term gain.' The deficit, he had argued, had to be brought under control. These became election issues and the government went down to defeat.[8]

Election campaigns usually give rise to new spending commitments without at the same time having the merits of ongoing programs fully debated. Among others, commitments were made by the winning party to child care in the 1984 election campaign, to the resources sector in 1980, to mortgage deductibility in 1979, to housing development in 1974, to the construction of new national parks in 1972, and to regional development in 1968.[9] These were all 'national' commitments designed to benefit all or most of Canada.

Election campaigns also give rise to regional commitments. All three parties have regional caucuses and election planning committees whose job it is to place their party in the most favourable light possible in their regions. Traditionally, this is done by committing the party to specific high-profile projects. Again, little effort is made to debate the most appropriate policy or set of policies to deal with perceived or real regional ills. And, again, in the absence of such a debate, a multitude of projects are held out. Examples abound. In 1984, the winning party promised new and stronger measures to develop the economy of Atlantic Canada; in 1980 the winning party promised new measures, including double-tracking rail lines, to develop the West; in 1979 the winning party promised a larger regional development department with a strong presence in three of the four major regions of the country; in the 1974 campaign the government pledged specific development measures for western Canada and a new agricultural policy, including larger cash advances and increased credit for young farmers; and in the 1972 campaign a 'blockbuster' commitment was made to Toronto, including plans for a new $30 million, eighty-acre waterfront park.[10] The list goes on.

There is yet a third level of commitment at the constituency level. There is never, for example, a lack of infrastructure projects to be financed, and an election campaign provides an opportunity for candidates to register their support. There are always ring roads for small urban areas, new community centres, new government offices, and so on. Typically candidates will also pledge to bring new economic activity and prosperity to their constituencies, if elected. If some federal activities in the constituency are rumoured to be threatened, candidates will inevitably pledge their determination to fight for their continuation.

Conversely, it is rare indeed for any candidate to suggest that a particular program, level of services, or a specific initiative in his or her constituency should be cut back. The same is true at the regional or even national levels where the party leadership will avoid identifying specific program cuts during an election campaign. A party leader may, as Brian Mulroney did during the 1984 campaign, call for a better control of government spending. When asked where cuts would be made, however, opposition parties invariably point to government overhead and the bureaucracy. Governments seeking re-election seldom talk about cutting back programs since they had every opportunity to do so while in power.

The result is that newly elected members of parliament arrive in Ottawa with a string of spending commitments for their constituencies. These are of course in addition to commitments their parties made at the national and regional levels. However, few possible cuts have been identified and virtually no debate of substance on policy has been engaged in. With an eye always on the next general election, MPs, especially those on the government side, continually pressure relevant line ministers and departments to deliver on their commitments. In piloting their spending proposals through the government approval process, those who are appointed cabinet ministers obviously have a distinct advantage.

There is now a great deal of literature on the practices of cabinet making in Canada, and there is no need to go over all the points here.[11] Suffice it to say that talent and experience are not the only criteria. Many other factors come into play, not least of which is the regional factor. All provinces are now 'entitled' to at least one representative in cabinet. Prince Edward Island, with only four MPs, is assured of one seat. Quebec has more cabinet ministers than any other province except Ontario, which still has the most. Subregions now also expect their place at the cabinet table. The Gaspé region, the Lac Saint-Jean area, northern Ontario, eastern Ontario, rural Alberta, and so on are now traditionally represented in cabinet. Even when a province fails to elect any government members to the House of Commons, the government usually turns to a senator from the province to sit in cabinet. Such was the case for three western provinces under the last Trudeau government and for Quebec under Clark's.

Ability then is not necessarily its own reward. Some government MPs may well be ideally suited for a particular portfolio but be overlooked for the appointment because of the need for a regional balance in cabinet.

BEING THERE

The *Toronto Star* reported that Canadian 'politicians don't fall from heaven. They are the folks next door.'[12] A cursory look at the background of cabinet ministers in 1988 reveals that seven of forty were in the teaching profession before they entered politics, ten practised law, and fourteen were in business. Few had any solid government experience. Thirteen had served briefly in the cabinet of the short-lived Clark administration, and two had some brief government experience as public servants. None, however, had served for any length of time in senior-level positions in government.

There is no special training required to be appointed to cabinet. About all that is required is a security check, which is now carried out on all possible cabinet appointees to see if any criminal charges are pending. Once appointed, officials from the Privy Council Office will brief new ministers. This briefing can cover a wide range of issues, including conflict of interest, the status of ministerial exempt staff, and the role of cabinet committees.

The day someone is appointed to cabinet, however, he or she inherits all the trappings of the office of the minister. A chauffered automobile is immediately made available and an exempt-staff budget is granted from which funds are available to hire at least half a dozen people with scarcely any restrictions on who can be hired. One exempt-staff position, that of chief of staff, is now a very senior position by the standards of the federal public service and commands a salary equivalent to that of an assistant deputy minister (the second most senior position in government). A minister also has a number of other privileges, including access to a government jet, departmental staff, and special briefings on virtually any public policy issue of interest.

Overnight, then, it is possible for a teacher, a small-town lawyer, or a small businessperson to be appointed to cabinet and be asked to direct the work of a large sprawling department with several thousand employees and a billion dollar budget. He or she will have little specific direction on what is expected and on the long-term direction of the department. The prime minister does send out a mandate letter to all ministers appointed to a new department, but these are usually vague and hardly a guide for action.

In being named to the cabinet, a minister is also asked to work with his cabinet colleagues as a team to manage the government. This in itself is no easy task. The operations of the federal government are larger than for the top twenty Canadian companies combined. Government operations and its machinery, as we saw in earlier chapters, are complex. Guiding a policy or a program change through the machinery is no small achievement. It takes knowledge, skill, and determination on the part of the minister and, above all, cooperation from the department.

Shortly after taking the oath of office, ministers meet their deputy ministers and other senior department officials. They will be given several briefing books and offered numerous oral briefings on the work of the department. The officials will be highly educated and extremely well versed in the operations of government – likely with some twenty years experience in government, including some in central agencies.[13] None of these officials, however, has been or will be appointed by the minister. The deputy minister is appointed by the prime minister on the advice of the clerk of the Privy Council and other officials are appointed by the Public Service Commission. Some of the more senior ministers in any government *may* be consulted on the choice of their deputies, as were Marc Lalonde and Allan MacEachen by Trudeau, and Don Mazankowski by Mulroney. Similarly, deputy ministers can only be removed or transferred by the prime minister on the advice of the clerk of the Privy Council. It is not at all uncommon to have several ministers at any one time trying to change deputy ministers, but few are successful.[14]

Little wonder then that a minister described his feelings when he was first appointed to cabinet in this fashion: 'It's like I was suddenly landed on the top deck of an ocean liner and told that the ship was my responsibility. When I turned to the captain [i.e., deputy minister], I was told that he was appointed there by someone else and any decision to remove him would be made elsewhere. When I turned to others on the ship, I soon found out that they all report through the deputy minister, owe their allegiance to him and, more importantly, their future promotions. When I asked for a change in the ship's course, the ship just kept on going on the same course.'[15] Thus, it would be foolhardy for ministers to assume that they could walk into their departments and reorient substantially their policies and programs. There are several reasons for this. For one thing, ministers are soon overwhelmed by the demands of cabinet, parliament, caucus, their constituencies, interest groups, and their own staffs so that little time is left for departmental matters. A former clerk of the Privy Council warned cabinet ministers that, 'having many roles, you will be under constant and unremitting pressure to allocate some of your time to this or that worthy endeavour. They [ministers] must establish priorities and the time frame within which they want to accomplish them and allocate their time accordingly. If they don't do this, and do it well, they will be lost.'[16] He added that ministers work between seventy and eighty hours a week but that 'surveys indicate that they often have only three hours a week to spend with their Deputy Ministers.'[17]

However, usually the only hope for a minister to influence the ongoing policies and programs of the department is to rely on departmental officials. Ministers have been bluntly told that 'on a more practical level, you simply do not have the time to have problems with your Deputy Minister.'[18] Senior departmental officials not only have the expertise but they also prepare the groundwork – including cabinet documents for changing policies and programs – and, in the end, it is they who must implement policy decisions. The minister is then at the head of an organization staffed by permanent officials who are very knowledgeable and make the policy and decision-making process work. Often, however, 'the reverse side ... is the conviction that a lifetime of service and study has given them insights that transcend the contained and shallow-rooted views of political appointees.'[19] Anyone with even a cursory knowledge of how Ottawa decides will know that considerable tension can and does exist between ministers and officials.

There are a variety of methods that can be used to circumvent the wishes and the policy directions of a minister. A former senior official who occupied a number of positions in the federal government explains: 'Bureaucracy by its nature includes a tendency to want to make the decision itself, to want to have things go its way. This tendency is greater in times of big government ... The usurpation of the politician's authority by the bureaucracy is done in countless ways: by providing incomplete information, by precooking among officials, by playing ministers off against one another, by controlling process, by introducing delays or suddenly imposing deadlines, and so on and on.'[20]

In short, the size and complexity of the federal bureaucracy has reached the point where often only insiders can understand the policy-making process, let alone master it. Heclo and Wildavsky, in their detailed study of British politics and government, commented that 'Ministers fail to become more involved [in the policy-making process] because civil servants prefer it that way.'[21] The same is also true for the Canadian government. With few exceptions, ministers are viewed as short-term appointees, short on ideas, and short on appreciation for the department's long-term interests.[22] One senior deputy minister explained: 'Most ministers are not as bright as the officials they are leading ... A minister in Canada is typically a former small businessman or a walk-up lawyer or a farmer; he or she has little or no executive experience and little by way of shared values with a department.'[23]

The inability of ministers to redirect departmental policies and programs may be even more pronounced in Canada than elsewhere. We saw that Canadian political parties are 'organized around leaders rather than around political principles and ideologies.' Certainly, Canada's two major political parties have no set posture and ideology from which to assess government policies, programs, and proposals for new initiatives. The Progressive Conservatives, who are said to favour less government intervention in the economy than do the Liberals, were the party that launched the most ambitious and costly government programs ever undertaken to promote economic development in western Canada, northern Ontario, Quebec, and Atlantic Canada. Thus, senior public servants can well argue that they are never certain precisely what it is the party in power wants to accomplish and where it stands on a host of public policy issues. With little cohesion or firm direction coming from cabinet, public servants are left to operate in a vacuum from which they inevitably will influence policy and program decisions. In the absence of strong, sustained, and clear political direction, government program managers will quite naturally push for their areas of concern. They may well want to carry out clear-cut political instructions with loyalty, but the instructions are rarely clear-cut.

This is not to suggest that ministers are without power and influence in Ottawa. Some veteran ministers in the Trudeau government, for example, had operated at their level longer than any deputy ministers had at theirs. They had as good a knowledge of 'how the system operates' and 'how to make things happen' as anyone. Still, while ministers always have the power to say *no* to their department and to refuse to sign their proposals, including cabinet documents, some are quite happy to let their departments carry on with their work. They are simply not prepared to 'take on their officials' and 'to look their deputy minister eyeball-to-eyeball and have the confidence to say that they may have been doing things no longer appropriate.'[24]

In the absence of political ideology to guide the work of cabinet and the thinking of ministers, one must look at what it is that motivates ministers. Their individual personalities and how they relate to their departments are important. It is of course not possible to divide all ministers neatly into specific groups according to type of personality and motivation. Obviously, various forces enter into play, all of which cannot possibly be categorized. As well, a minister who plays a relatively passive role in one department may become much more involved if appointed to another whose policies are of greater personal interest.

Still, it is possible to group most ministers under four broad categories: *status*, *mission*, *policy*, and *process* participants.[25] Some ministers can be found in two or more categories: for instance, a minister generally considered a mission participant can also be seen by departmental officials as a status participant. With most, however, it is possible to discern a dominant characteristic.

To department officials, the status participants are, paradoxically, the least troublesome ministers and the most difficult to please. All ministers, of course, know the importance of good press. As Maurice Lamontagne once observed: 'If a minister enjoys a good press, he will be envied and respected by his colleagues. If he has no press, he has no future.'[26] Status participants, however, take public visibility to the extreme. They are the least troublesome ministers in that they are never a threat to the department's A base and programs, rarely questioning ongoing policies and programs. If anything, they are likely to encourage the department to do more of what it does, if only to capture attention.

Their main preoccupation is visibility. One senior official explained: 'All my minister really cares about is getting good press. If we could orchestrate things so that his photo appears in a favourable light on the front page of the *Globe and Mail* and "The National" once a month, then we would have absolutely no problem with him.'[27] Thus the focus is almost always on appearances and, from a public policy perspective, the superficial. The emphasis of status ministers is not on what they might do in government or what they might achieve, but on how they appear to the electorate and to their colleagues.

Officials find these ministers difficult to please because they are never completely satisfied with the department's ability to sell itself, its policies, and, by extension, its minister. Status participants and their staff are continually on the prowl in the department in search of new initiatives to announce. If Treasury Board approval is required, they will happily take up the challenge and lobby their colleagues on the board. They will volunteer to make announcements and give speeches.

Status participant ministers have an obvious impact on spending. They can never be counted upon, however, to support cuts in spending or in the level of service. They may in a general discussion in cabinet or in caucus voice their support for controlling spending, but they will shy away from discussing specific program cuts. They will also strongly oppose any suggestions that their own programs should be cut or even reduced. In short, they only want to be the bearer of good news.

The personality of status participant ministers also usually inhibits their challenging departmental policies and programs. Generally, they will try to avoid confrontations with their own staff, their cabinet colleagues, or even their departments. They will not want to jeopardize any opportunities to be cast in a favourable public light. A long-running debate with the department over policies and programs (over which they usually have only a limited interest in any event) could well divert attention away from initiatives involving the media and public relations.

Mission participants make quite different cabinet ministers. They will certainly seek a favourable press, like all politicians, but that is not their all-consuming purpose. They bring to the cabinet table strongly held views and they usually do not avoid confrontation if their views are challenged. While these views are not always politically or ideologically inspired, they do 'seek to serve a cause' which is brought to the cabinet table. It is widely known, for example, in parliament, in cabinet, and in the public service that Jake Epp, Brian Mulroney's minister of health and welfare, holds strong religious views. It can be assumed that he will take a strong position on moral issues coming before cabinet, such as abortion, or even matters involving integrity in government, such as procurement policies.

Mission participants can have an important impact on government spending. They are particularly tenacious in pushing their causes or their point of view and they are likely to keep trying long after other ministers would have given up. Rarely, however, does their impact reduce spending.

To be sure, there can be mission participants in both the spenders' and the guardians' camps. Those in the latter camp, however, will find the going difficult. Mission participants who regard cuts in government spending as their principal reason for being in politics had better hope that they will be appointed to either Finance or the Treasury Board. In these portfolios, they will have a specific place in cabinet, together with bureaucratic support to advance their views. But there are only two such positions in cabinet, and now, even they have a spending function which both ministers are expected to support.

Mission participants seeking to reduce the role of government but heading spending departments face a formidable challenge and a strong test to their tenacity. Their departments will inevitably resist cuts to their own programs or organization. If the minister should persist, officials may well, as mentioned above, attempt to undermine political direction by 'providing incomplete information, by precooking among officials, by playing ministers off against one another ... '[28] They will also attempt to delay any discussions with their ministers if departmental programs are threatened. With the many other demands on ministers' time, this is usually not difficult. Officials also know full well that a minister's stay in a department is usually limited. General elections, but especially cabinet shuffles, ensure that ministers are changed frequently. In addition, if they are unable to submit their own departmental programs to a thorough review for possible cuts, there is little hope that they will have much of an impact on the programs of other departments.

Mission participants who have been successful in the past have been spenders. Great causes usually cost money. They are also the ministers who held the same portfolios for a long time. Eugene Whelan, Roméo LeBlanc, and Monique Bégin were all mission participants in the Trudeau administration, as was John Wise in the Mulroney government. Whalen, LeBlanc, and Wise continually pushed the interests of farmers and fishermen and Bégin those of the elderly and the disadvantaged beyond what senior government officials would consider 'reasonable limits.' Mission participants are insistent in cabinet discussions and offer little room for compromise. In championing their causes, they are usually impelled by their forcefulness into conflict with some of their colleagues – at times with other mission participants holding diametrically opposed views, such as the guardians.

Mission participants, however, often have a strong standing in cabinet and within their own political party. Thus, when they speak in cabinet or in political strategy meetings, they are listened to carefully. Inevitably, mission participants will have little concern for the work of the guardians. In fact, they are likely to regard guardians as uncaring, insensitive, politically naive, and captive of the country's business establishment. Mission participants in spending departments are also likely to support each other's initiatives. Thus, it is more difficult for the guardians to keep spending in check when confronting several determined and collaborating spenders rather than one. It also makes the situation difficult for the prime minister. He knows that he must support his minister of finance in cabinet but he also knows that mission participants have a political following in the party and with the electorate, and he must be careful not to be seen to offend their client groups. At times, he must give in on some measures and the minister of finance also has to know when the prime minister will yield since, if he is to remain effective, he cannot often afford to go to war and lose.

Policy participants are rarely numerous in cabinet and they usually have limited success. One former deputy minister explained: 'My experience as often as not was that the minister had no view (on policy).'[29] The few real policy participants in cabinet, however, profess to be in politics precisely to influence and shape public policies. These ministers usually welcome long policy debates with their officials. They often have a specific area of expertise and come to office equipped with more than the generalities of their own party election platforms. This is not to suggest, however, that their having a specific field of interest will ensure their even making it to cabinet, let alone being appointed to the post for which they are best suited. Don Johnston, one of Trudeau's ministers, for example, would fall under the policy participant category. He has some definite policy views and is an expert in tax policy. He was never, however, appointed minister of finance or even of national revenue.

There are other reasons why policy participants have limited success.

Having an interest and even some expertise in public policy is one thing. Knowing how the policy process works is quite another. The policy process and the machinery of government are now fields of specialization in their own right. It usually takes several years for permanent government officials to understand them fully and to feel at ease working in them. The result is that most ministers must rely on their own departmental officials to help them through the maze. Officials are likely to argue that single ministers cannot possibly make policy or launch major initiatives on their own and will seek to dissuade them from getting too far ahead of their colleagues or the 'process' on any policy issue, all the while arguing that it is in their own interest not to forge ahead without political and bureaucratic support. Certainly one would be hard pressed to identify many major federal policy initiatives in recent years that were inspired by a single minister. The major policy revisions in fisheries, in regional and industrial development, in defence, among other areas, were not inspired by a single minister, but were the result of group efforts, often involving task forces, outside consultants, and provincial governments.

Those policy participants who have been cabinet ministers and who have later written about their experiences often report their disenchantment with the deep frustration over their inability to change policy.[30] They point to officials in the Prime Minister's Office, the Privy Council Office, Finance, and elsewhere as inhibiting their efforts to introduce real change. Those who claim some success report that they had to go through extraordinary lengths to bypass the formal policy process.[31]

The most successful and the most numerous cabinet ministers are (for want of a better term) the process participants. They rarely question policy or the policy process itself. Their purpose is to make deals for a designated clientele. They usually understand how parliament works, enjoy parliamentary jostling, get along well with most of their colleagues, and take particular delight in striking deals. They are often politically partisan and willing to help out one of their own who might be in some difficulty in his or her constituency.

Policy content, political ideology, government organization, management issues – and even government programs themselves – are all of limited interest to the process participants. The notion that government spending should be reduced may make for an interesting discussion in cabinet, but it holds little real appeal. Projects are what matters and the more the better. They will look to their own departments to come up with specific projects for their own ridings or for the regions for which they are responsible. Process participants have no interest in challenging their departmental policies and officials, generally viewing officials as allies in getting their projects through the approval process. They will have difficulty with their officials only if the latter are uncooperative in putting deals together. Process participants are generally easy-going extroverts. Nothing pleases them more than having a project to announce at the end of the week. Like mission participants, process participants will, when possible, collaborate with each other and seek to strike alliances among themselves. Such alliances, however, are never as solid as they are between mission participants, in part because they do not relate to a fundamental purpose as do those of mission participants.

Still, they are clearly on the side of spenders. When the minister of finance briefs P & P or full cabinet on the fiscal plan, it is the process participants who will speak about the political importance of spending, particularly in selected ridings. Some departments are particularly well suited to process participants: Public Works, Employment and Immigration, Fisheries and Oceans, Supply and Services, Agriculture, Secretary of State, and the regional development agencies provide ample opportunities for spending.

Process participants are particularly popular with government backbenchers. They are the ones turned to for help on a particular project. It is rare to see a government backbencher not having at least one riding project for which he or she is lobbying ministers hard. As one minister explains:

Backbenchers always have what I call a do-or-die project. They committed themselves in the election campaign to high-profile projects and when elected they must deliver or, in their opinion and that of their chief political organizers, they will be defeated at the next election. They usually come to us with this line of argument – look, I need this project very, very badly. Get me this one and I will not be back for more. They are also likely to argue that the project is not that expensive and insist that the government blows a hell of lot more money every day on worse projects. If I deliver on a project, the backbencher is very grateful and will tell his colleagues what a great guy I am. If I don't, well I am dismissed as someone who can't deliver.[32]

The minister went on to explain that government backbenchers are often able to determine why their projects are not getting approved. 'If a minister stands in the way, he will likely get a barrage of criticism from the MPs and, if the project is big enough, from the regional caucus.

Often someone in the department is blamed and then the minister is earmarked as one who is unable to control his bureaucrats.'[33]

It is possible to define other types of ministers or participants. For instance, some are labelled 'departmental participants' because after only a few weeks in a department they begin to espouse its long-standing policy lines. They suffer from 'departmentalitis' because of their preoccupation with their own department to the exclusion of all other considerations, including the fortunes of their political party, their cabinet colleagues, and government backbenchers. Ministers suffering from departmentalitis are usually convinced that, by following departmental advice, they will seldom get themselves in political difficulty, since most publicized political problems stem from ministers dismissing advice from their officials. Examples abound and include 'the tuna affair,' Mirabel land deals, Nova Scotia lobster fishing licences, the West Edmonton mall project. Thus, ministers suffering from departmentalitis will ruthlessly pursue their department's interest. This, too, costs money, since it is never in a department's interest to cut its programs or budget. Departmentalitis, however, has never been widespread in Ottawa, particularly in recent years. The level of distrust between ministers and permanent officials has increased notably, and ministers now often seek advice from their own staff and elsewhere before promoting the department's position. In any event, ministers suffering from departmentalitis are quickly spotted by their colleagues and they will find it more difficult to be heard in cabinet.

Virtually all federal departments are organized along sectoral lines, such as fisheries or agriculture, whereas political institutions are organized along regional lines. Thus, ministers are less and less willing to identify themselves with sectoral interests. In fact, if there is one thing that transcends personalities and types of participants, it is the regional factor. Politicians are elected to represent a region, not a sector. Given Canada's vast geography, its uneven economic development, and the lack of strong political ideologies or even policy preferences in our political parties, the regional factor is perhaps more important in Canadian politics than in any other country. As Richard Simeon writes: 'Regional divisions ... are a continuing threat through Canadian history ... Regional jealousies [are now being] fanned by federal grants and subsidies seem to favour one region over another ... regional tensions are built into the Canadian political economy and institutional structure; they, along with region, will remain central problems for governance in the future.'[34]

Certainly, regionalism is a main motivating force for all types of participants, with the possible exception of those afflicted with departmentalitis. Regional concerns are central to process participants. The deals they seek to strike are invariably for the benefit of their own ridings, or of their party colleagues. Status participants are more often motivated by the desire to be seen to be doing things for their regions rather than for economic sectors or specific client groups. For one thing, it is easier to target one's efforts for the benefit of a specific region than for a client group. For another, the local media will give more prominence to a politician bringing projects to the region than to a national constituency. Finally, status participants know full well that it is the voters in their own riding who in the end will decide whether they return to parliament or not. Even mission participants are often motivated by regional concerns. Roméo LeBlanc admits: 'Although I was fisheries' minister, I did not consider that my interest in New Brunswick was limited to fish and fishing matters only. In fact, I pushed my regional role as hard as I could.'[35]

As noted earlier, regional cabinet ministers are now a central part of the policy-making process in Ottawa. As Herman Bakvis explains, 'in earlier times, influencing appointments to boards and commissions and the location of wharves and post offices continued to be fair game; but it was soon discovered, larger objects such as aircraft maintenance hangars or factories relocating under the Regional Development Incentives Act (RDIA) incentive programs, could also be levered into position, providing one had the appropriate fulcrum.' He goes on to define regional representation in cabinet as 'obtaining as many visible projects as possible for their particular region. Personal ambition and the wish to do things for one's region, to help redress the economic imbalances within confederation, merge into one. In this respect, it demonstrates that federal leaders can be just as regionally centered, perhaps even parochial, if not more so, as their provincial counterparts.'[36]

The place of regionalism and the role of regional ministers in federal government spending have not received the attention they deserve in the public policy literature in Canada. Some have even questioned the relevance of the limited importance we have attached to these. Donald Smiley, for one, argues that the cabinet minister's role in 'aggregating and articulating the interest specific to their provinces and regions ... has been vastly diminished.'[37]

Anyone who has attended a cabinet or cabinet committee meeting – particularly the Economic Development Committee – knows full well that the clash of regional interests dominates the discussion. He also knows that regional ministers are as determined as are provincial premiers in advancing the case for their provinces. Even conflicts over language, which can be very difficult, do not compare in intensity with regional conflicts over economic development and the competition for new projects. They are also usually very difficult for the prime minister to manage politically. Brian Mulroney did away with the designation of 'regional ministers' in the hope that it would attenuate regional tensions in his cabinet when he first came to power, only to reinstate it a few years later. A number of regional issues debated in both Liberal and Conservative cabinets have spilled over into the public area. The rivalries between Quebec and Ontario over building the F-18 aircraft, Quebec and Manitoba over its maintenance contract, Ontario and Quebec over new automotive plants, Quebec and New Brunswick over a frigate contract, and Ontario and the Atlantic and western regions over the level of DRIE funding for industrial development are some examples.

In the early 1980s, Prime Minister Trudeau asked officials in the PCO and the FPRO to consider new measures to 'manage regional tensions' within the government because there was a concern that they were becoming as unmanageable within cabinet as they were at the federal-provincial conference table. For instance, DREE was perceived by both Atlantic and western ministers as weak and ineffective. 'The best DREE could ever do for us,' explained one senior Atlantic minister at the time, 'was to provide us with a penalty shot from time to time. Most of the scoring was taking place in Ontario and Quebec.'[38]

DREE was disbanded and a new organization for economic development – MSERD–was established. Provincial offices were set up and headed by senior public servants. This office was designed to do more than negotiate federal-provincial economic development agreements and manage regional development programs as the provincial DREE office had done. The MSERD office was being asked to provide regional intelligence, to develop federal economic development strategies for the provinces, and to coordinate federal development efforts. In addition, the 'regional minister' was being asked to play a lead role on behalf of the provinces in the new organization and the senior official in the province 'became a quasi deputy minister working for this [the regional] minister.'[39] The result was that even relatively weak regional ministers gained influence.[40] DREE had never operated like this in the past. Provincial and regional DREE offices had reported to the deputy minister who in turn had reported to the minister. Some consultation had taken place between the regional minister and the head of the local DREE office, but the arrangements were never fully satisfactory. Regional ministers often argued that local DREE offices were a lot closer to provincial premiers and provincial governments than to them.[41] It thus marked for the first time ever that regional ministers had direct access to permanent officials whose purpose was to promote the interests of their provinces. Officials in sectoral departments take a strictly sectoral perspective and can offer only limited assistance to their ministers in promoting regional interests. Fisheries officials, for example, have no expertise in regional matters. As Peter Aucoin explains, 'in the organizational design of the portfolio and departmental structures of the government of Canada, organization by place has not assumed great importance as a design criterion. Rather, portfolios and departments have been structured primarily on the basis of purposes, persons and processes.'[42] Permanent officials, unlike politicians, relate to purposes and economic sectors.

Under the new decentralized central agency, regional ministers could compete head to head with provincial premiers. All premiers have economic advisers in their own central agencies who can advise them on the health of the provincial economy and provide all kinds of 'facts and figures' to show that the province is not receiving its fair share of federal spending. Regional federal ministers now also had such advisers and all sought to make the most of it. It did not take long for central agency officials left in Ottawa to wonder if what they had created was not worse than what it had replaced. Senior officials who had been perfectly sensible working in sectoral departments in Ottawa were now 'going native' in the regions, arming regional ministers not simply with new spending measures but with arguments suggesting that their province was being short-changed by the federal government.[43]

Regional ministers and even those with no regional responsibilities welcomed the change: mission participants who made the development of their province their major cause now had allies in the bureaucracy; status participants could turn to the office to generate new announcements; process participants had an agency which could support new projects and more deals; and policy participants had a place to turn to for position papers and for new economic development strategies. Some of Trudeau's ministers, notably Lloyd Axworthy, Marc Lalonde, Roméo LeBlanc, Pierre De Bané, and Allan J. MacEachen, proved particularly adroit at working with the new organization and in bringing new federal spending to their regions.

When John Turner came to power, he immediately abolished MSERD on the advice of central agency officials. Nor was it reinstated by Brian Mulroney when he assumed power after defeating the short-lived Turner government. The same officials who had urged Turner to rethink MSERD were not about to recommend to Mulroney that it be reinstituted. Mulroney, however, quickly concluded that he had to do something new on the regional front. The economy of central Canada was buoyant, while those of the West and Atlantic Canada were slow to come out of the 1982 recession. While the Mulroney guardians – Wilson, and de Cotret, both from central Canada – were insisting on spending cuts, leading members of the western and the Atlantic caucus were reporting to the prime minister how difficult things were economically and, by extension, politically in their regions.

To the dismay of some senior federal government officials, Mulroney went outside the bureaucracy for advice on possible new measures for the regions. He subsequently unveiled a new organization for promoting economic development in Atlantic Canada and later announced a similar agency for western Canada. Both agencies, as we have seen, would spend over $1 billion of new money. Another economic development agency was announced for northern Ontario and later a special regional development fund was set up for Quebec.

The Atlantic and western agencies represent a major innovation in Canadian public administration. Both are headed by senior deputy ministers, both have headquarters outside of Ottawa, and both have been given considerable autonomy and decision-making authority to make and implement plans without reference to central agencies in Ottawa. Ministers from both regions are consulted regularly in the operations of the agencies. Both agencies are 'organizations by place' and, again, regional ministers have access to officials whose purpose is to promote the development of their regions rather than an economic sector. The agencies and the regional development fund have also proved attractive to the status, mission, process, and policy participants.

The new money for the agencies and the regional development fund only tell part of the story. DRIE's reference level and existing federal-provincial economic development agreements for each province have also been transferred to the agencies. Some departments also allocate special reserves or spending to programs with a strong regional appeal. Examples range from the small crafts and harbours programs in Fisheries and Oceans, to special employment creation measures in Employment and Immigration, to funding for a host of associations and special programs in the Department of Secretary of State.

Many officials, especially those in Finance and central agencies, consider it impossible to satisfy the appetite of ministers for regional projects – regardless of the political party they represent. As far as they are concerned, the cabinet table is the market-place where ministers compete to win projects for their constituencies or regions. 'Like successful business people,' explained one senior official, 'they are never content to sit on the profits they have realized. They always come back for more.'[44]

Some ministers are particularly skilful at getting projects for their regions. It is well known, for example, that Allan J. MacEachen was a master at the trade, 'collecting IOUs for his adroit handling of the Commons during his stint as House Leader, ensuring that there was no dissent in the Maritime caucus and carefully identifying and then stalking the desired object, whether it be an oil refinery or a heavy water plant.'[45] Roméo LeBlanc, who knew how to marshal his provincial caucus to press other cabinet ministers for projects for New Brunswick, provides another example.[46] LeBlanc also made full use of his departmental programs in Fisheries and Oceans, Public Works, and CMHC as bargaining chits to negotiate new projects for his constituency and his region.

The result is that some regions are now blessed with numerous projects, financed by federal funds. Winnipeg, for example, received through the efforts of Lloyd Axworthy a high-profile core area initiative designed to redevelop the downtown area. Funding was initially secured from DREE, but more money from MSERD, Public Works, and Air Canada was later added. Montreal has received funding for a host of projects, including office buildings, water and sewage treatment plants, and special federal industrial incentives programs. Such projects have not been limited to major urban areas. Some rural constituencies have received marinas for pleasure-boat owners, new four-lane highways, golf courses, special community buildings, and so on, all financed at least in part by the federal treasury.[47] Most regional ministers will readily admit that they do not hold back when it comes to projects for their own ridings. When asked if he may not well have gone overboard with costly projects for his own constituency, one regional minister responded:

No doubt, I went for the Cadillac model instead of the Volkswagen model in the case of the golf course, the marina, the highways, the bridges, and so on. Yes, I had some second thoughts about the cost of it all. But that second thought lasted for all of five seconds. All you have to do is sit at the cabinet table and watch ministers from Toronto, Ottawa, and Montreal grab everything that goes by. If I went for the Cadillac model, they went for the Rolls Royce model. Compare, for example, what I did for my riding to what the National Capital Commission does for Ottawa every year. A piece of road in the Gatineau park and recreational facilities for Ottawans is no more justifiable or rational than they are for my own riding. I saw that whenever support for the party in Toronto dropped two points it sent Toronto ministers running around everywhere for new projects. I made sure that my region would get its share of federal spending. And you know, when I look at what other regions got, I am convinced that I could have done more. If Toronto ministers couldn't show restraint surely you don't expect me to do so.[48]

In effect, ministers practise the art of grabbing at whatever they can, believing that others will take the opportunity if they do not.

Strong regional ministers with the reputation of being able to deliver for their regions usually gain influence in cabinet. In turn, they are usually able to secure for themselves a strong political base at home. As Richard French explained, a strong political base and influence in cabinet go hand in hand.[49] This, obviously, is not lost on ministers. Strong regional ministers are invariably invited to sit on the powerful Priorities and Planning Committee and they are usually invited to play a key role in planning the election campaign. Provincial premiers quickly sense if their federal regional ministers have clout and are able to deliver for their provinces. If they have such power, then the premiers and their ministers will show some deference when they come calling in Ottawa.

STAYING THERE

Strong regional ministers have shown a remarkable staying power. Allan J. MacEachen was first elected to parliament in 1953 and re-elected in every election from 1962 until he decided not to run again in 1984. A number of regional ministers from the Trudeau era also managed to withstand the strong Mulroney tide in 1984. Bill Rompkey who, as regional minister for Newfoundland, was able to bring to his own riding a special economic development plan – the coastal Labrador subsidiary agreement at a cost of $39 million – was re-elected.[50] André Ouellet from Montreal won his seat again, as did Lloyd Axworthy, the only Liberal elected in western Canada in that election. Herb Gray, Ontario's regional minister in the last Trudeau government, also won his own riding. Though Roméo LeBlanc chose not to run again, his riding was the only one in New Brunswick that still voted Liberal in 1984.

Successful ministers, particularly strong regional ministers, remain active in their constituencies, knowing full well that they can be MPs without being a minister but cannot be ministers without being MPs. Ministers can lose their seats at the cabinet table in three ways: they can resign because of a policy difference; they can be moved in a cabinet shuffle; or they can lose their seats at election time.

It is rare indeed for a federal cabinet minister to resign over a policy difference. Suzanne Blais Grenier reportedly resigned in 1985 over her government's unwillingness to do more for Montreal. But it was widely rumoured in Ottawa that Prime Minister Mulroney had been on the verge of asking for her resignation for various reasons, including an expensive trip to Europe apparently unrelated to her work. In any event, in Canada, it is better to resign because you are standing up for your region, as did Grenier, than over a policy issue. Other resignations over the past twenty years include those of James Richardson and Jean Marchand, both over the Liberal government's language policy, and Eric Kierans and Paul Hellyer because of major policy disagreements on housing and the economy. In the case of Hellyer, however, it has been suggested that his resignation had less to do with policy than with his losing the party leadership to Pierre Trudeau. Other ministers who have resigned over the past twenty years, such as Donald Macdonald, have done so simply because they wanted to go on to another career.

Policy then has claimed few ministerial casualties. In a virtually non-ideological political arena such as Canada, where federal election campaigns are fought with few genuine policy debates, ministers who claim to have major policy differences with their cabinet colleagues are regarded more as troublemakers, incapable of loyalty, than as serious public policy actors. Ministers who do resign over policy are usually quickly forgotten and rarely make a successful political comeback. In Canada, 'resignations from our federal Cabinet rarely make a big blip on the political screen.'[51]

It is much more frequent to see a minister being asked to resign or dropped from cabinet in a shuffle because of poor performance. In the first instance, the prime minister is usually told that the media are onto a serious wrongdoing. The prime minister calls in the minister concerned, confronts him or her with the case put together by the Prime Minister's Office, and suggests that resignation would be appropriate.

In the second, a minister may be dropped from cabinet because he or she consistently stumbles in question period in the House or with the media. Ministers are never, however, asked to step aside because the prime minister senses that their policy preferences diverge from those of their cabinet colleagues or because they have overcommitted their departmental budgets or made spending commitments in a region. The departments of Regional Industrial Expansion and Indian and Northern Development, as we saw earlier, both overcommitted their budgets in recent years. No minister – or for that matter, deputy minister – was asked to step down. It is also unheard of for a minister to be dropped for fighting for his or her region and constituency, even though committing the government to too much new spending.

The greatest potential for ministerial casualties is at election time. Ministers, of course, know this. As one put it, 'the constituency is where the rubber meets the road.' He went on to report that 'my constituents were singularly unimpressed with my exotic trips abroad or any brilliant paper I might have tabled in the House. Most of them had trouble going beyond 100 miles from where they live. They may read about your accomplishments abroad or in government with some interest but they do not think that it has much to do with them.'[52] Ministers themselves also tend to identify what they can do for their constituency or for 'back home' as their most important goal. As one minister explained: 'When I am done with this game, I would like to be able to sit back on the veranda of my house back home with my grandchildren and tell them what I was able to accomplish for their community.'[53] Ministers, one senior official contends, 'are always on the lookout for things they can be remembered for after they have left politics. They are rarely satisfied with what they get and invariably report that they are going to run again to try one more time. They keep coming back for more things to be remembered for and it keeps on costing more and more money.'[54] At times, this is even formalized in the policy-making process. A priorities-setting exercise held in the mid-1970s by officials from the Privy Council and Prime Minister's offices posed two questions to all ministers: 'What does the government have to do during its mandate in order to win the next election? and what do you want to be remembered for having done should the government lose the next election?'[55] Such questions invariably bring suggestions for new spending and rarely elicit proposals for cuts.

Serious policy debates, particularly in the economic field, hold little potential for electoral success in Canada. Given the country's regional economic and social diversities, a wide-ranging debate on the role of government in society would hold too many minefields for ministers, and even for most MPS. It would, for instance, be political suicide for a senior cabinet minister to state in the House of Commons that government should allow market forces and outmigration to resolve Canada's regional problems. Imagine, if you will, the howls of outrage from all three political parties representing Atlantic, and much of rural, Canada.

In short, electoral success in Canada requires government spending. Ministers are regarded as strong only if they can deliver projects for their regions. Prime Minister Mulroney, for one, quickly discovered this and declared in his first campaign for parliament in a Nova Scotia by-election that 'when it comes to government largesse in Central Nova, I will make Allan J. MacEachen look like a schoolboy.'[56] A senior and long-serving minister in the Trudeau cabinet summed up his view of Canadian political life in this fashion: 'In politics the only thing that succeeds is success and success is measured in what you deliver first to your own riding and second to your region. If you can't get elected in your own riding and help your colleagues in your region you are just whistling in the wind. It is that simple.'[57] It also appears that ministers can never do too much for their regions. For instance, when Gerald Merrithew went to his riding to announce that Saint John had been awarded a contract to build new frigates for the navy, someone in the audience shouted, 'Way to go Gerry, now go get us the nuclear submarines.' The comment was widely applauded.[58]

9

Departments: On the inside looking in

There are over eighty federal government departments and agencies in Canada. They vary considerably in size, from the Department of National Defence with 37,000 civilian employees to a small agency employing a dozen or so. They all have a distinct mandate and clientele. The prime minister holds the power to initiate change, to revise their respective mandates and roles, and even to transfer a program from one department to another. There has been, however, remarkable stability over the years, with few departments being abolished without another being created to take its place. The few exceptions over the past two decades include the ministries of State for Urban Affairs, for Economic and Regional Development, and for Social Development.

A new department can now only be established by an act of parliament. Typically, however, the legislation setting up a department is brief and by design its mandate is defined in a broad fashion, the argument being that in the modern era departments must have flexibility to respond to changing socio-economic conditions. No longer is it possible to predict problems and situations that may crop up within six months, let alone a few years down the road. If the legislation is restrictive, the department will be unable to deal with unanticipated issues. Going back to parliament to amend its enabling legislation is not an option, given the crowded legislative agenda.

Government departments have been classified in various fashions.[1] The most widely employed divides them in terms of traditional horizontal coordinative portfolios (Finance, External Affairs), junior horizontal coordinative portfolios (Ministry of State for Youth, Forestry, Mines, etc.), administrative coordinative portfolios (Revenue Canada, Public Works), and line, or vertical, constituency portfolios (Agriculture, Fisheries and Oceans, National Defence). The latter are the big spenders for they deliver programs to client groups – in fact, they account for the bulk of federal government spending. Still, all departments have a somewhat similar organizational structure and all follow established management and budgetary practices. As well, all must abide by the provisions of the Financial Administration and the Public Service Employment Acts.

PROTECTING THE TURF

I do not accept the cynical view that government departments and agencies are concerned entirely with the growth of their own budgets and organizations. At the same time, I reject the view that they are solely devoted to delivering their programs in the most efficient way possible, or that they welcome and abide by political direction even if this direction would reduce the scope of their programs and the size of their budgets and organizations. The truth lies somewhere between. A retired public servant who had been deputy minister in a few departments agrees with this assessment, observing that: 'Looking back, I would say that protecting the department's turf took an awful lot of my time and energy!'[2]

Much has been written about 'empire building' and the lengths departments will go to survive when threatened. Richard Simeon has written: 'One might ... explore how much bureaucratic expansion is now a central force in the growth of government.'[3] Likewise, Sandford Borins argued: 'Among new mandarins, the game is very different. Politics is played by bureaucrats as well as politicians. Each player has his preferred policies, his own style of play, a territory to enlarge or defend, ambition, ego, and reputation. The result, particularly when resources are limited, can be one of all against all.'[4]

To be sure, one would be hard pressed to identify departments or agencies that have been disbanded as a result of recommendations from the organization itself. Those that have been disbanded over the years, including DREE and DRIE, resulted from recommendations coming either from outside government or from central agencies. In both cases, however, the staff were able to relocate to the new, replacing departments. Organizational units within departments are also not wont to offer themselves as a means of cutting spending – even if they no longer serve a purpose or if they can see that they are less important than another unit in the department or elsewhere in government.

The Department of Veterans Affairs is one example. It has been argued that 'while its *raison d'être* just fades away, the Department of Veterans Affairs is flourishing. It continues doing old jobs that are fast becoming obsolete. It also tries hard to think up new ones.'[5] There are approximately 600,000 veterans still alive, of whom something like one-fourth are eligible for benefits. The department has 3675 authorized person-years which means that there is about one permanent official for every 45 eligible veterans. The veteran population is decreasing rapidly and some programs and divisions have seen their workload decrease substantially. For example, lending under the Veterans Local Administration Act, initially established to assist returning veterans to buy a home or start a business, was stopped altogether in 1977. There are now 19,500 accounts with an outstanding principal of $118 million to be collected. Still the person-year complement for the program rose to 137 in 1988–9 from 127 the previous year.[6]

But there are other, less obvious examples. When the Mulroney government came to office, it quickly indicated its desire to transfer a number of industrial incentive programs to provincial governments. The intent was to transfer not just the programs but also a set spending level. The proposed transfer, however, meant that a number of officials would either have to transfer with the programs or be declared redundant. Two things happened. First federal officials slowed the process down – deliberately, some insist. After several months, key ministers (status participants) began to lose their desire to transfer the programs and began to express deep concern over the likely loss of public visibility for spending. Secondly, while discussions were taking place about the proposed transfer, policy papers were being prepared outlining the 'new role' for officials previously delivering the programs. In future, the policy papers argued, they would be freed from the time-consuming task of processing applications so that they could do what they ought to have been doing all along. That is, to assist business people to identify new business opportunities, to guide them towards new technologies, and to identify new markets abroad. In the end, however, the programs were never transferred.

For senior departmental managers, it is of course vitally important to protect not only the department's budget, but its person-year complement as well. Even ministers are expected to defend the department's interest before Treasury Board. A minister who comes from a Treasury Board or cabinet meeting to report that the department's budget and person-year complement have been reduced will quickly be dismissed as weak and ineffective. Similarly, a deputy minister who cannot protect the department's interest before central agencies will lose credibility within the department and even among his or her peers.

Protecting departmental interests in many instances means protecting the A base which is akin to money in the bank. If ministers want their departments to do more, it will have to be paid for from the policy or operating reserves. They will not look to their own A base to support new or unforeseen initiatives. For example, when the Department of National Defence was asked to bring special equipment to the North for a papal visit, it went to the Treasury Board to request some $20,000 from the operating reserve rather than using its own budget, which stood at about $10 billion. Again, when the department needed two person-years to oversee a new development in the frigate program, it came to Treasury Board, rather than looking to its own existing 130,000 person-years (civilian and military combined).[7] This approach is by no means limited to the Defence Department. When the Mulroney government sought to implement its campaign commitment to provide more assistance to taxpayers in filing their income tax reports, Revenue Canada sought and obtained all the required person-years from the Treasury Board rather than using its own complement.

Few departments see any reason to employ their own A base to support new measures, to accommodate increases in workload or caseload, or to reflect changing priorities. Meanwhile, a handful of officials in the Treasury Board secretariat (let alone overworked ministers invariably preoccupied with other, more pressing issues) cannot possibly challenge the position of line departments. The two or three secretariat officials usually available to work on a request from a department for more person-years or for funding from the operating reserve will be pitted against hundreds of analysts and financial advisers representing the large spending department.

In the British television satire 'Yes Minister,' the permanent secretary scolded one of his subordinates for putting forward the wrong question on internal departmental management. The subordinate had asked how they would justify the department's person-year levels and over-head costs before the parliamentary committee. The permanent secretary explained that he was asking the wrong question – the point, he insisted, was for the parliamentary committee to demonstrate that the department did not require these resources and not the other way around. 'Let it try,' he boasted. It is not too much of an exaggeration to suggest that this resembles the real world of the federal government.

Ministers and central agency officials are too busy with current or emerging political issues and also lack the necessary information to mount a strong challenge to departmental A bases and person-year counts.

Once departments are able to secure new resources and person-years for new initiatives, they quickly become part of their A base. They join other resources 'in the bank' for the department and are not easily freed up. This is even true for the guardians. For example, when the government established the two central agencies MSED and MSSD and senior committees (that is, mirror committees) of deputy ministers in introducing PEMS, the Treasury Board secretariat established some new senior positions. The thinking was that existing senior officials would otherwise be spending most of their time at mirror committee meetings. When the central agencies and mirror committees were disbanded, however, the Treasury Board secretariat did not, in turn, abolish the positions.

Departments will invariably report to central agencies, parliamentary committees, and their ministers that their resources are stretched to the limit and that little can be done to improve the efficiency of their operations. Some central agencies appear to agree. The Public Service Commission observed in the early 1980s that government was growing because, with the downturn in the economy, more people were required to deliver existing programs and services because more people were resorting to these services.[8] The commission neglected to explain why government had also grown in the late 1960s when the economy was expanding. One is left with the daunting prospect that, if left to the Public Service Commission, government would continue to grow in both good and bad economic times.

Officials insist that the system is not designed to encourage managers to prune their organizations. For one thing, senior officials command a higher classification and salary if they manage a greater number of people and large budgets. For another, those who seek to run a highly efficient organization are rarely rewarded. Often, they are penalized. One former manager in the Department of Supply and Services explains: 'The deputy minister asked all of us to look carefully at our budgets and human resources to see if we could identify expenditure cuts. Resources were tight, he explained, and the Department wanted to launch new initiatives. I went back and reorganized my division. I was able to cut four person-years, including my own secretary. The other directors were not as successful, with most of them reporting that there was nowhere to cut. Several months later, we had an across the board cut and all divisions had to cut x resources and person-years. It was a lot easier for the other divisions to absorb the cut than it was for mine. That day, I learned a lesson that I will never forget.'[9]

The lesson is clear: if you make cuts in your own organization, not only do you run the risk of having your own position reclassified downwards, but you also make life more difficult for yourself when across-the-board cuts are called for. Guardians in central agencies are well aware of this dilemma but they have precious few solutions. A former secretary of the Treasury Board recently posed a series of questions to guide the future of public administration. He asked: 'How can we recognize and reward a manager who recognizes that a program is no longer relevant and takes the initiative to disband it, thereby freeing up scarce resources?'[10] This question is frequently asked by people outside government, although seldom within it.

Many outside government insist that more could be done in government with less. Some government employees who have moved to the private sector believe there is still considerable fat in the system. Many journalists report that the federal bureaucracy is bloated and unproductive. One wrote bluntly that 'the current perception is ... that public administrators are parasites, ill-adjusted, and boring.'[11] Academics who have studied public sector management and carried out extensive interviews with senior officials also report that there are likely far too many public servants for the work at hand. One suggested that the federal government was probably overstaffed by 25 per cent.[12]

In my consultations, most senior officials accepted that the federal public service was probably overstaffed. Dealing with the problem, however, does not rank high in their list of priorities. For one thing, they are likely to argue that there is more fat in the next department than in their own and that, if the government was truly serious about cuts, it should start there. One senior official of the Employment and Immigration Commission suggested that the department could probably operate as efficiently with 4000 or 5000 fewer person-years than the current base of 24,000. But, he added: 'If they want to cut back person-years, then they should look at some of the other departments. They should, for example, look at Defence, with well over 30,000 person-years whose main purpose is only to look after 90,000 military personnel.'[13] Other officials suggest that any savings realized from cuts would, in the end, only be employed to create a 'political slush' fund for ministers and never to lower the deficit. 'Why should we offer ourselves as sacrificial lambs to politicians,' asked one, 'when all they will do is turn around and spend the money on high-profile political projects?'[14] Another argued: 'Not infrequently, the manager sees the government announce $200 million worth of subsidies or grants or programs for a purpose that is widely known to be absolutely futile and unjustified. Here he is being asked to cut down on his resources by a few hundred thousand dollars while on the other hand the government is wasting literally hundreds of millions of dollars. The effect on motivation is severe. People either give up in disgust or they became completely cynical.'[15] Still others accept that there are 'far too many public servants chasing too few jobs' but they argue 'all large organizations are bureaucratic and lend themselves to waste.'[16] They also insist that the problem never enjoys priority status in government and that, in any event, they simply do not have the management tools to deal with it. More will be said about this later in the chapter.

Ministers and ministerial staff disagree. Many of them argue that, try as they might to give the matter priority, the bureaucracy will never respond properly. When asked why cabinet was not looking at the bureaucracy in its attempt to restrain government spending, a senior cabinet minister in the Trudeau administration responded: 'We were told time and again that cutting in the bureaucracy would only save nickels and dimes and that if we really wanted to cut, we should look at the big spending programs on the social side.'[17] A cabinet minister in the Mulroney government reports that he and his colleagues were told the same thing. A senior political adviser in the Mulroney government adds that, when the new government came to power, it was handed reams and reams of briefing papers, few of which identified options for cutting back on government operations and in the bureaucracy. Still, he continued, when the cabinet took a decision to cut 15,000 person-years from the public service, ministers just 'grabbed the number from thin air.' The chief of staff to another senior cabinet minister reports that ministers always want to 'cut the bureaucratic fat while officials constantly try to steer them away from there to the big social and federal/provincial programs.'[18] Officials, he went on, 'have a profound dislike of ministers mucking around in personnel matters. In their minds, it is really none of their business.'[19] It is true that although the Treasury Board delegates a great deal of authority to ministers, personnel matters are delegated directly to deputy ministers.

Ministers themselves report that whenever they raise the possibility of cutting back in the public service, they are invariably told two things:

first, it would take too much effort and, in the end, little in the way of savings would actually be realized; second, whenever cuts are raised, officials always point to meat inspectors, national park attendants, and the clerks who send out widows' pensions. Explained one minister, 'I have never heard one deputy minister talk about all the staff positions in Ottawa called policy analysts, policy coordinators, policy advisors, and so on. They all talk about the impact on the officials on the front line in our riding whenever we talk about cutting back government. We know that this is going on and that there is fat there, but what can we do? They tell us that there is very little saving that can be realized in cutting back in the bureaucracy. Who are we to say that they are wrong and how far can we push this view, considering everything else we have to deal with?'[20] A minister in the Trudeau cabinet had this explanation:

Bureaucracy always creeps up, always grows. You never see it happening. You add fifty person-years here, another hundred there, but you never realize how big it is growing until it is too late. I have a perfect example of this. When Trudeau came to power in 1968, we all knew his disdain for officials in External Affairs. He kept saying, even in cabinet meetings, that if you really want to know what is going on abroad, read the London *Times*, the *New York Times*, or *Le Monde*. Their articles are better written and more informative than anything External can put together, he claimed. The fact of the matter is, however, that when Trudeau came to power, there were 4000 officials in External. When he left, there were nearly 6000. Had he been told in 1968 that External would grow by that much during his stay in office, he would have had a fit.[21]

Ministers may well have a point when they argue that the cost of running the government is more than nickels and dimes and that there are a great number of officials who do not deliver any programs or services to the public. Part II of the 1988–9 estimates provides for over $119 billion in net expenditures. This figure excludes revenue credited to specific spending votes and unallocated reserves for new spending. Some $32 billion is allocated for debt charges, an item which requires little overhead cost to government. From the remaining $87 billion, some $20 billion are earmarked for federal transfer payments to the provinces for fiscal equalization payments, medical care, post-secondary education, and social services, which also require few people to administer. One could go even further and isolate the bulk of the federal transfers to individuals and the numbers required to deliver the programs. For example, $17.6 billion was earmarked for the income security program and family allowance and some 2768 person-years were required to deliver these programs. This leaves less than $50 billion in proposed spending. Out of this amount, the total personnel cost, including salaries and overtime and the cost of various employee benefit plans, amounted to $15.35 billion and $1.8 billion for travel expenses and communication. It is not possible to isolate the net cost of office space, utilities and supplies, and professional services. It is possible to assume, however, that the total cost of salaries, travel expenses, telephone, postage, office rentals, supplies, and professional services amounts to at least $20 billion a year.

It is also not possible to divide neatly into two groups those officials in a staff capacity and those in a line capacity, delivering programs. However, in September 1987 the official languages branch of the Treasury Board secretariat set about to identify all positions that were involved in providing services to the public. The branch surveyed 221,434 positions, attempting to identify all jobs that had at least some responsibilities to deal with the general public, even if that 'some' amounted to only 10 per cent of the total work or responsibilities. It found a total of 92,480 such positions.[22] This is not to suggest for a moment that all of the remaining 128,954 positions are staffed by policy analysts, coordinators, advisers, or administrators. Still, we know that a good number of them are. For instance, the 1987 government telephone directory reveals that in DRIE some twenty-five organizational units carried the word *Policy*, *Liaison*, *Coordination*, or *Evaluation*, or a combination of them. Looking at it from the outside, one suspects that the numbers and layers of units are excessive but how is one to demonstrate conclusively that this is so? Those in a position to know would be the senior executives and the program managers actually operating the programs. But there is obviously little incentive for them to admit to it. As Lee Iacocca, who has had some firsthand experience at pruning an organization, observed: 'If you wait for a manager to *volunteer* a cut in his budget, you're going to be an old man before it happens.'[23]

The few who have worked in policy and coordination units and who have gone on to write about them have been anything but positive. John Chenier and Mike Prince, in an article entitled 'The Rise and Fall of Policy Planning and Research Units,' observed that 'our analysis and that of others suggests that over time, policy units become the victims of organizational infighting, slowly losing any effectiveness in the policy process.'[24] H.L. Laframboise argued that 'there is a need for a return to simplicity, clarity and speed of decision making in the arrangement of functions and authorities, and a willingness to forego the highly ornamental refinements that have given a rococo cast to our organizational designs ... The merits of the coordination function are in my view overrated.'[25] Chenier and Prince concluded their essay by suggesting: 'We suspect that many government agencies have already determined the problem [i.e. that policy units are not very effective].'[26] They may well have, but the organizational charts of federal departments and agencies show that little has been done about it.

This is not to suggest that officials in these units merely go to work every day and do nothing. Some are kept busy, but working hard is not necessarily what matters. One must ask if the work is contributing positively to the work of government. One such official in DRIE remarked bluntly: 'To be frank, I am being kept busy at turning cranks not connected to anything. But what do you expect me to do? Walk up to the Treasury Board and say cut my position because it is really not necessary? Ministers blow more money on strictly political things in one day that my salary will ever cost taxpayers for twenty years.'[27]

One can hardly overemphasize our inability to assess the work of certain organizational units in government, notably those in a staff capacity who are performing research, policy planning, and coordination functions. There are rarely clear-cut criteria to measure the success of these units. Within the universities, it is possible to have at least some appreciation of the research being done, depending on whether the work gets published in the right places. But not so in government. It is quite possible that a great number of policy units are producing material that has virtually no value to society or even to the government. It may be fair to compare it to the output of the heavy water plants of Cape Breton, which was put in storage immediately on production with little hope of its actually being sold. The difference, of course, is that it was relatively obvious that the cost of the Cape Breton product to the federal treasury was of no value. The minister of finance explained: 'The heavy water plants in Glace Bay and Port Hawkesbury are recognized as striking symbols of government waste and mismanagement. We will move immediately to close the plants.'[28] The issue was simple and clear cut. There was a tangible product that could not be sold. If the product of certain units in the federal government could be judged on the same basis, we could well discover some similar examples and identify potentially important savings to the federal budget. Moreover, unlike heavy water, the unreviewed output of policy and evaluation units can slow down decision making.

Certainly, the multitude of long-range research and planning and policy units in federal economic departments, not to mention the resources of the Department of Finance ($102 million and 822 person-years in the 1984–5 estimates), which is responsible for federal economic policy, or those of the Economic Council of Canada ($7.6 million and 133 person-years in the 1984–5 estimates), did not prevent Ottawa from establishing a royal commission at a cost of over $20 million to study Canada's economic prospects and come up with policy recommendations. Since two costly central agencies, MSERD ($23.5 million and 291 person-years in 1983–4) and MSSD ($6.8 million and 119 person-years in 1983–4), armed with well-staffed policy and planning units were also operating at the time, one can only conclude that they could not provide the kind of long-range policy advice the government was seeking. They were both disbanded in 1984 and no one seems to be the worse for it. The question that comes to mind is how many other agencies or units could be disbanded with little impact on society other than potential savings.

This raises another important issue of government organization, that of the number of units loaded with 'think' positions. These exist in all economic and social programming departments. H.L. Laframboise wrote: 'We have created "think" positions in numbers far out of proportion to the availability of individuals with the talents needed to fill them. The result is that analytical and developmental work is cluttered by thousands of individuals who, in a more rational world, would be filling routine positions more consistent with their limitations. Since no policy is better than bad policy, the overall quality of developmental work would be raised immensely if we could discipline ourselves in future to limiting "think" positions to a number more in line with the availability of individuals with the necessary intellectual, judgemental and communications skills.'[29] It is also important to bear in mind that bureaucracy does not lend itself to creative thinking, to challenging the departmental policies and programs and the way things are done. It does appear that a great deal of energy is spent in these units in keeping an eye on other departments to ensure that no one is encroaching on their own mandate and programs. One official explained: 'they [departmental officials] spend part of their energy protecting their own territory and part to grab at that of others. There is not much left to do the job ... '[30]

In our consultations, the majority of ministers (especially the policy, mission, and process participants) and their staffs expressed deep disappointment with the advice coming from their departmental policy and research units. One senior minister said that 'the biggest letdown in government was the lack of creativity and clear thinking on the part of the permanent officials. I imagined while in opposition that it was the Trudeau cabinet that was stifling the public servants in their attempts to come forward with new ideas and new solutions. I was wrong.'[31] He went on to insist that he can usually predict what government planners will have to say on any number of topics. 'Those in departments will urge us to stick with the status quo and those in central agencies will simply give us twenty reasons why we can't pursue something.'[32] Another argued that 'cabinet documents are poorly written, bland, and unimaginative.'[33] Yet another reported: 'Every time I ask for something that is more than a few pages long or that breaks out of the narrow operating mode of the department, officials always tell me that they have to go to an outside consultant for the work. All in all, we have a pretty stale bunch in government.'[34] For their part, officials readily admit that there can only be an 'imprecise notion' of the success of policy advice in government. Some also insist that the criteria for the success of policy units must go beyond pleasing a minister. It is important, they argue, in an organization as large as the federal government for policy, research, and coordination units to achieve the respect of other departments.

It is clear, however, that the biggest disappointment ministers and their staff have with policy and research units is their inability to challenge the status quo in their department. Central agency officials also tend to agree with this assessment. This is why, for example, Treasury Board secretariat officials insist on staying close to departmental programs. Otherwise, it would be impossible to provide ministers with 'real choices' when program cuts have to be made. When asked to propose cuts, departments will invariably suggest their most politically appealing or high-profile programs – the 'musical ride' approach, so-called after the hugely popular RCMP musical ride, whose demise would cause an uproar.[35] For instance, ministers in the Mulroney government were embarrassed when cutbacks to the CBC's budget resulted in the cancellation of the popular children's television program, 'The Friendly Giant.'[36]

It is well known that the forces of the status quo in government are strong. Some even suggest that, by definition, bureaucratic behaviour seems to denote caution and opposition to change.[37] But there are also other factors in society that favour the status quo. Interest groups are increasingly active players in the policy- and decision-making process in Ottawa. These groups now 'constitute a principal channel through which various major interests in the country can participate in the making of public policy, [and] they help to legitimize not only specific policy outputs but also the system which produces those policies.'[38] The most successful groups have established strong two-way contacts within the public service. In a number of instances, interest groups and government departments will reinforce each other. In fact, a good number of interest groups now owe their existence to government, without whose financial support some of the best-known would not exist. These include groups promoting linguistic rights, women's issues, environmental and multicultural concerns, native development, the disabled, and youth. None of these are likely to argue that government funding for their causes should cease. They will either favour the status quo or go about demonstrating the inadequacies of existing government programs. Remedying these inadequacies inevitably costs money.

The existence of interest groups make it difficult for the government to launch a policy of retrenchment. A. Paul Pross argues that interest groups are more and more important actors in policy making because, in the modern economy, individuals are deeply concerned with problems associated with the economic sector where they are employed. Not only does government still have to deal with the ever present regional dimension, but also increasingly with economic sectors, because interest groups are usually organized along sectoral lines. They also often have articulate and high-profile representatives to present their case to government.[39] Governments are finding it difficult to define the more diffused and universal issues in the face of individual interest groups. One could ask whether the government is appropriately organized to deal with a pluralism which, in the words of one keen observer of Canadian society, 'has to some extent run amok.'[40] One could even ask if the way government is structured has contributed to our pluralism running amok.

Our government is divided along sectoral lines with programs scaffolded on top of each other in individual departments. The interests of individual departments often go hand in hand with those of special interest groups, and ministers are expected to take up the cause of their departments and their client groups with their cabinet colleagues. A former British cabinet minister explains: 'Of course, it is necessary for you to pursue the interests of your Department: that is why you are there. And little can arouse greater pleasure in a Department than the return from a Cabinet Committee of a minister who has gained a majority for his Departmental view.'[41]

In Canada, one only has to recall the strong reaction of the arts community when Marcel Masse, a newly appointed minister of communications, expressed his interest in hanging a question mark next to some government-supported arts programs. How could he do that? the arts community asked. After all, he was 'their' representative in cabinet. Masse quickly won the confidence of the community, however, as soon as it became publicly known that he was defending the arts before his colleagues.[42] A former environment minister, Suzanne Blais Grenier, also had some trying moments with environmentalists and the media after she had publicly supported cuts in environment programs. Cuts in programs can never safely be announced or even supported except by the guardians.

What the above suggests is that the structure of government itself may increase the difficulty of mounting campaigns for the general public good. The structure may be such that senior departmental officials and, over time, some ministers may regard the fortunes of the department as more important than those of the government. And what constitutes the fortunes of departments is often shaped by the interests of special pressure groups or the industry the department is serving. One former federal minister explained: 'I became aware of the intimate relationship that existed between the civil service, the Canadian Transport Commission (CTC) and the airline industry soon after being appointed to the transport portfolio.'[43] This is not to suggest that ministers usually take a stronger interest in what a particular industry or an interest group is pursuing than in their regions. They know, however, that a well-organized interest group can create great political problems for them in the national media. Even just cutting back the level of support given a particular interest group will more than likely bring a minister unfavourable press in the country's leading newspapers.[44]

Quite apart from the fact that departments may serve as conduits for pressure groups to the cabinet table, having large departments with program activities scaffolded on top of one another may not be the best means to deliver goods and services in current economic circumstances. Organizationally, government departments still have structures designed for the delivery of routine, large-scale services – like the delivery of mail. Yet economic and social forces are evolving at a far quicker pace than they were even twenty-five years ago. It may well be that we ought to look at radical changes to the administrative structure of the federal government. John Manion, a respected senior public servant who headed both a large line department and a central agency, asked two fundamental questions along these lines when he wrote: 'Is it still appropriate to organize policy, planning, research, and evaluation units the way we organize the units that deliver programs or routine services? Do the hierarchical chains of command and the multi-layered administrative structures inhibit creative thinking and the ability to question the continuing effectiveness of existing programs?'[45]

MANAGING THE TURF

Though there are variations, all government departments are basically organized along the same lines. The deputy minister is the administrative head of the department. In some, one or more associate deputy ministers may be appointed to assist the deputy minister. There are usually several assistant deputy ministers reporting directly to the deputy, including one responsible for policy development and coordination, another for administrative, financial, and personnel services, and others for a geographic area or a specific program operation. Reporting to the assistant deputy minister are directors general or executive directors, and reporting to them are directors. Managers and group chiefs usually complete the departmental hierarchy. Figure 5 is an organizational chart, down to the assistant deputy minister level, of the Department of Indian and Northern Affairs.

All policy advice and all financial management issues going to the minister from the department, whether large or small, go through the deputy minister, who is the link between the political world of the minister and political advisers and the public service. The deputy minister is at once the minister's chief policy adviser, the department's general manager, and a key participant in the collective management of the government. The Privy Council Office has laid out the responsibilities of deputy ministers under three categories: 'the responsibility for managing the internal operations of the department ... the duty to support and participate in the collective management responsibilities of the government ... [and] the duty to provide the minister and the government with policy advice.'[46]

The job of deputy minister is not for the faint of heart. A deputy minister is constantly being pushed and pulled in several directions. He or she must above all serve the minister and learn to navigate in the waters dividing the political and bureaucratic worlds. This is no easy task. As Timothy Plumptree points out: 'Above, there is the political culture, where optics and impressions are often more important than

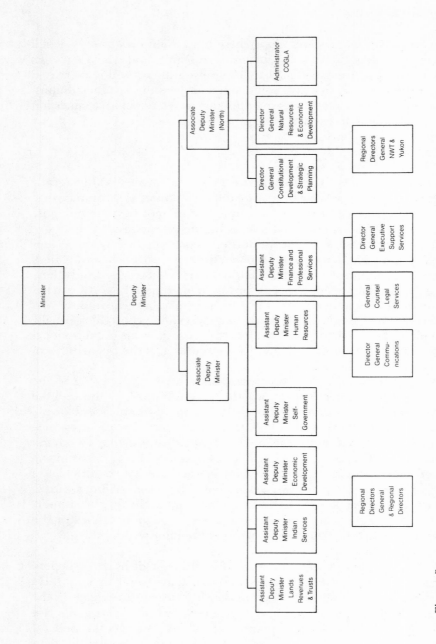

Figure 5
Organizational structure: Department of Indian and Northern Affairs

objective reality. Below there is the bureaucratic environment, composed of large administrative operations that rely on stability, constancy of purpose and a professional and rational analysis of public issues.'[47] Deputy ministers have a certain assurance that they will be able to work with the officials down the line. If there are problems, the deputy minister is usually able to organize a quiet transfer for the 'troublemaker' and then bring in others with whom an easy working relationship can be established. There are reasons to believe that this takes place if one is to judge by the limited departmental reorganizations or changes at the senior management level that usually follow the appointment of a new deputy minister.

But their relationship with ministers is not so easy. As one deputy minister put it, 'in this line of work you do not pick and choose who you are going to work for.'[48] Another went further and said that 'a deputy minister is extremely vulnerable – for example, you may get an incompetent minister to serve ... Or you may suddenly find yourself reassigned to a portfolio that is not of great interest to you ... If , as a senior official, you do a hell of a good job, this may or may not be to your advantage tomorrow.'[49] In some instances, the working relationship between ministers and their deputies is excellent, in others less so, and in a good number it is anything but engaging. Whatever the relationship, the department expects the deputy minister to protect its interests before the minister and his colleagues.

Perhaps the best way to illustrate the various relationships a deputy minister must juggle with is to reproduce the accountability relationships framework published in Timothy Plumptre's *Beyond the Bottom Line* (see figure 6). A former clerk of the Privy Council and secretary to the cabinet explains that 'deputy ministers see themselves as accountable to the Prime Minister, the Treasury Board and the Public Service Commission, as well as to their ministers. In addition, Deputy Ministers recognize that they have special responsibilities to officials such as the Auditor General and the Official Languages Commission, as well as having an obligation to coordinate and cooperate with other departments.'[50] He could well have added the Public Accounts Committee, the Prime Minister's Office, the Privy Council Office, and the Access to Information Commission. What this suggests is that anyone wanting a clear mandate in the day-to-day work environment ought not to aim to become a deputy minister. It is, of course, impossible for them to give equal importance to all these individuals and agencies.

Successful deputy ministers will want to ensure that their relationships

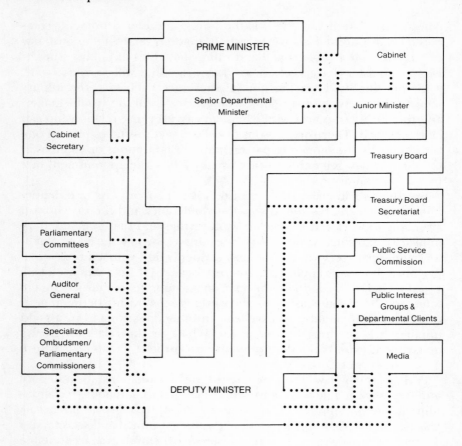

Figure 6
Formal and informal accountability relationships of a Canadian deputy minister
Source: T. Plumptre, *Beyond the Bottom Line* (1988)

with their ministers and the prime minister through the clerk of the Privy Council Office are well protected. Deputy ministers pride themselves on being able to keep 'their ministers out of political trouble.' This is important not just for their own relationships with their ministers, but also for their credibility with their peers. All deputy ministers have regular breakfast meetings and they prefer walking in to these meetings knowing that their minister is in no political controversy or difficulties.

One senior deputy minister boasted: 'I have never lost one minister and I have worked with several. One of my colleagues has lost every single minister he or she has ever worked with. That tells you something.'[51]

Deputy ministers must also ensure that two-way communication exists between their offices and the Privy Council Office. For one thing, their next promotion depends to a large extent on what the clerk of the Privy Council will recommend to the prime minister. For another, they know that an untoward action by their minister can have a far-reaching impact. At times, a matter strictly internal to a department can mushroom into a government-wide political problem. The so-called 'tunagate scandal,' for example, started innocently enough with the minister and Department of Fisheries. It was not contained, and eventually the prime minister became directly embroiled in the controversy. A deputy minister must, then, be able to read signals, to know which are important, and to understand the concerns or perspectives of other departments and central agencies.

In practice, deputy ministers have to establish good working relationships with a wide variety of people and continually seek to create 'a happy family out of a complex group.'[52] The focus of this complex group is invariably on new policies, programs, or initiatives. Ministers, whether they be status, mission, process, or policy participants, will focus on new initiatives and rarely on spending cuts. According to a senior official, they 'may well want to rant and rave about the fat in the Ottawa bureaucracy and about mismanagement in government but when push comes to shove they will put those concerns aside and push their officials to come forward with new initiatives.'[53] 'The object of the game,' added another, 'is to keep your minister happy. How do you do that? There are only two ways – keep him out of political trouble and get him new initiatives to announce – it is truly that simple.'[54] 'What counts for politicians,' said yet another, is the announcement of a new program. These announcements are what the minister is recognized for. No one is really interested to know if the program is efficient or effective.'[55] As a result, there is little opportunity or even requirement in the total scheme of things for deputy ministers to focus on good management, or on human and financial resources. The political priority is clearly new initiatives. Thus, the task of briefing ministers to enable them to respond to criticism in question period in the House or in the media crowds out management and administrative concerns. There are also only so many hours in the day. In government, the urgent inevitably crowds out the important.[56]

Managing political crises demands far more time from senior departmental managers than is generally assumed outside government. It is not simply the minister and the political staff who must spend hours diffusing a potentially explosive situation. Permanent officials must constantly monitor crises and prepare briefing materials with which to advise their ministers. Such instances as the Tamil boat refugees, the Franco-Canada fish dispute around Saint-Pierre-Miquelon, and the tunagate scandal, among many others, take up many hours. Senior officials in Ottawa with 'good instincts' for dealing with political situations are in great demand, and the prime minister on the advice of the Privy Council will often ensure that they are appointed to departments with junior or weak ministers. The importance attached to their capacity to advise ministers and cabinet on politically difficult situations is illustrated by a presentation on how to manage political crises made by the deputy minister of fisheries to a one-day meeting of assistant deputy ministers held in Ottawa. In his presentation he identified four stages that all such crises usually go through. Little was said, however, about improved management practices.[57]

The road to the top for federal public servants is often easiest for the policy and policy process specialists. Well over half the deputy ministers appointed during the past three years have come from central agencies, notably the Privy Council Office. In getting to the top, the policy specialists rarely stay in one position for much longer than two years. What is important to stress here is that ambitious public servants are eager to come up with proposed solutions and initiatives, not least because this brings greater career rewards. However, there is considerably less visibility, less prestige, and, consequently, fewer opportunities for advancement for those left behind to implement the initiatives. Ambitious public servants are no different than their private sector counterparts. They will quickly sense the fastest way to the top and adjust their career paths accordingly. One senior public servant explained: 'The fact is that more emphasis has been placed on policy considerations and indeed on growth and expansion than on frugality. The facts show that the rewards are going to those who gave their time to developing imaginative policies and programs. And where the real rewards go, effort will follow.'[58] Departments continually seek to dominate the policy agenda in government if only to protect or expand their turf. To dominate the agenda, departments must recruit the best and the brightest to send to interdepartmental meetings.

Yet, frequently, proposed solutions that appear on the face of it well suited to the problem at hand will break down in the implementation stages. The policy analysts responsible for coming up with the proposals in the first place who have gone on to greater heights elsewhere can always claim that, while the initiative was conceptually sound, it was never implemented properly. Thus, dazzling policy initiatives, well packaged, persuasively argued, forcefully negotiated, often costly, and unveiled in a blaze of publicity, may, a few years down the road, show little in the way of actual benefits. Well-packaged policy announcements and genuine policy reforms are two very different things. One could easily put together a hefty catalogue of failed major policy initiatives. A case in point was DREE's major policy shift in 1973, involving the decentralization of its operations to field offices. Few would argue that this initiative lived up to expectations.[59] Again, some ten years later, the prime minister announced a major policy shift in the area of economic development and moved to amalgamate the former Department of Industry and Commerce with DREE, shift the trade function to External Affairs, and restructure a central agency. A well-packaged backgrounder to the announcement laid out all the benefits of this initiative.[60] Again, one would be hard pressed to demonstrate that many of the identified benefits have been realized. A more recent example is Canada's job strategy, which was launched with great promise. A few years later, however, the program has come under heavy criticism. It is costly ($1.5 billion), it is 'bogged down by complicated paperwork,' and it has been discovered that Canadians pass up temporary jobs so that they 'can stay unemployed long enough to qualify for training.'[61] There are numerous other examples. All in all, the lack of interest in policy implementation and in improving government organization, as well as management and program practices, is understandable.

Quite apart from promotions, it is also true that job classifications with a policy component command higher salaries than those in the administration, personnel, or financial categories, or even program management. It is not uncommon, for example, to see economists or commerce officers at the desk level of analysts in a staff position earning more than the lowest level in the management category. John Meisel describes the new breed of policy analysts in Ottawa: 'They are less specialists in the substance of any one area than experts in the general art of policy analysis and in the folkways of bureaucracy. They are ever ready to exclaim – Have tools! Will travel ... [they] have become less oriented to certain policy areas and more concerned with their own advancement in the invitingly open and evermore rewarding hierarchy of the governmental priesthood.'[62]

It is hardly possible to overemphasize that the management of financial and human resources in government is often forced to take a back seat to politics and the policy process. Former clerk of the Privy Council Gordon Osbaldeston acknowledges this and goes on to argue that it should be the case. He writes: 'Another problem with the management standards approach to accountability is that by concentrating on good performance in specific functions, we can lose sight of the purpose for which the department was created, and thus reduce the capacity of the department to respond to the legitimate purposes of the ministers ... Management standards must be tailored specifically to each department's situation, and must be viewed as only a small part of the requirements of managing an organization which is intended to support and serve the Minister and the government.'[63] With so little emphasis on management, there ought to be little wonder that the federal government is having considerable difficulty attracting top people to financial and personnel management. Top accountants and financial experts are more likely to be found in the private sector where their talents are recognized. There are not many boards of directors or senior management cadres of large private firms that do not have at least two or three such persons. There are, however, many government departments in which the top echelon contains no one with such a background. But even if one wanted to stress good management practices in the federal government, one would come up against numerous constraints. There are more 'incentives to manage badly' in the federal government than there are to manage well.[64]

One incentive to manage badly is year-end spending. As we saw earlier, parliament approves funding for one fiscal year. If financial resources are not spent in that year, they lapse and are not available for the following year. There is a 'stigma attached to lapsing funds at the end of a fiscal year. The reason is that this can be taken as an indication of a manager's inability to budget and plan properly.'[65] Managers are, therefore, constantly on the look-out to ensure that all funds are spent. If they are not, the deputy minister and the Treasury Board secretariat will consider the program to be cash rich and that it should be cut back. If this is done, the money does not necessarily stay with the manager who has been frugal. It either goes to the deputy minister for reallocation in the department or to the centre (the guardians). Thus, the resources that a frugal manager has worked hard to free up may well be turned over to spendthrift managers who never lapse any funding. Worse still, the frugal manager may see some of the freed-up resources go to a 'new politically-motivated boondoggle announced in the media (which will) simply reinforce the determination of civil servants to protect their budgets and programs. Who wants "their" program resources used for a project designed to purchase the re-election of the Government?'[66]

Another incentive to manage badly is that management positions are often directly linked to the portion of the departmental budget involved and the number of persons reporting to them. The more people a manager supervises, the higher the classification for his or her position. The following observation by a senior official explains the dilemma very well:

We had a supervisor and two subordinates. We could see that we had more people than we needed. The supervisor came up with an idea whereby he could move our two subordinates and handle it by himself, just to improve work methods. We implemented this, but what happens – Classification and Staffing hear about it and we get instructions to lay off one of the two officers. So we end up by laying off one guy, we force the second guy to move. We red-circled the supervisor who thought of the idea, because he lost his subordinates. He lost so many points out of his job description that he went from a CR7 down to a CR6. Now here is a guy who saved us two full year salaries and our thanks to him was one of our staff got laid off, one of our staff got transferred, and he got slapped. I would imagine he would not have another good idea for the rest of his career. And you can't blame him one bit. So there is still a real incentive to get as many people under you as possible. If you are a PM2, you should be looking to hire 18 people, not 8. You get to be a PM3 with 18 people.[67]

Quite apart from the incentives to manage badly, management in the federal government is mostly one of process rather than substance. That is, managers are confronted by a myriad of complex government procedures and regulations which, many claim, makes it virtually impossible to manage effectively. Some suggest that it is only the process, not management authority, that is delegated to them: that is, management accountability is based on how well the process is respected, rather than on results. The process and prescriptions on how to handle virtually any conceivable administrative, personnel, and financial issues are laid down in thirty-four voluminous loose-leaf binders circulated to all departments. Two federal public servants who have looked at the constraints to management in the federal government explain:

Treasury Board determines how departments budget, classify positions and organize functions. The Public Service Commission prescribes how managers will hire and promote staff. The Comptroller General sets guidelines for internal audit and evaluation. The Department of Supply and Services establishes procedures for making purchases. Public Works has responsibility for the acquisition and maintenance of accommodation. Departmental staff groups tell the manager how to plan, deal with personnel, administer regulations, keep accounts, measure performance. Audit groups check for weaknesses and make recommendations for change. Each of these groups has some authority to prescribe how managers should act, yet assumes little or no responsibility for the results of managers' actions, should they turn out to be unsatisfactory because of conflicting demands.[68]

One could also add to the list the requirements of the Office of the Commission of Official Languages, the Office of the Auditor General, and the Access to Information Act. Rules, regulations, and processes have a purpose. They promote equity and reduce criticism and embarrassment. This is important if only to protect the minister before the media and in question period in the House. But they do not always provide for quick, imaginative, and flexible management decisions.

Figure 7 illustrates the accountability relationships between departmental management and other organizations. The result is that there is little room for managers to exert discretion, be flexible, or adapt to special situations. The cost of such procedures and regulations is also high, with some suggesting that it accounts for 20 to 30 per cent in unnecessary overhead. One official reported: 'I have about 237 person-years in the organization in personnel and administration and a lot more in Finance. And they are there because I have to have very heavy management systems in order to serve the central agencies. But they are largely overhead and the costs of this overhead are much too large ... So I have to carry some extra staff. But as long as ... they [central agencies or the guardians] are willing to pay for it to meet central agency requirements, then I'm willing to accept that additional cost.'[69] Managers are quick to point out that they did not originate these regulations.

Still another problem with the various regulations and procedures is that they make it more difficult to judge who is a good manager. It is

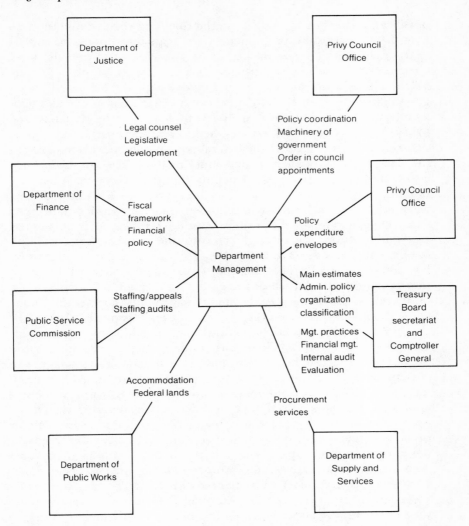

Figure 7
Accountability relationships
Note: This does not include special agencies such as the Office of the Commissioner of Official Languages, the Office of the Auditor General, and the many relationships each department has with other departments and provincial governments.

possible for someone to abide by all the rules and regulations but over-look the substance. Respecting rules and regulations does not usually lead a manager to prune his or her organization or to find the most effective means to deliver a particular service. One senior official bluntly asked: 'How the hell are you going to judge a good manager? If he's a good manager, what has he got to manage? He's got money, he's got people, he's got facilities, and so on. But in these areas he often has little to say. In terms of capital fixtures, he has nothing to say.'[70]

Nowhere is a manager in the federal government more hampered in the day-to-day work than in personnel matters. The constraints are everywhere and apply even to deputy ministers. To establish a new position, the manager must produce an inordinate amount of paper-work. A job description must be prepared, then a linguistic profile must be attached, and finally the position must be classified. All in all, the red tape that must be gone through can consume an extraordinary length of time – on average, several months. This fact no doubt explains why few positions are ever abolished. Better to adapt a vacant position to new requirements, if at all possible, than to create a new one. Once a position is available for staffing, the manager must contact the Public Service Commission. However, the staffing process can be slow, espe-cially in the later 1980s because of the lengthy redundancy lists a man-ager must go through. (These lists result from the reduction in the public service effected by the Mulroney government.) The manager will also discover that government staffing policies are designed to serve a multitude of objectives and may well wonder if the merit principle still applies. The various selection criteria may be related only vaguely to job competence in that there are now special provisions in the staffing process designed to ensure linguistic balance, a capacity to serve both official language groups, special efforts to recruit disabled persons, visible minorities, natives, and women. Should there be a conflict between the operational requirements of the manager and government-wide personnel objectives, the latter will likely prevail. Government-wide objectives are either enshrined in an act of parliament or are laid down as government policy by the Treasury Board. Notwithstanding employment equity measures and personnel policy objectives, the man-ager must guard against recruiting people who are not up to the posi-tion. It is difficult to deal with non-performers and, in this, central agencies are not helpful.

There is now in the federal government a general disinclination to confront problems of non-performance among employees.[71] The reasons are varied. For one thing, it is widely assumed, even by managers, that public servants should be protected against dismissal. For another, disciplining individuals for failure to perform is an extremely difficult and time-consuming task. Every manager in the federal government has heard horror stories about failed attempts to dismiss an employee. Even when an attempt has been successful, however, it is widely believed that it was not worth the effort.

The Public Service Employment Act gives deputy ministers and, through them, their managers the power to appoint an employee who 'is incompetent in performing the duties of the position or is incapable of performing those duties ... to a position at a lower maximum rate of pay or be released.'[72] To do this, however, the manager must document the employee's incompetence. This takes time.[73] Once the incompetence has been documented and, after the employee has been informed in writing of his dismissal, the employee 'may appeal against the recommendation of the deputy head to a board established by the [Public Service] Commission.'[74] Few managers can be bothered going through the process. In addition, those who seek to discipline employees are not assured of success. The secretary of the Treasury Board in 1985 sought to dismiss two officials who had set up a government lobbying firm while continuing to be employed. The officials organized seminars on weekends to show how business people should deal with the government to obtain more contracts.[75] The two officials appealed and won their jobs back. The message was not lost on federal government managers. If the secretary of the Treasury Board could not make the dismissals stick, there is little hope that anyone else will be successful.

All managers are expected to review the performance of their employees at least once a year. Employees can perform at the following levels: outstanding, superior, fully satisfactory, satisfactory, and not satisfactory. Something like 30 per cent of all employees are assessed at the outstanding and superior levels, with the great majority of them evaluated as superior. The bulk of the remaining employees are evaluated as fully satisfactory. Hardly anyone is assessed as not satisfactory, simply because it would then be impossible for the manager to 'shop around the employees to other departments.'[76] The result is that few employees are ever dismissed for incompetence. In 1987, for instance, out of well over 200,000 employees, only 58 were fired for incompetence or incapacity; none of the 4521 top-ranked managers were released for any cause.[77] The punishment for non-performance or inappropriate behaviour in the federal government is now 'with rare exception, non-promotion rather than demotion or dismissal.'[78]

The alternative to dismissal is to abolish the incumbent's position, but this involves a high price. The manager loses the position, possibly forever, since there are always plenty of others in the department eager to grab the freed-up person-year. In addition, the unions would strongly object if they had any reason to believe that a manager had cut a position to get rid of an employee. In any event, even if the position were successfully cut, there is no assurance that the employee would be forced to leave the government. When a position is declared redundant, the employee must receive a minimum six months' notice. After this period, the employee is placed on a priority list at the Public Service Commission, and every effort is made to place him or her in a comparable position in government. The commission's success in placing displaced employees is very high.[79]

Many observers have pointed to the demoralizing impact non-performers have on government departments. One wrote: 'People who do not measure up, and who are allowed to get away with it, are like an acid eating at the innards of an organization ... People who are paid less but who know they work harder and better than a non-performer are constantly reminded (by his or her presence) that their employer does not believe in treating employees equitably.'[80] Another wrote: 'Although the burden on the taxpayer of retaining incompetent or lazy public servants is not zero and the effect on the morale of others is not trivial, perhaps the most serious burden is the amount of time and effort required by the competent and ambitious to "work around" the deadwood in order to get on with the job.'[81]

That said, there is little outside pressure and, as we have seen, precious few incentives for managers to deal with non-performers and to prune their organization. The Office of the Auditor General will point to specific programs that have been badly mishandled and that invariably cause political embarassment. The office, however, will never single out a particular manager who may have too many person-years for the task at hand, simply because the auditor general is rarely in a position to build up a case to make this point. The ones who are in a position to say if an organization is overstaffed are the departmental managers themselves, but they are unlikely to make the case.

Another important management problem in government is, as mentioned above, how to measure success. It is relatively easy to see who is incompetent but much harder to determine who are most competent. The most ambitious will attempt to assess the 'attitudes and actions of others in order to be able to assist them, thwart them or remain passive ... because ... a knowledge of ever-changing alliances frequently makes the difference between success and failure.' The lack of objective criteria is such that 'favourable reputations, upon which promotion ultimately hinges, can be manufactured by false advertising just as surely as reputations can be destroyed by false rumour.'[82] One senior official of the Privy Council Office acknowledged this and added that 'in this game, theatre is important. The Deputy Minister who goes to meetings and makes an excellent presentation, reassures ministers that an answer to their problems is just around the corner and who can stroke central agencies will be tagged a success story. Whether the department is well managed and whether things are actually getting done is quite another story.'[83] Otto Brodtrick compares management in the federal government to organized anarchy and illustrates his point by way of a soccer game with highly flexible ways of determining who wins: 'The team plays on a round field that is ringed by numerous goals. There is no fixed number of players. Players enter and leave the field sporadically. There are several balls in the game, and each one is of a different size and shape. The players vigorously kick the balls toward one or another of the goals, and sometimes balls are even kicked from the outside. During all this, there are men in green overalls who are busy moving the goals around to different positions on the field. The players sometimes judge themselves, and sometimes they are judged by others, but always according to ambiguous and variable scoring systems.'[84]

A flare for theatrics may be important for deputy ministers to get ahead, but there is also evidence to suggest that things are not well with lower-level managers. A great deal has been said of late, for example, about the length of time deputy ministers spend in departments. It is been suggested that they are appointed with little advance knowledge of the department's activities, since the great majority of them are now appointed from outside the department – more often than not from central agencies. Worse still, it is argued that they do not stay long enough in the department to acquire a sufficient degree of knowledge of the department's activities or its employees to manage properly. There is no doubt some truth to these charges. 'In 1966, when most Deputy Ministers were appointed from within their departments, the average number of years that a Deputy Minister had spent in that position in a department was 4.5 years. By 1986, the average time that

Deputy Ministers were in their positions in a particular department was 1.4 years.'[85] The prime minister may well make changes at the deputy minister level for reasons only remotely related to good management. For example, it is perhaps easier to change deputy ministers than to fire those who may appear to have been too close to a previous government. The prime minister may also change deputy ministers to ensure fairer representation for francophones, women, and visible minorities: 'in 1976 only 23 percent of Deputy Ministers were Francophones and only 3 percent were women. By 1986, 37 percent were Francophones and 17 percent were women.'[86]

Frequent changes at the top, however, can have an unsettling effect on departmental managers. It has been argued, for example, that the difference in attitudes between middle management and those higher up the ladder suggests that they belong to 'separate management cultures.'[87] One mid-level manager reported (no doubt, with some cynicism) that he always likes to see a minister appointed to his department 'because some of the ministers insist on a walkabout to meet the managers. In that way, I and some of my people get to meet the Deputy Minister.'[88]

The evidence of two separate management cultures manifests itself in many different ways. Deputy ministers are invariably preoccupied with the views of the cabinet, the Privy Council Office, and other central agencies and departments. They regularly put in seventy-hour weeks and receive less compensation than private sector counterparts. They see the assistant deputy ministers working just as hard and wonder why the public service is subjected to so much criticism from the 'media, academics, and politicians.'[89] Managers down the line, however, see the non-performers at first hand. As one explained: 'In my shop as elsewhere in government, about 25 per cent of the workers take on 50 per cent of the work, another 50 per cent of the workers assume just about the rest of the work while the remaining 25 per cent frankly don't do much.'[90] Yet, at the same time, managers down the line are likely to be far more preoccupied with the future of the department than are deputy ministers who are just passing through for a year or two. A recent survey of attitudes of public and private sector managers carried out by David Zussman and Jak Jabes revealed that 'private sector managers view their leaders as committed to the future of the organization. In the public ranks, as few as 42 percent of managers view deputy ministers in the same category.'[91] The survey also revealed that there is a 'serious morale problem' among public sector managers, with one in five often thinking about quitting, compared to one in fifty in the private sector.

The morale problem among managers and elsewhere in the federal public service is caused by a number of factors. The perceived lack of strong, stable, and committed leadership at the top is one thing. Others have pointed to 'management layering' as a fundamental problem. Many, including senior officials inside government, recognize that there are excessive layers of management.[92] One official put it this way: 'It is possible to run the Roman Catholic Church with five layers of management (i.e., the pope, cardinals, archbishops, bishop, and the parish priest). In the federal government we have at least eight (i.e., minister, deputy minister, assistant deputy minister, director general, director, manager, group chief, and supervisor).'[93] Layering, it has been suggested, contributes to 'low morale, clogs up decision making, inhibits communication, discourages productivity, limits initiative, diffuses accountability, and increases operating costs.'[94] It is certainly intimidating for a junior employee who may well have a good idea to look up and see what he or she will have to go through to sell the idea in the department.

These problems and other criticism directed at the federal public service, including lack of productivity, have not gone unnoticed by political leaders. Mulroney pledged in the 1984 election campaign to encourage 'creative and efficient management' in government and to challenge managers to come forward with proposals to achieve greater value for money. It will also be recalled that private sector representatives on the Nielsen Task Force reported that perhaps their most important recommendation was for the government to introduce a 'make-or-buy framework policy' to its operations. In July 1986, the Treasury Board approved such a policy.

CHALLENGING THE TURF

One of the purposes of the government's make-or-buy policy is to encourage competition between the public and private sectors for the delivery of government services.[95] The policy goes hand in hand with the government's privatization plans. The make-or-buy policy is designed to challenge government agencies to produce services for the public, for themselves, or for other government departments or agencies at a cost comparable to what private sector firms would charge for performing the same service. If fully implemented, the policy would force government departments and agencies to contract out to the private sector any services that they could not produce at a comparable or lower cost. Thus, a key part of the policy is to find a way to compare the actual cost of delivering the same service by government and the private sector. In addition to competition tendering between the public and private sectors, the policy also provides for employee takeovers, joint ventures, and proposals from community enterprises. The make-or-buy policy was borrowed from the United Kingdom and the United States, where governments have registered actual savings of over $50 million and $770 million, respectively, in six years. It was decided early on that in Canada the make-or-buy policy would be phased in through pilot projects, with departments invited to participate on a voluntary basis. To assist in implementing the policy, a small secretariat was established in the Treasury Board secretariat. In addition, some funding was made available to retain the services of consultants to determine the most cost-effective organization to deliver current government services.

The make-or-buy group in the Treasury Board secretariat was quick to argue that most government services are amenable to make-or-buy policy, or at least to some form of restructuring of the delivery of services. It also argued that important savings could be realized by challenging the in-house delivery of such services as training, claims processing, facility management, and even program delivery, including growing seed grains, research, laboratories, and health care for prison inmates. The process is intended to work in this fashion: first, specifications for a job or what is actually being done is described in a detailed fashion; secondly, a 'most efficient organization' study then looks at alternative sources of supply and expected cost (this study is usually conducted by an outside consultant to ensure, among other things, that the study is impartial); thirdly, bids from the private sector are solicited; and fourthly, the most efficient option, either private or public, is implemented.

By mid-1988, a dozen pilot projects had been launched, including one on the hydraulic laboratory in Environment Canada, another on Dorval airport, another on health care for inmates, and yet another on the Blainville Vehicle Test Centre. The results of all pilot projects point to important potential savings, ranging from 12 to over 20 per cent.

Still, little has been actually accomplished under the make-or-buy policy. Early on, the Treasury Board secretariat identified the surveys and mapping services and the Canada Centre for Remote Sensing in the Department of Energy, Mines and Resources and the Canadian Hydrographic Service with the Department of Fisheries and Oceans as ideal candidates. The three centres employ 1300 employees, mostly in Ottawa. Some preliminary discussions were held with the Montreal consulting firm Lavelin Inc. and with Bell Canada to see if they would be interested in putting together a joint proposal under the make-or-buy policy. The thinking was that a private sector consortium could not only run the centres more effectively, but also use them as a springboard to develop a world-class firm to challenge American and especially European firms. Word quickly leaked to the media, however, and it became front-page headlines in the Ottawa newspapers.[96] Area MPS, including those on the government side, publicly denounced the proposed transfer to the Lavelin-Bell consortium and the possible loss of jobs to Sherbrooke, which the consortium had identified as a possible site to develop the services further. Ministers, in turn, denied any suggestion that the centres would be 'privatized' and reassured Ottawans that their city would not lose any public service jobs. The minister of state, Gerald Merrithew, declared that the 'Government has never discussed privatization in the strict sense of the word' with Lavelin-Bell.[97]

The public controversy dampened the interest the government had in its make-or-buy policy. From that moment on, the Treasury Board secretariat abided strictly by the rule that pilot projects would have to be identified by *departments* on a *voluntary* basis. For supporters of the policy, the results have been disappointing. Though all pilot projects have pointed to important potential savings, none has been acted upon. In addition, departments and agencies are proving reluctant to volunteer for the pilot project stage. There are reasons other than the regional factor to explain this reluctance. In Canada, implementation of the policy has been voluntary and there is no burden of proof on managers to justify retention of in-house delivery. In contrast, government managers in the United States and the United Kingdom, when challenged, are required to demonstrate cost-effectiveness for all commercial functions to keep them in-house. In the United Kingdom, for example, competitive tendering is mandatory for certain activities.

Government managers, of course, see no incentives and plenty of discentives to transfer an activity to the private sector. Pilot projects which have been identified by departments have been geared mostly to see if they could absorb at least some of the reductions in person-years set for them. The thinking was that if a service could be transferred to the private sector, it would show a net reduction in the department's total person-year complement, even if it meant transfer of some of its financial resources to the private sector to carry out the service. This remains about the only incentive for deputy ministers to implement the government's make-or-buy policy. In short, managers are more interested in reducing person-years as a way of meeting their assigned reduction targets than in reducing total financial costs. They are likely to reject out of hand the notion that the make-or-buy policy can lead to important savings. They are more likely than not to argue that if the government is truly interested in saving money, it should look to other departments (where there is always more fat), and will also imply that any potential savings would only be turned over to ministers to support their slush funds for high-profile projects. The make-or-buy policy, however, holds plenty of disincentives for managers. Some are administrative, such as penalties on pension transferability for affected government employees. Others are much more visible, including opposition from public service unions. Still others are the impact a transfer of a particular unit or service to the private sector is likely to have on all government managers, from the assistant deputy minister down the line. Such a transfer will no doubt, at least in time, have some negative impact on their classification levels and hence on their salaries.

There are also some broader issues that need to be addressed. Government managers will invariably argue that it is unfair to compare the cost of running their operations with the private sector. They will point to various government policies and measures over which they have little control that serve to increase the cost of their operation. These include employment equity, the Official Languages Act, access to information, the requirements of central agencies, the Public Service Employment Act. Few private sector firms have similar restrictive measures on their activities.

There is yet another problem. Senior government managers will quite naturally look upon a make-or-buy policy with deep concern. They are likely to view it as a vote of no confidence in the public service on the part of the politicians. And yet, if the public service has become inefficient and costly over the years, it is because of various measures the politicians themselves put in place, from the establishment of the Office of the Comptroller General to access to information. A good number will consider it unfair that politicians would now seek to dismantle their institution by hiving off parts to the private sector. They are also likely to link the make-or-buy policy to morale problems and to the less-than-healthy state of the federal public service.

PROSPECTS

We now know that the make-or-buy policy has not been successful, that departments favour the status quo and spend considerable time and energy 'protecting their turf.' We also know that there are probably more incentives to manage badly in government than to manage well. Finally, we know that there is a morale problem plaguing the federal public service, that it is on the defensive, and the object of a barrage of criticism from 'the media, academics, and politicians.'[98] 'Bureaucrat-bashing,' a senior federal government official declared, 'has become a popular sport' in Canada.[99]

It has become almost trite to say that the federal public service no longer commands the respect it once did. The extend to which it has lost prestige is brought home by the comments of Dr John Evans, former president of the University of Toronto and member of the Rhodes scholarship selection committee, when he learned that a Rhodes scholar had decided to make the public service his future. He expressed his deep disappointment that the young man had chosen such a 'parasitic' profession.[100]

What then can we expect from the public service in terms of public spending and improved financial and management practices in government? There are few reasons to be optimistic. 'Public servants are like everybody else,' one senior central agency official observed: 'when they feel threatened, they will pull their wagons in a wide circle and defend themselves. It is basic human nature to be defensive and protect whatever you have left when you are threatened.'[101] A former federal deputy minister recently declared publicly that 'there is a malaise, and institutionally, I've been surprised at the lack of willingness to "fess up." '[102] Public servants are likely to say that politicians need to be more committed to sound financial management before they can be. If it is waste and mismanagement one is looking for, they will argue, one should look to the 'political boondoggles' and not to the bureaucracy. If the finger is pointed at their own department, they are likely to point their fingers at another where, they will claim, waste is even more spectacular.

There is also good reason to believe that the federal public service in future will be even more reluctant to accept change than it has been in the past. Its personnel is ageing, and the infusion of young or new blood has been severely cut back. Ten years ago, 14 per cent of public servants were younger than 25. Today, only 3 per cent are. The proportion in their 30s has increased to 36.9 per cent from 22.5 per cent in the same period. In 1974, 46,000 public servants were hired from outside government. In 1987 the number had dropped to 8892, with about half of the appointments being to term positions or to a non-permanent status.[103] As the public service ages, there are fewer and fewer promotions available (the annual number of promotions per hundred employees has dropped to eight from seventeen in ten years). The first year that there were more lateral transfers (when an employee moves to another position with the same classification and pay level) than promotions was 1985. Moreover, even lateral transfers have declined in recent years, falling from about 21,000 in 1982 to about 17,000 in 1986. In addition, as the public services ages, fewer and fewer people leave it. The percentage leaving ranges from a high of 17.5 per cent at age 19 and below to a low of 1.9 per cent at age 41. Separation rates stay at about 2 per cent for those between 41 and 49 and, from there, the rate increases to 3.8 percent by age 53.[104] The Nielsen Task Force reported that risk-taking in an entrepreneurial sense is actively discouraged in the federal government and that the fear of failure leads to the excessively bureaucratic procedures. An older public service increasingly subjected to outside criticism holds little promise for a greater entrepreneurial spirit, for new approaches to management, for challenging the government's A base, or for the continuing relevance of ongoing government programs.

10

Crown corporations: Financing the jewels

'Over the years,' the Economic Council of Canada reports, 'Canadian soil has ... been relatively conducive to the blossoming of state enterprise,' and 'now the concept of public enterprise is deeply embedded in the fabric of Canadian society.'[1] So deep is it, according to the council, that 'public and private sectors have worked in partnership' to build the Canadian nation.[2] The establishment of the Canadian National Railways (CNR) in 1919 constituted the federal government's first major venture into public enterprise.[3] The government has since made numerous other ventures, particularly during and after the Second World War. Today there are 53 parent crown corporations and 114 wholly owned subsidiaries. They employ about 180,000 people and have assets totalling approximately $60 billion.

Many people, particularly in more recent years, have expressed deep concern about the operations and accountability of crown corporations. Some prominent politicians have labelled them 'the hidden government deficit.' Others have suggested that crown corporations are 'out of control' and still others have called for new measures to control the 'flow of public funds' going to them.[4] Although major revisions to the operations of crown corporations were introduced in 1984, they have not served to satisfy many critics. Increasingly, we hear calls for the privatization of crown corporations and, in 1985, a secretariat was established to promote a government-wide privatization plan. This chapter reviews these developments, the operations of crown corporations, and their financing from public funds.

NOT ALL CROWNS ARE EQUAL

One of the last pieces of legislation enacted into law during the final days of the Liberal government in 1984 was a major overhaul of the operations of crown corporations. The Financial Administration Act (FAA) was amended to provide 'a stronger and more comprehensive framework for improved control and accountability of Crown Corporations to Parliament, to the government and to the public.'[5] Many, including the auditor general and the Lambert Commission, had written at length about the problems of identification, classification, and accountability of federal crown corporations. Some, Lambert had pointed out, operate much like government departments or branches of departments. Others operate at arm's length and still others have a relationship with the government which differs little from that maintained by private sector organizations.[6] This, the commission concluded, makes it difficult for the government to develop sound financial controls. To Lambert and others, the rules of the game for crown corporations were not all clear and, when they were, they did not apply equally. One can easily appreciate how this situation came about.

Crown corporations were not established in an orderly fashion or based on clear criteria that would automatically trigger either their establishment or their divestiture. The CNR was established in 1919 to 'safeguard the government's large investment in the railways [and] to protect Canada's image in foreign capital markets.'[7] Later, in 1932, fearing that Canadian broadcasting would be dominated by broadcasts originating in the United States, the Bennett government set up the Canadian Radio Broadcasting Commission to administer a national broadcasting service. Still later, the Mackenzie King government saw that the private sector was unwilling to launch a new enterprise to provide domestic air services and established Trans-Canada Airlines (TCA), now Air Canada. It was only during the Second World War, however, that the government began to make extensive use of crown corporations. At the start of the war, there were fifteen crown-owned corporations. Thirty-two were added during the war years because it was felt that they were better suited to lure business people to manage war programs than a typical government department would be. In addition, key cabinet ministers, notably C.D. Howe, felt that implementing a successful war effort required a highly decentralized form of administration. All of the thirty-two corporations established during the war years were incorporated under federal companies legislation under the authority of the War Measures Act or the Department of Munitions and Supplies Act. Because of the urgency of the war effort, none was established by an act of parliament.

Although most of the crown corporations established during the war were later disbanded, some continued, including Polysar and Canadian Arsenals Limited. In addition, new ones were created to participate in the post-war reconstruction, and many of these were established under various statutes rather than by act of parliament. The Canadian Mortgage and Housing Corporation (CMHC), for example, was created during this period to promote new housing construction. By 1951, there were still thirty-one federal crown corporations. Yet there was no model for their establishment or procedures by which they could be held accountable for their spending. Crown corporations that did not require parliamentary appropriation to finance operations, for example, could completely avoid parliamentary scrutiny. The story does not end here, however. There was an accelerated increase in the number of crown corporations in the 1960s and 1970s.

The government amended the Financial Administration Act in 1951 to strengthen its financial control over and direction of crown corporations. The amendments classified and listed the crown corporations for the first time. Schedules attached to the FAA classified corporations as follows: schedule B listed all departmental corporations that were treated in the same way as government departments, such as the Economic Council of Canada and the National Gallery of Canada; schedule C listed agencies responsible for the trading or service operations on a quasi-commercial basis, including Atomic Energy of Canada Limited (AECL), Canadian Arsenals, the Canadian Film Development Corporation (CFDC); and schedule D listed those responsible for the management of commercial and industrial operations, such as Air Canada, Eldorado Nuclear, as well as corporations (for example, FBDB) responsible for the management of lending or financial operations. Crown corporations operating after the FAA amendments were granted varying degrees of independence. Schedule B corporations were designed to function much like typical government departments. Accordingly, the responsible minister and the Treasury Board could exert financial control and direction as for a department. Schedule C corporations had more autonomy but still had to obtain approval from the appropriate minister and the Treasury Board president for their annual operating budget. At the other end of the spectrum were schedule D crown corporations. Air Canada, Petro-Canada, and Canadian National, for instance, could operate very much at arm's length from the government's financial controls. In some instances the government would not approve, or even see, their annual budgets and was not involved in any way in the day-to-day management. It would, however, review capital spending proposals.

By the late 1960s and 1970s many observers were calling for further revisions to the FAA with regard to crown corporations. The auditor general, in particular, stressed time and again the need for greater 'direction, control and accountability' of crown corporations.[8] Even the federal cabinet got into the act when the Privy Council Office issued a paper in 1977 proposing major 'improvements' in the way crown corporations report to parliament and the government. The paper began by asking the question: 'How can increased responsiveness to public policy be reconciled with the arms-length relationship which the theory of public enterprise requires government, ministers, and Parliament to maintain with Crown Corporations?'[9] It did not provide a completely satisfactory answer and no one since has been able to. Striking the right balance between giving crown corporations enough independence to perform their jobs, or in some instances to compete in the market-place, and at the same time ensuring that they can be held accountable for their spending of public funds is an elusive task. No one formula could possibly satisfy all parties. Some corporations would ask for more autonomy while some ministers and government officials (notably the guardians in Finance, Treasury Board, and the Privy Council Office) would seek greater government and financial controls.

Still, virtually everyone who took a look at the operations of crown corporations – including officials in the Privy Council Office and the Treasury Board secretariat – concluded that the 1951 FAA amendments were inadequate. Many even argued that they were flawed from the beginning. The schedules in the amendments did not cover all crown corporations and thus the amendments could not apply to them all. In addition, subsection 68(1) of the act stated that its provisions did not apply in the event that they were inconsistent with those of any special act of incorporation. The government had argued in 1951 that parliament should have the ability to place 'special or extraordinary' provisions in any special act of incorporation even if they were inconsistent with the FAA amendments. The government pledged, however, to amend wherever possible existing acts and draft new ones to bring them into line with the FAA amendments.

The opposite was to occur. Almost every new bill introduced in parliament from 1951 on to create new corporations was at least in part at variance with the FAA amendments. In addition, by the mid-1970s, the FAA applied to only fifty-four crown corporations. But it was clear to everyone that there was a great deal more to the story. From 1968 on a large number of companies, either wholly or partially owned by the federal government, were established under federal or provincial companies legislation without statutory authority. There was no government centre for the coordination or approval of the acquisition or incorporation of new crown corporations. Worse still, there was little government control over entities that had the power to expose the government to heavy liabilities.

The 1951 amendments had failed to provide an appropriate definition of what constituted a crown corporation, simply stating it to be 'a corporation that is ultimately accountable, through a minister to Parliament for the conduct of its affairs.'[10] This vague definition caused no end of confusion. Because it was so vague, several corporations had asked to be exempted from any crown corporation policy and, in fact, not be designated as crown corporations at all. For example, the International Development Research Council (IDRC) had never been listed on any schedule to the FAA. It asked to be exempted on the grounds that to be treated as a crown corporation *comme les autres* would hamper its international credibility and operations. Yet, then as now, the IDRC was a corporation, was wholly owned by the federal government, and was funded by the federal government. Similarly, Canadair had asked to be excluded from the application of any crown corporations bill, on the grounds that inclusion might detract from its ability to market its products abroad, especially in the United States.

The Conservative government moved in 1979 to place stronger financial control on crown corporations and, on 28 March, the Treasury Board issued a minute designed to restrict ministers and departments from creating or acquiring new corporations without cabinet and parliamentary authority.[11] A few months later the clerk of the Privy Council and secretary to the cabinet wrote to all crown corporations to request them not to incorporate or acquire a subsidiary without first obtaining Treasury Board approval.[12] He explained that the board would wish to ensure that the proposed subsidiary's undertakings were consistent with the mandate of the parent crown corporation and that the new incorporations would not serve to dilute or avoid government control and direction.

But these could only be stopgap measures. More far-reaching changes were required. The Privy Council Office had prepared a 'blue book' on crown corporations which recommended sweeping changes. The auditor general and the Lambert Commission had also made numerous recommendations designed to strengthen the government's financial control over crown corporations. A task force was established to prepare a comprehensive policy on crown corporations and was asked to report by the summer of 1979. The task force included representatives from Finance, the Treasury Board secretariat, the Office of the Comptroller General, and one crown corporation, and was chaired by the Privy Council Office.

It, too, recommended sweeping changes and urged the government to introduce a new crown corporations bill. The government agreed and, in November 1979, introduced a bill detailing far-reaching changes to the operations of crown corporations. The government, however, fell in the House shortly after and the bill died on the order papers.

When Trudeau was returned to power, there was little indication that the operations of crown corporations ranked high on his list of priorities. Some watered-down legislative measures were introduced to parliament on 30 June 1982. But they went nowhere. However, pressure to do something was kept up by the opposition, particularly by the Progressive Conservatives (who had introduced major reforms a few years earlier), by the media, and by the auditor general. And, as already noted, the government did introduce major reforms to the operations of crown corporations in 1984 for which parliamentary approval was finally secured. It did not, like the Clark government had in 1979, seek to put in place a Crown Corporation Act. Rather, as in 1951, the government again amended the Financial Administration Act. It did, however, accept a number of recommendations made by the 1979 special task force. As recommended, its wholly owned corporations were divided into three categories or groupings. The first group comprises those that are, in effect, departments of government with corporate form and essentially subject to the same regime of financial management and control as established for government departments by the FAA. These are called departmental corporations. The remaining corporations – that is, the crown corporations – are grouped into two broad categories: those that operate in a competitive environment and are ordinarily independent of the Consolidated Revenue Fund for the financing of operating expenditures, and those that do not fit into either of the previous two groupings. Of the two groups (schedule c, parts I and II respectively) a more rigorous regime of financial management and control is imposed over part I corporations. This distinction is based on the notion that ministers have a clear responsibility to account to parliament for the expenditure of public funds and also have a clear duty to protect the integrity of the Consolidated Revenue Fund. Accordingly, when either of these is directly involved, ministers must have at hand effective mechanisms to fulfil their responsibilities. Those mechanisms are not as necessary when public funds or the integrity of the Consolidated Revenue Fund are not directly involved. Thus the government embraced the view that governmental financial direction and control of crown corporations should in part at least be proportional to their dependence on the Consolidated Revenue Fund. (See appendix 4 for schedule B and C corporations, as outlined in the FAA 1984.)

With respect to control over policy, however, the government argued that all crown corporations are instruments for the achievement of public policy objectives. Accordingly, it did not wish to distinguish them as policy instruments and felt that the mechanisms of policy direction and control should be constant for all crown corporations.

The government's principal concern in revising the FAA was to tighten its financial management and control of crown corporations.[13] Under the new legislation, parliament is required 'to approve the creation, mandate and financing of new parent Corporations.' Crown corporations now must obtain government approval before they can acquire or establish new corporate entities, and (for schedule C, part 1 corporations) the government now approves annual corporate plans as well as operating and capital budgets. The 1984 amendments also enabled the government to prescribe the form, content, and timing of corporate plans, as well as the operating and capital budgets. In general, each corporate plan provides information on the corporation's growth and market strategies, their consistency with statutory mandates and stated government objectives, the financial implications of such strategies, and their time frames. The plans are to be structured on a three- to five-year basis and are tailored to the operations of individual corporations. In addition, direct responsibility for the management of crown corporations is now supposed to rest with their board of directors and chief executive officers.

In respect to corporate financing information, the 1984 FAA amendments provide general authority to the minister of finance to approve borrowing activities of any wholly owned corporation. The government also strengthened its authorities to require financial information consistent with its role as shareholder and frequently banker of crown corporations.

With respect to direction, the government enshrined in the FAA a provision that grants it the same rights and powers of direction as exercised by the sole shareholder (or proprietor) of a private sector company incorporated under the Canada Business Corporations Act. There is, however, no requirement for the government as shareholder to approve the by-laws, although it can veto them. Shareholders' rights involve prerogatives in relation to binding direction under a unanimous shareholder agreement, appointment and removal of directors, and appointment of auditors. The government also served notice that it would employ this authority, when and if necessary, to require audits of management systems. [14]

The power to issue a directive proved to be highly controversial and the government was forced to retreat somewhat. In many ways, this power goes against the long-established principle that crown corporations operate at arm's length from government. The obvious purpose behind the principle is to insulate crown corporations from political intervention in their operations. Yet the notion that the government can issue a directive to crown corporations is based on the premise that ministers either collectively or individually have powers no less than those of a sole shareholder in the private sector. Especially during the 1970s parliament, the media and the general public began to hold ministers to a higher standard of responsibility about the actions of individual crown corporations than had previously been the case. Ministers were often asked in parliament to account for controversial developments in several crown corporations, notably Air Canada, Canadian National, AECL, and Polysar. In the case of Air Canada, specific charges were made in the mid-1970s over the lack of financial controls. The government responded by establishing an independent commission of inquiry 'to investigate ... [the] financial controls, accounting procedures and fiscal management' in Air Canada. [15] Ministers were now more and more of the view that if they were to be held accountable for actions by crown corporations, then they should have some powers of direction to ensure that certain practices are followed.

In addition, there was a growing realization in parliament and elsewhere that the majority of crown corporations require either budgetary or non-budgetary financing from the Consolidated Revenue Fund. In such cases, if the responsible minister agrees with the financing request or proposals put forward by a crown corporation, he must support them both before Treasury Board and his fellow MPs. Thus, the ministers involved felt that they should have a say on the appropriateness of the requests for funding. The minister of finance also has a special responsibility for the funding of crown corporations to the extent that it impacts upon the Consolidated Revenue Fund. For this reason the Department of Finance argued that it must have available the means to protect the fund against unforeseen liabilities.

Yet crown corporations had traditionally taken the position that they only report to parliament 'through' a minister. The 1951 act appeared to confirm this. It stated, it will be recalled, that a crown corporation is 'a corporation that is ultimately accountable through a minister, to Parliament.' As a result, the role of a minister responsible for a crown corporation had been relegated to that akin to a 'post box.' Thus, most corporations strongly resisted any changes that would strengthen the role of the ministry in their operations. Some have been successful. Cultural corporations, such as the Canada Council and the CBC, expressed deep concern over the government's power, as sole shareholder, to issue directives. The government, they argued, should have no authority over program priorities and types of projects to be funded. The opposition agreed and, to secure parliamentary approval for amending the FAA, the government exempted several crown corporations from certain provisions of the new legislation. All are funded almost exclusively from government appropriations, including the Canada Council, the CBC, the CFDC, the Canadian Institute for International Peace and Security, IDRC, and the National Arts Centre.

This is yet another sign of the diversity in the relationship of wholly owned corporations to the government and of their funding. It is simply not possible to write about corporations as one can about government departments. The latter must all follow the same rules and processes to obtain funding for continuing programs and new initiatives. This is not so with crown corporations.

Departmental corporations seek funding in the same way departments do. But because they have arm's length status, ministers usually do not go to bat for them at the cabinet table to the extent they do for departments. Nor do the corporations compete to the same extent as departments for new funding from the policy reserves and cabinet committees. Still, schedule B corporations, including the Economic Council of Canada, the AECB, and the NRC, must submit their MYOPS to the Treasury Board secretariat where they are assessed in the same way departmental MYOPS are. They get a reference level for their expenditure budgets, and any increases must be justified on the basis of workload, adjustments for salary increases, and so on. The cultural or the exempted corporations also secure their funding from the Treasury Board through MYOPS.

All schedule C crown corporations must submit corporate plans. This is true for parent crown corporations that operate in a competitive environment and are not supposed to be dependent on government operating subsidies, as well as for corporations that are dependent on parliamentary appropriations. The Treasury Board and its president both play key roles on behalf of the ministry in the government management of crown corporations. The former recommends corporate plans for cabinet approval, approves capital and operating budgets, considers individual program and investment proposals, and can make regulations on form and content of annual reports. The Treasury Board president receives notification of important corporate developments, such as acquisitions or divestiture of shares, and tables an annual consolidated report on activities of crown corporations and other government holdings.

To support the Treasury Board and its president, a crown corporations' directorate has been established in the Treasury Board secretariat. The directorate reports to both the Treasury Board and the Department of Finance. It serves as the main contact between crown corporations and the central agencies of the government in overseeing the applications of Part XII of the FAA. Corporate plans and requests for funding from crown corporations are always submitted to the Treasury Board by the relevant line minister.

The cost of crown corporations to the government is substantial. Table 9 reports that the actual total budgetary funding for C-I, C-II, and unscheduled corporations amounted to $4.692 billion in the year ending 31 July 1987. The net cost is somewhat lower since a few crown corporations pay dividends to the government. For instance, CN paid over $23 million in 1985, although no dividend was reported in 1986 because it registered a loss. In addition to budgetary funding, crown corporations can obtain loans, investments, and advances from the federal government and from lending institutions in the private sector. As of 31 March 1987, they had nearly $16 billion in outstanding obligations to the government of Canada and nearly $20 billion to the private sector. Air Canada, Petro-Canada, and Canadian National alone owed $6.5 billion to the private sector.

Most observers nevertheless agree that the 1984 amendments to the FAA have put in place an effective accountability and control framework for crown corporations. The proliferation of crown corporations wit-

TABLE 9
Parent crown corporations budgetary funding (for years ending on or before 31 July 1987)

FAA schedules	Year end	Budgetary funding from Canada ($ millions)
C-I corporations	31 December 1986	0.7
Atomic Energy of Canada Ltd	31 March 1987	217.6
Canada Deposit Insurance Corp.	31 December 1986	
Canada Harbour Place Corp.	31 March 1987	13.6
Canada Lands Company Limited	31 March 1987	
Canada Lands Co. (Mirabel) Ltd	31 March 1987	6.8
Canada Lands Co. (Le Vieux-Port de Montréal) Ltd	31 March 1987	3.3
Canada Mortgage & Housing Corp.	31 December 1986	5.0
Canada Museums Construction Corporation Inc.	31 December 1986	1355.1
Canada Post Corporation	31 March 1987	66.0
Canadian Arsenals Limited	31 March 1987	486.1
Canadian Commercial Corporation	31 March 1987	
Canadian Dairy Commission	31 July 1987	16.1
Canadian Livestock Feed Board	31 March 1987	292.2
Canadian National (West Indies) Steamships, Ltd	31 December 1986	17.2
Canadian Patents & Development	31 March 1987	nil
Canadian Saltfish Corporation	31 March 1987	nil
Canagrex	31 March 1987	nil
Cape Breton Development Corp.	31 March 1987	163.9
Defence Construction (1951) Ltd	31 March 1987	13.2
Export Development Corporation	31 December 1986	nil
Farm Credit Corporation	31 March 1987	nil
Federal Business Development Bank	31 March 1987	54.8
Freshwater Fish Marketing Corp.	30 April 1987	nil
Great Lakes Pilotage Authority	31 December 1986	nil
Harbourfront Corporation	31 March 1987	1.0
Internationl Centre for Ocean Development	31 March 1987	4.0
Laurentian Pilotage Authority	31 December 1986	1.3
Marine Atlantic Inc.	31 December 1986	127.0
Mingan Associates, Ltd	31 December 1986	nil
National Capital Commission	31 March 1987	62.4
Northern Canada Power Commission	31 March 1987	nil
Pacific Pilotage Authority	31 December 1986	nil
Petro-Canada International Assistance Corporation	31 December 1986	23.5
Royal Canadian Mint	31 December 1986	nil
St Anthony Fisheries Limited	31 March 1987	nil
St Lawrence Seaway Authority	31 March 1987	13.2

TABLE 9 – *continued*

FAA schedules	Year end	Budgetary funding from Canada ($ millions)
The Standard Council of Canada	31 March 1987	6.7
Via Rail Canada Inc.	31 December 1986	506.0
Total C-I corporations		3457.2
C-II corporations		
Air Canada	31 December 1986	
Canada Development Investment Corporation	31 December 1986	13.0
Canada Ports Corporation	31 December 1986	19.8
Canadian National Railway Co.	31 December 1986	
Halifax Port Corporation	31 December 1986	
Montreal Port Corporation	31 December 1986	
Petro-Canada	31 December 1986	
Port of Quebec Corporation	31 December 1986	
Prince Rupert Port Corporation	31 December 1986	
Saint John Port Corporation	31 December 1986	
St John's Port Corporation	31 December 1986	
Teleglobe Canada	31 December 1986	
Vancouver Port Corporation	31 December 1986	0.5
Total C-II corporations		33.3
Total schedule C corporations		3490.5
Exempt (unscheduled) corporations		
Canada Council	31 March 1987	85.5
Canadian Broadcasting Corp.	31 March 1987	855.1
Canadian Film Development Corp.	31 March 1987	86.0
Canadian Institute for International Peace and Security	31 March 1987	3.0
Canadian Wheat Board	31 July 1987	58.0
International Development Research Centre	31 March 1987	100.0
National Arts Centre Corp.	31 August 1986	14.8
Total, exempt corporations		1202.4
Grand total, parent crown corporations (except Bank of Canada, 2320 employees)		4692.9

SOURCE: Public Accounts of Canada, 1987, vol. III: The president of the Treasury Board, Annual Report to Parliament on Crown Corporations and Other Corporate Interests of Canada

nessed in the 1960s and 1970s has ended. As is the case for government departments, crown corporations have significantly improved their cash management. There have been few stories of fiscal and administrative mismanagement of the kind that surfaced during the 1970s. The great majority of crown corporations have tabled the required documents in parliament as prescribed in the FAA amendments.[16] In 1986, for example, 218 documents were tabled and only 22 were still outstanding at the end of the year. Ministers sign off all corporate plans, and these plans now contain performance expectations. The overall cost to the government of supporting crown corporations is also down (see figure 8).

This is not to suggest that all is now well with the financing and operation of crown corporations.[17] Many companies in the private sector still object to some crown corporations being able to compete with them in the market-place, with the full backing of the government. They argue that crown corporations do not have to keep watching their bottom lines. If they cannot turn a profit, the argument goes, they simply draw on the Consolidated Revenue Fund. They point to numerous examples. AECL, for instance, has not been able to secure new orders for its CANDU reactors. Yet it has successfully resisted cutting back its research activities on the grounds that any significant loss of key staff would imperil its survival and also Canada's long-term prospects in the nuclear industry. The federal government has continued to support the company year after year by at least $200 million a year. If AECL were operating according to the rules of the market-place, the business community maintains, it would have had to downsize its operations substantially or it would be out of business.

The competition with crown corporations, they also insist, can never be fair. As mentioned above, the private sector never has access to the Consolidated Revenue Fund to borrow from or to shoulder any loss. They also object to crown corporations raising capital from other sources. It will be recalled that the government urged crown corporations to borrow from outside markets to limit its total spending to less than the growth in GNP. The Canadian Manufacturers' Association (CMA), for example, was quick to ask the government to restrict crown corporation long-term financing from capital markets, arguing that they 'scoop' the market because of the implicit back-up of the Consolidated Revenue Fund.[18] CMA also insisted that because of the privileged status of crown corporations in capital markets, they can never feel the full weight of market forces.

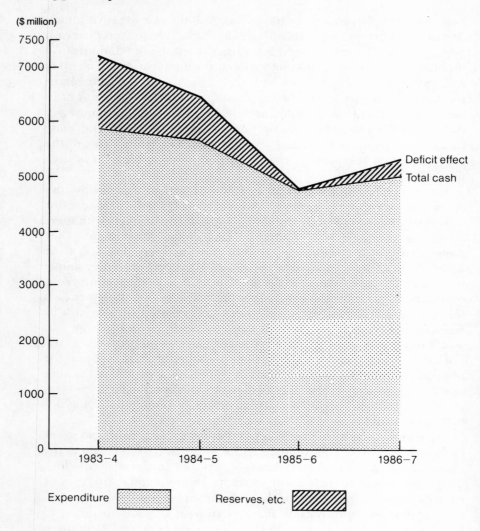

Figure 8
The cost of crown corporations
Source: Treasury Board Secretariat, 1988
Note: Expenditure or total cash is the total government outlay in support of crown corporations less dividends. Reserves or deficit effect represent an amount placed in reserve to pay for defaults on loans.

There are other criticisms. Many private sector representatives challenge the view that crown corporations are created or continue operations to perform tasks private companies could not or would not undertake. Trans-Canada Airlines might have been created because no one in the private sector was prepared at the time to launch air services across the country. But such is no longer the case. They also argue that not all crown corporations serve a public policy objective. Many frequently point to Petro-Canada as a case in point. Petro-Canada, it has been reported, 'was established in response to concerns raised about the world oil crisis in 1973–74 which for the first time brought into serious question the security of Canada's oil supplies.'[19] Canada, it was decided, needed a window on the oil industry. In addition, it was argued that the country could no longer rely exclusively on foreign firms for a secure oil supply, and it was felt that a publicly owned oil company was needed to promote exploration and development. However, Petro-Canada has become more of a major oil and gas retailer than an explorer. It has had only limited success in exploration for new oil and gas discoveries. Yet it has purchased Petrofina, BP Refining, and Gulf Canada. The Petrofina purchase was financed by the federal treasury through the Canadian ownership account at a cost of between $1.4 and $1.6 billion. All in all, the total cost to taxpayers has amounted to over $4 billion. One observer suggests that 'it is hard to imagine a single advantage we have gained for our investment, except a modicum of exploration – most of it paid for ... by exploration grants.' He concluded that Petro-Canada has not and does not serve any public policy objectives. 'It looks,' he claims, 'much like any other oil company.'[20]

For their part, crown corporations argue that although they may have access to the Consolidated Revenue Fund, they are often compelled to operate under difficult circumstances unknown to the private sector. Crown corporations, including those that are expected to be competitive in the market, must adhere to a host of government policies that can prove costly. As in the case of government departments discussed earlier, parent crown corporations and their wholly owned subsidiaries are now subject to the provisions of the Official Languages Act. They have also been directed to plan 'within a reasonable period of time ... special measures to enable designated groups – women, persons with disabilities, aboriginal peoples and members of visible minority groups – to participate equitably in employment and career advancement opportunities.'[21] Subsequently, the Treasury Board established quotas for crown corporations to meet.

Crown corporations are also expected to generate 'all kinds of briefings and papers' to feed the Ottawa system. There are the various reports that are now required to be tabled in parliament, in addition to numerous special requests for information from the relevant line departments, central agencies, and ministers.

A more important factor, however, is that crown corporations are not always able to conduct their operations solely on the basis of commercial practices and principles. Their operations are subjected to a degree of public scrutiny and expectation that is unheard of in the private sector. The political imperatives of Canadian regionalism also often weigh heavily in their decision making. An example will illustrate the point. In the mid-1970s, the large Canadian retailer, Eaton's, closed its catalogue operations in Moncton, NB, throwing 1000 people out of work. Monctonians essentially looked on the matter as a business decision and there was little protest by the local media and community leaders. Governments were asked to intervene with special job creation measures but there were no demonstrations against Eaton's itself, and the company was not asked to keep open its catalogue operations.

In contrast, however, when CN decided in the early 1980s that it no longer required its repair and maintenance shops in Moncton, Roméo LeBlanc, a powerful minister in the Trudeau cabinet representing the riding adjoining Moncton, made it clear to CN that closing 'the Moncton shops would not be acceptable – period.'[22] CN knew full well that it would not be any easier to close the Winnipeg shops, a city represented by Lloyd Axworthy, another powerful minister in cabinet, or those in Montreal, which was represented by Marc Lalonde.

With the election of the Mulroney government, CN again sought to close the Moncton shops and this time there was no longer any senior cabinet minister to fight for Moncton. With only one junior minister representing New Brunswick at the time, CN was finally able to announce its decision to close the Moncton shops. The reaction in Moncton was swift, highly vocal, and determined. The local member of parliament was asked to resign, a 'Save Our Shop' committee, consisting of leading community spokespersons, was established, several widely reported demonstrations took place, and the matter dominated the local media for three years.[23] Municipal, provincial, and some federal politicians insisted that the 'federal government' was treating Moncton unfairly. CN subsequently announced a delay in implementing the shop closure and unveiled a special fund to attract new jobs to Moncton. In short, Monctonians had one set of expectations for government, even crown corporations operating in a competitive environment, and another for the private sector. When a leading member of the Moncton community was asked to comment on this discrepancy, he responded that 'business must make business decisions. There is a bottom line to look after. Otherwise the business will not survive long. Eaton's is a business and it must compete. In government, especially in the federal government, there is a great deal of waste and inefficiency. Moncton is not getting its share of the waste. In losing the CN shops, we are now getting even less of our share.'[24]

There are numerous other examples. Terra Transport, a subsidiary of CN, consistently loses money in operating a passenger and freight service in Newfoundland. It lost $39 million in 1987 and $41.3 million in 1986. CN, however, knows that it simply cannot act as a private firm might and cancel the service. After several years of federal-provincial negotiations, the federal Ministry of Transport announced in June 1988 that CN would close down its Terra Transport operation. In turn, the federal government agreed to spend 'over $800 million in new money ... to improve Newfoundland's Transportation system and for labour and community adjustment.'[25]

Air Canada has had to reassure Manitobans time and again that its maintenance facility in Winnipeg will not be transferred elsewhere. At one point the deputy prime minister stood up in parliament to say that Air Canada would not close its maintenance facility in Winnipeg even if the company were to purchase new equipment requiring less and different maintenance than at present.[26]

Ministers can influence crown corporations, even schedule C, part II corporations, in three ways. First, they can make their views known to management. Secondly, they have a say in naming members to the board of directors. Thirdly, and most important, they have to approve corporate plans. This last controlling device is by far the most effective, though not all ministers seek to influence crown corporations' decisions. In fact, officials report that ministers rarely attempt to intervene in policy matters or broad corporate strategy decisions or seek ways to cut back spending. They intervene mostly on the location of economic activities, and some are even prepared to hold up corporate plans from going to Treasury Board to make their point. Examples abound. In 1983, for instance, the minister of transport was able to secure a decision from Air Canada to locate new computer facilities for its financial services in Winnipeg. Another minister of transport held up CN's corporate plan until the company rescinded a decision to close down regional operations and offices in less-populated areas.[27] Thus, while the 1984 FAA amendments have ensured greater financial control over crown corporations and their corporate plans, they have also strengthened the hands of powerful regional ministers in their dealings with crown corporations and in securing the location of certain economic activities.

Schedule C, part 1 corporations (or corporations that are dependent on government subsidies) must also contend with regional issues. Some were created precisely to deal with such issues. The Cape Breton Development Corporation (DEVCO), for example, was established to serve the economic well-being of a geographic area, rather than of a particular industry. It was first set up to promote industrial development in light of the closing of coal mines and because of problems in the local steel industry. The federal government earmarked $20 million to develop new industry and $25 million to develop the mines in 1967. It has since provided new funding every year except in 1984–5. In 1986–7 alone, the federal government contributed $163.9 million in subsidies.[28] Numerous studies, including a 1983 TBS assessment, have documented management and financial problems at DEVCO. Suggestions, however, that the corporation should be cut back were for a long time dismissed by Allan J. MacEachen, a power in the Trudeau cabinet. When the Mulroney government came to office, it was widely assumed in Ottawa that government funding to DEVCO would be reduced substantially. But, explained one central agency official, 'after the Mulroney government cut the heavy water plants in Cape Breton, Atlantic ministers and Nova Scotia politicians began insisting that the region had contributed more than its share to government restraint and that if further spending cuts were required then we should look elsewhere. After a while most people simply stopped talking about cutting back subsidies to DEVCO.'[29]

There are other examples of regionally sensitive issues, and not all of them are in economically depressed areas. In 1972, for instance, the federal government delineated a harbourfront in Toronto by assembling land it owned and by expropriating other lands. It then established in 1978 a crown corporation, Harbourfront Corporation, to develop the site. The corporation has put together a series of cultural, recreational, and educational activities. In addition, it has signed agreements with private sector firms to lease some land and it has also sold air rights. Notwithstanding these initiatives, the corporation has consistently received annual subsidies from the federal government for its operations – $14 million in 1983–4, $20.9 million in 1984–5, $6.1 million in 1985–6, and down to $1.0 million in 1986–7.[30]

Crown corporations must also contend with public pressure to extend their services and activities in the regions. Often they are criticized not so much for what they do but rather for where they do it. The premier of New Brunswick, for example, has been highly critical of the CBC, not over policy or program content, but over the limited presence the corporation has in the province compared with the other provinces. Frank McKenna suggested it was 'absolutely and totally shameful' that the CBC could find $220 million to outfit the corporation's new Toronto headquarters and 'pour money into richly endowed Ontario but was unable to find the $10–$20 million needed for New Brunswick.'[31]

Though the 1984 FAA amendments went a long way towards tightening up crown corporations' financial controls, some suggest that not enough has been done, arguing that only in exceptional circumstances should the government substitute itself for private sector actors. Privatization has become a key word in the political vocabulary in the western world, and Canada is no exception. Privatization, explains Jeanne Laux and Maureen Molot, fits 'within a broader political agenda for the Conservatives, who saw their impressive mandate as an expression of Canadian exasperation at the Liberal legacy of soaring government deficits ... intrusive government and sluggish, uncertain economic growth.'[32]

ROMANCING PRIVATIZATION

Few were surprised that the Mulroney Conservatives would make the privatization of public enterprise a key part of their agenda in government. After all, 'the Tories had spent the better part of the previous decade in opposition criticizing Crown Corporations.'[33] As soon as Brian Mulroney became leader of the party in 1983, he appointed a five-person task force on privatization. Although its report has never been made public, it is now widely known that it recommended selling numerous crown corporations, including Petro-Canada, CN, Air Canada, and AECL. In his first major economic statement as finance minister barely seven weeks after coming to office, Michael Wilson declared: 'Although each corporation was established to serve what, at the time, might have been important public policy purposes, we must ask ourselves whether that remains the case. If it does not, it is surely important to consider whether the corporations should be retained.'[34] In his first budget speech, he declared that 'Crown Corporations with a commercial value but no ongoing public policy purpose will be sold.'[35] Privatization was seen as highly supportive of the government's strategy for economic renewal which was based on promoting private sector growth and restoring the government's fiscal flexibility.

The concept of privatization was not new to central agencies and government departments. As noted above, the Trudeau government had undertaken a privatization review in 1976, as had the Clark government in 1979. Several crown corporations had been identified as candidates for privatization and for in-depth analysis. And, once again, in the last days of the Trudeau administration, several crown corporations, including Air Canada, had been earmarked for possible privatization. But further action was never taken. Still, central agency officials, particularly in the TBS and Department of Finance, had a basis to work from. They also readied themselves in the summer of 1984, knowing that a Conservative government would want to push this issue on coming to office. Their main concern, however, was 'how to privatize,' rather than 'what to privatize.' They sought to identify general, financial, policy, and procedural issues with which any privatization program would have to deal.

The Mulroney government was quick off the mark. Within weeks of coming to office, the minister of DRIE announced that the government would sell Canadian Development Investment Corporation (CDIC), Canadair, de Havilland, Teleglobe, Eldorado Nuclear, and CDIC's interests in Massey-Ferguson. A few weeks later, the government approved the sale of the Northern Transportation Corporation, a crown corporation providing marine, tug, and barge services in the North. Several inactive crown corporations were also dissolved, including Canadian Sports Pool Corporation, Canagrex, and Loto Canada. In 1985, the government sold Canadian Arsenals and 21.8 million shares of the Canadian Development Corporation.[36]

The government's privatization initiatives, however, were soon in difficulty as charges of favouritism were hurled at the government by the opposition and the media over the handling of some sales. Word also leaked out that the bidding process of other sales was 'in chaos.'[37] The sale of Teleglobe ran into problems when government-imposed guidelines included limits on foreign ownership. One observer labelled the sale 'Act First, Think Later.'[38] De Havilland, in the words of another observer, was 'pushed into the hands of Boeing [still] leaving the government potentially responsible for $400 million in debt.'[39]

Mulroney and his most senior ministers sought to put order in the government's privatization initiatives by establishing a new ministerial task force on privatization chaired by the Treasury Board president, with a small secretariat inside the Treasury Board to support the task force. In June 1986 the task force was turned into a cabinet committee and a minister was asked to establish a new Office of Privatization. The office's mandate was expanded to include regulatory affairs and a deputy minister was appointed in August. These initiatives, it was hoped, would ensure that the sales of crown corporations would be properly planned, timed, and implemented and also provide a voice at the cabinet table so that privatization would always be central to the government's agenda.

The secretariat and later the Office of Privatization and Regulatory Affairs immediately set out to 'manage better' the various activities, including overseeing the preparation of necessary legislation of the sales already announced. It also pressed ahead, at the request of Priorities and Planning, with the development of a privatization plan. The plan has been updated and been brought before P & P on several occasions. Essentially, it calls for a series of initiatives, some of which could be carried out quickly (that is, over six months), and others over the medium and longer term. The thinking was always to have plans for the privatization of crown corporations 'on the shelf' so that initiatives could be pursued when the economic and market conditions were right. In preparing the plan, it was decided that all crown corporations would be considered for privatization and that the onus was on ministers to explain why they ought not to be involved. Candidates for privatization would be identified on the basis of two principles: if they were no longer serving public policy purposes, or if they had sufficient financial viability and prospects to attract investors.

The office quickly identified two 'flagship' candidates – Air Canada and Petro-Canada – and about fifteen others. It argued, for example, that CN hotels, among others, hardly contributed to a public policy objective. It also recommended that two subsidiaries of AECL – Radiochemical Company and Medical Products – be sold. It urged the sales of Eldorado Nuclear, the government's share in CN/CP Telecommunications, Terra Nova Communications, the loan portfolio of the FBDB, Telesat Canada, the Toronto Harbourfront Corporation, and others. It also suggested that several crown corporations be removed from schedule C of the FAA. The office argued that some of their functions could be taken over by a government department or be redesignated as schedule B corporations and thus managed in much the same fashion as departments. Candidates included Defence Construction Limited (which manages property construction projects), the Standards Council of Canada, and the Canadian Dairy Commission.

Notwithstanding the establishment of a privatization office, the development of a comprehensive plan, and the big push in the first months in office of the Mulroney government to act quickly on the issue, the *Financial Post* reported in late 1987 that 'the process of privatizing Canada's Crown Corporations has virtually ground to a halt!'[40] Only two major crown corporations were sold in 1987, Fishery Products International and Teleglobe Canada. The Mulroney government had committed itself publicly to sell Teleglobe early in its mandate. In February 1988, the government also announced that it would merge Eldorado Nuclear and Saskatchewan Mining Development and that a public share offer would follow within one year.[41] Plans to sell the two above-mentioned subsidiaries of AECL were also announced in 1988. But these were small firms and no action was being taken on the two flagships – Air Canada and Petro-Canada.

However, in a cabinet shuffle in the spring of 1988, the powerful deputy prime minister, Don Mazankowski, was appointed minister responsible for privatization. Within weeks of his appointment, he announced the partial privatization of Air Canada with a public offering of 45 per cent of the shares. Observers and critics were quick to dismiss the announcement as a political ploy. One veteran Ottawa journalist wrote: 'Before Mazankowski rushed into the Commons with his red herring, the Mulroney Government had been drifting into danger over language policy and the Meech Lake constitutional deal.'[42] The opposition declared that the announcement came so late in the government's mandate that there was little hope that the necessary legislation could be approved before a general election was held. To some parliamentarians, there was a sense of déjà vu in the announcement. The former transport minister in the previous government had told the Commons Transportation Committee that the time had probably arrived when Air Canada should be broken up or privatized to improve its efficiency. But the 1984 general election had 'deprived him' of the chance to pursue the matter.[43]

Still there were some strong forces pushing the government towards the privatization of Air Canada. For one thing, the government needed to rejuvenate its lagging privatization program, and Mazankowski had the clout to ram the initiatives through the cabinet decision-making process. In addition, Air Canada urgently required equity infusion to upgrade its ageing fleet of airplanes and urged the government to come up with $300 million or turn to privatization. The government could either dip into the Consolidated Revenue Fund, provide a loan to the company, or arrange further financing from the private sector to which Air Canada already owed about $2.5 billion. It decided to make a share offering, which was expected to raise $400 to $550 million. The government also agreed that Air Canada could keep the proceeds from the sale rather than have all the funds go to the Consolidated Revenue Fund.[44]

That the government needed to rejuvenate its privatization plan was clear to everyone.[45] Many in government were saying that the work had gone more smoothly when there were no secretariat and no office to guide it – and it is true that since their establishment few announced sales have been made. In addition, few of the crown corporations identified as potential candidates for privatization have been sold, and the government has yet to unveil plans for privatizing them. Examples include Petro-Canada, Harbourfront, FBDB, and Telesat Canada.

There have also been some new crown corporations established in recent years and some existing ones have expanded. The International Centre for Ocean Development, for example, was set up in early 1985 to assist less-developed nations. Other new corporations include Marine Atlantic, the St John's Port Corporation, and the Saint John Port Corporation. The government has also considered the setting up of yet another crown corporation, this one to publish primary school textbooks. It announced that if the u.s. firm Gulf and Western Inc. is unable to find a Canadian buyer to purchase its Canadian subsidiary, Ginn & Co., then it would purchase a 51 per cent stake in the firm.[46] Petro-Canada has added three new subsidiaries and has received approval for the purchase of Gulf Canada's refineries and service stations in western Canada. All in all, the dismay in government ranks over the lack of progress on privatization initiatives after a 'few months of flurried activities' early in the mandate has now been widely reported.[47]

Why has the government's privatization plan not lived up to the government's own expectations? First, the issue is far more complex than was initially envisaged. In many instances, privatization requires specific legislation, and in all cases it requires long-term financial planning if the government is to secure the best possible deal. The capacity of Canadian capital markets to absorb large equity sales is limited. As a result, when privatization of large corporations involves public share issues it must proceed in stages.

It was initially believed that privatization would help get the government's fiscal position in order. It was soon apparent, however, that the impact of privatization on the deficit was, in the short term at least, not substantial. In fact, the impact of receipts from sales could be negative in cases where the government's investment exceeds market value. For example, the government carries Petro-Canada in its public accounts at $4.3 billion, which represents the total investment in cash or assets by Canada in common and preferred shares of the company. If the government were to sell Petro-Canada outright or an interest in the company, it would have to obtain more than it had invested for there to be a positive impact on the deficit. There is every reason to believe that rather than recovering all of its investments if it sold Petro-Canada, the government would actually increase its total deficit.

But there have been more important forces working against privatization. The minister and Department of Finance – the guardians – have insisted that all proceeds from the sale of crown corporations or subsidiaries should go to the Consolidated Revenue Fund. Other ministers, their departments, and the crown corporations strongly object to this view. And, as ministers have become more familiar with their departments and the crown corporations for which they are responsible, they have resisted increasingly the Department of Finance position. For example, the minister of energy argued that the proceeds from the sales of the two AECL subsidiaries should be ploughed back into the parent company, which had serious financial problems, rather than be put in the Consolidated Revenue Fund. Finance's view, however, has prevailed. The one exception is the announced sale of 45 per cent of the shares of Air Canada: Finance agreed that the proceeds should go to purchase new equipment. The generally prevailing Finance view may well have helped dampen ministers' enthusiasm for privatization.

Ministers and departments also looked on with some concern when the privatization program was centralized in a Treasury Board secretariat and later on in an office headed by its own minister. This structure has heightened the suspicions of line ministers (and their departments) who feel that they should take the lead in privatizing the crown corporations for which they were responsible. The greatest concern of ministers with privatization, however, has been a regional one and there has been strong resistance to any privatization that would risk depriving regions of economic benefits. They fear facility shutdowns, layoffs, and cancelled investments. 'Certainly the regional factor,' said one senior official directly involved with the government's privatization progam, 'is always very present in any discussion ministers have about selling one Crown Corporation or another.'[48]

Examples will illustrate the point. The Toronto Harbourfront was initially identified as an ideal candidate for privatization. It owns choice and high-priced property in downtown Toronto which could be easily sold within one year, a conservative estimate suggesting that it could bring in over $100 million. However, Toronto-area ministers have consistently resisted its sale. They argue that Harbourfront was a 'gift' from the federal government and that it could not simply be turned over to the private sector – that to do so would be tantamount to taking back a gift. At a minimum, Toronto ministers insist that, if Harbourfront were to be sold, a good part of the proceeds, something like 25 per cent, should be set aside in a trust fund to continue financing the cultural and recreational activities on the site. This certainly has not gone unnoticed by ministers from other regions. One senior minister from Atlantic Canada summed up the situation this way:

Here we have a situation where we could not sell the most expensive real estate in the wealthiest city in the country. To sell it, we had to put aside money so that people in the richest city could keep going to live concerts. Yet these same people (i.e., some Ontario ministers), see nothing wrong with cutting back the jobs of coal miners in DEVCO and heavy water plant workers in Cape Breton or CN workers in Moncton. I quickly discovered the rules of the game and I began to play the game like everybody else. There is no way I am going to put up with cutting more jobs of average Canadians struggling to make a living for their families in Atlantic Canada while people in Ottawa are worried about what may happen to live jazz concerts on the Toronto Harbourfront.[49]

It will also be recalled that Quebec ministers, particularly those from the Montreal area, have successfully resisted the suggestion that FBDB be privatized. They argued that the head offices of all major banks were located in Toronto and that it was important for Montreal to have one of its own. Quebec ministers also resisted the privatization of Air Canada, in part because the company's head office is in Montreal and also because they feared that a privatized Air Canada may well in time show less and less concern for Canada's official languages policy.

The list of problems goes on. In the words of one official, any discussion on the privatization of crown corporations 'always gets ministers looking at which regions will win and which ones will lose. It is inevitable.'[50] Another suggested that privatization produced such 'an explosive regional political minefield for the government that it probably surprised even the most seasoned politician in the Mulroney cabinet.'[51]

11

The provinces and the regions:
A federal responsibility

Former Canadian Prime Minister Mackenzie King once observed that 'other countries suffer from too much history. Canada suffers from too much geography.'[1] Leading students of Canadian politics have pointed to regionalism as a central characteristic of Canadian society.[2] It was, after all, the political forces of regionalism that led our founding fathers to adopt a federal form of government in the belief that the centralizing tendencies of the Constitution Act 1867 would ensure the paramountcy of the national government and the national interest over regional interests. Actual political experience has, of course, shown that the British North America Act has not been as successful as first envisaged in establishing the paramountcy of either the national government or the national interest.[3]

This chapter looks at the forces of regionalism and their impact on the federal government expenditure budget. It considers the role first ministers' conferences play in bringing pressure to bear on the federal government to loosen its purse-strings, and it reviews the evolution of federal-provincial programs. It also points to other regional forces, such as municipalities, which place added pressures on the federal government to spend.

CONFEDERATION: WHO BENEFITS?

Many have sought to determine which regions or provinces have bene-fited the most from Confederation. No one has been able to state pre-cisely which have gained the most or by how much. The battle of the balance sheet has been anything but clear. At the height of the sovereignty-association debate in Quebec, for example, studies were produced in Ottawa, Quebec, and Toronto which showed Quebec to be both a major winner from Confederation and a major loser.[4] The problem is that, even if one could measure total federal taxes collected from a region and total spending, including tax expenditures, it would still not be sufficient to conclude whether the region has benefited from Confederation or not. There are many non-spending policies that have a direct impact on the economic structure of the regions. These include tariff policies, energy price controls, human resources policies. In addition, it may not be appropriate to look at Confederation as a zero sum game with gains and losses coming out to zero. One can assume, for example, that the free flow of goods between the provinces generates a national surplus, that the sharing of overhead cost for, say, defence and transportation is more efficiently provided by the federal government than by the regions, and that the federal government is able to strike a better trade deal at the international bargaining table than the provinces could alone.[5] This, however, has not prevented provincial governments from insisting that their regions have been short-changed by Confederation and that federal policies favour certain regions – notably, the more populous provinces of Ontario and Quebec. Nowhere is this more evident than in the economic development field.

All provincial governments have over the past twenty-five years denounced federal policies for their negative influence on the course and pace of the economic development of their provinces. Provincial governments in western and Atlantic Canada are convinced not only that federal policies favour central Canada, but that they even retard their own development. One student of Canadian federalism writes: 'The premiers have obviously mastered the rhetoric of regional alienation, and the positions of governments in the Maritimes and western Canada are firmly rooted in the belief that Ottawa's policy retards regional development, ignores salient differences among the provinces, and ultimately serves the interests of central Canada. The bitter resentment of sparsely-populated hinterlands toward the more heavily populated areas is of course a longstanding feature of Canadian politics.'[6] Former Premier Hatfield of New Brunswick summed up the view of his Atlantic colleagues when he argued that 'there is an attitude here in Ottawa ... that there are certain things that we cannot do down there because we are not so capable of doing them, but there are only certain things that we can do and we should stick with them.'[7] Western premiers have been equally strident in their criticism of the federal government, consistently arguing that Ottawa has been either unwilling to lessen their regions' dependence on natural resources or ineffective in its attempts to do so and that federal policies have held back the development of their energy sector.

In more recent years, Quebec has argued that federal policies favour Ontario's economic development at its expense. Quebec politicians do not deny that large sums of federal money are spent every year in their province, but they insist that the better part of these funds are nonproductive. For example, they point to the considerable federal funding of unemployment insurance in the province and the federal attempt to prop up the textile sector. They also argue that most of the federal funding for industrial development, particularly in the future-oriented field of high technology, is spent in Ontario, as are its efforts to lure new auto plants to Canada.

The Ontario government meanwhile has also been critical of federal regional development efforts. Successive premiers have warned that Canada's industrial structure may become distorted through industrial development 'designed to reduce regional disparities.'[8] In sum, all ten provincial governments blame federal policies for at least some of their economic difficulties and, in the case of Atlantic Canada, its underdevelopment.

Not only is it widely believed that federal economic policies are discriminatory, but it is also assumed that it is within the power of the federal government to alter significantly the economic conditions of the different regions of the country. Before the late 1950s, Ottawa's efforts at promoting regional development centred on the fiscal capacities of the provincial governments. In 1957, however, the Gordon Commission urged Ottawa to shift its focus to 'the developmental approach to regional disparities' and to develop 'the economics of the region(s) rather than merely compensating provinces for lower rates of economic growth than those achieved by the country as a whole.'[9] The newly elected Diefenbaker government pledged to move away from the previous government's 'GNP mentality,' which, it argued, had overlooked 'major pockets of Canadian society.' All successive federal governments have since pledged to 'alleviate regional disparities' and have introduced their own schemes, ranging from Funds for Rural Economic Development (FRED) under the Pearson administration, to the establishment of DREE under Trudeau, to the Special Regional Development Agencies under Mulroney.

Certainly provincial governments believe that the federal government can and should 'alleviate regional disparities.' This belief has led to wildly exaggerated calls for federal action. One senior finance official reports that a provincial minister of finance called on the federal government at a federal-provincial meeting in the 1970s 'not to rest until all the regions, and all the provinces have economic performances above the national average.'[10] Such expectations have led to intense pressure being placed on the federal treasury. Premier Peckford, for example, said in 1981: 'If Newfoundland is to even equal the national average earned income by the year 2000, a growth rate of double the national average will be required each year ... [Even then] Newfoundland will still not catch the three leading provinces by the year 2000.'[11] The sheer futility of such an objective is made evident by the fact that between 1946 and 1979 Alberta's earned income did not increase at anywhere near that pace, despite intense energy-related economic activity. Still, the argument goes that Newfoundland (or any other province) is capable of performing better economically if only the federal government would do more and spend more in the province. This view is also held by some federal government officials. In 1987 a senior intergovernmental committee of officials reported on federal efforts at promoting regional economic development over a twenty-year period. It concluded that 'expenditures ... were in the order of 3 percent of total federal economic expenditures ... Greater expenditures could well have had significantly greater results.'[12] How the officials arrived at this conclusion is not clear. In fact, they did not even present a convincing case that the money had been wisely spent, that it had had a lasting impact, or even that there were any economically promising projects that were not undertaken because of a lack of federal funds.

The regional unevenness of Canada's economic development has also given rise to countless debates at federal-provincial conferences. In turn, federal-provincial relations have certainly contributed to the notion of an equitable regional distribution of the economic benefits of Canadian federalism and have ensured that our economic debates would not simply be concerned with the functional efficiency of national economic policies. But they have also fuelled resentment between the sparsely populated peripheral regions of the country and the heavily populated and highly industrialized centre. The centre-periphery dichotomy of the Canadian economy has also created among the country's residents different perceptions of their own economic interests, and federalism has created a framework that has served to promote these differences. Ontarians tend to favour tariff protection, as does the Ontario government; western Canadians and their provincial governments favour free

trade; Atlantic Canadians see a need for special measures to correct /
regional economic imbalances, and so do their provincial governments.

Provincial premiers can always count on the support of their electors
whenever they take aim at federal policies to explain the underdevelopment of their regions. In fact, for many premiers, this spells good
politics. It is often said that more than one provincial premier was able
to win election and re-election on the back of the federal government.
By the end of the Trudeau regime, for example, not one provincial
Liberal party held power. A few years after the Mulroney government
came to power, provincial Liberals held office in four provinces and had
made impressive gains elsewhere. With peripheral regions convinced
that the federal government always favours central Canada, it is relatively easy for several premiers to build up a case against Ottawa. One
leading journalist explained: 'Many Maritimers still blame the betrayals
that followed the Confederation deal for the flight of their people and
capital, the collapse of their industries, the feebleness of their economy,
and the fact that their social services are poorer and their pay cheques
smaller than those other Canadians get. They know they live in a dependent colony of the Canadian empire, and that their plight is a direct
result of a gigantic double-cross.'[13]

Both Atlantic and western Canadians can point to a series of specific
federal government initiatives to explain the development of central
Canada and their own underdevelopment. They can argue, for example, that C.D. Howe led the war effort and the accompanying government investments to central Canada, which explains in large part the
region's rapid industrial growth and also helps to 'illuminate the process
by which regional disparity is created.'[14] During the war, government
policies on coal, steel, shipbuilding, ship repair, and manufacturing
industries, the argument goes, invariably favoured central Canada so
that 'by July 1, 1945, five percent of the funds had gone to the six
Maritime and Prairie provinces. Ontario had received forty-five percent,
Quebec thirty-two.'[15] For the peripheral regions, the federal government can never do enough to rectify long-standing grievances, including
enshrining equalization in the constitution, and any suggestion that its
funds are wasted in these regions is rejected out of hand 'in light of the
billions the feds have poured into central Canadian benefits such as the
St. Lawrence Seaway, the Mirabel Airport boondoggle, fast trains on
the Windsor-Montreal corridor and assorted subsidies and tax breaks
for auto plants, aircraft factories ... '[16]

PUTTING OTTAWA ON THE DEFENSIVE

Provincial governments nearly always evaluate federal government policies and initiatives in terms of their impact on their own provinces and regions. Allan Tupper argues that 'the provinces' singular obsession with their own well-being often leads them to discount the possibility that federal decisions, while not necessarily conferring equivalent short-term benefits on all the provinces might, over the long term, strengthen the national economy.'[17] Indeed, when a provincial government considers that the federal government has slighted the province's economic interest, it will make a case to Ottawa for appropriate compensation. Indeed Ottawa often does try to compensate the province and such compensation invariably costs the federal treasury. Meanwhile, provincial governments continue to have ample opportunities – some under the glare of the national television cameras – to show where and how federal government policies are inappropriate for their provinces.

Regional premiers from the Atlantic and western provinces now meet regularly and always conclude their meetings with a press conference, or a the very least a press communiqué. The Western Premiers' Conference meets annually, usually in the spring. The Council of Maritime Premiers has its own permanent secretariat. Both the council and the conference frequently issue press releases condemning federal economic policies or requesting federal funding for 'regional' projects. For example, the Council of Maritime Premiers, in response to cutbacks in Via Rail personnel in the region, publicly asked 'federal agencies not to lay off people,' arguing that 'jobs were lost in the Maritimes in order to protect or create jobs in other provinces.'[18] On many occasions, the three premiers unite in a common front to ask for federal funding for highway construction, economic development, post-secondary education, health care, agriculture, fisheries, and so on. Though less structured and formal, the Western Premiers' Conference is also often intensely critical of federal economic policies. In recent years, federal government purchasing policies have been accused of 'discriminating against' the western provinces.[19]

All ten premiers now also meet once a year at the Premiers' Conference. The first such meeting was held in 1887, and others followed in 1902, 1910, 1913, and 1926. The birth of the annual conference was in 1960 when Premier Jean Lesage of Quebec convened a meeting in Quebec City and suggested that there be an ongoing conference. At the

1960 meeting, the participants agreed that the event 'should not be viewed as hostile to the federal government' and declared their intention to examine provincial and interprovincial questions.[20] However, particularly since the election of the Parti Québécois to power in Quebec in 1976, the Premiers' Conference has been involved in issues that go much beyond the provincial sphere. A review of its agenda since 1976 reveals three dominant themes: the national economy and federal government policies, federal-provincial fiscal relations (such as shared-cost programs), and constitutional questions. Few would deny that several of the Premiers' Conferences since the early 1980s have been hostile to the federal government. In 1960 the prime minister was invited to attend the conference, but no such invitations are now issued. In fact, in the early 1980s, federal government officials were deliberately stopped from attending the conference as observers. A great deal of effort is now spent at the Premiers' Conference to prepare positions and where possible 'a common stance' for the federal-provincial First Ministers' Conference.

Though it took close to forty years before the prime minister would call a First Ministers' Conference (FMC), there have been sixty such conferences since – over half of them in the last twenty years. In March 1984, former Prime Minister Trudeau chaired the last of the twenty-three such conferences he had held in a sixteen-year period. Between 1983 and 1987 there were eight FMCs, an average of two a year. It was agreed at the Regina FMC in 1985 to hold 'an Annual Conference of First Ministers during a period of five years renewable for another five years.'[21] The first ministers went further in formalizing the FMC in signing the Meech Lake Accord on 3 June 1987. It was agreed then that the prime minister would be 'required' to convene an FMC at least once a year to discuss 'the state of the Canadian economy and such other matters as may be appropriate.'[22] The premiers insisted on 'requiring' the prime minister to hold an FMC at least once a year in large part because the decision to hold an FMC was always the prerogative of the prime minister. Prime Minister Mulroney acknowledged that this in itself was a 'source of federal-provincial tension ... Premiers spend a good deal of energy and time promoting the need for an FMC.'[23] FMCs are now major events in Canadian politics and are held both in and outside Ottawa, attract well over 200 government delegates and advisers, and are major national media events.[24] Since 1968, FMCs have been televised live, coast to coast, and it is because the federal government is thus publicly and invariably placed on the defensive that many federal politicians and officials have become less than enthusiastic about holding FMCS.

The structure of FMCS, particularly those on the economy, with its *tour d'horizon* of economic issues, is ideally suited to the premiers' public posture. It provides each of them with the opportunity to appear dynamic and make statements on those two or three issues crucial to their particular regional economies, while forcing the federal government to present consistent policy positions applied to all ten regional economies, and thus across each premier's short list of 'fighting issues.' Many in Ottawa believe that, courtesy of national media coverage, each premier appears to be involved in national deliberations without having to venture beyond the narrow role of regional spokesman. In short, FMCS provide the premiers with an ideal national forum to point to all the shortcomings of federal economic policies when viewed from the perspective of ten provinces. Some premiers have brought up real or perceived historical grievances regarding the impact of federal policies on their economy. Others have blamed national economic policies for the weakness of their industrial sector. Some have insisted that their provinces are not getting their fair share of federal purchases. Others have argued that national defence spending in their provinces is inadequate when compared with the national averages, and still others have argued that there are more federal public servants located in Ontario, the richest province, than in their own. The list goes on. Each provincial premier can easily find at least one area of federal government responsibility that is lacking in his province. As one political columnist and former senior official in the FPRO puts it: 'Premiers use them [FMCS] mainly as a national platform from which to engage in fed-bashing or to air concerns that are primarily provincial.' He went on to conclude: 'They nag that Ottawa does not spend enough in their provinces or that national policies are benefitting every province but their own. The result is moderately good television, but lousy policy-making.'[25]

Criticism has been directed at the federal government in every FMC since the mid-1970s. By way of example, the 1982 FMC on the economy was widely described as a disaster for the federal government because all premiers took turns attacking Ottawa for high interest rates and for misjudging the state of the national economy. (The federal budget three months earlier had predicted the economy would grow by 2.27 per cent in 1982, but it contracted by 3.2 per cent; the unemployment rate was predicted to be 7.8 per cent when it shot up to 11 per cent; and so on.)

The 1985 FMC saw all premiers criticizing Ottawa for cutting back on transfer payments. The 1986 FMC saw the Manitoba premier attack Ottawa for awarding a $1.4 billion maintenance contract for CF–18 jets to Quebec rather than to Manitoba.

FMCS not only give premiers a chance to point out shortcomings in federal economic policies, they also provide 'a chunk of television time they would not get otherwise.'[26] They also inevitably provide favourable publicity for the electorate back home. As one senior government official put it: 'it is always good for your own political·fortune when you can be seen on national television back home taking on the big bad feds because of what they are not doing for your province. If it were not for FMCS, some of the premiers may never make it on national television for months on end.'[27]

For the federal government, FMCS are essentially a one-way street. They give provincial governments a national audience to discredit federal policies and to demand more for their provinces; however, they do not lend themselves to a critical review of provincial government policies. There is a tacit understanding between provincial governments that they will not be critical of one another's policies or position. The focus is always on federal responsibilities and seldom on what provincial governments do. Thus, the prime minister or his ministers are rarely able to comment on what provincial governments may be doing in their own fields of responsibility. The issue before the cameras is invariably whether federal government funding is adequate in, say, education; rarely is there a debate on the appropriateness of provincial policy on education.

Thus, FMCS can give rise to intense public pressure on the federal government to spend more on federal-provincial programming and to increase federal activities in the regions. There is also pressure on the federal government to be even-handed in distributing its activities across the ten provinces. The result is that regions represented at the FMC table will inevitably get more federal funding and activities than regions that are not. The Gaspé region, for example, with three times the population of Prince Edward Island, gets less visibility for its economic woes.

The public pressure stemming from FMC debates tends to spill over not only into the media, but into the federal cabinet and the government caucus as well. It also fuels already volatile and intense interregional competition for federal government projects. One can easily put together a catalogue of federal projects that have tested cabinet solidarity and party loyalty in caucus. If, for example, a provincial premier makes the case at an FMC that his province is getting less than 5 per cent of federal purchasing and procurement while it accounts for 9 per cent of the Canadian population, as has Alberta, the regional federal minister will be asked to pursue the cause with his colleagues. Such tactics at FMCs are considered fair game. The same would not be true, however, were the prime minister or a senior cabinet minister to suggest that the Ontario or Quebec government does not direct enough of its procurement to northern Ontario or the Gaspé. Similarly, no provincial government would ever agree to hold an annual conference on the economy to which all regional and municipal governments would be invited, since they are not likely to lay themselves open to accusations that the lack of economic performance in their province is the fault of their own governments or themselves. It is easier and safer to focus on what the federal government, with all its resources, could do for the province than to allow their own misguided or badly implemented policies to come under scrutiny. Local observers and the local media will invariably applaud a premier's intervention on behalf of his province and push the federal regional minister to rectify the situation. The *Financial Post*, for example, reports that 'Cabinet members from the West and Atlantic provinces are always under enormous pressure from their provincial counterparts to produce more federal business for their region.'[28]

Regional competition for federal projects, however, is not limited to the West and the Atlantic provinces. Intense political competition erupted between the Quebec and Ontario governments over a federal 'decision' with regard to the location of its own space agency. When word got out that the federal government was taking another look at whether it could still financially support a new space agency, a former federal cabinet minister from Quebec jumped on the issue, believing that it was an Ottawa ploy because that city might have lost out to Montreal. She declared: 'When it's a question of finding $1 billion to bail out a bank in Alberta or $1 billion for Saskatchewan farmers, there's no problem ... But when it's a question of rebuilding Montreal's industrial structure ... they can't find [the money].'[29]

If a region should lose out on the location of a federal enterprise, then a call is immediately made, usually by the premier, for compensation. The decision to have a New Brunswick–based shipyard build the last six frigates immediately drew howls of protest from Quebec politicians. The leader of the opposition in the Quebec National Assembly argued: 'How can the (federal) government give $2.5 billion worth of direct subsidies to farmers in the West, and not even bother to use the proven expertise of Quebec shipyards?' He added that the federal decision to favour 'New Brunswick is made even less acceptable by the the fact that Mr. Côté [minister of supply and services] is the minister responsible in the federal cabinet for the Quebec City region.'[30] The Quebec premier, Robert Bourassa, while strongly disapproving of the decision, reported that he had received assurances from Prime Minister Mulroney and his chief of staff that 'several other important contracts were in the making' for Quebec.[31]

The press will also highlight federal government decisions that favour one region over another. Numerous articles appeared in the print media, for instance, on the decision to designate Montreal and Vancouver – but not Toronto – as international banking centres. With such wide coverage of this and similar decisions, criticism in the Commons is sure to follow. Opposition members will query ministers with great indignation during question period, asking why the government has decided against a particular region and then go on to demand compensation with special economic development efforts. One senior government official recently wrote that, because parliamentary proceedings are televised, such questions put increasing pressure on them to come up with 'plans to see a community's economic woes resolved in a 20 second clip on the National.'[32] Yet, when ministers do announce special development efforts, they rarely meet with the approval of the opposition or the local media. They are inevitably dismissed as insufficient or no longer relevant. For example, when the industry minister, de Cotret, announced a special plan for Montreal's east end, amounting to $35 million, an opposition MP from Montreal immediately declared the plan 'too little, too late and an insult to area residents, and Le Devoir in reporting the story ran a headline stating: 'De Cotret n'accouche que d'un maigre $35 millions.'[33]

Even some government members have been known to criticize their own government's regional plans. For example, when the Mulroney government announced its special $1.2 billion Western Diversification Office, government member David Kilgour labelled it 'insufficient' and published a paper detailing how the federal government was shortchanging the West in research and development, in procurement, in tourism, and so on.[34] Unless the federal government comes up with promising projects for a region – from the most economically developed to the poorest – it is assumed either that federal ministers representing the region are too weak or that the government has written off the region politically. Several months after the Mulroney government came to office, it announced a number of new projects for Atlantic Canada, in response to which, the magazine *Atlantic Insight* ran an article lamenting the departure of former 'heavyweights' in cabinet from the region, such as Allan J. MacEachen, Don Jamieson, and Roméo LeBlanc. Atlantic ministers in the Mulroney government, it concluded, simply do not measure up. Again, when the federal government failed to put in place a series of projects for Toronto, a columnist wrote: 'The popular wisdom ... is that Tory strategists have simply written off the city. Otherwise, the reasoning goes, why is Prime Minister Brian Mulroney's Government hedging on money for Toronto's new ballet and opera house? Why exclude Toronto as an international banking center?'[35]

THE PROVINCES AS SPENDERS

Federal government transfers to provincial governments make up an important part of the federal expenditure budget. If all payments to the provinces and the associated costs in delivering them, together with the tax points transferred, could be eliminated overnight, the federal government would eliminate its deficit.

A.W. Johnson has recently documented how the federal government began, after the Second World War, to increase its transfer payments to provincial governments.[36] By 1988–9, over $22 billion under several major intergovernmental budgetary arrangements, including equalization, Established Programs Financing, Canada Assistance Plan, Canada Health Act, and Economic and Regional Development Agreements, was being transferred. As Johnson explains, the federal government emerged from the Second World War with a vision of social security in Canada. This vision called for universal or near-universal medical care, as well as financial assistance for the unemployed. The federal government knew full well, however, that the provinces held jurisdiction in key social policy fields and that it could intervene only through its spending power in light of its constitutional responsibility for 'peace, order and good government.'

The federal government did not hesitate, particularly in the 1960s, to make full use of its spending power to encourage provincial governments to share in its vision of social security. At the least, it accelerated the introduction of spending plans in provincial governments by pressing them to undertake major health and welfare programs and by helping to finance growth in spending through contributions to program costs, and increased equalization payments. This growth also served as a basis for still further spending plans by the provinces by giving them greater analytical and managerial skills. It gave the provincial governments a new importance in the eyes of residents, a greater capacity to speak on a wide range of matters, and a new capacity to question federal policies and their impact on regional economies.

This is not to suggest that, initially at least, all provincial governments welcomed federal intervention in their fields of responsibility. Johnson writes, for example, that 'medicare was enacted ... in the teeth of opposition from many of the provinces. Indeed, the opposition was so bitter that Prime Minister Pierre Trudeau was to declare at a future constitutional conference: 'There will be no more medicare.'[37] The federal government waited another twenty years before introducing a new major federal-provincial program in the social policy field. Its contribution to the new national day-care package will amount to over $6 billion, over seven years. This time, however, the provincial governments greeted the initiative with enthusiasm and, in fact, urged Ottawa to earmark still more new federal funding for day care.

In the mid-1970s the federal government sought to limit 'its liability' to the provinces and to manage better the problems of federal-provincial shared-cost programs.[38] The Established Programs Financing (EPF) Act of 1977 was designed to let the provinces decide on priorities and expenditure levels for health insurance and post-secondary education, with the federal government transferring the amounts paid under previous arrangements with a limit on its escalation. EPF transfers funds in the form of cash payments and tax points. A tax-point transfer is a reduction in federal income tax with a corresponding increase in provincial income tax. For the medicare program, however, the federal government insisted on retaining the principles of 'universality,' comprehensiveness, portability, and public administration. The objective of EPF was to close the door on the use of shared-cost programs 'as vehicles for developing, or at least of maintaining, Canada-wide programs, with national standards.'[39] By the early 1980s, however, the federal government was complaining that provincial governments were not spending the EPF payments in the programs they were designed for and were, in fact, diverting part of these payments to other programs.

Federal shared-cost agreements in the economic development field soon followed those in social policy. Initially, such agreements were modest and were directed to economically depressed rural areas. By the late 1960s, the agreements were also being signed for urban areas, although the bulk of the funds were still going to Atlantic Canada. By the late 1970s, economic development agreements could be found in all ten provinces, covering virtually every economic sector and the most-developed areas of the country, including Montreal, parts of southern Ontario, and Alberta. A change of government in Ottawa in 1984 did not dampen the federal desire for signing economic development agreements with all provinces. Shortly after the Mulroney government came to power, it signed a comprehensive ten-year agreement with Ontario. The scope and the variety of projects sponsored by these agreements during the past fifteen years are, in the words of one federal official, 'truly mind-boggling.' In fourteen years, over $10 billion has been committed, to finance anything from industrial parks, to marinas for pleasure-boat owners, highway construction, dry-dock facilities, recreational parks, consultant reports, water treatment facilities, historical villages, and steel production facilities.[40]

In the case of the four Atlantic provinces and Manitoba, these agreements have over the years supported the great majority of B budget items, or new projects in the economic development field. Federal funds have financed anywhere from 60 to 90 per cent of the cost of such agreements in these provinces. Elsewhere, the federal contribution is usually 50 per cent of the cost. It has, however, quickened the pace of signing new economic development agreements with the provinces significantly over the past several years.

Still, the greatest impact has been in the have-less provinces. There, virtually all new government initiatives are designed with potential federal cost-sharing in mind. New initiatives, however desirable they may be from the provincial government perspective, are often scrapped for others which are less desirable but which stand a better chance for cost-sharing. Though the negotiation process allows the federal government to make proposals, this does not occur often. In many ways, in this respect, Ottawa acts like the Treasury Board – it reviews proposals, accepting some and rejecting others. There were concerns at one point that provincial governments, particularly the smaller ones, did not have the analytical capacity to define viable economic plans. The federal government signed a series of planning agreements to fund planning initiatives and shared the cost of salaries of provincial public servants to encourage the province to hire more planning and economic analysis staff. Throughout, however, the federal government has played the role of 'provider' of funds for the agreements. In some instances, federal departments have believed that the federal government was financing projects for provincial governments to implement that should have been delivered by federal departments themselves. A former federal minister of fisheries, for example, often questioned why economic development funding earmarked for provincial fisheries agreements could not be transferred to his department because, as he explained: 'I found it difficult ... [to accept that] ... what I could not do in my defined area of responsibility I find another department [transferring funds] to the provinces to do the job.'[41] The economic development agreements were adjusted in the early 1980s to enable federal departments to 'deliver directly' projects under the agreements. The adjustment has only had a limited impact, however, and the federal government continues to play essentially a Treasury Board role in managing federal-provincial agreements.[42]

All provincial governments approve of this approach to economic development. Premiers have come and gone, but they have all insisted that the federal government must continue with this method and, if anything, add more funding to it. Premiers Loughheed, Hatfield, McKenna, Lee, Buchanan, Peckford, Pawley, Davis, among others, have all publicly declared their support. The only time the premiers have been critical was when the federal government declared that it would deliver some of the projects directly.

The approach has spawned new organizational models for the federal government which have had far-reaching implications for regionalization and for the federal expenditure budget. New departments and even a central agency have been set up to promote a regional perspective and dimension in federal economic development activities. In more recent years, new agencies, located outside Ottawa, headed by deputy ministers and reporting directly to a minister, have also been established.

In all instances, large provincial offices with considerable decision-making authority have been set up to negotiate and implement economic development agreements with all ten provincial governments. Unlike other federal departments, these offices have a regional, rather than a sectoral or national, perspective. Their objective, much like that of the provincial governments, is to promote the economic interests of their provinces. The competition for projects and for new funding from Ottawa has been as intense between these federal government offices in the provinces as it has been between provincial governments. Many in Ottawa, particularly in central agencies, believe that officials in these offices have become too imbued with a provincial attitude. They are thought to be simply echoing provincial government priorities and to be no longer able to bring a national or even interprovincial perspective to their work.[43]

Federal officials in provincial offices readily admit that their main goal is to promote the interests of the province. They are often consulted by senior provincial government officials who wish to marshal arguments and data for their premiers to address at FMCs. The flow of information between the offices is constant and hardly inhibited by questions of jurisdiction. There have also been instances of close collaboration that raised eyebrows in Ottawa. For example, the New Brunswick government decided that, unlike the other provincial governments, it could not afford to open and staff a booth at Expo '86 in Vancouver to promote the province as a place to invest. The provincial DRIE office decided that it would be manifestly unfair to have other provinces represented at the fair and not New Brunswick. As a result, DRIE opened, financed, and operated a New Brunswick booth.

Though many in Ottawa have expressed concern that these offices are too close to provincial governments, many federal cabinet ministers, notably those with regional responsibilities, have struck alliances with them. Some have been particularly adroit at this practice and have been able to secure important new funding for projects in their ridings and provinces. The great majority find these offices well suited to their political needs, since it is rare indeed to find federal officials who wish to promote regional progams, rather than sectoral ones. When ministers do find such officials, they often strike close alliances. And, when pushed to make a choice between a regional or a sectoral perspective, ministers will often choose the regional one. For example, when Environment Minister Tom McMillan was forced to choose between promoting a fixed link to Prince Edward Island, his province, or responding to environmental concerns flowing from the building of the fixed link, he quickly decided to promote the fixed link. He wrote to the prime minister to request that he be 'relieved of all ministerial responsibilities having to do with the fixed link and specifically with the environmental review process as it relates to the fixed link.'[44]

Quite apart from the issue of federal offices located in provincial capitals and the natural tendency of federal ministers to favour a regional perspective, federal-provincial shared-cost programs have led to a multitude of federal-provincial committees and countless intergovernmental meetings. It is estimated that about 200 'senior' federal-provincial conferences and meetings are held every six months. There are many more 'working-level' meetings. Not only are such meetings costly in their own right, but officials on these committees have, for the most part, programs and activities to protect. The process, argues Alan Cairns, is biased in favour of big government. It has given rise to either conflict or collaboration, but in either case it is staffed by a bureaucratic elite 'possessed of tenacious instincts for their own preservation and growth.'[45] Cutting back federal-provincial programs managed by communities of federal and provincial officials is a far more complex and difficult exercise for the guardians than is cutting federal programs.

Cheque-book federalism is now firmly entrenched everywhere, and federal funding of programs is important for all ten provinces. It represents anywhere from 15 to 50 per cent of total revenues for provincial governments, with the smaller provinces highly dependent on federal transfer payments for their operations. However, the larger and wealthier provincial governments also depend on transfer payments. Ontario, for example, received in 1984–5 nearly 20 per cent of its revenues from federal cash transfers alone. By 1987–8 the Ontario government was receiving nearly $5 billion in federal cash payments, including $2.8 billion under the EEP. Because of the robust Ontario economy in the mid-1980s, federal cash payments as a percentage of total provincial revenues fell to about 15 per cent. However, federal tax points transferred to the province as a result of the EPF agreement represented an increasing share of the province's revenues. By 1986–7 the value of federal tax points to Ontario under EPF was about equal to the value of cash transfers.[46]

All provincial governments have strongly resisted any suggestions by Ottawa that federal cash payments to the provinces be reduced. Provincial premiers and their ministers of finance (of whatever political party) have made clear their objections to any such cuts in their own legislative assemblies, at interprovincial meetings, and at First Ministers' Conferences. They give various reasons for their opposition. In 1981, the Ontario treasurer, for example, stated in his budget speech that 'for a number of valid reasons we believe that large-scale retrenchment in fiscal transfers to the provinces is both unjustified and unwise.'[47] He explained that transfers to the provinces 'have not been a significant cause of federal ... fiscal difficulties [and] that ... Ottawa has the capacity to avoid precipitous cuts in transfers.'[48] Premier Ghiz of Prince Edward Island, a province highly dependent on federal transfer payments and lacking the obvious fiscal strength of Ontario, was blunter about possible cuts to his province. He argued: 'The federal government is a big spender and we want our share in Atlantic Canada. Transfer payments are not a negotiable item. They cannot be reduced substantially without bringing irreparable damage to the credibility of the federal government. If the federal government has a fiscal problem then it should look elsewhere for solutions. It simply cannot transfer what is a national problem to the provinces.'[49]

FINANCING THE MUNICIPALITIES

Canada's constitution makes clear that the provinces have 'exclusive' responsibility for 'municipal institutions.' Municipal governments are the creations of provincial governments and have no link with the federal government. It is often said the the rigidity of Canada's constitution is such that the federal and provincial governments have had to turn to 'cooperative' federalism to circumvent the country's constitutional niceties in putting government programs in place. In addition, there are policy fields, such as agriculture, fisheries, and immigration, where jurisdiction is shared. In some instances, the constitution does not deal explicitly with a policy field. Economic development is one such example, and most observers agree that concurrent powers exist. In other areas, such as social policy, the federal government has sought to introduce national programs. There ought to be no need for federal-provincial programs for municipalities, however, because there is no doubt that they are clearly the constitutional responsibility of the provinces and have limited impact on the national interest.

Canada's constitution also makes it clear that federal property should not be subject to municipal property taxes. Section 125 of the Constitution Act 1867 states: 'No land or property belonging to Canada or any province shall be liable to taxation.' The fathers of Confederation in this instance simply followed precedents elsewhere. The United States government, for example, has never and still does not pay municipal property tax. Jurisdiction notwithstanding, on 1 January 1950, the federal government instituted a restricted 'grants to municipalities in lieu of taxes.' This decision resulted from intense pressure from municipalities and some MPs. The government announced that grants would be paid to municipalities on departmental properties and then also directed crown corporations to make similar 'payments' on a basis that would be 'fair and equitable.'

Payments, however, were limited to 75 per cent of real property taxes and were applicable only in respect of property in excess of a specified threshold that consisted of 4 per cent of the combined value of all taxable property and federal property in the municipality. The threshold had the effect of excluding most municipalities and only about seventy qualified for annual grants. Federal property excluded property that, 'in the opinion of the Minister, was wholly independent of a municipality in respect of the services that the municipality customarily furnishes to lands in the municipality.'[50]

It was not long, however, before the federal government extended the scope of the program, largely as a result of pressure from MPS representing communities not eligible for the grants. In 1955, therefore, the Municipal Grants Act was amended and the threshold lowered from 4 per cent to 2 per cent. The government also began, under the legislation, to pay grants on federal properties occupied by an employee or member of the Canadian Forces and used as a domestic establishment. These grants were not subject to the 2 per cent threshold. Following these changes, approximately 600 local taxing authorities qualified for annual grants. In 1957, the Municipal Grants Act was amended once again and the threshold was dropped entirely. Following this change, the number of local taxing authorities qualifying for annual grants increased to about 1350.[51]

The program was revised once again in 1980. Federal properties that had been ineligible under the program were now all designated as eligible for grants. These included the Houses of Parliament, historic parks, libraries, reclaimed lands, water consumption and irrigation projects. By 1988–9 the program was costing the federal treasury nearly $300 million for 'departmental' properties alone. A public works official reports that one could add nearly another $100 million for other agencies and non-commercial crown corporations.[52]

The federal government has also, since the 1950s, supported a host of municipal infrastructure projects. Funds were first made available for the municipalities by a special winter works program and by the Canadian Mortgage and Housing Corporation. Between 1961 and 1980, when the last CMHC municipal infrastructure program was terminated, CMHC provided about $2 billion in loans and $750 million in grants for sewage, water treatment, and storm and water distribution systems under a bloc-funded program which gave the provinces the flexibility to choose among components.[53] By the late 1960s, DREE was financing water and sewage projects and highway construction in 'designated' municipalities or growth centres. A decade later, DREE was no longer restricting itself to 'designated' centres and contributed towards a water treatment plant for Montreal.

By the late 1980s, the 400-member Federation of Canadian Municipalities was asking the federal government to participate in a $12 billion
(1986 dollars) program to reconstruct sewage and water treatment facilities, roadways, and bridges.[54] The federation proposed that the federal
government pay 50 per cent of the cost, the provinces 25 per cent, and
they the remaining 25 per cent. It made numerous representations to
the prime minister, the ministers of public works and the environment,
and the leaders of both opposition parties.

But the responsibility for municipal infrastructure and its financing
rests clearly with the provinces and the municipal governments themselves. Why then would the federation, with the support of the provincial
governments, turn to the federal government not only for financial
assistance, but with a request that it pay 50 per cent of the cost? There
are, it appears, several reasons. The municipalities know that the federal
government has supported municipal infrastructure projects in the past.
If the federal government decided to ignore constitutional niceties when
it wanted to implement the growth pole approach to economic development, it should not be able to hide behind the constitutional division of
responsibilities when the provinces and municipalities bring forward
their own priorities. The municipalities also argue that their proposal
holds considerable promise for stimulating real economic growth when
compared with other federally sponsored initiatives and programs. It
argues, with the aid of specialized economic impact studies, that 'if
municipal services work, the economy will work, putting Canadians to
work.' It insists that the proposal would have a highly 'positive' impact
on 'output,' 'employment,' and 'incomes.' Finally, both the municipalities and provincial governments assume that only the federal government has the fiscal strength to support 'large' spending items, such as
a multi-billion-dollar municipal infrastructure proposal. In other words,
it is not so much who is responsible for what that is important, but rather
that the federal government should be involved if a particular proposal
involves billions in spending.

A cursory look at debt-to-revenue ratios, however, reveals that the
provinces and the municipalities have a greater capacity to absorb debt
than has the federal government. While provincial and municipal ratios
have remained relatively stable over the years, the federal government
has seen a jump of over 18 per cent. Debt service charges as a percentage
of *revenue* have changed as follows between 1975 and 1985: the federal
has risen from 11.8 to 30.2 per cent; provincial from 6.3 to 10.3 per
cent; and local from 7.2 to 8.8 per cent.[55]

FEDERAL SPENDING POWER REVISITED

Much has been written about the spending power of the federal government under our constitutional arrangements. Provinces have argued that the federal government has on numerous occasions simply spent its way into their areas of responsibilities. The 1987 constitutional accord made specific reference to this development. Some observers have suggested that federal government spending could be limited if its spending power came under closer scrutiny.

It is unlikely, however, that federal spending will decrease or even be restricted because of any constitutional arrangements. Historically, the constitution has not inhibited provincial governments, municipalities, associations, or individuals from making demands on the federal government for new spending. In Canada, when considering spending power, it may be useful to think of government as having a dual personality. One has all the attributes of a normal person; it can buy property, engage in business, give gifts, or hire employees. It is from this aspect of its personality that the spending power comes. In its second personality, a government acts as a legislature or regulator; that is, it legislates rules to regulate the conduct of individuals and sometimes of itself. This is why the spending power does not mirror legislative jurisdiction, and why the courts have said the only limit on federal (or, by implication, provincial) spending power is when it is used to legislate (or regulate) in areas where it is not constitutionally entitled to do so.

Both levels of government in their capacity as 'normal persons' can spend money to engage in activities subject to the regulatory jurisdiction of the other. In this regard, the provincial spending power is as broad as is the federal, and provinces do spend in areas of exclusive federal jurisdiction. For example, they spend considerable sums of money on foreign trade and in the field of communications, such as public broadcasting (TV Ontario, British Columbia's Knowledge Network, and Access Alberta).

Because of this dual personality and the fact that the two different functions of government flow from quite different underlying principles, disputes can be never-ending about the category into which a particular exercise of the spending power falls. For example, it is argued that the National Film Board, National Museums, and the National Library are all improper federal expenditures because the federal government does not have constitutional authority to regulate film productions, museums, or libraries. The response often made is that the government is justified in spending for these agencies because they are national in scope and only the federal government could create a 'national' agency of this type. If one accepts that line of reasoning, one must also accept the argument that only the federal government can develop a national pension program, a national medicare system, or a national education system.

It is precisely this concern over the ability of the federal government to move in with spending plans to undertake initiatives that are 'national in scope' that led the provinces to insist that a new provision be included in the 1987 Constitutional Accord. Section 106A(1) of the accord reads: 'The Government of Canada shall provide reasonable compensation to the government of a province that chooses not to participate in a national shared-cost program that is established by the Government of Canada after the coming into force of this section in an area of exclusive provincial jurisdiction, if the province carries on a program or initiative that is compatible with the national objectives.'

The intent of the provision clearly is not to inhibit the amount of federal government spending, but rather to limit *how* Ottawa can spend. The clause establishes a bargaining relationship between the federal and, provincial governments, and it is designed to stop the federal government from introducing a national plan in areas of provincial jurisdiction, such as medicare, and have it apply everywhere with no possibility of provincial governments opting out with compensation. In other words, the federal government could in future define national objectives for, say, a new major social program, but any province could set up a parallel program and still collect money from the federal government. Provinces are given greater opportunities to opt out of federal programs, but 'to opt out of a program, any province *must* agree to spend federal money in the same field.'[56]

Experience has already shown that the clause has had limited impact in terms of provincial opting out and no impact in terms of government spending. By 1988, as noted above, well over one year after the constitutional accord was agreed to by all first ministers, the federal government was putting the final touches to a multi-billion-dollar child care program, which falls within provincial jurisdiction. There is little chance that provincial governments would wish to challenge the constitutional right of the federal government to make funds available for programs falling under the jurisdiction of the provinces. J.A. Corry wrote some time ago that 'a little reflection will show that proof of unconstitutionality of federal spending for objects outside federal legislative powers would prove far too much for almost anybody's comfort.'[57] Little has changed since he wrote this over twenty years ago. If anything, the spending power of the federal government has been strengthened. If the 1987 constitutional accord is ratified, the federal government will have for the first time full constitutional recognition to spend in areas of exclusive provincial jurisdiction.[58]

12

The private sector: Grabbing with both hands

Especially since the early 1960s, governments have put in place a variety of incentive programs for the private sector. We have now reached the point where, in certain areas of the country at least, there is a government subsidy available for virtually every type of commercial activity. Government intervention in the economy is particularly pervasive in Canada because both the provincial and federal levels of government have become involved in decisions about the location of new or expanded economic activities by the private sector. Market forces alone no longer dictate a firm's response to emerging opportunities or its decision with regard to location.[1] With their shareholders' best interests in mind, firms will search out government programs to see if public funds are available to assist in promoting their development strategy. *Canadian Business* summed up the situation when it observed that 'some firms are in the happy position of being able to employ staff or consultants whose sole function is to sniff out all the juicy morsels the politicians and policymakers throw into the public trough.'[2]

The federal government supports the private sector in numerous ways. It gives cash grants, funds federal-provincial agreements designed solely to assist the private sector, and makes tax incentives available. Other federal measures include special grants to support firms facing economic difficulties and to organizations or groups established to promote the views of the private sector.

FINANCING THE PRIVATE SECTOR

Early Keynesian economists believed that government could fine tune the economy through incentives to the business community. Some federal government assistance programs, including the Maritime Freight Rates Acts, date back to the depression years. But it was only in the late 1950s and 1960s that government grants to the private sector became fashionable. Before that time, the federal government had considered that the best means of adjusting fiscal policy lay in offering generous subsidies to provincial governments for public works. Ottawa felt that this alone would allow a concerted attack on unemployment. Later, it introduced equalization payments to poorer provinces to even out the fiscal capacities of all provincial governments. This policy was intended to reduce disparities between regions, to achieve a national standard in public services, and at the same time to equalize provincial government revenues.[3] It was only during the Second World War that the federal government sought to act as a high-profile economic manager and to intervene in private sector decisions. The extent of the government's involvement in the economy during the war years has been documented elsewhere.[4] Suffice it to say that under the direction of C.D. Howe, the 'Minister of Everything,' the government intervened in numerous ways. When, for example, the private sector proved reluctant to produce synthetic rubber for the allied war effort, the federal government established Polymer, a crown corporation, solely to establish a rubber industry in Canada.[5]

When the war came to an end, however, the federal government withdrew and let the private sector set the pace of economic development. While C.D Howe's influence did not wane until Louis St Laurent's Liberal government was defeated in 1957, he essentially had a businessman's view of the limits of government programming and of Canadian economic development. Michael Bliss writes that Howe 'did not really believe that governments could or should force the pace of development faster than the private sector could support and was content to see relations between government and private business fall into a much more America-like mould, with the private sector being more the engine and architect of development.'[6] He adds: 'Howe worked in the public sector, but he seemed to have a bias in favour of private enterprises ... [he] was happy to wield public power vigorously to help private enterprises achieve what seem like national goals.'[7]

A Conservative government under John Diefenbaker came to power in 1957 with no single minister with the stature of C.D. Howe to shape government-business relations. Shortly after coming to power, however, it was confronted by a recession and was greatly in need of innovative solutions. The previous government had already appointed a Royal

Commission on Canada's Economic Prospects (Gordon Commission) which, reporting in 1957, urged that a bold, comprehensive, and coordinated approach to development was needed to resolve the underlying economic problems of Atlantic Canada. The report advised that a federally sponsored commission be set up to provide infrastructure facilities to encourage economic growth. The report also called for measures to increase the rate of capital investment in the region. In many ways the proposal to involve the private sector in promoting development in slow-growth regions was breaking new ground. Perhaps for this reason the commission remained cautious in its recommendations: 'Special assistance put into effect to assist these areas might well adversely affect the welfare of industries already functioning in most established areas of Canada.'[8]

The new Diefenbaker government did not immediately embrace proposals inspired by a Liberal-appointed commission. However, as the recession worsened, the persistence of regional imbalances was once again underlined. All regions felt the effects of the recession, but nowhere was it as severe as in the four Atlantic provinces. This helped convince the federal government that undirected financial transfers in the form of equalization payments were simply not sufficient to bring about structural changes in the slow-growth regions. Certain ministers in Ottawa were also pointing to what they viewed as unacceptable levels of poverty in numerous rural communities and arguing for special corrective measures.[9]

The 1960 budget speech unveiled the first of many measures Ottawa has since developed to assist the private sector. The budget permitted firms to obtain double the normal rate of capital cost allowances on most of the assets they acquired to produce new products – if they located in designated regions (with high unemployment and slow economic growth).[10]

Other measures quickly followed. The Agriculture Rehabilitation and Development Act (ARDA) was passed in an attempt to improve the depressed rural economy. ARDA began as a federal-provincial effort to stimulate agricultural development in order to increase income in rural areas. It aimed to increase small farmers' output and productivity by providing assistance for alternative use of marginal land, creating work opportunities in rural areas, developing water and soil resources, and setting up projects designed to benefit people engaged in natural resource industries other than agriculture, such as fisheries. ARDA, however, was widely criticized because, among other things, it lacked an appropriate geographical framework. It was, in the words of one federal official, 'all over the Canadian map.'[11] The Fund for Rural Economic Development (FRED), introduced in 1966, was intended to deal with this concern.[12] The program could be applied only in designated regions, those with widespread low incomes and major problems of economic adjustment. Only five such regions were identified.

The FRED program, as it was applied in northeast New Brunswick, broke new ground in that it provided special inducements to private enterprise. Assistance was given to projects that were considered capable of creating long-term employment in the natural resources and tourism sectors, but that could not be carried out without some form of public assistance. An interest-free forgivable loan of 50 per cent of approved capital costs of up to $60,000 for new manufacturing or processing industries and up to 30 per cent for modernization or expansion was available. It was explicitly designed to encourage new entrepreneurs and expansion of small existing businesses.[13]

The federal government introduced in 1962 yet another development initiative, the Atlantic Development Board (ADB). Largely inspired by the Gordon Commission, the board was given a special Atlantic development fund to administer. By and large, the fund was employed to assist in the provision or improvement of the region's basic economic infrastructure.[14] It did not provide direct assistance of any kind to private industry, as the Gordon Commission had recommended, and, on this point, the ADB was heavily criticized.

The federal government dealt with this criticism by providing 'limited' and 'direct' assistance to the private sector. To do this, it introduced the Area Development Incentives Act (ADIA), and the Area Development Agency (ADA) within the Department of Industry. Legislation establishing ADIA was passed in 1963.[15] The central purpose behind these initiatives was to turn to the private sector to stimulate growth in economically depressed regions. Regions of high unemployment and slow growth were the target, and only regions reporting unemployment rates above a specified level would be eligible. Manufacturing and processing firms were then invited to locate or expand operations in these regions. Three kinds of incentives were applied sequentially: accelerated capital cost allowances, a three-year income-tax exemption, and higher capital cost allowances. In 1965, a program of cash grants was introduced over and above the capital cost allowances.

Assistance was provided automatically on a formula basis. It was applied in a non-discretionary manner to areas chosen solely on the basis of unemployment levels, and Ottawa was told that it had limited potential as a development tool. Virtually no opportunity existed to relate assistance to development planning. In addition, because of the program's regional formula, the areas eligible for assistance did not include main population or industrial centres within slow-growth regions, where new manufacturing initiatives could be expected to have a better chance of success.

In 1968, Pierre E. Trudeau became leader of the ruling Liberal party. Shortly after assuming office, Trudeau called a general election and campaigned vigorously on the theme of national unity, his central preoccupation. For Trudeau, national unity extended well beyond English-French relations. He boldly declared: 'Economic equality ... [is] just as important as equality of language rights.'[16] When the Liberal party was returned to power with a strong majority after five years of minority rule, there was no doubt that the government would give increased priority to regional employment. Trudeau appointed Jean Marchand, a close friend and trusted Quebec lieutenant, to his newly established Department of Regional Economic Expansion (DREE).

Marchand immediately set out to 'modernize' the government's incentive program to the private sector. He decided to build the new incentives package from the existing ADA program by taking from ADA most of its positive attributes and discarding its less desirable features. First, the new program would be discretionary. Secondly, grants would now be available for selected sectors only. The program, however, would also be available over a much wider area, by providing incentives in growth centres and in selected urban areas. Other features were added. The new program would confine itself to development grants; would set a maximum level, but also provide for offers at less than the maximum if circumstances warranted; and would establish a two-part grant structure, one for capital costs and the other according to the number of jobs created. Maximum levels for both were also more generous for the Atlantic provinces.[17]

Not surprisingly, the most contentious issue confronting the new program was its geographical applicability. Marchand was adamant on two points: first, that the regions designated be sufficiently limited so as not to dilute the effectiveness of the program, and, secondly, that unlike the ADA program, it should apply in growth centres – Halifax, Moncton, Saint John, and St John's, among others.

Regions designated for the program included all the Atlantic provinces, eastern and northern Quebec, parts of northern Ontario, and the northernmost regions of the four western provinces. Thus, regions were designated in all ten provinces, and for a three-year period ending 30 June 1972. The regions designated accounted for about 30 per cent of the Canadian labour force, and the average per capita income within them was approximately 70 per cent of the national average. On the face of it, this coverage may appear excessive in terms of the program's regional applicability. However, initially at least, Marchand got what he wanted. He was successful in limiting the program's coverage to the areas he had first envisaged. Parts of Ontario, Alberta, and British Columbia were also designated, but more as a gesture to ensure that they would not feel completely left out. As well, Marchand feared that these provinces, given their relatively strong fiscal positions, might establish their own incentives programs, thereby greatly inhibiting the new federal initiative.[18]

It was not long before strong political pressure was exerted on Marchand to extend the program's regional designations further. Cabinet ministers and MPs from the Montreal area frequently made the point that Montreal was Quebec's growth pole and that, if DREE were serious about regional development, it ought to designate Montreal under its industrial incentives program. Montreal's growth performance rate was not keeping pace with expectations, particularly those of the large number of Liberal MPs from the area. The city's unemployment rate stood at 7 per cent in 1972, compared with 4.6 per cent for Toronto. Further, Quebec's economic strength, it was argued time and again, was directly linked to Montreal, and, unless new employment opportunities were created there, little hope was held for the province's peripheral areas. Montreal required special measures to return to a reasonable rate of growth.

In the end, Marchand chose to include Montreal in a special region, known as 'region C.' In this newly designated region, which consisted of southwestern Quebec, including Hull and Montreal, and three counties of eastern Ontario, the maximum incentive grant was lower than elsewhere. The grant could not exceed 10 per cent of approved capital cost, plus $2000 for each direct job created. Elsewhere in the designated regions of Quebec and Ontario, the maximum incentive grant was fixed at 25 per cent of approved capital costs and $5000 for each new job created. A third level of assistance was established for the Atlantic region, which called for a maximum grant of 35 per cent of capital cost and $7000 per job created. Finally, the changes stipulated that region C's special designation was to be for two years only. This, it was felt, would be sufficient to help Montreal return to a 'reasonable rate of growth.'[19] The changes, however, extended the designated regions to cover about 40 per cent of the population. Still, Marchand assured his colleagues that the special Montreal designation was temporary and committed his department to de-designate the city after two years.

But, by 1976, Montreal-area MPS were pressing Marcel Lessard, the then DREE minister, to re-designate their city under DREE's incentive program. Unemployment in Quebec had risen to 300,000, half of it in the Montreal region. The election of the Parti Québécois in November 1976 resulted in a sudden downturn in private investment in the province and the widespread fear that head offices of major companies would leave Montreal because of proposed language legislation.[20]

When Lessard first went to the cabinet with the proposal to designate Montreal, he met with stiff opposition. If DREE could justify a presence in Montreal, why could it not also justify one for Vancouver and Toronto? Fundamental questions were asked about DREE's mandate and its role in alleviating regional disparities. Cabinet ministers from the Atlantic provinces remembered well Marchand's comment about the necessity of spending 80 per cent of DREE's budget east of Trois-Rivières. How would a Montreal designation affect other regions? Would it still be possible, for example, to attract firms into depressed regions if they could obtain a cash grant for starting new production in Montreal?

Lessard now reports that, with considerable help from seven ministers from the Montreal region, he was finally able to convince the cabinet to designate Montreal under the RDIA program. In June 1977, DREE introduced, under the authority of the DREE Act, a discretionary incentives program for selected high-growth manufacturing or processing facilities. Only certain industries could qualify, including food and beverages, metal products, machinery, transportation equipment, and electrical and chemical products. Projects would be limited by a lower maximum grant than elsewhere: 25 per cent of total capital cost.[21]

In obtaining cabinet approval for the Montreal designation, Lessard promised his colleagues to look at the possibility of designating other regions, including northern areas of British Columbia and the Northwest Territories. He also committed DREE to undertake special development efforts in eastern Ontario, notably the Cornwall area.[22]

By the early 1980s, the regional incentive program in the private sector had been pulled and pushed to cover fully 93 per cent of Canada's land mass and over 50 per cent of the population. Candidates for parliament from all parties pledged, if elected, to make every effort to see their riding designated for regional incentives. Local chambers of commerce and other business groups continually applied pressure on their MPS and the DREE minister to have their communities designated. From the time the program was introduced in the late 1960s until the early 1980s, the federal government spent well over $1 billion in cash grants to the private sector.[23]

The constant pull to extend the government's regional incentives program to the private sector, among other things, led Ottawa to revamp its regional and industrial programs and its delivery mechanism. DREE was disbanded and a new department – the Department of Regional Industrial Expansion – designed to combine both industrial and regional 'perspectives' was established. The newly appointed minister of DRIE, Ed Lumley, rose in the House of Commons on 27 June 1983 to report that he had finally solved the designation problem for regional incentives to the private sector. He unveiled a new program, labelled the Industrial and Regional Development Program (IRDP), which would apply *everywhere* in the country. Lumley told the house that IRDP was 'a regionally sensitized, multifaceted programme of industrial assistance in all parts of Canada. This is not a programme available only in certain designated regions. Whatever riding any Member of this House represents, his or her constituents will be eligible for assistance.'[24] The program can accommodate a variety of needs, he also reported. It could be used for investment in infrastructure, for industrial diversification, the establishment of new plants, and the launching of new product lines.

An important distinguishing characteristic of IRDP is the 'development index,' which is designed to establish the needs of individual regions, as far down as a single census district. All are arranged in four tiers of need. The first, for the most developed 50 per cent of the population, covers districts with a need for industrial restructuring. In this tier, financial assistance is available for up to 25 per cent of the cost of modernization and expansion. At the other end of the spectrum is the fourth tier, which includes the 5 per cent of the population living in areas of greatest need (based on level of employment, personal income, and provincial fiscal capacity). In this tier, financial assistance is available for up to 60 per cent of the cost of establishing new plants.

The program can provide financial assistance to both business and non-profit organizations through cash grants, contributions, repayable contributions, participation loans, and loan guarantees. This assistance is available for the various elements of 'product or company cycle': economic analysis studies; innovation (including product development);

plant establishment, modernization, or expansion; marketing (including exact development measures); and restructuring. Lumley saw this as another of the program's selling points. He claimed that through this program the government could be involved in every stage of the development of a business – from start-up, to expansion, modernization, and restructuring.

Tier 4 regions are eligible under all program elements; tier 1 regions are not. Financial assistance under tier 4 can amount to 70 per cent of costs, while tier 1 varies from 20 to 50 per cent. When the Mulroney government came to power in 1984, only some relatively minor modifications were made to IRDP. Restrictions were imposed on tier 1 regions, or the most developed regions of this country, so that 'modernization' and 'expansion' projects would no longer qualify for assistance. It was clear by then that the private sector was taking full advantage of the government programs, even firms in the most developed regions of the country. For the first full year of operation, for example, the program was more successful in the Windsor-Quebec corridor than elsewhere, and the estimated number of jobs created or maintained under tier 1 was well over twice the number estimated for tiers 3 and 4 combined. In terms of financial resources, DRIE funds earmarked for tier 1 projects alone amounted to over $229 million, compared with $23 million for tier 4, $46 million for tier 3, and $74 million for tier 2.

In time, the program favoured tier 1 regions (or the more developed regions of the country) even more, so that by 1985–6 over 70 per cent of DRIE funds for IRDP went to Ontario and Quebec.[25] This led to a series of charges from both the Atlantic and western regions that private sector firms in central Canada were being given preferential treatment. DRIE was disbanded in 1988 after separate Atlantic and western agencies had been established. The focus of both agencies, with their billion dollar budgets of new money over five years and the inclusion of ongoing programs begun under DRIE, is on the private sector. Both now have programs in place which can fund virtually any conceivable private sector plan or initiative. In addition, a new department, this time labelled the Department of Industry, Science and Technology (DIST), was also established in 1988. DIST is present in all regions of the country and also makes cash grants available to the private sector.

Cash grants to the private sector have not by any means been limited to regional incentives programs. The federal government has, since the 1960s, made cash grants available to businesses in the shipbuilding industry, energy exploration, and the defence industry, to name just a few. It also provides cash grants to the private sector for human resources training and development, for research and development, and for transportation. Under various federal-provincial programs, cash grants are also available to the private sector for almost any kind of business activity. Tourism, agriculture, fisheries, and mining have all benefited. In addition, whenever a sector is experiencing difficulties, the federal government often moves in with its own program or enters into a federal-provincial agreement to assist firms in 'adjusting to new or emerging circumstances.' There are numerous examples. Agreements were signed in the late 1970s and early 1980s with the provinces of Ontario ($180 million), Quebec ($282 million), New Brunswick ($42.5 million), Nova Scotia ($21.7 million), and Newfoundland ($33 million) to fund pulp and paper firms to modernize their operations.[26] Another example is the major appliance industry. By the early 1980s it was obvious that this industry, located in southern Ontario and Quebec, was in difficulty and was the least likely to survive tariff cuts. In January 1987, the government announced a $15 million assistance package to help restructure the industry.

The minister of finance also revealed in his 1980 budget speech a major initiative 'to promote industrial restructuring and manpower retraining and mobility in areas of particular need.'[27] Communities were designated on the basis of need, as measured by the number of layoffs from an industry, whether the adjustment was recent or chronic, and whether the layoffs were structural or cyclical. Communities with recent adjustment problems were favoured on the grounds that other programs existed to help those with more long-term problems. Assistance under the Industrial Labour Adjustment Program (ILAP) applied to various sectors, including the auto parts industries.

Yet another regionally oriented initiative was the Adjustment Assistance Benefit Program, which granted some $250 million over a five-year period. Ottawa sought to update its textile and clothing policy, last revised in 1978. At that time, it had negotiated nine bilateral arrangements and it later concluded eight more. The seventeen arrangements were to expire on 31 December 1981, and Ottawa had stated its preference for freer trade and for the removal of special protection measures over the long term. The new program was 'to revitalize the economies of those communities most vulnerable to foreign competition' in the textile and clothing industries. A newly established Canadian Industrial

Renewal Board (CIRB), made up of senior business leaders, as well as labour and government representatives, was made responsible for implementing the program.[28]

CIRB provided for contributions of up to 75 per cent of the costs of consultants for new development projects, and for loans of up to $1.5 million, at preferential rates. Firms wishing to establish a new manufacturing and processing activity in a designated region could receive repayable interest-free contributions of up to 50 per cent of the capital costs and up to 50 per cent of preproduction expenses. Under CIRB, the federal government sought to attract firms 'which had a comparative advantage in the economy of the 1980s – high productivity, high-technology industries.'[29]

But CIRB often came face to face with competition from other federal and provincial government programs also designed to attract high-productivity and high-technology industries. Though observers insist that Canada has never been able to put together an industrial development strategy, all eleven governments have, often in competition with one another, attempted to lure industrial winners with cash grants to force the pace of structural change in the economy. Throwing money at old industries is necessary to assist firms through a transition period, but governments also believe that there is more payoff in terms of employment creation if they 'pick winners and throw the money at the attractive new infant industries.'[30]

All in all, there is now a plethora of government programs for the private sector. The Nielsen Task Force reported that there were 'some 218 distinct federal or federal-provincial programs costing in aggregate $16.4 billion in 1984–85 and requiring the services of more than 68,000 federal public servants.'[31] The task force concluded that programs to business were overly rich, overlapping, and required rationalizing. It argued that there were compelling reasons to change incentives programs to make them more efficient, and that there were many existing programs that would probably 'not be invented today.' It will be recalled, however, that the task force held out little hope that redundant programs would actually be dropped, insisting that the 'problem is that at the political and senior bureaucratic levels there do not seem to be rewards for doing more with less. In fact, middle managers now are all too aware that their pay and classification levels depend in part on the number of people they supervise and the dollars they spend. Such incentives have predictable results.'[32]

It is wrong to assume that all cash grants to business are targeted to slow-growth regions or communities facing difficult adjustment problems. There are several that favour firms and prosperous communities in southern Ontario and Quebec. The Defence Industry Productivity Program (DIPP) is designed to promote economic growth through defence-related exports, to provide a defence industrial base, and to maintain a defence technological capability. The program provides four types of assistance, including research and development, source funding to establish a qualified supplier of defence-related products, capital assistance, and market feasibility. The main beneficiaries of the program are large multinational corporations located in southern Ontario and Quebec. The 1984–5 DIPP budget, for example, amounted to $197.8 million with firms from Ontario and Quebec able to claim $187.6 million.[33]

There are other similar examples. The bulk of federal shipbuilding subsidies have been directed to firms in Ontario and Quebec. Programs designed to assist 'high-technology' have largely funded companies in the more developed areas, notably Ottawa, Toronto, and Montreal.[34] Duty remission schemes have also benefited firms in central Canada. In some instances, the federal government has offered a combination of cash grants and duty remission to lure new firms and new economic activity to, or to keep existing firms in, the highly developed economy of southern Ontario.[35]

There are also a battery of provincial government programs, some financed jointly with the federal government, designed for the business community. All provincial governments have a host of programs of their own to quicken the pace of private sector development, to attract footloose industries to their own provinces, and to assist firms adjusting to new economic circumstances or even to competition. Admittedly, in the case of the 'have-not' provinces, virtually all such programs are covered by federal-provincial agreements. In the case of the larger and wealthier provinces, however, provincial governments are assuming the full cost. Marchand's hope that having the federal regional incentives program apply to all provinces would ensure that provincial governments would not come forward with competitive programs has proved fruitless. Ontario, for example, introduced its own Equalization of Industrial Opportunity Loans (EIOL) in 1967, which made available 'forgivable' loans to manufacturing firms locating in designated areas. By the 1980s, however, the Ontario government had in place several assistance programs to the private sector, regardless of where firms located in the province. Quebec also has several programs of its own, including a variety of mixed (public-private) enterprises.[36]

The spectacle of the provinces competing with federally funded programs for industry has been frowned upon by many observers. There is little doubt that provincial governments have engaged in bidding wars. The lure of government grants and the consequent 'shopping around' by the private sector has resulted in 'windfalls' for corporations. Governments have no assurance that a firm will not request assistance for a particular location, even after a corporate decision has already been taken to locate there. How is a government to know, for example, if McCain's chose to place a number of production facilities in northwestern New Brunswick because of government cash grants or because the McCain family is from the area? More important, how is a government to know whether McCain's would not have located its plants in the area, with or without government grants?

Those who have attempted to assess the effectiveness of government incentives to the private sector suggest that the programs tend to have a limited impact. The Economic Council of Canada, for example, found that the incrementality of projects under the federal regional incentive scheme was between 25 and 59 per cent and that of jobs between 35 and 68 per cent. (An investment project is considered incremental if the firm, without assistance, would not have undertaken the project or would have undertaken it outside the designated region.) The lower rates, 25 and 35 per cent, represent, according to the council, a conservative estimate of success. On the whole the council found the program beneficial, with a benefit-to-costs ratio of between 3 and 19 to 1.[37]

David Springate found that regional incentives grants had relatively little influence on the investment decisions of large firms, concluding that the grants produced few changes in the timing, size, or technological improvements of the projects he studied. Carleton Dudley suggested that the grants were not sufficiently generous to offset the added operating cost of locating in designated regions and estimated their potential for reducing the operating cost of a firm to be between 1 and 5 per cent of sales, substantially less than the added cost of operating in designated regions, estimated to be between 5 and 20 per cent.[38]

However, how to measure incrementality is controversial. Dan Usher explained the difficulty: 'Normally one is taxed or subsidized for doing something regardless of whether one would do it or not in the absence of the tax or subsidy. It is as though the family allowances were restricted to children who would not have been conceived in its absence, or Crow's Nest Pass rates restricted to grain that would not have been grown if freight rates were higher.'[39]

Those who have looked at government incentives for industries such as auto parts and major appliances also report limited success, if any. Harold Crookell examined the federal government's efforts to assist the latter industry and concluded that, in the end, the government was not pursuing 'national economic welfare (goals) ... (it was) primarily (concerned) with narrower, more parochial interests ... This intervention has probably set the industry back five years in its pursuit of improved productivity.'[40]

The call by the Nielsen Task Force to rationalize and cut back government programs to the private sector has been largely ignored, as task force members had suspected would be the case. The government, for example, still operates its Industrial and Regional Development Program (IRDP) – although it claims that this program will be replaced. The replacement programs, however, are likely to be more costly and even more open-ended than IRDP. The two development agencies operating in Atlantic and western Canada will have, in their own words, extremely 'generous' and 'flexible' assistance programs to the private sector. The newly created Department of Industry, Science and Technology also declared its intention to introduce a multifaceted program of its own for the private sector. In addition, the federal-provincial economic development programs under the ten-year umbrella agreements with all provincial governments continue. That said, the federal government did adopt as policy the Nielsen Task Force recommendation that in future 'Crown assistance for any private investment from tax expenditures, ERDA's and grants does not exceed 50 percent of a project's cost or 75 percent of a Research and Development project except with the explicit approval of the responsible minster.'[41] In the past, according to federal officials, some firms, by shopping around the available programs, had been able to secure government funding for well over 80 per cent of the cost of their projects.

It is often difficult for the officials operating incentives programs to determine precisely what kind of tax incentives a firm will enjoy once it has received a cash grant. The worlds of tax incentives and cash grants in the federal government are quite separate and work in near complete isolation from one another. Tax incentives are administered by Revenue Canada, and cash grants by a variety of departments and agencies. There is virtually no contact between the groups. Revenue officials treat all tax returns and correspondence with clients with the utmost confidentiality. They are even reluctant to release total tax expenditure figures for a particular region, such as Cape Breton, let alone information on a particular firm.

Still, we do know that tax incentives and tax credits, though less visible, can be even more lucrative for firms than cash grants. We also know that tax expenditures are estimated to amount to at least $30 billion annually. We also know that before the major tax revisions were introduced in 1988, tax expenditures for businesses were the second largest, trailing only those of Health and Welfare, which include items involving income maintenance and registered pension and retirement savings plans. The tax incentives available to businesses are varied, ranging from lower income tax on small businesses, to rapid depreciation allowances for buildings and modernization, to fast write-offs for Canadian exploration and development expenses. The Nielsen Task Force reviewed twenty tax expenditure programs for business and estimated that something like $7 billion of revenue had been forgone in one year alone. We know little about the success of tax incentives or whether tax credits are meeting their objectives. With only limited data available, few researchers have looked at their impact. Those who have are less than enthusiastic about their likely success. Neil Brooks, for example, argues that 'there is astonishingly little evidence that these tax breaks are effective.' He adds that corporate tax incentives in manufacturing amounted to $2.5 billion between 1972 and 1975, but the additional amount of investment only amounted to between $340 and $846 million.[42]

Though the federal government does commit well over $25 billion annually to the business community through cash grants, tax incentives, and a host of schemes under federal-provincial agreements, there is more. Special federal funding for the use of the business community also exists for infrastructure facilities. There are, for instance, a multitude of industrial development parks in several provinces, a good number of which, especially in rural areas, now stand empty or nearly empty.[43] The federal government's attempts to promote industrial development through the funding of industrial parks has been likened to the following 'cargo cult' story.

During the Second World War, natives of some Pacific islands saw the arrival of American troops. The Americans cleared and levelled an oblong piece of the jungle, set lights along the edges, and, lo! after a while, a giant silver bird arrived, bearing all manner of valuable things. This gave rise to a 'cargo cult' among the natives, who, having seen what the Americans had done to attract the silver bird, similarly set about clearing portions of the jungle and then waited by their fires, patiently and reverently, for the arrival of the bird.

It has been suggested that, in practice, our industrial and regional development policies represent a cargo cult mentality. In areas where we wish to attract economic development, industrial parks are constructed and cash grants offered. It is then time to sit back and wait for the silver bird of industry. No one knows for sure where the mysterious bird is to come from. Rarely does it come and, when it does, it seldom stays for long. This approach to industrial development, mechanistic in its instruments, thinks magically about outcomes. In the cargo cult ethos, the population of the designated region plays a passive role, except for the government officials who simply prepare the runway. If the silver bird comes, the people will provide the labour but the organization and promotion of economic activity comes from the outside.[44]

There is more. The federal government has also intervened, particularly during the past several years, with special funding to rescue firms experiencing serious business difficulties. This is beyond the special assistance provided for specific sectors, such as the heavy appliances or auto parts industries, which, as mentioned above, have at one point or another experienced economic problems. Though the practice is highly controversial, the government has bailed out a number of firms. One would be hard pressed to find a rationale to explain why all or even some of the firms were selected.

BAILING OUT FIRMS

Textbook economics suggest that bankruptcies are normal in a private enterprise economy. By weeding out the unsuccessful firms, bankruptcy provides additional room for growth by the more productive, job-creating businesses. When a company fails, its shareholders lose their investment and unsecured creditors obtain less than full compensation for their loans, with the company's assets being sold to other firms at depressed prices. But those assets, in turn, if placed in the hands of energetic managers, lower the cost of production. Productivity and international competitiveness thus are both increased, with the result that sales grow and new employment is created. Accordingly, government intervention to save a failing firm is considered to be counterproductive.

The federal government, however, has tossed aside textbook economics on many occasions, opting instead for intervention. Among others, Chrysler Canada, Massey Ferguson, Cooperative Implements, Maislin Industries, Lake Groups Inc., CCM Inc., White Farm Equipment, Consolidated Computer Inc., Electrohome Ltd, Pelromont Inc., National Sea Products, H.B. Nickerson & Sons Ltd, Fisheries Product International, and General Motors of Canada, without government aid, would not exist in their present form or would have gone bankrupt earlier than they eventually did.

The federal government responded on several occasions to requests for financial assistance from failing corporations in the early 1980s in the midst of world recession. It will be recalled that, during the recession, interest rates were both high and unpredictable. In Canada, something like two-thirds of corporate earnings went to pay interest. With weak markets, several major corporations had inadequate earnings to meet their interest payments.

Faced with certain bankruptcy, the firms turned to Ottawa for help. Often the appeals came at the eleventh hour, which put enormous pressure on the government. Financial deadlines (especially loan repayment dates) could not easily be postponed without causing damaging stock market reactions. Ministers, particularly those representing the affected regions, either had to push the cabinet for a quick decision to support the firms, despite the limited information available, or risk seeing thousands of workers in their ridings or regions being laid off. Inevitably, they chose the former course. But once the government bailed out high-profile corporations in central Canada, such as Chrysler and Maislin, other regions insisted on equal or better treatment for their firms, given their weaker industrial structures. Having assisted these once-solid corporate citizens, it was extremely difficult for Herb Gray, the minister of industry, and Marc Lalonde, the minister of finance, in the Trudeau government to oppose similar assistance for Co-op Implements Ltd in western Canada and National Sea in the east. Similarly, after bailing out corporate giants in central Canada, it became difficult to turn down pleas for aid from smaller companies, also facing bankruptcy. Numerous small firms, including some in the retail business, did receive special assistance through various federal and federal-provincial programs.

The government bail-out of firms has not been limited to the recession years of the early 1980s. The practice has continued (though with less frequency, given the upturn in the economy and the consequent lower interest rates). We saw, for example, in an earlier chapter, that the Mulroney government intervened to bail out banks in western Canada. As well, when General Motors raised the possibility of closing its Sainte-Thérèse plant in Quebec in 1987, the government intervened with a special $110 million interest-free loan to keep the plant open. The Quebec government matched the federal effort, and General Motors unveiled a $330 million project to upgrade and retool its plant. When Mulroney was able to announce that the government had 'saved 3,500 assembly line jobs,' both opposition parties supported the initiative.[45]

FINANCING THE VOICE OF THE PRIVATE SECTOR

Many observers insist that the business community has not been successful in influencing broad government policy. Michael Bliss argues, for example, that 'in the battle for public opinion on big questions of national economic policy, business was defeated years ago and on the big general questions such as the growth and effectiveness of government ... business has nothing effective to say.'[46] It has not been, however, for want of trying. There are now numerous lobby groups whose only purpose is to represent the views of the business community to governments. There are also other groups whose mandate is to explain government economic policy and identify emerging economic circumstances and trends to the business community, and still others whose function is to encourage strong two-way communication between governments and business.

One of the best known of the lobby groups in Ottawa is the Business Council on National Issues (BCNI). Established in 1976, BCNI is an élite organization, comprising the chief executive officers of the one hundred largest firms in Canada, and is 'dedicated to the development of public policy in the national interest.' It has, in recent years, championed several causes, including the Mulroney government's free trade initiative with the United States, lower federal government deficits, and a continuing check against inflation.[47] While taking care not to point to specific expenditure cuts to lower the deficit, BCNI was among those who urged the government not to reduce the deficit on the 'backs of the elderly.' The government, it will be recalled, later backed away from its announced cuts to old age pensions. One observer who applauded the BCNI call for a lower deficit noted wryly that one sure way to achieve this would be for corporations to pay a fairer share of taxes. But, he reported, 'BCNI is silent on this point.'[48]

The same is not true for a good number of other private sector groups. The Atlantic Provinces Economic Council (APEC) and the New Brunswick Economic Council (NBEC) are two of the most important voices representing the interests of the private sector in Atlantic Canada before government. Both have made numerous pleas that the federal government turn to the private sector to stimulate economic development in their area, arguing that past efforts have been dominated far too much by governments. They report that both they and their members are anxious to show the way to a more self-reliant economy in the region. They have also, however, pressed for more federal funding to the private sector to ensure that such development take place. The president of the NBEC, for example, declared that the $1 billion new money earmarked for the new development agency for Atlantic Canada 'is clearly insufficient to resolve Atlantic Canada's problems.'[49] He suggested that $3 billion was a more appropriate figure and went on to urge that the private sector in the region be permitted to take the lead in deciding how the money should be spent.

Both groups also receive a major portion of their funding from the two levels of government. The federal government alone, for example, has provided over 50 per cent of the expenditure budget of the NBEC since it was established in the late 1970s. Again, it is unlikely that APEC would exist today in its present form had the federal government not intervened with a special multi-year funding scheme in 1981.

It is not just business groups from Atlantic Canada that depend on federal government funding to operate. The Conference Board of Canada also benefits. Calling itself 'an independent research group responding to the needs of Canadian leaders,' it provides research and information on 'economic-forecasting and analysis compensation and human resources, corporate and public issues, (and) international business and tourism.'[50] One would assume that the federal government with all its expertise in these areas (notably, Finance and the Economic Council of Canada) could only draw limited benefit from the Conference Board. The board of directors, which is highlighted in its annual reports, reads as a veritable Who's Who of Canadian business, and the private sector flavour of its orientation is evident in all its work and publications. Yet provincial governments and over forty federal departments and agencies are members of the board and contribute over $600,000 annually in funding to its operation. In addition, the federal government began in 1987–8 to give a special annual grant to the Conference Board, amounting to $165,000.[51] This is not to suggest that the work of the Conference Board is lacking or not up to standards found in government or elsewhere. The Conference Board, for example, provides an excellent non-government look at provincial government finance. The point is that an organization that prides itself on having a private sector perspective has no reservation in applying for a special federal government grant to support its activities. This grant is over and above other government support, including membership dues.

A small group of business leaders based in Toronto and Ottawa got together in 1987 to launch a new group, the Public Policy Forum. Its purpose is to encourage the private sector to 'seek ways of using its knowledge and experience more directly in charting national policies.' To encourage this, the forum wishes to foster strong two-way communication between senior government representatives and the business community. To secure the necessary funding to operate, the group enlisted some eighteen corporate sponsors, including some of Canada's largest firms – notably, Gulf Canada, IBM Canada, Imperial Oil, and the Royal Bank of Canada. It also obtained the support of three federal departments. The level of support received from government and the private sector to pay the operating costs of the Public Policy Forum, however, has not been evenly distributed. More than half of its total funding comes from the federal government.[52]

WHY?

The role of the federal government in the business community and in business decisions has increased by leaps and bounds since the late 1950s. The helping hand of the federal government can now be found in virtually all types of business activities, in all economic sectors, and in all facets of business decisions, from feasibility studies and market surveys, to being the lender (often the lender of last resort), to being responsible for the closing of redundant or obsolete plants, and even to holding off bankruptcies, if only temporarily. Of late, its helping hand can even be found in the setting up and financing of organizations and groups that trumpet the virtues of the business community in the economy.

Some statistical comparisons are quite revealing. In 1961–2, federal government grants to the manufacturing sector amounted to $8 million, or $11 million in constant 1971 dollars. By 1970–1, the total had shot up to $159 million, or $171.7 million on constant 1971 dollars. By 1979–80, it was $410 million, or $203.9 million in constant 1971 dollars. As a percentage of manufacturing investment, the grants amounted to 0.3 per cent in 1961–2, 3.8 per cent in 1970–1, and 3.6 per cent in 1979–80.[53] A senior official in DRIE reports that the total has nearly doubled from 1979–80 to 1987–8. It is worth repeating once more that data on tax incentives are not easily accessible. Still, it has been estimated that federal corporate tax incentives in the manufacturing sector alone went from $83 million in 1961, or $115.3 million in constant 1971 dollars, to over $1 billion in 1979, or $540 million in constant 1971 dollars.[54] Another observer reports that total federal tax expenditures more than doubled from 1976 to 1979. By 1980, total corporate tax incentives amounted to $6.2 billion, while total federal corporate income tax collected in 1979 amounted to $7.2 billion. Corporate tax revenues as a percentage of federal revenues declined from 15 per cent in 1951 to 13 per cent in 1977. They dropped to 13.5 per cent in 1981 and still further to 11.5 per cent in 1987.[55]

As we have seen, those who have looked at the value of government programs designed for the business community, in the form of either cash grants or tax expenditures, have been less than enthusiastic about the results. Why then do such programs continue to exist and why are new ones added? Are we to believe that King Canute–type politicians and officials will always resist the tide of economic change? We know that the corporate culture found in most government departments will ensure that the status quo is favoured. We also know that ministers and politicians generally have a never-ending desire to be seen to be announcing new government measures. Is there more to it than that? One keen observer suggests that the private sector cannot possibly meet the expectations of the public and the media to provide jobs. This brings an almost unrelenting pressure on governments to force the creation of new employment. He writes: 'The almost universal use of unqualified percentage rate of unemployment ... meant that the government would be subjected to intense criticism for not having done enough, would be constantly reminded that private business was *failing* to provide enough jobs.'[56]

The great majority of new jobs created in recent years has been in small business. These jobs are often created one by one and seldom will the workforce rise dramatically when a small business expands. Such developments rarely receive much coverage in the local media. How-

ever, possible closures with hundreds of employees thrown out of work
or an entire economic sector, such as textiles, in decline will command
media attention for weeks and even months. The pressure on the government to do something, especially from the affected workers and
communities, is immense.

But what about the private sector? Why would business seek out
government grants and tax incentives and even employ staff and consultants to sniff out 'juicy morsels' that governments 'throw into the public
trough'? After all, the business community is the most self-reliant in
Canada. Surely, if one group is capable of making it on its own without
government help, it is the business community. Indeed, one frequently
hears business people and private sector groups calling for less government. They do not, however, always identify specific areas where cuts
could be made. On the question of government grants and tax incentives
for economic development, they are often silent. They have, however,
often expressed a preference for tax incentives. They claim the tax
incentives are more appropriate because they encourage profitability
and efficient operations. A cash grant, the argument goes, favours all
companies that apply and grants are awarded to firms whether they are
efficient or not. Tax incentives, meanwhile, only benefit those able to
compete in the market-place and to turn a profit. Accordingly, tax
incentives encourage firms to reach maximum profitability and efficiency. In addition, tax incentives need little additional government
personnel to administer, since they are merely adjuncts to the national
tax system.[57] Although the private sector is not wont to highlight this
aspect of tax incentives, they are also often hidden from public view.
Thus, they do not entail the stigma of admitting government aid to
business.

But this still does not answer the question: why would the private
sector seek out cash grants and tax incentives? I put the question to
several business people. Though hardly a representative survey, their
answers were revealing. Typically, their response was: we turn to these
programs because they are there. One explained: 'If I don't take advantage of government handouts, my competitor surely will. The business
game is one of survival and a good businessman can't let his competitors
get a leg up on him.'[58] A recurring theme from Atlantic Canada was that
federal government grants to the region's business community hardly
compare with what Ottawa makes available to business in other regions.
They pointed to past cash grants and current tax incentives to the
energy sector in western Canada and current ones to the manufacturing

sector in Ontario and Quebec. A leading member of the New Brunswick business community suggested that 'the federal government can spend more in one day to keep one General Motors plant open in Quebec and on tax expenditures in Toronto than it does in one year on the whole manufacturing sector in all of New Brunswick.'[59] A business person from Ontario observed that government grants are attractive for two reasons: 'first, they cut down substantially any risk in new investments, and second they are a great alternative to the equity market. Government grants can provide an infusion of capital without having to sell shares of your own company.'[60] The majority, however, insisted that government spending in support of business is far more appropriate than in virtually every other policy field. One echoed the views of all the others when he claimed that 'compared to what the federal government wastes on purely political schemes, on hopeless causes and make-work projects inside government, we get very little. At least what we do get we put to good use. We create real productive jobs that generate wealth rather than consume wealth.'[61] Not one business person, however, argued in favour of cash grants or even tax incentives on the basis of the programs' real or perceived merits.

Although the business community seldom argues that government programs for the private sector are viable or even necessary in their own right and few outside observers believe that the programs meet their objectives, cash grants and tax incentives to business continue to expand. There was a momentary pause in their expansion in 1984 when the Mulroney Conservatives came to power. The new government made it clear that it was unhappy with the plethora of economic development programs it had inherited from the Liberals, arguing that 'some programs designed to assist investment have the perverse result of distorting investment decisions and leading to the establishment of companies that are viable only with continued tax payer support.'[62] It will also be recalled that the government announced a series of cuts to DRIE during the first eighteen months of office. The cuts were to be spread throughout the department, and were to include major reductions in the IRDP budget. However, some thirty months later, cabinet approved a series of special funding measures to replenish DRIE's budget, because, it will be recalled, the department had seriously over committed its budget, particularly with respect to IRDP. In addition, early in the government's mandate, the then energy minister, Pat Carney, abolished the National Energy Policy, together with its generous incentives program to the oil and gas companies. She 'boasted that the Department of Energy would wither away because it was no longer necessary.'[63] There would be no need for a large Department of Energy simply because from now on the private sector would be left on its own to develop the oil and gas industry. In short, 'never again (would the government) ... interfere in the sacred laws of the oil marketplace.'[64] The Department of Energy, however, is still very much in operation. By 1988–9 the department had nearly 5000 person-years – about the same as it had in 1983–4 – and a budget close to $1 billion.[65] Its budget is also destined to grow substantially in coming years as a result of the announced major energy projects on the east coast and in the West, all of which require government assistance.

The government's proposed free trade agreement with the United States does not appear to have dampened its appetite for business-oriented programs. After three years in office and just about the time the free trade negotiations were reaching a conclusion, the Mulroney government unveiled a massive overhaul of federal government economic development programs. However, instead of reducing the scope of the programs for business, it enlarged them. It did abolish DRIE, but at the same time it established several new agencies, all designed with the private sector in mind. It established, it will be recalled, The Atlantic Canada Opportunities Agency (ACOA) which inherited existing government programs in the region, together with their funding levels, in addition to over $1 billion of new money. It established a similar agency for western Canada but gave it slightly more generous funding. It set up a new development office in northern Ontario and agreed to share the cost of a special $1 billion economic development plan for Quebec. Finally the government announced the establishment of a new Department of Industry, Science and Technology. Plans are to give the department at least $1 billion funding annually. Its mandate is to assist business in six areas: training, market penetration, technology, supplies, financing, and transportation and communication. In securing a new funding level for the department, the newly appointed minister, Robert R. de Cotret (the former Treasury Board president), made it clear early on that 'the federal deficit will not be balanced at the expense of DIST.'[66] It took only a few months for de Cotret to make the transition from guardian to spender.

The Mulroney government also in time cast aside its early conviction that the government should not interfere 'in the sacred laws of the oil marketplace.' It chose, for example, not to let the market-place dictate the pace of development of the Hibernia oilfield. Analysts suggest that the price of oil must be at $22 u.s. for the project to break even. The federal government moved in to kick-start the project when the price was at $14 u.s. It put together a $2.66 billion package of cash grants and loan guarantees to a consortium of five major oil companies.[67] The Newfoundland government also provided assistance to Hibernia in the form of reduced royalty payments and sales tax exemptions and reductions. The total cost of the project is estimated at $5.2 billion, with governments picking up as much as $1 billion in grants, $1.6 billion in loan guarantees, and the rest in reduced royalty payments for a total of $3.5 billion and the private sector consortium $1.7 billion. While representatives of the oil companies attending the announcement applauded the generous assistance provided by government, they did say that they had hoped for even more. The chairman of Mobil, a leading member of the consortium, reported, for instance, that there 'were several more things the oil companies wanted from the federal government but were unable to get, including more protection from losses because of (possible lower) oil prices.'[68] All of this prompted one political observer to sum up the economic policies of the Mulroney government with those of its predecessors as: 'plus ça change, plus c'est la même chose.'[69]

The Mulroney government has continued and even expanded an approach which took hold in government in the early 1960s. Initially, the federal government had let the market-place operate where and when it liked the results, intervening with modest cash grants where and when it did not. Over time, however, virtually every sector was to receive ever more generous cash grants, new loan guarantees, and tax incentives. The motivating force is less and less the desire to correct the where and when of economic activity. How could it be, when programs apply everywhere and at all times? Rather, it has become a political game in which non-designated communities, regions, and sectors look enviously at the designated. Politicians representing the regions or constituencies with a large number of employees in a given sector have happily taken up the cause. Whether or not the programs being expanded were successful has mattered little.

The business community, always ready to criticize big government (and especially government spending on social programs), has not, we have noticed, objected to incentive programs for the private sector. Would-be and full-fledged entrepreneurs, small, medium-sized, and big business, including large multinationals, have quite happily lined up for public largesse. Government programs have all but taken the hazard out of commercial investments. Indeed, there is little investment risk, if any, for the new 'energy projects' in western Canada, the tire plants in Ontario, the General Motors plant in Sainte-Thérèse, or the private sector consortium developing the Hibernia oilfield – let alone a host of less spectacular enterprises in all regions of the country. Even firms and plants teetering on the verge of bankruptcy or closure can often turn to government for assistance. As noted earlier, when asked to justify these wide-ranging and generous programs for the private sector, business people are likely to assert that such use of public funds is money better spent than if it were allocated to other groups in society.

PART IV

Towards an explanation

13

The ghost of spending past:
Revisiting the guardians and spenders

Many economists, students of public policy and public administration, and other observers argue that the most important challenge facing the federal government in the next decade is to manage restraint and to bring down the deficit.[1] And well they should. The accumulated debt is over $300 billion. With nearly 30 per cent of its expenditure budget – and increasing yearly – allocated to servicing the debt, the federal government is leaving itself precious little room to manoeuvre to stimulate the economy in the event of an economic downturn. But the alarm bells over the growth in spending have been ringing for years. It was, after all, an attempt to get a better handle on the problem that led to the introduction of PPB and PEMS. This study clearly shows that neither lived up to expectations. Their biggest failure was their inability to solve 'the incremental character of expenditure decision making.'[2] No minister and no official has willingly given up resources 'in order that other ministers might use them, whatever the rhetoric of the PEMS philosophy.'[3] Doug Hartle explains that ministers 'face a prisoner's dilemma problem: if they are forthcoming with proposed cuts, there is no assurance that the other members will not free ride – hoarding their own departmental surplus to finance new initiatives that would not be funded out of "new" money.'[4]

Little has changed since the days of the classical budget process. The focus, the energy, the competition, and, inevitably, the decisions are all geared to the margin, to the amount of 'new' money made available most years to support new initiatives. Once the battles have been fought, the winners walk away with their share safely tucked away in their A base. The process begins when new money is made available in policy reserves or when it is pryed away from the guardians. The A base, however, entails much less give and take. Central agency officials are far more interested in policy issues and in ensuring that ministers and departments follow 'due process' than in carrying out analyses of ongoing expenditures.

The Treasury Board secretariat does have an opportunity to look at the A base when it reviews departmental Multi-Year Operational Plans (MYOPS). But, as we saw, MYOP reviews in practice do not constitute a challenge to departmental programs and they are usually guided by across-the-board increases for inflation. Discussions with departments much more often centre on requests for new funding to cope with workload increases than on possible spending cuts.

Yet even a cursory look at the expenditure budget reveals how the process really plays at the margin. In the best of times for new funding, when the government knows that it will be implementing a major new initiative, such as child care, unallocated reserves never amount to more than 4 per cent of the total expenditure budget.[5] But that is the exception: the norm is anywhere between less than 1 per cent and 2 per cent. The result is that over 95 per cent of the budget is usually not subject to change.

If one looks at the expenditure budget process in the federal government as a struggle between guardians and spenders, one sees clearly that the spenders have had the upper hand. Although the guardians occupy positions of prestige and influence, the forces fuelling spending are formidable and can hardly be held in check by even the most powerful and determined guardians. Guardians in Ottawa have traditionally been the most senior and able cabinet ministers, numbering among their ranks such skilled politicians as Mitchell Sharp, Allan J. MacEachen, Jean Chrétien, Marc Lalonde, and Michael Wilson in the finance portfolio, and Bud Drury, Herb Gray, and Don Mazankowski as presidents of Treasury Board. All had served in cabinet before being appointed to these positions and all were well versed in the ways of the spenders, having themselves excelled as spenders.

EXPLAINING THE DEFICIT

The expenditure budget process and the struggle between guardians and spenders do not operate in a vacuum. Increased government spending is not the only reason for Ottawa's large annual deficit and accumulated debt. Deficits are also a product of the economic environment and revenue choices or, in part at least, the failure to tax. Indeed many observers point to these two forces rather than the expenditure side of the budget to explain in large part the federal government's deficit. An expanding economy, for example, brings in more revenues and also entails automatic decreases in spending.

The deficit can be divided into two main components: the cyclical and the structural. The cyclical component consists of that 'part produced by the gap between revenues and expenditures at the actual level of output in the economy and the amount of revenues and expenditures that would hypothetically exist at the full employment level of output. The structural component of the deficit results from the gap between the level of revenue generated by the tax system and other forms of government income, and the level of expenditures to which the government is committed. It constitutes the level of the deficit that would persist at the full employment level of output.'[6] Keynesian economics concentrates mainly on the cyclical component with deficits registered in the cyclical downswings in economic activity as a means of promoting higher levels of income and employment. When the pace of economic activity quickens, governments would cut back spending and produce surpluses. In time, budgetary surpluses and deficits would balance out. It is clear that this is pretty well what happened in Canada between the end of the Second World War and the mid-1970s. The Department of Finance points out that 'the federal budget balance fluctuated between surpluses and deficits in the 1950s and 1960s, averaging close to zero over the period as a whole. This pattern continued in the early 1970s. After a small surplus in 1970, there were small deficits in 1971 and 1972.'[7]

The deficit problem arrived to stay in 1975. The federal government recorded a deficit of $3.8 billion in 1975, rising to $21.1 billion in 1982 and again to over $30 billion by 1985. As noted earlier, some observers argue that the spending side of the federal government budget is only one of many forces fuelling the deficit and further that it is not the leading cause of the problem.[8]

Some observers suggest that the deficit problem coincided with the oil crisis of the mid-1970s and the resulting downward shift in growth trends in Canada and other western industrialized nations. The Department of Finance points to the severe recession that started in mid-1981 as another explanation. 'The estimates of the budget deficit adjusted for cyclical conditions indicate that 60 to 80 percent of the approximately $13 billion rise in the federal deficit that occurred in 1982 was due to automatic effect of lower activity levels on revenues and expenditures. In terms of levels, the estimates for 1982 suggest that the federal cyclically-adjusted or structural deficit might be in the $9 to $12 billion range, compared to an actual deficit of over $21 billion. This indicates that about half the federal deficit in 1982 was due to the impact of economic conditions on revenues and expenditures.'[9] One could add that the sudden increase in interest rates in the 1980s had far-reaching implications on the cost of servicing the public debt, thus contributing to the deficit problem.

Important changes to Ottawa's revenue system have also had important implications for the deficit. Lower corporate income tax, the two-year write-off for investments in the manufacturing and processing sectors, and the transfer of tax points to the provinces have been important. Of particular importance in explaining the slow growth in revenues was the federal government's decision in 1974 to index partially personal income tax.

It will also be recalled that tax expenditures – or spending by not taxing – became very popular soon after the government implemented a series of expenditure restraint measures in 1976. Tax expenditures were not counted in the total expenditure budget and so had no impact on the government's decision to limit the growth in spending to less than the growth in GNP. The result was that when spenders were told to limit spending increases, many of them shifted their efforts from promoting spending proposals to promoting tax expenditures. It is interesting to note that, when, at Finance's initiative, tax expenditures were placed in the appropriate spending envelope at the time PEMS was introduced, we saw the fewest number of tax expenditures introduced since they became a popular policy instrument in the mid-1970s. Under this system the minister bringing forward a tax expenditure proposal for regional development had the choice of either spending x million directly or through tax expenditures. This system was dropped only a few years after PEMS was introduced, largely as a result of spenders attempting all kinds of end-runs to gain support for new tax expenditures or because Finance feared that it was losing control over the approval of new tax expenditure schemes.[10]

There is no doubt that the various new tax expenditures introduced since the mid-1970s have entailed a significant revenue loss for the federal government. We saw earlier in this study that tax expenditures did not lose their popularity in the early 1980s when the country was confronting a deep recession and when Finance again took full control of the tax expenditure approval process. It will be recalled that tax expenditures were viewed as free money and 'more easily accessible' and that by 1985 it was estimated that Ottawa had over 300 tax expenditure items, compared with 200 in 1980. Revenue Canada reports that revenue losses in 1982–3 resulting from major tax reductions and tax expenditures stood at over $23 billion. The Department of Finance, Ottawa's leading guardian, acknowledged – albeit somewhat hesitantly – the impact of lost revenues on the deficit when it reported in the 1986 fiscal plan that the rise in the deficit 'was largely accounted for by an increase in expenditures that outstripped the growth rate of GNP, notably public debt charges, although declines in revenue contributed significantly as well.'[11]

It may well be that a good part of the deficit problem lies with the revenue budget rather than the expenditure budget, because of the severe recession of the early 1980s and the high interest that made servicing the debt very costly. It remains, however, that the spenders are responsible for the great majority of the tax expenditures introduced between 1976 and 1985. G. Bruce Doern documents the introduction of the Cape Breton tax credit and explains that the pressure for the new tax expenditures 'came from outside Finance and from a senior (spending) minister.'[12] The negotiations between the then minister of DRIE, Sinclair Stevens, and the finance minister, Michael Wilson, over the scope of the Cape Breton tax credit is akin to the struggle between guardians and spenders when shaping the expenditure budget. Indeed, Doern adopts a guardians-spenders framework to explain the development of the Cape Breton tax credit and reports that the push for new tax expenditures in the economic development field results in considerable negotiation between Finance and spending ministers.[13] This is in line with the findings of this study which suggest that the regional variable as it applies to economic development is much more important in explaining the growth of the expenditure budget than the literature has so far suggested.

It also remains that spenders have always had the upper hand in shaping the expenditure budget except when special spending restraint measures were introduced in the late 1970s and in 1984–5.[14] One only has to look at the number of programs and initiatives that have been added to the federal government budget compared with those eliminated to recognize that budgeting by subtraction has never replaced budgeting by addition in Ottawa. As well, the economy has been expanding for the past several years and the deficit remains at about $30 billion. A change of government in 1984 has also not fundamentally altered the federal government expenditure budget.

REVISITING THE 1984–8 YEARS

In the 1984 election the Progressive Conservative party won a majority of seats for the first time in twenty-seven years. Senior members of the new government made it clear early on that things would be different than they had been under the spendthrift Liberals. Treasury Board President Robert R. de Cotret explained within weeks of coming to power that the deficit was much too large and the government's focus in reducing the deficit would be on the expenditure side. He said: 'for too long the government has been spending money which it did not have ... The solution is clear. In a pragmatic, considered fair way, the government must review and reduce its expenditures.'[15] Finance Minister Michael Wilson added: 'Our immediate goal is to reduce the deficit through expenditure reduction and not through major tax increases.'[16]

When it sought a second mandate in November 1988, the Mulroney government claimed some success in reducing the annual growth in the deficit. As we saw, the government's biggest anti-deficit push came in the first months of its mandate and took the form of a combination of spending cuts and tax increases. Further spending cuts and new measures to raise additional revenues were announced in Wilson's first budget. The drive to get the deficit down, however, stalled after a few years. It is still growing at about $30 billion a year, although the latest fiscal plan calls for it to go down to about $20 billion by 1992.[17] However, this expectation is based on the assumption that Canada's gross domestic product will average about 3 per cent in real terms between 1988 and 1992. Many observers consider this to be overly optimistic.[18] Most economists predict slower growth than is suggested by the fiscal plan. The prediction of the minister of finance that the economy will grow by 3 per cent in real terms through to 1992 comes on the heel of five years of one of the strongest recoveries since the Great Depression. Economists expect a 'pause,' if not a recession, before 1992. Maureen Farrow, director of the C.D. Howe Institute, says: 'The picture presented (in the budget) for 1989 is overly optimistic and underplays the risks Canada faces from a slowdown in the U.S. and/or the world economy.'[19] On the spending side, major new commitments were made after the government's fiscal plan was tabled in February 1988. The finance minister did announce a $300 million cut in non-statutory spending. The cuts, however, will only be identified in 1989–90. It is true that major tax reforms are being implemented, but the government pledged that the reforms would be 'deficit neutral.'

On the revenue side, the federal government collected $27 billion in personal income tax in 1983–4 and $37.9 billion in 1986–7. Similarly, federal sales tax generated $6.7 billion in revenues in 1983–4 compared with $10.6 billion in 1986–7.[20] The list goes on. The growth in the economy was such that finance officials underestimated revenues. For example, federal tax revenues are estimated to bring in well over $3 billion more in revenues in 1988–9 than had earlier been projected. The annual growth in the deficit, however, will not decrease by the same amount. The finance minister reported that new revenues would go to pay for 'increased defence spending, for deficiency payments for grain farmers and the doubling of the child care deduction for individuals.'[21]

The federal government has, since 1984, also announced a series of tax increases and new revenue-generating measures. In his first budget, Michael Wilson imposed a deficit-reduction surtax on individuals and corporations and a two-year tax on the capital of large banks, and modified the indexation of personal exemptions and tax brackets to reflect only the annual increase in the consumer price index greater than 3 per cent. He also added new revenue-generating measures in every subsequent year, including a one-cent-a-litre increase in the excise tax on gasoline, to cover the cost of the day care program in his 1988 budget. In short, it is clear that an expanding economy, new taxes, and tax increases explain in large part the recent reduction in the annual growth in the deficit.

Canada is ill prepared to confront a recession. The federal government debt as a percentage of GDP stood at 26 per cent when Canada faced the last recession in the early 1980s. Today, after more than five years of economic expansion, it is 53 per cent of GDP. Many observers charge that the federal government has 'blown a rare opportunity' to use the revenue windfall (generated by a growing economy) ... to lower the deficit by several billions.'[22]

When the Mulroney government came to office, the accumulated debt was approaching $200 billion. Four years later, with the economy expanding throughout the mandate, the debt had risen to $300 billion. During Trudeau's last full year in office, the government ran a deficit of $32.4 billion. The Mulroney government ran a deficit of $34.4 billion in its first full year of office, but brought it down to $30 billion or slightly less thereafter.

How was the federal government able to cut back the annual growth in the deficit? Between 1984 and 1988, overall federal spending grew by 26 per cent. The growth in spending has been particularly strong since early 1987. As we have seen, starting in June 1987 a series of costly new measures have been announced in the area of economic development, energy, multiculturalism, drought relief for farmers, port development, defence, and child care, among others. The majority of these are not one-shot projects. They are being built into the A base or as part of the ongoing expenditure budget.

The guardians in the Mulroney government also benefited from favourable economic circumstances. Growth in domestic product shot up by 40 per cent and tax revenues jumped by 46 per cent between 1984 and 1988.[23] An expanding economy has obvious implications for the budget and the deficit.

REVISITING THE BUDGETARY SYSTEMS

We have seen in this study that new systems and processes were introduced from time to time in an effort to hobble the spenders. PPB was introduced because the classical budget process, which operated in Canada until the late 1960s, 'treated the expenditure base as given.'[24] Its focus had always been on additional inputs required and not on program objectives or effectiveness. It was hoped that PPB would change all this and 'usher in integrated top-down expenditure planning' by forcing managers to state their program objectives, to assess alternative means of achieving them, and to measure progress and effectiveness.[25] Programs that did not measure up would be either discarded or revised. In short, PPB with its sophisticated techniques was to unearth government waste and redundant programs, as well as point the way to restructuring costly programs. The guardians, notably the finance minister, heralded PPB as a 'budget breakthrough.'[26] It quickly became evident, however, that PPB had serious shortcomings. The approach proved difficult to implement, and many months were wasted as government officials tried to define quantifiable program objectives and performance criteria. However, the focus under PPB never shifted away from the traditional competition for new funds to a thorough review of existing programs. These simply continued and new programs were added on, much as in pre-PPB days.[27] There was a move away from a concentration on 'input costs' to broad policy discussions but, for the guardians, little apparent gain elsewhere. As Robert Adie and Paul Thomas observed, PPB led to 'very few program terminations or dramatic shifts in expenditure patterns.'[28]

If PPB was designed to check growth in government spending, there is little doubt that it failed and failed badly. The growth in spending in 1970–1 stood at 12.1 per cent over the previous year while growth in gross domestic product was 7.3 per cent and that in the consumer price index was 3.3 per cent. From 1970–1 to 1975–6, the annual growth in spending far outstripped both the growth in GDP and increases in CPI.

By the mid-1970s, it will be recalled, the government became increasingly concerned over growing inflation. Convinced that the growth in government spending was a notable cause of inflation, the government, in a major policy statement, pledged to hold growth in spending to less than the annual growth rate in GDP. Strong signals were sent to spending ministers, departments, and agencies to hold back the growth in spending. If new spending was required, departments were told, it must be found through a reallocation of resources within existing budgets.[29] It was apparent that PPB was considered a failure and that it could no longer be relied upon to do the job. The policy of holding back growth in spending to less than the growth in GDP, however, did meet with some success. As figure 9 shows, growth in spending was less than that in GDP in three of the four years between 1976–7 and 1979–80. Still, the spenders were able to find new ways to spend and, at the same time, to sidestep the policy. As we have seen, tax incentives were popular during this period. In addition, in introducing the Established Programs Financing Act in 1977, the federal government transferred tax points to the provinces rather than making new transfer payments. Notwithstanding these innovations, annual growth in government spending remained close to the increase in GDP and in 1977–8 it actually surpassed it. As well, growth in government spending was consistently higher than increases in CPI during this period.

The then prime minister, Pierre Trudeau, now more convinced than ever that growth in spending was fuelling inflation, returned from the Bonn economic summit in 1978 with plans for major spending cuts in hand. Without even consulting his guardians, Trudeau went before a national television audience to unveil the cuts. It was an unprecedented step and left no doubt that Trudeau was exasperated with the process in place. It explained his 'swift strike [which was] born of his own

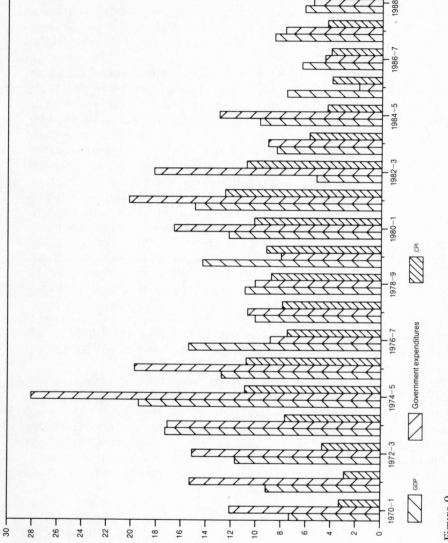

Figure 9

Growth of budgetary expenditures, GDP, and CPI

frustration at the civil service's reluctance to respond to his request for money saving ideas.'[30] Important spending cuts were made as a result of Trudeau's sudden decision, as we saw; however, some proved to be only temporary.

Trudeau's dramatic cuts, combined with concerns that 'Parliament and indeed the government had lost or was close to losing control of the public purse,' pushed the federal government to introduce PEMS, which was widely considered to hold great promise for curbing growth in spending. Cabinet committees were granted spending envelopes or expenditure limits and a policy reserve to be spent on new initiatives. If ministers and cabinet committees wanted to approve new spending beyond what was available in the policy reserve, they would have to review existing programs and free up resources from them. PEMS would thus place responsibility for saving squarely on the shoulders of those who spent. The thinking was that all ministers would act as both guardians and spenders. The envelope system would force each cabinet minister, within his committee, to participate in the budget process, to make trade-offs between introducing new programs and cutting back existing ones.

PEMS expanded the government's planning horizon by making spending projections by envelope available for four years into the future. New central agencies were set up to assist the policy committees, and mirror committees of deputy ministers were asked to review all proposals coming forward for funding from the policy reserve. The key characteristic of PEMS, however, from the guardians' perspective, was the envelope accounting system which confronted the cabinet and ministers with the fiscal consequence of their spending decisions. All in all, PEMS was an attempt to impose 'discipline and collective responsibility' on what had been an undisciplined process of spending funds.[31]

No one in Ottawa would argue that PEMS has lived up to expectations. Federal officials are now scrambling either to put PEMS back together again or to come up with yet another solution. It is obvious that ministers have not become both guardians and spenders. Finance and the Treasury Board are still the guardians, and spending ministers and their departments remain the spenders: competition between the two groups is as intense as it ever was.

Spending ministers and their departments have continued to channel all their efforts into competing for new funding from the policy reserves. It is true that, in principle, policy reserves can be set at negative values with a call made for reductions in an envelope's expenditure base.

In practice, however, ministers and their departments have proved reluctant to volunteer programs for reduction or elimination. When policy committees did initiate x budget exercises or actual cuts in spending, ministers returned the next day asking to be reallocated the funds they had just freed up. In addition, when departments were asked to cut spending, they had a tendency to meet their reduction quotas by cutting or deferring capital expenditure and maintenance spending so that they could preserve their program expenditures. The guardians, still finance and the Treasury Board secretariat, can suggest candidates for cuts but the poor quality of program evaluation and the lack of a formal mechanism to force such choices make this difficult. In an attempt to remedy this situation, the TBS will instruct departments to bring forward data on the performance of their programs. Departments quickly discovered, however, that compliance with such instructions often brings harsher punishments in terms of their budgets than does disobedience.

When departments are asked to take on new initiatives, however modest, they still seek new funding, from either the policy or operating reserves. This is evident from trivial dollar and person-year requests. Much as in pre-PEMS days, then, departments and agencies are reluctant to reallocate resources among their various programs to reflect new government-wide or sectoral priorities.

Moreover, the policy reserves have, if anything, strengthened the incremental forces in the budget process. The existence of policy reserves encourages departments to leave their A base intact and to come forward with proposals for new initiatives to compete for whatever funds are available. The majority of the proposals are not one-time spending projects and, once approved, their ongoing costs become part of the department's A base.

When cuts are required, the guardians still often call for across-the-board reductions, as they have always done. The longer-term implications of such cuts are that high- and low-priority programs are subjected to equal cuts. Yet PEMS was designed precisely to force decisions on program spending and avoid future across-the-board cuts.

PEMS's greatest failure, however, is that it has never been able to instil the kind of 'financial and qualitative' discipline that was envisaged. Policy committees have always been quick to approve new spending proposals and to spend their policy reserves. Once spent, ministers and departments do not always sit back and wait for reserves to be replenished in the next fiscal year. Many spending ministers have gone straight to the minister of finance and the prime minister in search of new funds. Many have been successful. Knowing that pressure for new spending would spill over from the policy committees, the minister of finance put aside a central reserve to accommodate the inevitable pressure from the spenders. Once the minister of finance agreed to fund one such proposal, however, he was in fact inviting other spending ministers to try the same route. A pattern has developed whereby the Department of Finance will support the big-ticket items, such as the development of the Hibernia oilfields and assistance to western grain farmers, and special development funds, while policy committees will handle the less expensive proposals. Ministers with clout also bypass PEMS when quick decisions are required. However, often decisions are made to approve initiatives without at the same time identifying the source of funds to finance them (for example, the Atlantic Accord). The result is that Finance is left to pick up the pieces. This has given Finance greater influence in shaping actual spending decisions than was first envisaged under PEMS. The overall cost to the guardians, however, has been less financial discipline.

The result is that PEMS today has become substantially different from when it was first introduced in 1979. It has been considerably diluted. Strategic overviews that set out departmental priorities and objectives have been replaced by ministerial letters detailing strategic priorities upon the request of the prime minister. The ministries of state supporting the social and economic cabinet committees have been disbanded, as have been the mirror committees of deputy ministers.

When a new Progressive Conservative government was elected in 1984 with an agenda to cut spending, it decided to bypass PEMS and its attendant cumbersome procedures. The new cabinet felt strongly that public sector spending had not been adequately controlled by the previous government. The minister of finance, Michael Wilson, made it clear in major economic statements and in his first budget speech that the government would cut spending.[32] The guardians clearly had the upper hand during the early months of the Mulroney government and important spending cuts were announced. Growth in spending in 1985–6 was held to below the growth in GDP and the increase in CPI, as figure 9 shows.

The Mulroney government also established the Nielsen Task Force and the Forget study of the unemployment insurance program. But, as we saw, by the time Nielsen and Forget had submitted their reports, the government had lost its appetite for cutting spending. The spending ministers had become familiar with their portfolios and saw greater merit in protecting their respective departments' A base and in generating new spending proposals than in collaborating with the guardians. They saw no reason to cut spending in their own departments, only to see the savings directed to other spending ministers or to support the general expenditure reduction exercises of the guardians. The Forget report which recommended that the unemployment insurance program be overhauled was rejected and, though some of the Nielsen Task Force's recommendations were implemented, it had limited impact on the federal government's expenditure budget. As a leading political columnist explains: 'The government pulled the fuse on almost all the controversial recommendations in the 21-volume study.'[33] Nielsen himself readily admits the limited impact of his review and explains that by the time he submitted his recommendations the government's 'political will had eroded.'[34]

The government's political will to continue with a policy of spending cuts also eroded over time. The minister of finance and the president of the Treasury Board proved incapable of convincing their colleagues to stick with a policy of restraint and, slowly but surely, spenders turned the tide against the guardians. A good number of cuts announced in late 1984 and in 1985 were later abandoned. Examples range from capital spending, old age pension indexation, subsidies to Via Rail, to industrial and regional development incentives. As well, after only some eighteen months in power, the Mulroney government began to announce a string of new and costly spending commitments. By the time the government tabled its 1988–9 main estimates, the victory of the spenders was complete. The increase in spending for that year was projected to be much higher than both the rate of inflation and projected increases in GDP.

What conclusions can we draw from this and from the inability of PPB and later PEMS to check the growth in government spending? We now know that the analysis of the expenditure budget on a program-by-program basis is not the best approach. For one thing, it has taken us to where we are today. Such an approach appears to be better suited when growth in spending is possible or even desirable. When the focus is on programs, spending ministers and departments have a double advantage. Departments can argue for more resources to operate and expand a successful program, while at the same time arguing for more funding to rectify problems when a program does poorly. In addition, there are now so many federal government programs that it is impossible for the guardians to get a handle on all of them in any given year so as to recommend which should be eliminated or cut back.

The basic role of central agency officials has not changed dramatically since the days of the classical budget process. Their function is still to refuse requests for incremental resources. They still play the role of guardians. But few have the analytical and political capabilities to challenge established policies and programs. Guardians are also relatively few in number, and they have limited time available to challenge departmental programs. A handful of Treasury Board and Department of Finance officials can hardly be expected to take on a battery of accountants, policy analysts, program evaluation specialists, and the like in, say, Defence, Transport, or Revenue Canada. The guardians have never been able, under either PPB or PEMS, to get the authority to go beyond merely responding to departmental proposals and questioning what departments are doing.

Departments can invariably predict that Treasury Board and Finance will have a knee-jerk reaction to all proposals involving new spending. Spending ministers and their departments will compete with one another to tap the policy reserves or, if it is a large, expensive project, Finance's centrally held reserve. If they are turned down, they can always attempt to bypass the guardians, to orchestrate end-runs with their ministers and their cabinet colleagues, or to appeal to higher authorities (the prime minister, his office, or one or two powerful regional ministers).

Central agency officials are viewed as great goaltenders, quite willing to try to stop projects but incapable of coming forward with any solutions. In short, theirs is an anti-spending, defensive strategy. They rarely initiate proposals and Finance, in particular, has 'failed to find any criterion of general economic policy more sophisticated than a reflex anti-spending posture.'[35] The Department of Finance has had nothing creative to suggest for years in such fields as regional or industrial development, energy, and federal-provincial relations. It was finance officials who took the lead in bringing Keynesian economics to Ottawa but, as John K. Galbraith reports, the time has passed for Keynes's theories.[36] Nothing of equivalent force has replaced them. For the spenders, therefore, the guardians simply represent an inviting target and a challenge to be overcome.

It is clear that ministers find it much less difficult to agree on levels of total expenditures, even the total dollar figure to be cut from the budget, than on where specific reductions should take place. It explains why both the Trudeau and Mulroney cabinets often agreed to across-the-board cuts when forced to announce expenditure reductions. It also explains why departments, having no specific direction on where to cut, have often responded by simply delaying capital budget and maintenance and operating spending, while avoiding cuts in program expenditures.

Some departments may well have had information in hand to justify cuts in their program expenditures. But there is little incentive to make this information available to the guardians. Better to absorb their share of the cuts like everyone else than to see their department lose more than the others. As Aaron Wildavsky observes: 'If a [department's] loss is [another department's] gain, why should [it] play this game?'[37]

It is also fair to say that many departments are not set up to foresee major developments and to plan for them. Access to policy reserves, to the operating reserve, and to special emergency allocations has provided little incentive for departments to undertake effective planning. Whatever planning has taken place, either in preparing strategic overviews or in responding to a prime minister's letter to outline strategic priorities, has taken the form of competition to get new incremental resources.

The setting of expenditure limits, or envelopes under PEMS, has not changed this situation. Spending ministers and departments still compete intensely for new incremental resources. It was hoped that spending limits would attenuate this competition. One observer wrote that 'the invisible hand of the envelope mechanism may lead individual ministers and program managers, through pursuit of their own interests, also to pursue the social goal of a more efficient allocation of resources, at least within the policy envelope.'[38] This view has proved naive. The truth is that spenders quickly learn to play under any rules, be it PPB or PEMS, and they are quite capable of circumventing the obstacles of any budget process, PEMS included.

The finance minister must, as never before, be on the look-out for end-runs by spending ministers. Either by design or because it felt it had little practical choice, Finance now has a reserve set aside to accommodate spending proposals beyond what is made available in the policy and operating reserves. Such proposals are funded outside the cabinet committee structure through bilateral negotiations between Finance and the spenders. These negotiations are not normally open to policy committee review, and the lack of consultation with all parties has no doubt restricted the government's ability to establish a broad framework in which competing demands for resources can be reviewed and trade-offs established.

If we have learned anything about the federal government expenditure budget over the past twenty-five years, it is that rational budget processes 'do not meet the tests of political rationality.'[39] We expect too much of them. Such processes, we have assumed, could identify unnecessary programs, highlight important issues, and prepare policy plans. They could provide an assessment of alternatives and control spending forces, as well as enable ministers to weigh trade-offs, so that only the most deserving proposals – those that support government priorities – are approved, while low-priority programs or activities are cut. We now know that the spenders are not so easily controlled.

WHY?

In the introductory chapter, I briefly reviewed some of the best-known theories explaining the growth in government activity and spending. I also argued that theories depend on generalizations, and government officials directly involved in the expenditure budget process insist that budget making is much too untidy a business for generalizations.

Still, the theories reviewed in that chapter have some relevance to the Canadian situation and explain in part the growth in spending in the federal government. My findings lead me to echo the comments of Robert Adie and Paul Thomas that 'there is no single, widely accepted explanation for the growth of government ... Rather there are many explanations, some competing, and others complementary, each containing, no doubt, some element of truth.'[40] Certainly Wagner's law, for example, is relevant to the Canadian experience. There is no denying that new economic activity, rising per capita income, urbanization, and the development of the modern economy have fuelled demand for services that government is best suited to deliver. As in other countries, technological change and new techniques of production have given rise to demands for new services and often for increased government control of new economic activities. Legal protection, research and development, and large infrastructure investment all point to more government intervention in the economy. Demographic change also holds obvious implications for Ottawa's expenditure budget. An ageing population inevitably places considerable strain on the budget, with new spending required for pensions and health care.

Incrementalism and the inability of politicians and officials to stop and start programs quickly also explain in part the growth in spending. As elsewhere, an important determining factor of the size of the main estimates tabled by the federal government is the previous year's main estimates. In Canada, however, federal ministers and officials have demonstrated a knack to start new programs quickly. Cabinet, especially when the party in power has a majority in parliament, can launch major new programs on short notice, and there have been many such cases. Cabinet has the same power to stop programs as quickly, but there have been few such cases. This begs the question: Why has cabinet proved to be unwilling to stop more programs than it has? Wildavsky's cultural theory of budgeting has some relevance to Canada. It no doubt explains the popularity of social programs among Canadians. It also likely explains Richard Johnson's findings that social programs are highly popular in Canada and that, on the whole, 'Canadians are an economist's version of *le bourgeois gentilhomme*: Keynesian without realizing it.'[41] It would also be difficult to disagree with Alan Cairns's view that eleven governments pursuing visions instead of one and 200 ministers building empires instead of 25 are bound to increase the scope of government.

Public choice theorists offer another explanation. They argue that government is 'a piece of machinery, like the market, that people can use to achieve their purposes.'[42] Politicians and public servants are regarded as rational, self-interested, and maximizing actors. Anthony Downs, as we noted in the introductory chapter, maintains that politicians 'act solely in order to attain the income, prestige, and power which come from being in office. Thus ... their only goal is to reap the rewards of holding office.'[43] W.A. Niskanen, meanwhile, claims that public servants are similarly motivated, always on the look-out to maximize their budgets, and their sponsors do not have access to the information to hold them in check.[44] There is little incentive to pursue efficiency, since most of the goals of public servants are related to the size of their budgets.

The public choice theory holds considerable appeal for those in Canada, as elsewhere, who seek to explain the growth in the federal government's expenditure budget once and for all. First, it is a simple theory, easily grasped by students of public policy and political science. Secondly, it is relatively easy to accept that most people – politicians and public servants included – are concerned about their material well-being most of the time.

Doug Hartle recently introduced a public choice/rent-seeking perspective to the federal government expenditure budget process. There is much in this study that supports Hartle's conclusions. My findings, for example, support Hartle's observation that 'the pervasive force of the status quo is surely a reflection of the endurance of well-entrenched rent-seeking groups.' I also agree with Hartle that personalities are important in shaping the expenditure budget process and the expenditure budget. There are also other similarities in our findings regarding the role and effectiveness of the central agencies, notably the Office of the Comptroller General and the Office of the Auditor General. The reader will also see other similarities in the studies regarding the operations of government generally. Hartle concludes his study by stating that 'modern public choice theory, of which rent-seeking is but an aspect, is less than three decades old. From the perspective of the study of economics, both concepts are in their infancy. The ideas are still evolving and do not yet constitute an integrated whole.'[45] The findings of this study in fact raise a number of issues on the application of the public choice/rent-seeking perspective to the Canadian experience.

It is clear that the public choice theorists have yet to deal with the regional variable adequately. Hartle, for example, hardly dealt with the issue. The findings of this study suggest that regionalism is an important force fuelling new spending and supporting the status quo. The force cannot be simply explained by suggesting that it is being fuelled by politicians seeking to deliver benefits to their constituencies to secure their own re-election and to marginal constituencies to secure the re-election of the government. Those with even only a cursory knowledge of Canadian regional development efforts – an ideal area of government activity to favour marginal voters and marginal constituencies – know, for example, that in actual experience government policies and programs have not favoured marginal constituencies. Some of the most high-profile regional development projects – such as Michelin tire plants, the Maritime forestry complex, Mitel expansion projects – have all gone to non-swing seats, the majority of which have been held by the opposition.[46]

The public choice theorists' focus on marginal constituencies to explain the behaviour of vote-seeking politicians requires more research, if not some revisions. Well-known spenders such as Roméo LeBlanc, Don Jamieson, Eugene Whelan, and, albeit less so, Allan J. MacEachen never had to worry deeply about their own re-elections. Even after deciding to leave politics, many made full use of their skills and abilities in government circles to secure more initiatives for their regions.

I detected another equally powerful force to explain the determined efforts of politicians to pry more funds from the treasury. Ministers individually hold a profound conviction that if they should show self-discipline before the federal treasury, they would be the only ones to do so. They all believe that their colleagues and permanent officials are far more wasteful of public funds than they are.

Ministers from Atlantic Canada and the West are firmly convinced that their colleagues from Ontario and Quebec have been much more adroit at milking the federal treasury than they have been or could ever be. Ministers believe that the bureaucracy wastes more money by maintaining ineffective and dated machinery of government than they themselves do with their high-profile projects. Public servants meanwhile see little merit in managing their operations more efficiently only to see savings going to support political 'boondoggles' rather than to lowering the deficit.

An exchange I had with a senior deputy minister is revealing. He claimed that 'officials can do everything for ministers, they can point to where programs can be cut, they can explain how the cuts can be made, but they can never give ministers the political will to do it. That is something only ministers can do.'[47] I reported this view to a senior cabinet minister in the Mulroney government. He reflected on the observation briefly and then shot back:

The official is absolutely correct. We are ultimately responsible for mustering the political will to do something that is basically unpleasant – cutting back programs. However, I know full well that there is a great deal of waste in the bureaucracy, that departments could be much better managed, and that important savings could be realized. I know that and my colleagues know that. Anybody that works in Ottawa for any length of time knows that. Officials, I am sure, know that as well. I can have discussions with them but I cannot rectify the situation. It takes bureaucratic will to deal with the problem. I cannot give them bureaucratic will – it is something only bureaucrats themselves can do.[48]

As we have seen, the prime minister, cabinet, and ministers individually are always under intense pressure to spend in the regions. The pressure comes from the local media, from their own caucus members, from their own local party organizations, from local economic associations and organizations, and always (with an eye on the television camera) from opposition members during question period. Pressure comes as well from provincial premiers who also appear on television at inter-provincial and at first ministers' conferences. Premiers will pounce on every opportunity to point out where the federal government is short-changing their province. Premier Grant Devine echoed the sentiment of his western and Atlantic colleagues when he declared that 'Southern Ontario is a great place ... they're doing really well, fat cats, full employment, going great guns. We just want our fair share. Why would anybody deny us equal footing?'[49] How does one get equal footing or a fair share? Simply by having the federal government spend more in the region. The measurement of Ottawa's commitment to economic development is no longer determined by the kind of policies it puts in place; rather the measurement is displayed on pocket calculators.

This focus on funding has given regional development a bad name in Canada. An editorial in the Toronto *Globe and Mail* dismissed out of hand the feasibility of the Hibernia energy project. Because it made no economic sense, the project was labelled a regional development project. The newspaper stated that 'Brian Mulroney did not even try to pretend ... that Hibernia was an energy project. It is a regional development project at heart ... in the full context of Canadian policy, the question is not whether Hibernia is good, but how good at this price?'[50] Regional development has degenerated into a 'grab' for federal funds and supports any number of totally unrelated and often undeserving projects. The result is that regional development in Canada is viewed, not in terms of strengthening the national economy, but in terms of redividing the national pie, with most regions in full competition to get a bigger piece.[51] We do not look at less developed regions with the intention of studying both regional problems and potential in order to develop realistic ways of using their resources. The test of Ottawa's commitment to the regions is judged simply by the amount of money and its own activities it is prepared to commit to the region. When the prime minister unveiled the Atlantic Canada Opportunities Agency and the Western Diversification Office, for example, the local press focused almost exclusively on the billion dollars of *new* money that would flow to the regions rather than on the new approach the agencies would adopt and how this might benefit the two regions.[52]

The recession of the early 1980s and its deep impact on Canada's industrial heartland changed the federal government's approach to economic development. The unprecedented softness in key economic sectors in central Canada pushed the federal government to intervene there, much as it had done earlier in Atlantic Canada. Again, the collapse of the oil and gas industries a few years later saw federal intervention in western Canada. The then minister of finance explained in his budget speech that regions that had previously enjoyed strong growth were now confronted with special problems of adjustment, so that problems existed in all regions. The solution he proposed was to make 'regional economic development ... central to public policy planning at the federal level.'[53] The government's solution was to make cash grants, loan guarantees, and tax incentives available to business and to finance an array of projects; at this point Atlantic Canada, seeing that funding for economic development was being spread out across the country, immediately clamoured for more.

The constant pull for federal funds extends far beyond regional incentives and regional development agreements. It permeates virtually every area of federal government activity, including defence, procurement, some social programs, such as unemployment insurance, and every economic sector from agriculture to forestry to industrial development. It also covers every region. Bill Rompkey, then Newfoundland minister in the Trudeau cabinet, issued a special pamphlet to his constituents to report that he 'was able to sign recently a $39 million pact ... to improve conditions on the Labrador coast.'[54] Meanwhile, the member of parliament for Toronto's Etobicoke North in a Progressive Conservative administration happily wrote his constituents to report that his riding had been able to secure $1.3 billion in contracts awarded by the federal Supply and Services Department.[55] The list goes on. In fact, a regular feature that government MPs send out to their constituents in the parliamentary newsletter 'Householders' is a breakdown of how much funding they were able to secure for their ridings.[56] Ministers, MPs, provincial premiers, and others are sure to keep a running tab on who gets what and, if they themselves are not getting their share, the federal cabinet is certain to hear about it.

Party policies matter little here. For example, a New Democratic MP from western Canada pushed the government hard in question period to explain why his region, with nearly 30 per cent of the population, was 'receiving only 11.8 percent of national contracts from the Department of Supply and Services.'[57] The deputy prime minister, Don Mazankowski, responded by saying that there was no doubt 'a problem' and that the government would try to turn things around.[58] A Progressive Conservative MP, also from the West, charged that the region was only receiving '22 percent of federal research and development" and that the situation needed to be corrected.[59] Quebec MPs meanwhile argue that federal government policy on science and technology invariably favours Ontario at Quebec's expense.[60] Ontario MPs point out that the federal government diverts 'much of its spending in agriculture to the West at the expense of Ontario ... farmers in Ontario ... receive less assistance from the federal government than anywhere else.'[61] This line of argument is not limited to politicians. Economists have produced various studies on 'net federal fiscal contribution' to calculate the net outcome of federal taxes and expenditures in each province. One of the authors of such a study argued that Alberta was being short-changed and suggested that 'Ontario has had the highest per capita income and the lowest unemployment since 1982. And yet, on a net basis, federal money has flowed into that province. If the federal government is running a deficit with Ontario, why not with Alberta too?'[62]

The regional variable in Canada is even more perplexing and difficult to explain because it appears that the provinces do not always view the competition for more federal funds as a competition among themselves. Rather, at times they appear to regard it much more as a competition between them (the ten provinces) and the federal treasury. Manitoba's former attorney general, for example, now reports that he would never have agreed to the proposed Meech lake constitutional agreement had he realized that it might be employed to trample on anglophone rights in Quebec. He explains that 'Manitoba was given the impression that the distinct society clause would simply permit Quebec to get tons of federal money to develop French culture.'[63]

The study also reveals, however, that 'spending by comparison' extends beyond the regional factor. Supporters of the federal day-care policy have argued for more funding and, in doing so, have referred to what Ottawa spends in defence to support their case. The defence minister, sensing that his plan to purchase new nuclear submarines was in jeopardy, shot back with comparative arguments of his own. He argued that 'the boats will cost an average of only $300 million per year, spread out over a quarter century ... an amount equal to one-half or one percent of Ottawa's social expenditures.'[64]

One of the most frequently heard arguments in cabinet and among officials in Ottawa to support a new spending proposal is 'compared with what the federal government spends on such and such, this is peanuts.'[65] The arts community, the film, tourism, and pharmaceutical industries, can all lament their relative lack of funding compared with other sectors and demonstrate that they could generate more benefits for Canadian society than the others with the same level of government funding.

This argument applies not only when new funding is being sought but also when expenditure cuts are contemplated. Officials will not deny that they could survive with fewer resources and person-years. But if it is waste that one is looking for, officials in one department are likely to point the finger at larger, and presumably more wasteful, departments.

Officials will also point to the constant stream of new spending commitments by politicians to explain the difficulty in keeping a firm grip on spending. This study reveals that most of the new spending over the past several years has been politically driven by spending ministers or by election campaign commitments. This was as true under Trudeau as it has been under Mulroney. The special economic program (SCRAP), special assistance to grain farmers, new defence spending, new economic development agencies, child care – to name just a few – all came from the political level. In virtually all instances, a number of senior public servants, particularly the guardians, urged ministers not to go ahead with new spending plans. In addition, some public servants have on occasion sought to cut down new spending plans. Officials in the Ministry of Transport, for example, requested the government to contract out airport security services because it would cost less than doing it in-house.[66]

That said, it is also possible to conclude that officials have resisted attempts to make the operations of government more efficient, or to cut back the size of departments and agencies. Everyone appears convinced that there are 'too many people in government departments chasing too few real jobs.'[67] Advances in information technology and in computer facilities, which are particularly well suited to large bureaucratic organizations like the federal government, appear to have had only a limited impact on the size of government (see table 10). While large private sector corporations, such as Dupont, have been able to shed numerous white collar jobs and management layers, the federal government has done neither.[68] Cuts in the person-year complement since 1985 have been politically driven and have not come from the bottom up. No one inside or outside government appears to be the worse for it. If some 9000 person-years have been cut from the federal payroll with limited impact on programs and services, how many more such jobs could be cut without anyone noticing? What, for instance, would have happened if Priorities and Planning had picked 40,000 rather than 15,000 as the reduction target? Those who are in a position to know precisely what

TABLE 10
Person-years in the federal government,
1970–1 to 1988–9

Fiscal year	Person-years*
1970–1	189,886
1971–2	195,844
1972–3	203,128
1973–4	220,040
1974–5	231,374
1975–6	238,873
1976–7	241,301
1977–8	241,749
1978–9	242,414
1979–80	237,503
1980–1	231,788
1981–2	234,829
1982–3	236,559
1983–4	238,935
1984–5	241,534
1985–6	242,086
1986–7	236,230
1987–8	233,125
1988–9	231,164

SOURCE: Treasury Board Secretariat, Ottawa,
May 1988
*These numbers refer to the levels of person-year
resources controlled by the Treasury Board. Prior
year figures have been adjusted to exclude person-
years which were previously controlled but which
no longer are, such as those of Canada Post, which
is now a crown corporation.

resources are required to deliver the services and programs are the managers themselves. But, as we have seen, there is a positive disincentive for them to speak up. In any event, in my consultations with permanent officials, I heard time and again: 'Why should we make all the efforts to run an efficient operation when politicians will simply turn around and squander the savings on high-profile political projects?'

This brings me to the findings of the public choice theorists who have looked at the work of permanent officials or bureaucrats to explain growth in government spending. W. Niskanen argues that a bureaucrat will always seek to maximize his budget and that the sponsor does not have access to the information or the incentive to challenge the position of the bureaucrats successfully. The findings in this study tend to support most of Niskanen's views. Politicians who reported that they took a strong interest in promoting efficiency in government operations – and certainly not all of them did – also reported that they could rarely get at the information or the proper advice to deal with what they suspected were and are redundant government bureaus and units. It will be recalled that ministers reported that officials, including central agency officials, will often try to steer them away from looking at government operations, insisting that they would only find 'nickels and dimes' in savings. It will also be recalled that a senior Trudeau minister reported his complete amazement at how much the Department of External Affairs had grown during the Trudeau years, knowing that senior ministers and Trudeau himself had a low opinion of the relevance and quality of much of the department's work. Trudeau and his senior ministers were less successful than they would have liked to be in checking the growth in External Affairs for two reasons. One was time constraints. They had more important matters to attend to in cabinet, in their own departments, and in their regions. Second was their inability to get at the necessary data and advice to deal with growth in the department. When data on spending were brought before cabinet and cabinet committees, they were mostly in aggregate form so that there was little opportunity to focus attention on the growth of person-years at External Affairs. Niskanen, it will be recalled, identified the lack of incentive and the inability to get the right information as the two main reasons why politicians do not block the bureaucrats' attempts to maximize their budgets.[69]

It would, in my view, be foolhardy to suggest that permanent officials or, in Niskanen's terminology, 'bureaucrats' are completely detached and unconcerned with their own personal material interest. Of course they are concerned. Bureaucratic politics, broadly speaking, favours the status quo, security of employment, and the growth of one's own budget.[70] This study suggests that bureaucrats give greater importance to the first two than to the third. Admittedly, the research for this study was carried out at a time when the government was trying to implement a 15,000 person-year cut so that the opportunities for growth were severely restricted. As a result, Niskanen's argument that 'a bureaucrat's life is not a happy one unless he can provide increasing budgets for his subordinate bureaucrats'[71] has less relevance today than it probably did when he wrote it in 1971.

I also accept Niskanen's observation that bureaucrats have a distinct advantage in the budgetary bargaining game to protect the status quo or to secure new funding. After all, the absence of profit and competition removes any strong evaluation criteria or benchmark to report if a bureau is performing well or not. It is important, however, not to overstate this point. Not all bureaucrats in Ottawa have common interests. There are officials in central agencies who view problems and situations from a very different perspective than do others operating in line departments. As André Blais and Stéphane Dion observe, 'conflicting interests act as constraints on bureaucratic influence.'[72] Blais and Dion go on to conclude, however, that 'Niskanen's model of bureaucratic behaviour is a simple one ... one should not expect it to explain every bureaucratic behaviour everywhere and in every context [but] there is a substantial kernel of truth [in Niskanen's model] ... and ... it would be unwise ... to dismiss [it].'[73] I agree. Still, however convincing the Niskanen model is, there are numerous instances where it does not apply, including many that I saw in the course of preparing this study. There are probably many more senior public servants in the federal government than is generally assumed who perform guardian-type roles or who seek to limit new spending. There are also senior officials in Ottawa, notably in central agencies, who hold a broad view of government operations and who make it their tasks to resist demands for new resources from departments. 'Their absence in the Niskanen model,' it has been observed, 'should be reckoned as a major failure.'[74]

It is also important to underline that politicians, officials, provincial governments, and interest groups are not alone in pointing the finger at others to explain their own demands on the treasury. Businesses happily pocket cash grants and tax incentives and shop around for still more government assistance, all the while arguing that public funds are wasted on less deserving projects and less worthy causes than their own. A former federal deputy minister of finance recently wrote: 'Present expenditures in loans, grants and subsidies, together with corporate income and sales tax expenditures, greatly exceed collections from the corporate income tax.'[75] He went on to report that there has been 'no persuasive evidence' to suggest that 'this set of arrangements' has made much difference in industrial adjustment.

When spenders go to the cabinet table they are supported by powerful forces favouring either new spending or the preservation of the status quo. These forces include provincial governments, interest groups, government departments, the private sector, communities, and members of parliament. The guardians have nowhere near the same forces working on their side. Other than the threat of tax increases and larger deficits, they are often left to their own wits to fend off the spenders.

Yet many spenders have walked away from the cabinet table convinced that they paid more, or that they gave up more of their resources, than they got in return. Many have also walked away determined never to let it happen again and later returned far more resistant to spending cuts and more intent on getting new activities for their departments. It is a learning experience to see other spending ministers, and even guardians, or other regions, even the wealthiest ones, demand and get the most expensive item on the menu.

This may explain why it was relatively easy for a new government in 1984 to cut spending in various areas. As time went by, however, it got more and more difficult, so that after a few years the tide had turned completely. By then, spending cuts had ceased and new spending plans were being announced regularly. In the first months, ministers had expected spending cuts but they also had expected fair treatment. There is little doubt, therefore, that the eyebrows of spending ministers were raised when they saw the minister of finance, a key guardian, pull a few levers and suddenly make available $1 billion to bail out banks. Some spending ministers, such as Don Mazankowski, when minister of transport, also felt that they themselves had played the restraint game to the hilt, while other ministers had simply gone through the motions.[76] Still others noted how easily the government could put an assistance package together to save a General Motors plant in Quebec while they had had to struggle for months to get a 'few millions' for projects in their own regions. Still more looked on with concern, if not envy, at the buoyant economy of southern Ontario which was pulling, like gravity, a good part of federal funds for industrial development programs. Every new federal project announced for southern Ontario or by a department that was perceived to have had more than its fair share of projects, such as defence, made other ministers still more determined to fight harder for their own regions and departments.

Everyone is drawing from the same pool of funds available to all comers and there is little individual incentive to curb demands on the federal treasury. In addition, all comers can now pick from an extremely varied menu. The federal government can and has financed virtually every conceivable kind of project, including those that fall under the full jurisdictional authority of the provinces. Individual citizens, provincial governments, municipalities, the business community, and interest groups can all turn to the federal government for cash grants, operating subsidies, transfer payments, and special funding. The variety of projects and measures the federal government has supported is limited only by one's imagination.

This, combined with the view that no one wants to miss out on the best food at lunch while having to pay for it for someone else, appears to have seriously undermined the collective discipline of cabinet. Spending limits as envisaged under PEMS remain an excellent idea but one that can only work if there exists a collective discipline to make it work. This discipline has been absent, and the guardians have not been able to guard the public purse effectively.

Few would disagree with John K. Galbraith that the time has passed for Keynes's theories and that nothing of equivalent force has replaced them. What is often overlooked, however, is that the machinery of modern government also flowed from Keynesian thinking. New departments and agencies and new 'think' positions have been established in Ottawa since the early 1960s with a Keynesian perspective of the role of government in society.

Before Keynes, regions, communities, and people felt that they were wholly responsible for their own economic well-being. If a community, a business, or an individual fell off the economic ladder, they had no one to blame but themselves. For the past thirty years or so in Canada, economic development and growth at the national, regional, and community levels have become the responsibility of governments, particularly the federal government. Provincial governments may insist on delivering the programs and whatever initiatives are required, but it is the federal government which often comes up with the solutions and much of the cash. The federal government now has numerous government departments and agencies responsible for employment, economic development, regional development, community development, among other things, to which businesses, provincial governments, communities, and individuals can turn to for help in climbing the economic ladder or for getting back on the ladder if they should fall off. We saw in an earlier chapter that interest groups and government departments often reinforce each other and that it is now hardly possible for anyone in government − except the guardians − to announce or support program cuts.

As the search continues for a new approach with the equivalent force of Keynesian theories, it will be important to search also for a new way to organize government departments and agencies. Apart from showing that the guardians have not been able to guard the public purse effectively, this study also shows that the way government is organized is rarely, if ever, politically or policy neutral. The way government is organized can set in motion forces that can affect the distribution of power within government, fuel regional tension, and unleash new demand for government spending and serve to protect the status quo in existing government programs.

POSTSCRIPT

In November 1988 the Mulroney government was returned to power with its second majority mandate. As I was completing this book in January 1989, the government announced a major overhaul of its expenditure budget process. The sweeping changes brought to the cabinet committee structure at that time signalled the end of PEMS, the Policy and Expenditure Management System. Mulroney's changes also did away with policy envelopes and shifted effective decision making away from policy committees of cabinet to a new Expenditure Review Committee, to the Operations Committee, and to Priorities and Planning.

The changes are far reaching in that now all cabinet committees, with the exception of Treasury Board which fulfils statutory duties, are placed under an enlarged cabinet committee on Priorities and Planning. In addition, all new spending must now be approved by P & P, although adjustments in spending requirements for authorized programs continue to be the responsibility of the Treasury Board. Before reaching P & P, however, new spending proposals must go through at least one other cabinet committee, the Operations Committee, chaired by the deputy prime minister, Don Mazankowski. This committee was established 'informally' during the first Mulroney mandate, but it has now been formally recognized and is a gatekeeper for P & P. The Operations Committee is responsible for 'scrutinizing the government's weekly agenda, responding to crises, guarding access to P and P and steering the committees down below.'[77]

There are now a good number of cabinet committees 'down below' – fifteen in all, including several new ones such as Economic Policy, Environment, Human Resources, Income Support and Health, Cultural Affairs, and National Identity.[78] These committees do not have spending power in their own right as similar committees had under PEMS, and one can easily speculate that in time they will become totally ineffective: members will skip meetings or will become lobbyists for spending in their own policy areas. It is highly unlikely that they will play any kind of 'guardian-type' role. It will be recalled, for example, that before the introduction of PEMS cabinet policy committees often approved new spending proposals and simply turned over the responsibility for finding ways to fund them to the minister of finance or the president of the Treasury Board.

One of the new committees established in 1989 was especially designed to assist the guardians in holding government spending in check. The Expenditure Review Committee, chaired by the prime minister, was set up to 'ensure that the Government's expenditures continue to be directed to its highest priorities, and that expenditure control continues to contribute to deficit reduction.'[79] Much was made by the prime minister, key cabinet ministers, permanent officials, and the media over the role of this new committee and its prospects for success. It was widely reported that Mulroney borrowed from both Margaret Thatcher and Australian Prime Minister Bob Hawke in 'centralizing absolute power for spending cuts into a new ... committee ...'[80] One journalist labelled the new structure as a 'setup to say no.'[81] A senior PCO official, meanwhile, observed that 'we are in an era of contraction (not) in an era of new initiative.'[82] Other officials argued that the new structure would 'wage preemptive strikes against ministers [who are believed] to be spending too much.'[83] Prime Minister Mulroney himself explained that the reorganization was simply a reflection of the need 'for prudent economic management ... [because] ... we are expecting some difficulties on the fiscal side.' P & P, he added, would have the final say on new spending so that plans 'won't be snuck in the back door.'[84] By chairing the Expenditure Review Committee himself, he gave a clear signal that his priority in the coming months was to reduce spending.

Though it could be interpreted that the establishment of the new Expenditure Review Committee would serve to weaken the position of the Department of Finance, Michael Wilson gave no sign that he was unhappy with the changes. Certainly, Finance would no longer hold chief responsibility for spending cuts. This would now be directed by the new committee. Finance and Treasury Board would provide support and advice, but key decisions on spending would no longer reside with them.

Wilson, at least publicly, applauded the new structure. Indeed, though little was said throughout the 1988 general election campaign about the growing accumulated debt, he served notice shortly after the election was won that deficit reduction would rank high on the government's agenda. Hardly a week went by in the first months of 1989 without a senior minister bringing up the subject. The media picked up the cue, and both print and electronic journalists ran story after story about Ottawa's precarious fiscal position. Typical headlines reported on the 'Crushing Deficit,' 'Getting to the Root of the Federal Deficit,' 'The Debt: Where Does All the Money Go?' 'Are We Sinking or Just Swimming in Debt?' 'Mathematics of Federal Debt Add Up to Necessity for Drastic Measures,' and so on.[85] Wilson himself made a special public plea for 'tougher action,' arguing that the debt situation had reached a 'critical mass' and that 'you don't have to be a financial whiz to know that when you have to borrow to pay interest to the bank, something is wrong.'[86] 'Too often,' he added, 'governments said yes to new programs when they should have said no. Short-term interests have sometimes taken precedence over longer-term consequences.'[87] Little wonder then that Wilson would look to the expenditure side as a means of dealing with the deficit. He himself had argued earlier that 80 per cent of any deficit reduction 'should come from spending cuts, not taxes.'[88] Certainly, the Expenditure Review Committee, with the prime minister in the chair, had the clout to assist the guardians in carrying out expenditure reductions.

The committee was quick off the mark; it held its first meeting only a few days after it was established and initiated a thorough review of the government's expenditure budget. As the minister of finance reported in his budget speech: 'The expenditure measures in this budget result from a comprehensive review of government spending carried out in the past three months by the Expenditure Review Committee.'[89] The review was similar in many respects to that undertaken in 1984 by the minister of finance and the Treasury Board president. As before, officials from the Department of Finance and Treasury Board secretariat divided the expenditure budget among themselves and prepared a series of potential spending cuts to put before the Expenditure Review Committee. In 1984, it will be recalled, they had presented their recommendations to both ministers, who had met with their colleagues to go over the suggested cuts. In many instances, however, spending ministers were free to suggest alternative cuts provided that they amounted to the same dollar figure identified by Finance and Treasury Board.

In the 1989 review, the minister of finance and president of the Treasury Board also met with their colleagues to discuss the proposed cuts to see if they could secure some understanding before putting them forward to the Expenditure Review Committee. Spending ministers accompanied by their deputy ministers were then invited to appear before the committee to go over the suggested cuts. Great care was taken to avoid leaks; invitations to appear before the committee were restricted to ministers, their deputy ministers, and a handful of central agency officials. The flow of paper to and from the committee was accordingly severely restricted. The fear was that if potential spending cuts were leaked to the media, client groups would mount lobby efforts to protect the status quo.

In the early days of the committee's work, it was widely assumed that the committee was making some tough decisions. When asked whether committee members were 'biting the bullet,' a senior official who attended the meetings responded that 'they are not only biting the bullet, they are chewing it.'[90] They had every reason to do so. For one thing, the minister of finance was reporting to his colleagues at P & P and full cabinet that the government's fiscal position was deteriorating rapidly as a result of interest rate increases. For another, there is no better time to make tough spending cuts than in the early months of a new majority mandate. It will be recalled that virtually all of the spending cuts in Mulroney's first mandate were carried out in the government's first eighteen months in office. In addition, the fact that the prime minister himself had decided to chair the committee was widely perceived as strong evidence that the political will was there. At no time before had a prime minister personally taken the lead in reviewing the expenditure budget.

However, the enthusiasm of ministers (including those on the Expenditure Review Committee) to cut spending waned over time. For one thing, spending ministers all found special reasons why their own departments ought not to be cut back. The most common reason given was the heavy cuts of the previous four years. This line of reasoning may explain why the two departments that in the end suffered significant cuts in 1989 were the two that had seen substantial increases in their budgets since 1984, Defence and Foreign Aid.[91]

Certainly, the familiar argument – 'you can cut spending, even perhaps in my own area, but it would make far more sense to cut elsewhere because there is more room or more fat to cut there' – was again heard in 1989. Ministers were told early on that there was no more room to cut in the federal public service or in the overhead costs of government; officials reported that they were still implementing the 15,000 person-year cut announced earlier and that, in any event, cutting back in the bureaucracy would only produce 'nickels and dimes' in savings. Again, many ministers proved reluctant to cut programs, especially those most relevant to their own regions.[92] In short, the lunch analogy, presented in the introductory chapter, remains valid.

Indeed, one can question whether the establishment of the Expenditure Review Committee has had much of an impact on the federal government expenditure budget. The observation of a senior central agency official cited earlier that no expenditure budgetary system, no approach to policy making, and no cabinet committee structure can substitute for political will remains accurate. But removing the responsibility for identifying specific spending cuts from Finance and Treasury Board to a committee of ministers may well have been counterproductive. The minister of finance and perhaps to a lesser extent the president of the Treasury Board have strong incentives to act as guardians of the public purse. It is, after all, their responsibility. If spending cannot be reduced and taxes must be increased, it is the minister of finance alone who must stand up in the House and present the budget. It remains that, no matter what changes are introduced to the budget process, the budget itself remains closely identified with the minister of finance. Thus we refer to the Wilson budget, the Lalonde budget, the MacEachen budget, and so on, never to a Mulroney or Trudeau budget. Ministers may well serve on an expenditure review committee, but this is not to suggest that they will play a guardian role to the extent that the minister of finance and the president of the Treasury Board traditionally do. Indeed, turning over this responsibility to a committee of ministers may well have compromised the ability of the guardians to manage the government's spending plans. Full cabinet and P & P must now look to at least two sources for advice on spending: the guardians (the minister of finance and the Treasury Board president) and the Expenditure Review Committee. The focus now is less on what can be afforded after the fiscal framework has been struck by the minister of finance and more on what the Expenditure Review Committee recommends can be pared down. One can assume that the committee (since the majority of its members are spending ministers) is less likely to come down hard on spending than would the minister of finance acting alone or in consultation with the prime minister and the president of the Treasury Board. One can easily speculate, for example, that Don Mazankowski, who chairs the committee in the prime minister's absence, could not easily dissociate himself from his spending portfolio, Agriculture, while sitting on the committee. The same observation applies to other spending ministers on the committee. In short, there is a risk that the Expenditure Review Committee will become a budget review committee. Tax increases will always hold greater appeal to spending ministers than spending cuts.

Certainly, Wilson's 1989 budget did not contain the kind of spending cuts that had been in his 1984 and 1985 budgets. To be sure, as he had in all his previous budget speeches, Wilson spoke at length about the need to bring down the annual deficit. A year earlier he had predicted that for fiscal year 1989–90, it would amount to $28.5 billion. The sharp increase in interest rates and the cost of servicing the debt led him to revise the figure upward to $30.5 billion.[93] The deficit would have been much higher still had Wilson not announced a series of tax increases and spending cuts totalling over $5 billion for 1989–90 and increasing to $9 billion in 1990–1.

The bulk of the measures introduced to deal with the annual deficit, however, are on the revenue side. The 1989 budget brought a series of tax increases, including raising the federal surtax by 2 percentage points, an additional 3 per cent on high-income individuals, revisions to the large corporations tax, an increase in the federal sales tax, as well as an increase in excise levies on tobacco and a one-cent-per-litre tax hike on gasoline. Total tax increases amount to $3.3 billion for 1989–90 and over $5 billion for 1990–1.[94] The budget also moved the full cost of the unemployment insurance program to employee-employer premiums. The government will now continue to contribute to the financing of the program only in difficult economic times 'when it is inappropriate to raise premiums.'[95] Accordingly, the cost of financing regional extended benefits and benefits for fishermen that are in excess of premiums they pay will, beginning in 1990, no longer be financed by the federal government. This shift in financing will bring in savings of $425 million in 1989–90 and $1.9 billion in 1990–1. Wilson also made known the government's intention to move ahead with a 'goods and services tax' beginning on 1 January 1991 – even without the participation of the provinces.

The budget reported spending cuts of $1.5 billion for 1989–90 and $2.079 billion for 1990–1. The cuts were spread over several departments, agencies, and crown corporations. There were no major program cuts in any one area and taken together they are not as extensive as the 1984 or the 1985 cuts. Once again, for example, cuts were to be made in the subsidies to VIA rail. This time VIA was asked 'to accelerate its report on the 20-year outlook for passenger rail service and to bring forward as soon as possible a business plan ... Options which will be considered by the government include increased fares, reduced service levels and closure, sale or transfer of substantial part of the system.'[96] Total projected cuts to the VIA subsidy amount to $50 million for 1989–90 and $75 million for 1990–1.

A close look at some of the cuts raises a number of questions, not only about their merits in terms of actual expenditure reductions but also as to whether they really constitute cuts at all. For example, a cut of $215 million for 1990–1 is identified as repayment of social transfers. In reality, however, this has no impact whatsoever on the government's expenditure budget, thus hardly qualifying as a spending cut. Government spending on both old age security and family allowances remains at current levels, although the budget proposes to recover payments from higher-income Canadians under these two programs. The measure is being phased in over three years so that by 1991 all payments over a $50,000 indexed threshold will be recovered through the tax system.

Other cuts are in reality only delayed expenditures. For example, the construction of a new prison for Newfoundland was delayed, not cancelled.[97] The call for tenders to build a new headquarters for Transport Canada was cancelled. It is doubtful, however, if that qualifies as an expenditure restraint measure, as the budget papers claim. The employees of Transport Canada will continue to be housed in leased buildings. Further, they will be housed in temporary quarters while asbestos is removed from the existing leased building, the cost of which is to be borne by the government.

The budget also announced a delay in implementing part of the government's child care strategy. This was reported as saving $370 millions over two years. The budget goes on to add, however, that 'before the end of its term of office, the government will act to meet its child care objectives.'[98] No mention is made of the one-cent-a-litre increase in the excise tax on gasoline announced in the February 1988 budget to cover the cost of the day care program.

The budget also made no mention of the $300 million spending cut announced in the February 1988 budget which was, it will be recalled, to be identified only in 1989–90. One assumes that the $300 million is included in the total spending cuts. The main estimates tabled on 28 April 1989 pointed to expenditure cuts totalling $1.230 billion for 1989–90. The remaining cuts of $315 million required either legislative changes ($140 million) or had no impact on the main estimates ($175 million for child care).[99]

The most important cuts found in the main estimates were $360 million from Official Development Assistance (ODA) and $575 million from defence. As noted earlier, however, both areas saw important expenditure increases during the first Mulroney government mandate. The government had set a funding target of 0.5 per cent of GNP for ODA. The strong growth in the Canadian economy saw ODA cash levels grow from about $2 billion in 1984–5 to nearly $2.8 billion in 1988–9, or an average growth in spending of about 7.4 per cent. The 1989 budget reduced planned ODA cash levels by $360 million, bringing them down to $2.44 million. The budget, however, revealed that growth in the ODA/GNP ratio will resume in 1990–1, with the ratio increasing to 0.45 per cent, followed by annual growth of 0.005 per cent thereafter.[100] When reviewing the spending cuts in ODA, it is important to consider a number of issues. First, as already noted, the cuts came on the heel of substantial expenditure increases in recent years. Secondly, the cuts are temporary, in that spending increases will resume in 1990–1. Thirdly, the regional factor in ODA spending is not as important as it is in other spending areas in that ODA spending is at least perceived to be spent abroad.

Similarly, defence spending grew from $8.8 billion in 1984–5 to $11.1 billion in 1988–9, or about 6 per cent annually. The budget proposes to reduce its rate of growth to 1.2 per cent in 1989–90 over 1988–9 and thereafter to 5 per cent annually to 1993–4. It also reported that defence spending beyond 1993–4 will increase compared with 'the real growth.'[101] It may well have to because the proposed purchase of nuclear submarines recommended in the defence white paper was one of the items cut in the budget. Conventional submarines currently in use are to be retired by 1995. The Canadian Navy reported that it was busy the day after the budget identifying alternatives to the nuclear submarine purchase.[102]

The Defence Department also reported plans to close or scale down fourteen military bases. One question that jumps to mind is whether the regional variable discussed at length in this study was at play here. It is interesting to note that the most important cut is the planned closure of CFB Summerside, which employs 1200 people.[103] Prince Edward Island is the only province not represented at the cabinet table in Ottawa. Its premier was quick to retort that, in shutting down the Summerside base, the federal government was 'picking on the baby of Confederation' and that, translated on a pro capita basis, it was equal to a job loss of 50,000 in southern Ontario.[104] He called a provincial election a few days later and made the planned closure a central theme of his re-election bid. Some federal ministers also report that the Summerside issue was a classic example of 'the musical ride syndrome' at play, in that officials deliberately brought forward only politically embarrassing spending cuts, the great majority of which would end up being rejected out of hand.[105] It is worth noting that the minister of national defence reported: 'It is important to understand that this decision (i.e., base closure) was not made by the minister of defence or the minister of finance. We simply accepted the advice and recommendations of Defence officials.'[106]

The only other possible important regionally sensitive spending cut contained in the budget was a 1 percentage point reduction in the growth of transfers to all ten provinces in the Established Programs Financing (EPF) program beginning in 1990–1. The budget, however, made it clear that 'legislated provisions will continue to ensure that growth of the total EPF transfer will not fall below the rate of inflation.'[107]

In short, despite the mandate of the new Expenditure Review Committee and the fact that the government was in its first year of a new majority mandate, the government still looked to the revenue budget rather than the expenditure budget to deal with the annual deficit. Even accepting the government's version of what constitutes a spending cut, the budget for 1989–90 only had $1.50 in spending cuts for every $3.50 on the revenue side, with the figures for 1990–1 being $2.00 and $7.00 Thus, it will now be less and less possible to point to the revenue budget to explain the annual deficit. Indeed, the 1989 budget papers claimed that 'the tax measures of the 1970s and early 1980s which reduced the tax base have been largely reversed since 1984.'[108]

APPENDICES

Main estimates, 1987–8

Indian Affairs and Northern Development Department
Northern Affairs Program

OBJECTIVE

To promote the political, economic, social and cultural development of the northern territories and in collaboration with the territorial governments and other federal departments, to effectively manage the orderly use, development and conservation of the North's natural resources and to protect the northern natural environment, for the benefit of all Canadians, northerners in particular.

ACTIVITY DESCRIPTION

Political, Social and Cultural Development
Management of Departmental/Territorial Governments relations in the areas of political development, devolution of responsibilities and fiscal relations, the support of Inuit art and artists, the support of Inuit culture and language, financial assistance to native organizations to enable them to develop positions in regard to economic development and social issues, and financial assistance to territorial governments to meet hospital, medical and housing (Yukon) costs of status Indians and Inuit.

Economic Planning and Development
Provides for the continuing analysis of the northern economy and progressive development of an overall economic strategy, planning and

analysis in regard to the Northern Canada Power Commission (NCPC) and northern energy subsidies, negotiation and implementation of Economic Development Agreements in each territory, maximization of benefits to northerners from resource development projects, promotion and support of native businesses, planning for northern transportation infrastructure, construction of northern roads and coordination of federal government review and regulation of major resource development projects.

Renewable Resources Management and Environmental Protection
Provides in a quasi-provincial manner, for the management of the water, forest and land resources of the North, and for protection of the northern natural environment. Management of renewable resources, owned by the Crown in right of Canada, is achieved through administration of Acts and Regulations, which involves processing of applications from companies, communities and individuals for legal rights to resource use, administration of rights in good standing, and inspections to ensure compliance with terms and conditions of use. In addition, resources management requires the Program to undertake inventories of the quantity and quality of renewable resources, so as to have a sufficient information base with which to deal effectively with applicants. The Planning Element also includes the preparation for and fighting of forest fires, the development of land use plans to accommodate diverse land use and deal with use conflicts, implementation of the Federal Environmental Assessment and Review Process (EARP) in the North, the regulation of environmental impacts of land use on vacant Crown lands and of offshore operations, and the conduct of supplied environmental research. It also includes the administration for DIAND of the Environmental Studies Revolving Fund, which conducts social and environmental research to ensure informed decision making on oil and gas activities and is entirely financed by levies on oil and gas interest owners on Canada Lands.

Non-Renewable Resources Management
Provides in a quasi-provincial manner, for the management of the mineral resources of the North, through the administration of legislation governing mineral rights acquisition, maintenance and recording, through provision of ecological services and through maintenance of policies designed to encourage mining in the North. Northern interests and concerns respecting oil and gas exploration and development are

factored into the operational activities of COGLA. The Northern Oil and Gas Action Program (NOGAP) of research in preparation for major hydrocarbon developments in the North is coordinated, and the Norman Wells Proven Area Agreement is administered.

Source: Canada, Main Estimates, 1987–88;
Part II: Treasury Board Secretariat

Main estimates, 1987–8, personnel requirements

TABLE 6
Person-year requirements by activity

	Estimates 1987–88	Forecast 1986–87	Actual 1985–86
Financial and management accounting and reporting	65	60	58
Management practices and processes	62	70	71
Administration	23	20	26
	150	150	155

TABLE 7
Details of personnel requirements

	Authorized person-years			Current salary range	1987–88 average salary provision
	87–88	86–87	85–86		
Management	73	74	68	51,400–100,700	68,355
Scientific and professional	2	4	4	15,116–67,700	65,865
Administrative and foreign services	43	43	47	15,635–64,521	55,434
Administrative support	32	29	35	13,569–34,304	22,763
Other		1	2		

NOTE: The person-year columns display the forecast distribution of the authorized person-years for the OCG by occupational group. The current salary range column shows the salary ranges by occupational group at October 31, 1986. The average salary column reflects the estimated base salary costs including allowance for collective agreements, annual increments, promotions and merit pay divided by the person-years for the occupational group. Year-to-year comparison of averages may be affected by changes in the distribution of the components underlying the calculations.

20 (Comptroller General)

3. *Net Cost of Program*
The Estimates of the Program include only those expenditures to be charged to its voted authorities. Table 8 provides details of other cost items which need to be taken into account to arrive at the estimated total cost of the Program.

TABLE 8
Total cost of the program for 1987–88 ($000)

	Main estimates 1987–88	Add* other costs	Estimated total program cost	
			1987–88	1986–87
Comptroller General	12,974	1,826	14,800	14,381

	($000)
*Other costs of $1,826 consist of	
– services provided without charge from Public Works Canada	1,658
– Supply Services Canada cheque issue services and TB Benefit Plans provided without charge	168

(Supplementary Information) 21

Source: Canada, Main Estimates, 1987–88;
Part III: Treasury Board Secretariat

The Treasury Board of Canada

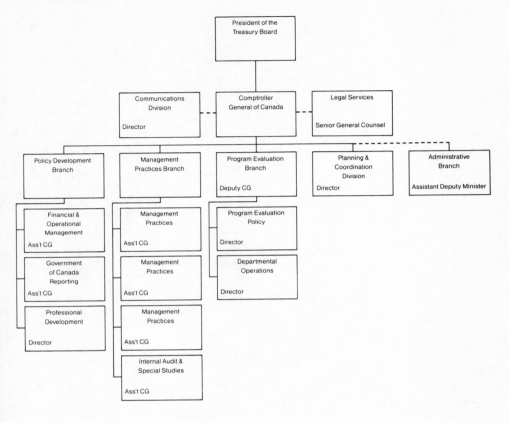

Figure 1
Office of the comptroller general
Source: Canada, Treasury Board Secretariat, October 1987

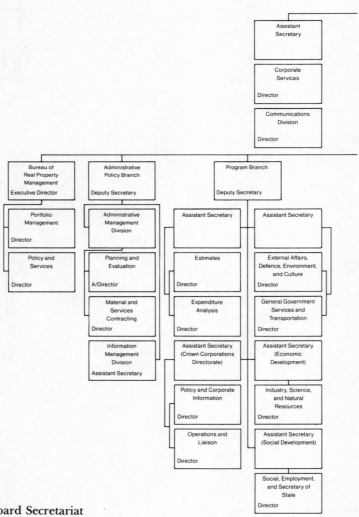

Figure 2
Treasury Board Secretariat

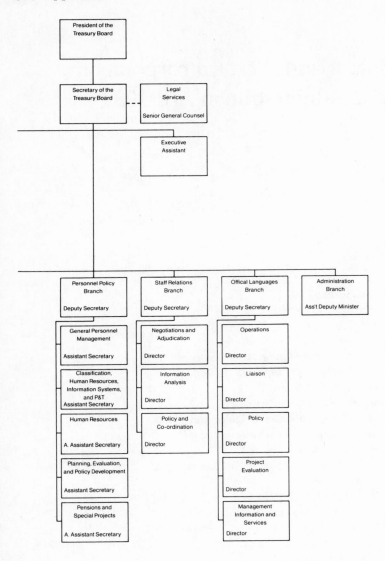

Source: Canada, Treasury Board Secretariat, October 1987

Schedule B and C crown corporations, Financial Administration Act, 1984

SCHEDULE B
(*ss. 2.2.1*)

Agricultural Stabilization Board
Office de stabilisation des prix agricoles
Atomic Energy Control Board
Commission de contrôle de l'énergie atomique
Canada Employment and Immigration Commission
Commission de l'emploi et de l'immigration
Canadian Aviation Safety Board
Bureau canadien de la sécurité aérienne
Canadian Centre for Occupational Health and Safety
Centre canadien d'hygiène et de sécurité au travail
Crown Assets Disposal Corporation
Corporation de disposition des biens de la Couronne
Director of Soldier Settlement
Directeur de l'établissement de soldats
The Director, The Veterans' Land Act
Directeur des terres destinées aux anciens combattants
Economic Council of Canada
Conseil économique du Canada
Fisheries Prices Support Board
Office des prix des produits de la pêche
Medical Research Council
Conseil de recherches médicales
The National Battlefields Commission
Commission des champs de bataille nationaux

National Museums of Canada
  Musées nationaux du Canada
National Research Council of Canada
  Conseil national de recherches du Canada
Natural Sciences and Engineering Research Council
  Conseil de recherches en sciences naturelles et en génie
Science Council of Canada
  Conseil des Sciences du Canada
Social Sciences and Humanities Research Council
  Conseil de recherches en sciences humaines

R.S., c. F-10, Sch. B; SOR/78–285, 378; 1980–81–82–83, c. 165, s. 38; 1984, c. 31, s. 13, c. 40, s. 28; SOR/85–108.

SCHEDULE C
(ss. 2.1, 2.2, 83, 103, 130, 141, 143)

PART I
Atlantic Pilotage Authority
  Administration de pilotage de l'Atlantique
Atomic Energy of Canada Limited
  Énergie atomique du Canada, Limitée
Canada Deposit Insurance Corporation
  Société d'assurance-dépôts du Canada
Canada Harbour Place Corporation
  Corporation Place du Havre Canada Inc.
Canada Lands Company Limited
  Société immobilière du Canada Limitée
Canada Mortgage and Housing Corporation
  Société canadienne d'hypothèques et de logement
Canada Museums Construction Corporation Inc.
  Société de construction des musées du Canada, Inc.
Canada Post Corporation
  Société canadienne des postes
Canadian Arsenals Limited
  Les Arsenaux canadiens Limitée
Canadian Commercial Corporation
  Corporation commerciale canadienne
Canadian Dairy Commission
  Commission canadienne du lait

Canadian Institute for International Peace and Security
Institut canadien pour la paix et la sécurité mondiales
Canadian Livestock Feed Board
Office canadien des provendes
Canadian National (West Indies) Steamships, Limited
Canadian National (West Indies) Steamships, Limited
Canadian Patents and Development Limited
Société canadienne des brevets et d'exploitation Limitée
Canadian Saltfish Corporation
Office canadien du poisson salé
Canadian Sports Pool Corporation
Société canadienne des paris sportifs
Canagrex
Canagrex
Cape Breton Development Corporation
Société de développement du Cap-Breton
Defence Construction (1951) Limited
Construction de défense (1951) Limitée
Export Development Corporation
Société pour l'expansion des exportations
Farm Credit Corporation
Société du crédit agricole
Federal Business Development Bank
Banque fédérale de développement
Freshwater Fish Marketing Corporation
Office de commercialisation du poisson d'eau douce
Great Lakes Pilotage Authority, Ltd.
Administration de pilotage des Grands Lacs, Limitée
Harbourfront Corporation
Harbourfront Corporation
Laurentian Pilotage Authority
Administration de pilotage des Laurentides
Loto Canada Inc.
Loto Canada Inc.
Mingan Associates, Ltd.
Les Associés Mingan, Ltée
National Capital Commission
Commission de la Capitale nationale
Northern Canada Power Commission
Commission d'énergie du Nord canadien

Pacific Pilotage Authority
Administration de pilotage du Pacifique
Pêcheries Canada Inc.
Pêcheries Canada Inc.
Royal Canadian Mint
Monnaie royale canadienne
St. Anthony Fisheries Limited
St. Anthony Fisheries Limited
The St. Lawrence Seaway Authority
Administration de la voie maritime du Saint-Laurent
Societa a responsibilita limitata Immobiliare San Sebastiano
Societa a responsibilita limitata Immobiliare San Sebastiano
Standards Council of Canada
Conseil canadien des normes
Uranium Canada, Limited
Uranium Canada, Limitée
VIA Rail Canada Inc.
VIA Rail Canada Inc.

PART II
Air Canada
Air Canada
Canada Development Investment Corporation
Corporation de développement des investissements du Canada
Canada Ports Corporation
Société canadienne des ports
Canadian National Railway Company
Compagnie des chemins de fer nationaux du Canada
Halifax Port Corporation
Société de port de Halifax
Montreal Port Corporation
Société du port de Montréal
Northern Transportation Company Limited
La Société des transports du nord Limitée
Petro-Canada
Petro-Canada
Prince Rupert Port Corporation
Société de port de Prince Rupert
Port of Quebec Corporation
Société de port de Québec

Teleglobe Canada
  Téléglobe Canada
Vancouver Port Corporation
  Société du port de Vancouver

R.S., c. F-10, Sch. C; R.S., c. 37(1st Supp.), s. 15; SOR/71–404; SOR/76–376; SOR/79–441; SOR/81–804; SOR/82–362, 363, 364; 1980–81–82–83, c. 121, s. 17; SOR/83–382, 658; SOR/84–54, 55, 89, 110, 427, 505, 506, 507; 1984, c. 31, s. 13, c. 40, s. 28; SOR/85–14, 48, 162, 208.

SCHEDULED

[Repealed, 1984, c. 31, s. 13]

Source: Canada, Financial Administration Act, 1984

Notes

CHAPTER 1 Introduction

1 Robert F. Adie and Paul G. Thomas, *Canadian Public Administration: Problematical Perspectives* (Scarborough, Ont.: Prentice-Hall 1982), 141
2 Interview with a senior official of the Treasury Board secretariat, Ottawa, 5 December 1988
3 Adie and Thomas, *Canadian Public Administration* (1982), 141
4 Canada, Department of Finance, *Economic and Fiscal Statement*, 8 November 1984, 4
5 Hugh Heclo and Aaron Wildavsky, *The Private Government of Public Money*, 2nd ed. (London: Macmillan 1981), lxi
6 Ibid., lxii
7 John L. Manion, 'New Challenges in Public Administration,' The 1987 Donald Gow Memorial Lecture, Queen's University, 25 September 1987, mimeo., 2
8 Ibid.
9 Heclo and Wildavsky, *Private Government*, lxiii
10 There are exceptions; see G. Bruce Doern, Allan M. Maslove, and Michael J. Prince, *Public Budgeting in Canada* (Ottawa: Carleton University Press 1988), and Douglas G. Hartle, *The Expenditure Budget Process in the Government of Canada* (Toronto: Canadian Tax Foundation 1978).
11 Douglas G. Hartle, *A Theory of the Expenditure Budgetary Process*, Ontario Economic Research Studies (Toronto 1976), 77
12 See Aaron Wildavsky, *The Politics of the Budgetary Process*, 3rd ed. (Boston: Little, Brown and Company 1979); see also Heclo and Wildavsky, *Private Government*.

13 Aaron Wildavsky, *Budgeting: A Comparative Theory of Budgetary Processes*, rev. ed. (Oxford: Transaction Books 1986), 12–13

14 Richard Bird, *The Growth of Government Spending in Canada* (Toronto: Canadian Tax Foundation 1970), and Hartle, *Theory*. For a neo-Marxist perspective, the reader should consult James O'Connor, *The Final Crisis of the State* (New York: St Martin's Press 1973).

15 Hartle, *Theory*, 77

16 Adie and Thomas, *Canadian Public Administration* (1982), 147

17 Quoted in Leslie A. Pal, *State, Class, and Bureaucracy: Canadian Unemployment Insurance and Public Policy* (Montreal: McGill-Queen's University Press 1988), 4

18 Hartle, *Theory*, 77

19 Wildavsky, *Politics of the Budgetary Process*, 13

20 Henry Aaron, 'Social Security: International Comparisons,' in *Studies in the Economics of Income*, ed. Otto Eckstein (Washington, DC: Brookings Institute 1967)

21 Harold L. Wilensky, *The Welfare State and Equality* (Berkeley: University of California Press 1975), xiii

22 Wildavsky, *Budgeting*, 367

23 Ibid.

24 Carolyn Webber and Aaron Wildavsky, *A History of Taxation and Expenditure in the Western World* (New York: Simon and Schuster 1986), 569

25 Ibid.

26 Ibid., 586

27 Anthony Downe, *An Economic Theory of Democracy* (New York: Harper and Row 1957), 28

28 James Buchanan and Gordon Tullock, *The Calculus of Consent* (Ann Arbor: University of Michigan Press 1962), 290

29 W.A. Niskanen, *Bureaucracy and Representative Government* (Chicago: Aldine 1971), 40. See also W.A. Niskanen, *Bureaucracy: Servant or Master?* (London: Institute of Economic Affairs 1973).

30 Lawrence H. Silkerman, 'Policy Analysis: Boom or Curse for Politicians,' in *Bureaucrats, Policy Analysts, Statesmen: Who Leads?* ed. Robert A. Goodwin (Washington, DC: American Enterprise Institute for Public Policy Research 1980), 37

31 Albert Breton, *The Economic Theory of Representative Government* (London: Methuen 1974), 130

32 Ibid., 162

33 Hartle, *Expenditure Budget Process*, 285

34 See, among others, Patrick Dunleavy, 'Bureaucrats, Budgets and the

Growth of the State: Reconstructing an Instrumental Model,' *British Journal of Political Science* 15, no 3 (1985): 299–328, and Peter Self, *Political Theories of Modern Government* (London: Allen & Unwin 1985), chapters 3, 6, and 7.

35 M.J. Trebilcock et al., *The Choice of Governing Instrument* (Ottawa: Minister of Supply and Services 1982)

36 Sandford F. Borins, 'Public Choice: "Yes Minister" Made It Popular, but Does Winning the Nobel Prize Make It True?' *Canadian Public Administration* 31, no 1 (spring 1988): 12–20. Another recent addition to the Canadian literature is Doern, Maslove, and Prince, *Public Budgeting in Canada*. The authors bring a multidisciplinary focus to government budgeting but give little weight to the public choice theorists. The authors argue that the process by which the federal government attempts to bring about more coordination between departments and agencies has resulted in what they label 'mezzo-budgeting.' That is, numerous forces both internal to government and external, such as trade pressures or new interest groups, have come together to create a 'typology of mezzo-budgeting.' They look at a wide array of 'attributes,' including the inherent flexibility of spending in relation to ingrained characteristics of spending in different policy fields. For example, the economic and regional development field is grant intensive, defence is capital intensive, foreign affairs is personnel intensive. They stress that some policy fields are highly visible (such as regional development), social programs enjoy widespread public support, and others (such as government operations) are hardly known to the public. They conclude that 'each attribute has some independent features, but they also quickly melt with the others to produce different dynamics through which budgetary choices are made at any given point in time.' See 205 and chapter 11.

37 Alan Cairns, 'The Other Crisis of Canadian Federalism,' *Canadian Public Administration* 22, no 21 (summer 1979): 189. See also Alan C. Cairns, *Constitution, Government, and Society in Canada: Selected Essays*, ed. Douglas E. Williams (Toronto: McClelland and Stewart 1988), 7–24; Samuel H. Beer, 'Political Overload & Federalism,' *Polity* 10, no 3 (1977): 5–17.

38 Robert B. Bryce, *Maturing in Hard Times* (Montreal: McGill-Queen's University Press 1986), chapter 6

39 Canada, Department of Reconstruction and Supply, *Employment and Income with Special Reference to the Initial Period of Reconstruction* (Ottawa: King's Printer 1945), 21

40 A.W. Johnson, *Social Policy in Canada: The Past as It Conditions the Present* (Halifax: Institute for Research on Public Policy 1987), 1

41 Ibid.
42 Quoted in Aaron Wildavsky, *How to Limit Government Spending, or* ....
   (Berkeley: University of California Press 1979), 169
43 Ibid., 173
44 Ibid.
45 J.E. Hodgetts et al., *The Biography of an Institution: The Civil Service Commission of Canada, 1908–1967* (Montreal: McGill-Queen's University Press 1972), chapter 7
46 See Donald J. Savoie, *Regional Economic Development: Canada's Search for Solutions* (Toronto: University of Toronto Press 1986), chapters 3 and 4.
47 Ibid., chapter 7
48 Quoted in Wildavsky, *How to Limit Government Spending*, 7
49 See Leo Pliatzky, *Getting and Spending* (Oxford: Basil Blackwell 1982), 51.
50 Quoted in *Dimensions*, winter 1986, 13
51 Jean de Grandpré, 'Public Budgeting Is Out of Whack – My View,' *Financial Post*, 27 July 1987. The article was based on an address he gave to the Harvard Business School Club of Toronto.
52 Royal Commission on the Economic Union and Development Prospects for Canada, *Report* (Ottawa: Minister of Supply and Services 1985), 3: 148
53 Hartle, *Expenditure Budget Process*, v
54 Alan Blakeney, for example, observed that 'the public seems to be reacting against big government' and went on to suggest that the New Democratic Party must adjust its policies. See 'Hard Times,' *Saturday Night*, April 1986, 13. The federal New Democratic Party also expressed concern over the federal deficit in the early 1980s and called for measures to reduce it.
55 'A New Direction for Canada: An Agenda for Economic Renewal,' presented by Michael H. Wilson, minister of finance, 8 November 1984, 15
56 Ibid., 19
57 Ibid., 15
58 Ibid.
59 See 'Statement by the Honourable Robert Andras, President of the Treasury Board on Expenditure Cuts,' 16 August 1978.
60 I also made use of the material I gathered for a report I prepared in 1987 on the establishment of the Atlantic Canada Opportunities Agency (ACOA). In preparing the report, I interviewed over one hundred individuals from the private sector, the universities, as well as politicians and permanent officials from the federal government and the four provincial

governments of Atlantic Canada. I should also point out that in 1987–8 I served as assistant secretary, Corporate and Public Affairs, in the Treasury Board secretariat. I also borrowed from the interview material Otto Brodtrick and Richard Paton put together in *Quotes* i and ii. The documents are a collection of selected quotes from 225 interviews with federal public servants, private sector executives, and academics on public sector management they carried out in the early 1980s. The material proved particularly useful for the chapters on ministers and departments for two reasons: they offered important reflections from senior public servants and they proved helpful in putting together questions for my own interviews with ministers and officials. See Otto Brodtrick and Richard Paton, *Quotes: Senior Executives Talk about Management in the Public Service*, and *Quotes ii: Public Sector Executives, Businessmen and Professors Talk about Managing in the Public Service* (Ottawa: Office of the Auditor General 1982, January 1984).

CHAPTER 2 The machinery

1 See Richard J. Van Loon and Michael S. Whittington, *The Canadian Political System: Environment, Structure and Process*, 3rd ed. (Toronto: McGraw-Hill Ryerson 1981); G. Bruce Doern and Richard W. Phidd, *Canadian Public Policy: Ideas, Structure, Process* (Toronto: Methuen 1983), and Richard D. French, *How Ottawa Decides* (Ottawa: Canadian Institute for Economic Policy 1980).
2 Consultation with a senior departmental official, Ottawa
3 Consultation with a former senior PCO official, Ottawa, 1987
4 Consultation with a PCO official, Ottawa, 1987
5 See, among others, Norman Ward, *The Public Purse* (Toronto: University of Toronto Press 1951).
6 Consultation with a government MP, Ottawa, 1987
7 Ibid. See also 'Bleak Picture Painted of Government Back Bench,' *Globe and Mail* (Toronto), 25 November 1985, A4.
8 Robert F. Adie and Paul G. Thomas, *Canadian Public Administration* (Scarborough: Prentice-Hall Canada 1987), 164
9 Consultation with an opposition MP, Ottawa, 1987. See also 'Bringing Down the House,' *Maclean's*, 30 November 1987, 8–9. A government member of parliament reported that he prefers working in his riding than in Ottawa because he commands more status there. He said: 'We feel more important in the riding. We are king here.' Quoted in 'Bench-warmers on the Tory Team,' *Gazette* (Montreal), 2 April 1988, B1.

10 Adie and Thomas, *Canadian Public Administration* (1987), 165
11 Ibid., 159–60
12 Consultation with a senior departmental official, Ottawa, 1987
13 Royal Commission on Financial Management and Accountability, *Final Report* (Ottawa: Minister of Supply and Services 1979), 387
14 Ibid.
15 Charlotte Gray, 'Sitting Bull,' in *Saturday Night*, April 1988, 11
16 Ibid., 13
17 Consultation with federal government officials, Ottawa, various dates
18 Canada, House of Commons, Standing Committee on Public Accounts, news release, 2 November 1987
19 Ibid.
20 Consultation with a senior departmental official, Ottawa, 1987
21 Canada, *Statutes*, 1977, c.34, s.7(2), The Auditor General Act
22 Canada, *Report of the Auditor General to the House of Commons for Fiscal Year Ended 31 March, 1987* (Ottawa: Minister of Supply and Services 1987), 1
23 Ibid.
24 Ibid.
25 'The Hunter of Smoking Guns,' *Vancouver Sun*, 28 October 1987, 8
26 Ibid. See also '12 Million Bullets Purchased by DND Don't Shoot Straight,' *Globe and Mail*, 28 October 1987, A6.
27 Quoted in Rod Dobell, 'How Ottawa Decides Economic Policy,' *Policy Options* 1, no 3 (September 1980): 15
28 Manion, 'New Challenges in Public Administration,' 6
29 See, for example, Douglas Hartle, 'Canada's Watchdog Growing Too Strong,' *Globe and Mail*, 10 January 1979, 7
30 Ibid.; see also S.L. Sutherland, 'On the Audit Trail of the Auditor General: Parliament's Servant 1973–1980,' *Canadian Public Administration* 23, no 4 (1980): 616–45.
31 Ibid.
32 Consultation with departmental officials, Ottawa, 1988. Still, some have suggested that IMPAC has been useful. An independent consulting firm, ABT Associates, concluded in 1985 that departmental management systems were improved as a result of IMPAC.
33 Consultation with an official of the Comptroller General's Office, Ottawa, 1988
34 See, among many others, M.J. Kirby, H.V. Kroeker, and W.R. Teschke, 'The Impact of Public Policy-Making Structures and Processes in Canada,' *Canadian Public Administration* 21, no 3 (1978): 407–17

35 Ian Clark, 'Ottawa's Principal Decision-Making and Advisory Committees,' Privy Council Office, Ottawa, 1 December 1983, mimeo., 4
36 Consultation with a central agency official, Ottawa, 1988. See also 'Operations Unlimited,' *Globe and Mail*, 19 May 1988, A6.
37 Ian Clark, 'Ottawa's Principal Decision-Making and Advisory Committees,' 9
38 Thomas S. Axworthy, 'Of Secretaries to Princes,' undated, mimeo., 9
39 Richard D. French, *How Ottawa Decides*, 6
40 For example, a proposal by DRIE in 1983 to provide financial support directly to industrial commissions in Quebec was turned down in cabinet after it had successfully gone through the cabinet committee system.
41 Clark, 'Ottawa's Principal Decision-Making and Advisory Committees,' 21
42 French, *How Ottawa Decides*, 7
43 See, for example, Van Loon and Whittington, *Canadian Political System*, 508.
44 Consultation with a former official of DRIE, Ottawa, 1987

CHAPTER 3 The expenditure budget process

1 See James Cutt and Richard Ritter, *Public Non-Profit Budgeting: The Evolution and Application of Zero-Base Budgeting* (Toronto: Institute of Public Administration of Canada 1984).
2 See Donald Gow, *The Progress of Budgetary Reform in the Government of Canada* (Ottawa: Economic Council of Canada 1973), chapter 2.
3 Ibid.
4 See 'Submission by the Treasury Board to the Public Accounts Committee,' 19 April 1941.
5 J.E. Hodgetts et al., *The Biography of an Institution* (Montreal: McGill-Queen's University Press 1977), 152
6 See Canada, Royal Commission on Government Organization, *Management of the Public Service*, vol. 1, abridged version (Ottawa: Queen's Printer 1962), 99.
7 See Gow, *Progress of Budgetary Reform*, 17.
8 See Royal Commission on Government Organization, 1: 1.
9 Ibid., 91
10 Ibid.
11 Ibid., 92
12 See Gow, *Progress of Budgetary Reform*, 22.

13 Ibid., 23–36

14 Ibid., 18

15 A.W. Johnson, 'PPB and Decision Making in the Government of Canada,' *Cost and Management*, March-April 1971, 16

16 Ibid.

17 See Adie and Thomas, *Canadian Public Administration* (1982), chapter 5; see also Verne B. Lewis, 'Reflections on Budget Systems,' *Public Budgeting and Finance* 8, no 1 (spring 1988): 1–12.

18 Hartle, *Expenditure Budget Process*, 59

19 A.W. Johnson, 'Planning, Programming and Budgeting in Canada,' *Public Administration Review* 33, no 1, 24

20 Donald J. Savoie, *Budgeting in the Government of New Brunswick* (Fredericton: Queen's Printer 1971)

21 Edgar Benson, 'The New Budget Process,' *Canadian Tax Journal*, May 1968, 161

22 Johnson, 'PPB and Decision Making,' 14

23 Canada, Treasury Board, *Planning, Programming, Budgeting Guide*, C.M. Drury, president, July 1968, revised September 1969

24 Johnson, 'Planning, Programming and Budgeting,' 26

25 See Adie and Thomas, *Canadian Public Administration*, 171.

26 Ibid., 172

27 Consultation with a senior federal government official, Ottawa, December 1987

28 Kenneth Kernaghan and David Siegel, *Public Administration in Canada* (Toronto: Methuen 1987), 532

29 Canada, *Report of the Auditor General of Canada to the House of Commons for Fiscal Year Ended 31 March, 1976* (Ottawa: Supply and Services 1976), 10

30 See Canada, Treasury Board, *Policy and Expenditure Management System Manual*, undated, 1.

31 The operation of PEMS has been fully explained in R. Van Loon, 'Stop the Music: The Current Policy and Expenditure Management System in Ottawa,' *Canadian Public Administration* 24, no 2 (1981); also, 'The Policy and Expenditure Management System in the Federal Government: The First Three Years,' *Canadian Public Administration* 26, no 2 (1983); with Richard French in *How Ottawa Decides: Planning and Industrial Policy Making, 1968–84* (Toronto: James Lorimer & Company 1984), chapter 9; and chapter 4, 'Ottawa's Expenditure Process: Four Systems in Search of Co-ordination,' in *How Ottawa Spends*, ed. G.B. Doern (Toronto: James Lorimer & Company 1982). See also R. Dobell, 'Pressing the Envelope,' *Policy Options* 2, no 5 (Nov.-Dec. 1981); Sandford

Borins, 'Ottawa, Expenditure Envelopes: Workable Rationality at Last,' in *How Ottawa Spends*, ed. G.B. Doern; G.B. Doern and Richard Phidd, *Canadian Public Policy* (Toronto: Methuen 1983).

32 See G.B. Doern and R. Phidd, 'Economic Management in the Government of Canada: Some Implications of the Board of Economic Development Ministers and the Lambert Report,' paper presented to the Canadian Political Science Association, Saskatoon, May 1979.

33 Consultation with a senior Treasury Board official, Ottawa, January 1988

34 Van Loon, 'Stop the Music,' 189

35 Ibid.

36 Canada, Treasury Board, *Guide to the Estimates of the Government of Canada* (Ottawa: Minister of Supply and Services 1983)

37 Van Loon, 'Stop the Music,' 177

38 See John A. Chenier, 'The Partners Change: Does the Dance Remain the Same? The Need for Reform in the Policy Expenditure Management System,' February 1985, mimeo.

39 Ian Clark, 'PEMS and the Central Agencies: Notes for a Presentation to a Seminar on Making Government Planning Work, Sponsored by the North American Society for Corporate Planning,' 27 October 1983, 16

40 See 'Trudeau-Pitfield Bureaucracy First Item on Turner's Overhaul,' *Globe and Mail*, 2 July 1984, 5; see also Canada, Office of the Prime Minister, 'Government Organization Measures,' news release, 30 June 1984.

CHAPTER 4 Finance: The keeper of the public purse

1 See W. Irwin Gillespie, 'The Department of Finance and PEMS: Increased Influence or Reduced Monopoly Power?' in *How Ottawa Spends 1984: The New Agenda*, ed. Allan M. Maslove (Toronto: Methuen 1984), 189–214.

2 Interview with an official of the Department of Finance, Ottawa, December 1987

3 See Gillespie, 'Department of Finance and PEMS,' 190.

4 See Jean Chrétien, *Straight from the Heart* (Toronto: Key Porter Books 1985), 117.

5 Interview with a Treasury Board secretariat official, Ottawa, December 1987

6 'According to the former Deputy Secretary (Plans) to the Cabinet, CCDM is designed to keep informed of what other servants of the collectivity are doing and for others to be aware of the views of the Secretary to the

Cabinet on matters pertinent to the collective decision making process.'
See Ian Clark, 'Ottawa's Principal Decision Making and Advisory Committees,' Privy Council Office, Ottawa, 1 December 1983, mimeo., 21.

7 Quoted in Christina McCall-Newman, 'Michael Pitfield and the Politics
of Mismanagement,' *Saturday Night*, October 1982, 35

8 French, *How Ottawa Decides*, 67

9 See McCall-Newman, *Saturday Night*, 34.

10 See Canada, Office of the Prime Minister, news release, 21 October 1982.

11 Consultation with a former member of the Priorities and Planning Committee, Ottawa, 11 January 1988

12 Donald Johnston, *Up the Hill* (Montreal: Optimum Publishing 1986), 67

13 See Robert B. Bryce, *Maturing in Hard Times: Canada's Department of
Finance through the Great Depression* (Montreal: McGill-Queen's University Press 1986), 236.

14 See Canada, Department of Finance, *This Is Your Department of Finance*,
undated.

15 See Canada, Department of Finance, *The Development of a Fiscal Plan*, a
briefing paper prepared by the Fiscal Policy Division, undated.

16 David A. Good, *The Politics of Anticipation: Making Canadian Federal Tax
Policy* (Ottawa: Carleton University, School of Public Administration
1980), 122

17 Richard W. Phidd and G. Bruce Doern, *The Politics and Management of
Canadian Economic Policy* (Toronto: Macmillan 1978), 229

18 Quoted in ibid., 210

19 Quoted in Colin Campbell and George Szablowski, *The Super-Bureau-
crats: Structure and Behaviours in Central Agencies* (Toronto: Macmillan
1979), 86

20 Consultation with a former official of the Department of Finance, Ottawa,
19 November 1987

21 French, *How Ottawa Decides*, 31

22 See Savoie, *Regional Economic Development*, chapter 7.

23 Consultation with a senior cabinet minister in the Trudeau government,
Ottawa, 12 December 1987

24 Consultation with a senior central agency official, Ottawa, 20 November
1987

25 Ibid.

26 Consultation with an official of the Department of Finance, Ottawa, 18
February 1988

27 Hugh Heclo and Aaron Wildavsky, *Private Government*, 161

28 Consultation with a senior central agency official, Ottawa, 20 November 1987
29 Chrétien, *Straight from the Heart*, 118
30 Ibid.
31 Ibid.
32 Consultation with a senior central agency official, Ottawa, 8 December 1987
33 Ibid.
34 Hartle, *Expenditure Budget Process*, 11
35 Consultation with a senior central agency official, Ottawa, 8 December 1987
36 Consultation with an official of the Department of Finance, Ottawa, 16 February 1988
37 Ibid.
38 Albert Breton, 'Modelling the Behaviour of Exchequers,' in *Issues in Canadian Economics*, ed. L.H. Officer and L.B. Smith (Toronto: McGraw-Hill Ryerson 1974), 107–13
39 French, *How Ottawa Decides*, 30
40 Richard Van Loon, 'Planning in the Eighties,' *How Ottawa Decides*, ed. Richard D. French, 2nd ed. (Toronto: James Lorimer & Company 1984), 168
41 Consultation with a senior official of a line department, Ottawa, 14 December 1987
42 A special energy envelope was set up under PEMS in the early 1980s. See, among others, Johnston, *Up the Hill*, and Van Loon, 'Planning in the Eighties,' 180–1.
43 Ibid.
44 Consultation with a senior central agency official, Ottawa, 3 December 1987
45 Canada, 'A New Direction for Canada,' presented by Michael Wilson, minister of finance, 8 November 1984, 55, 69
46 Van Loon, 'Planning in the Eighties,' 180–1
47 Ibid.
48 Peter Aucoin, 'Organizational Change in the Canadian Government: From Rational Management to Brokerage Politics,' *Canadian Journal of Political Science* 19, no 1 (1986): 17
49 Ibid.
50 W. Clifford Clark was at Queen's University immediately before being appointed deputy minister of finance; however, he had been a key

senior adviser to the department for months leading up to his appointment. See Johnston, *Up the Hill.*

51 Consultation with a senior federal government official, Ottawa, 10
December 1987

52 Consultation with a senior central agency official, Ottawa, 7 December
1987

53 Quoted in Good, *Politics of Anticipation*, 65

54 Ibid., 66

55 Consultation with a senior official of a line department, Ottawa, 14
December 1987

56 See Good, *Politics of Anticipation*, 80–1

57 Ibid., 82

58 Consultation with an official of the Department of Finance, Ottawa, 18
February 1988

59 Canada, Department of Finance, *Tax Expenditure Account*, December
1980, 1

60 Allan M. Maslove, 'The Other Side of Public Spending: Tax Expenditures
in Canada,' in *The Public Evaluation of Government Spending*, ed. G. Bruce
Doern and Allan M. Maslove (Montreal: Institute for Research on Public
Policy 1979), 149

61 Canada, *Tax Expenditure Account*, 9–28

62 Canada, *Report of the Auditor General of Canada, Fiscal Year Ended 31 March
1986*, 417

63 Consultation with an official of the Department of Finance, Ottawa, 18
February 1988

64 Federal Government Reporting Study, A Joint Study by the Office of the
Auditor General of Canada and the United States General Accounting
Office, *Detailed Report*, Office of the Auditor General, 21 March 1986,
Cdn. 60

65 See for example, '$2.6 Billion Final Cost of Tax Credit Scheme for
Scientific Research,' *Globe and Mail*, 29 January 1986, A16; see also
Canada, Department of Finance, *Account of the Cost of Selective Tax Measure*,
August 1985, 39–72.

66 Diane Francis, 'Wilson Cleans up Research Tax Credits,' *Financial Post*
(Toronto), 9 February 1988, 3

67 Canada, *Report of the Inquiry into the Collapse of the CCB and Northland Bank
by the Honourable Willard Z. Estey* (Estey Report) (Ottawa: Minister of
Supply and Services 1986), 479

68 See Robert B. Bryce, *Maturing in Hard Times*, 33–34.

69 Estey Report, 479

70 Consultation with a senior finance official, Ottawa, 11 February 1988
71 See, among others, 'Estey Blames Managers, Auditors and Regulators,' *Globe and Mail*, 25 October 1986, A1.
72 Ibid.
73 Ibid., see also 'Bid to Rescue Failed Banks Is Defended,' *Globe and Mail*, 25 October 1986, A1.

CHAPTER 5 The Treasury Board: Keeper of the expenditure budget

1 See Financial Administration Act, 1985, c.116, s.1
2 Douglas J. McCready, 'Treasury Board: Lost Influence?' in *How Ottawa Spends 1984: The New Agenda*, ed. Allan M. Maslove (Toronto: Methuen 1984), 219
3 Ian Clark, 'PEMS and the Control Agencies,' background notes for a presentation to a seminar on making government planning work, 27 October 1983, 11
4 Canada, Treasury Board, *Policy and Expenditure Management System Manual*, undated, 2.7; see also Canada, Privy Council Office, *Policy and Expenditure Management System Envelope Procedures and Rules* (Ottawa July 1980), 2.
5 French, *How Ottawa Decides*, 141
6 Canada, *1988–89 Estimates*, Part I: The Government Expenditure Plan, and Part III: The Treasury Board Secretariat (Ottawa: Minister of Supply and Services 1988)
7 Consultation with an official of the Treasury Board secretariat, 14 December 1987
8 Consultation with a senior official of the Office of the Comptroller General, 24 February 1988
9 Consultation with an official of the Treasury Board secretariat, 14 December 1987
10 See Canada, Office of the Prime Minister, 'Reorganization for Economic Development,' news release, 12 January 1982.
11 See Donald J. Savoie, *Establishment of the Atlantic Canada Opportunities Agency* (Moncton: Atlantic Canada Opportunities Agency May 1987).
12 Canada, Treasury Board, *Policy and Expenditure Management System Manual*, 6.1
13 Consultation with an official of the Treasury Board secretariat, 14 December 1987
14 Ibid., 16 December 1987
15 Ibid., 7 January 1988

16 See Gérard Veilleux and Donald J. Savoie, 'Kafka's Castle: The Treasury Board of Canada Revisited,' March 1988, mimeo., 15.

17 Consultation with an official of the Treasury Board secretariat, 26 November 1987

18 See 'Managing the Business of Government,' notes for an address by the Treasury Board president, 24 August 1987.

19 See Canada, Treasury Board, 'Special Measures Approved for Employment Equity' news release, 22 January 1988.

20 Consultation with an official of the Treasury Board secretariat, 26 November 1987

21 See 'Special Measures Approved for Employment Equity,' 22 January 1988.

22 Consultation with an official of the Treasury Board secretariat, 9 December 1987. See also Treasury Board secretariat, 'Report to the Standing Committee on Public Accounts on the Management of Job Classification in the Public Service of Canada,' 30 April 1986. The report was in direct response to the serious concerns the House of Commons Standing Committee on Public Accounts expressed 'over the state of job misclassification in the Public Service.' The report on a comprehensive audit of job classification revealed that 11.4 per cent of positions in the public service were misclassified, with overclassifications accounting for 7.5 per cent. See also Canada, Treasury Board, 'Treasury Board President Announces Stringent Measures to Reduce Classification Error in the Public Service,' news release, 26 April 1984.

23 Kenneth Kernaghan and David Siegel, *Public Administration in Canada – A Text* (Toronto: Methuen 1987), 572

24 See Veilleux and Savoie, 'Kafka's Castle,' 22.

25 See Canada, Treasury Board, *Role of the Treasury Board Secretariat and the Office of the Comptroller General* (Ottawa March 1983).

26 See 'Managing the Business of Government,' 16.

27 Ibid.

28 Sonja Sinclair, *Cordial but Not Cosy* (Toronto: McClelland and Stewart 1979), 128

29 Ibid., 139

30 Ibid., 142

31 Canada, Office of the Auditor General, *Annual Report, Year Ended 1976* (Ottawa: Minister of Supply and Service 1976), 9

32 Ibid., 11

33 See Sinclair, *Cordial but Not Cosy*, 144.

34 Ibid.

35 Consultation with a senior official from a line department, 16 November 1987
36 H.L. Laframboise, 'Government Spending: Grappling with the Evaluation Octopus,' *Optimum* 9, no 4 (1978): 39
37 See Canada, *Estimates*, Treasury Board of Canada, Office of the Comptroller General, Part III, various dates.
38 See Canada, Office of the Comptroller General, *Program Evaluation Newsletter* 10 (July 1984): 2–3.
39 Canada, *An Introduction to the Process of Program Review* (Ottawa: Minister of Supply and Services March 1986), 23
40 See, among many others, comments of Rod Dobell and Allan Maslove in Canada, Office of the Comptroller General, *Program Evaluation Newsletter* (various numbers).
41 Consultation with a senior official of the Treasury Board secretariat, Ottawa, 14 October 1987
42 Canada, *An Introduction to the Process of Program Review*, 23
43 Consultation with a senior official from a line department, 8 December 1987
44 Ibid., 16 November 1987
45 See 'Audit Prompts Call for Policy Review,' *Free Press* (Winnipeg), 22 September 1987, 1.
46 Progressive Conservative Party of Canada, 'Towards Production Management,' background note, undated, 1
47 Peter Aucoin and Herman Bakvis, *The Centralization-Decentralization Conundrum: Organization and Management in the Canadian Government* (Halifax: Institute for Research on Public Policy 1988)
48 See Canada, President of the Treasury Board, 'Notes for an Address to the Financial Management Institute,' 18 November 1986.
49 Canada, Department of Finance, *The Fiscal Plan* (Ottawa February 1986), 26
50 See R.R. de Cotret 'Notes for an Address to the Financial Management Institute,' 7.
51 Ibid.
52 See Veilleux and Savoie, 'Kafka's Castle,' 36.
53 Consultation with an official of the Treasury Board secretariat, 14 December 1987
54 Ibid.
55 Ibid.
56 Consultation with an official of the Privy Council Office, 10 December 1987

57 Consultation with an official of the Treasury Board secretariat, 14 December 1987
58 Ibid.
59 Ibid.; see also 'Mazankowski Shoulders Too Much of Government Burden,' *Globe and Mail*, 31 August 1987, 2.
60 Ibid.
61 Consultation with a senior official of a line department, 18 February 1988
62 Ibid., 20 January 1988
63 Quoted from Public Policy Forum, *Newsletter* 1, no. 2, 2
64 Quoted in Canada, Office of the Auditor General, *Annual Report, Year Ended 31 March 1983* (Ottawa: Minister of Supply and Services 1983), 61
65 Consultation with a senior official of a line department, 18 February 1988
66 Consultation with an official of the Treasury Board secretariat, 14 January 1988
67 Consultation with an official of a line department, 18 February 1988
68 Ibid.
69 Ibid.
70 Consultation with an official of the Treasury Board secretariat, 20 January 1988
71 Ibid., various dates
72 Ibid., 12 January 1988

CHAPTER 6 From Glassco to Nielsen: Inquisitors from the private sector

1 Consultation with a senior government official directly involved in the work of the ministerial task force program review, Ottawa, 16 March 1988
2 Ibid. See also Stanley H. Mansbridge, 'The Lambert Report: Recommendations to Departments,' *Canadian Public Administration* 22, no 4 (1979): 530.
3 Consultation with a former official of the Treasury Board secretariat, Toronto, 19 January 1988
4 Ibid. See also Mansbridge, 'Lambert Report: Recommendations,' 530.
5 J.R. Mallory, 'The Lambert Report: Central Roles and Responsibilities,' *Canadian Public Administration* 22, no 4 (1979): 517
6 Michael Hicks, 'The Treasury Board of Canada and Its Clients: Five Years of Change and Administrative Reform – 1966–71,' *Canadian Public Administration* 16, no 2 (1973): 204
7 Mallory, 'Lambert Report: Central Roles,' 517

8 Ibid., 194
9 Canada, Treasury Board, 'Statement by the Honourable Robert Andras, President of the Treasury Board, on the Royal Commission of Inquiry on Financial Organization and Accountability in the Government of Canada,' 22 November 1976, 4
10 Ibid.
11 Canada, 'Andras Announces Royal Commission on Financial Organization and Accountability,' Treasury Board, news release, 22 November 1976, 2
12 Ibid.
13 Ibid.
14 Ibid., 1
15 See Canada, Royal Commission on Financial Management and Accountability, *Final Report* (Ottawa: Minister of Supply and Services, 1979), 549–60.
16 Ibid., 7
17 Ibid., 21
18 Ibid., see chapter 9.
19 Ibid., 68
20 Ibid., see chapter 7.
21 Ibid., 117
22 Ibid.
23 Ibid., 127
24 Ibid., 114
25 Consultation with a senior official of the federal government, Ottawa, 19 February 1988
26 Ibid., 12 January 1988
27 Mallory, 'Lambert Report,' 527
28 Consultation with senior officials of the federal government, Ottawa, various dates
29 Mallory, 'Lambert Report,' 526
30 Quoted in Canada, *An Introduction to the Process of Program Review*, 1
31 Canada, 'Speaking Notes for Tabling of Study Team Reports,' Erik Nielsen, deputy prime minister, news release, 11 March 1986
32 Quoted in Canada, *An Introduction to the Process of Program Review*, 1
33 Ibid., 2
34 See Canada, Task Force on Program Review, Private Sector Advisory Committee, news release, Ottawa, 11 March 1986. See also Canada, 'Letter to Members of the Private Sector Advisory Committee and to the Study Team Leaders of the Ministerial Task Force on Program Review

from the President of the Treasury Board,' dated 23 February 1988. The letter was made public on 8 March 1988 by the Treasury Board secretariat.

35 Consultation with a senior government official directly involved in the work of the ministerial task force program review, Ottawa, 16 March 1988

36 Ibid.

37 See, among others, 'Tories Won't Wait for Review of Reports,' *Globe and Mail*, 14 March 1986.

38 Consultation with a central agency official, Ottawa, 12 February 1988; see also 'Beyond the Headlines,' *Globe and Mail*, 7 April 1988, A6.

39 Ibid.

40 Consultation with a former official with the Canada Mortgage and Housing Corporation, Ottawa, October 1987

41 Consultation with a senior government official directly involved in the work of the ministerial task force program review, Ottawa, 16 March 1988

42 Consultation with a senior official of the Treasury Board secretariat, Ottawa, 17 March 1988

43 Consultation with an official of a line department, Ottawa

44 Consultation with a federal cabinet minister from Atlantic Canada, Ottawa, 1988

45 Canada, *Economic Growth – Services and Subsidies to Business* (Ottawa: Minister of Supply and Services 1986), 21

46 Ibid., 22

47 Canada, Commission of Inquiry on Unemployment Insurance, *Report* (Ottawa: Minister of Supply and Services 1986), chapter 1

48 Ibid., 333

49 Ibid., chapter 12

50 See, for example, Conseil économique du Nouveau-Brunswick, *Bulletin*, November 1986, 3–4.

51 Crosbie added: 'There is no question of this Government reducing the sums we invest in the unemployed'; quoted in 'UB Benefits Secure until May, Bouchard Says,' *Globe and Mail*, 5 December 1986, A3.

52 Consultation with a member of parliament from Atlantic Canada, Ottawa, 18 November 1987

53 Consultation with a federal government official, Ottawa, 13 December 1987

54 Ibid., 12 January 1988

55 Ibid., 15 January 1988

56 Ibid., 10 February 1988
57 Consultation with a federal cabinet minister, Ottawa, various dates

CHAPTER 7 Cuts from above: On the road from Bonn and Toronto

1 Canada, *An Introduction to the Process of Program Review*, 26
2 Consultation with a senior central agency official, Ottawa, 25 March 1988
3 Canada, 'Attack On Inflation – A Program of National Action,' policy statement tabled in the House of Commons by Donald S. Macdonald, minister of finance, 14 October 1975, 1
4 Ibid., 7
5 See Canada, Treasury Board, text of remarks by Jean Chrétien, president of the Treasury Board, in the House of Commons, 18 December 1975, 3.
6 Consultation with a former Treasury Board secretariat official, Ottawa, December 1987
7 Canada, Treasury Board, 'Chrétien Identifies Federal Expenditures Reductions,' news release, 2 July 1975
8 Ibid.
9 See Canada, Treasury Board, text of remarks by Jean Chrétien, president of the Treasury Board, in the House of Commons, 18 December 1975, 4–10.
10 See Canada, Treasury Board, 'Chrétien Calls for Co-operation of Business Leaders to Restrain Federal Spending,' news release, 2 May 1976.
11 Canada, Treasury Board, statement by Robert Andras, president of the Treasury Board, on the tabling of the 1977–8 main estimates, 16 February 1977, 2
12 Ibid., 3
13 Canada, Treasury Board, statement by Robert Andras, president of the Treasury Board, on the tabling of the 1978–9 main estimates, 22 February 1978, 2
14 Ibid., 3–5
15 See Canada, Treasury Board, 'The Impact of Administrative Restraint,' released 27 February 1978.
16 Canada, Budget, May 1977
17 See Canada, 'Federal Expenditure Policy in Fiscal Year 1977–78,' notes for a speech by Robert Andras, Treasury Board, 23 February 1977. See also Canada, Treasury Board, *Estimates Fact Sheets* (various), main estimates 1976–7 and 1977–8.

18 Jean Chrétien, *Straight from the Heart* (Toronto: Key Porter Books 1985), 117

19 'Mr. Trudeau Tries Again,' *Globe and Mail*, 3 August 1978, 6; see also 'Fed-Up – PM Pledges Postal Shakeup,' *Globe and Mail*, 2 August 1978, 1.

20 Chrétien, *Straight from the Heart*, 118

21 Consultation with a senior departmental official, Ottawa, 29 March 1988

22 Chrétien, *Straight from the Heart*, 118

23 Canada, Department of Finance, *Budget Speech*, 16 November 1978, 5

24 Canada, statement by Robert Andras, president of the Treasury Board, 16 August 1978

25 See Canada, *Evolution of the Budget Process in Canada*, a document prepared by the Treasury Board secretariat for OECD, undated.

26 See 'Are Cuts Real, or Are They an Imaginary Total?' *Globe and Mail*, 9 September 1978, 1.

27 'Ottawa Will Be Insistent with Provinces,' *Globe and Mail*, 27 November 1978, 10

28 Canada, Department of Finance, statement by Finance Minister Jean Chrétien, news release, 24 August 1978

29 See Canada, *Evolution of the Budget Process in Canada*, 11.

30 Ibid., see also 'Are Cuts Real, or Are They an Imaginary Total?' *Globe and Mail*, 9 September 1978, 1.

31 See, for example, *Regional Poverty and Change* (Ottawa: Canadian Council on Rural Development 1976), 1.

32 Canada, Department of Finance, *Budget Speech*, 16 November 1978, 7

33 Canada, Department of Finance and the Treasury Board, *Briefing on Federal Expenditures*, 20 July 1979, 1

34 See, among others, John Sargent, Research Co-ordinator, *Fiscal and Monetary Policy*, Royal Commission on the Economic Union and Development Prospects for Canada, Research Studies vol. 21 (Toronto: University of Toronto Press 1986), 27.

35 Ibid., 28

36 See Canada, *Evolution of the Budget Process in Canada*, Task IV, 1–14.

37 Ibid.

38 Canada, *Briefing on Federal Expenditures*, 3

39 See Canada, *Evolution of the Budget Process in Canada*, Task IV, 1–14.

40 See Canada, *An Introduction to the Process of Program Review*, 22.

41 See Canada, Treasury Board, *Expenditure and Program Review*, November 1984.

42 See Peter Aucoin, 'Canadian Government: From Rational Management

to Brokerage Policies,' *Canadian Journal of Political Science* 19, no 1
(1986), 17

43 'Background notes for an Address by Brian Mulroney, P.C., M.P.,'
Toronto, Ontario, Progressive Conservative Party, 28 August 1984; see
also *On the Issues: Brian Mulroney and the Progressive Conservative Agenda*
(Ottawa: Progressive Conservative Party July 1984), 8.

44 Canada, Treasury Board, *Expenditure and Program Review*, November
1984, 1

45 Ibid.

46 Canada, Treasury Board, 'Freeze on Staffing and Discretionary Spending Announced,' 24 September 1984

47 Canada, Department of Finance, *Economic and Fiscal Statement*, 8 November 1984, 3–4

48 Ibid., 7

49 Canada, Department of Finance, *Budget Speech*, 23 May 1985, 18

50 Canada, Treasury Board, *Expenditure and Program Review*, November
1984, 5

51 Ibid.

52 Ibid., appendices A, B, C, D, E, F, and G

53 Canada, *Budget Speech*, 23 May 1985, 18

54 Consultation with Department of Finance and Treasury Board secretariat officials, Ottawa, various dates

55 Canada, Department of Finance, *Budget Papers*, 23 May 1985, 36

56 Ibid., 72

57 Canada, Minister of Health and Welfare, *Child and Elderly Benefits –
Consultation Paper*, January 1985

58 Ibid.

59 See, for example, David Zussman, 'Walking the Tightrope: The Mulroney Government and the Public Service,' in *How Ottawa Spends: 1986–
87, Tracking the Tories*, ed. Michael J. Prince (Toronto: Methuen 1986),
250–83.

60 Consultation with a cabinet minister, Ottawa, various dates

61 Consultation with a federal government official, Ottawa, various dates

62 Canada, *Budget Speech*, 23 May 1985; see also, Canada, Treasury Board,
'Federal Government Cash Management,' news release, 7 March 1988.

63 Canada, Department of Finance, *The Budget Speech*, 26 February 1986, 5

64 Ibid., 7–8

65 Canada, Privy Council Office and Treasury Board, 'Tighter Resource
Management: A New Corporate Culture,' 27 February 1986

66 Consultation with a former official of the Treasury Board secretariat, Ottawa, various dates

67 Canada, 'Expenditure Reduction in the Treasury in the February 1986 Budget,' news release, 18 November 1986

68 Canada, Department of Finance, *The Budget Speech*, 10 February 1988, 7–10

69 'Bureaucrats the Bunglers within DRIE, Audit Says,' *Globe and Mail*, 28 August 1987, A4.

70 See James J. Rice, 'Restitching the Safety Net: Altering the National Social Security System,' in *How Ottawa Spends: 1987–88*, ed. Michael J. Prince (Toronto: Methuen 1987), 211–36.

71 See 'Look after the Pennies and the Pounds (or Dollars) Will Look after Themselves,' *Thompson News Service*, Ottawa, 14 March 1988; see also Canada, Treasury Board, *Management Improvements*, Fact Sheet No 6, 27 February 1986, and Canada, Treasury Board, *Federal Government Cash Management Savings*, 7 March 1988.

72 Canada, Treasury Board, 'A New Commitment to Public Sector Management,' notes for an Address by Don Mazankowski to the Public Policy Forum, 14 April 1988, 7

73 Canada, Treasury Board, 'Work Force Adjustment Policy Reviewed,' news release, Ottawa, 31 March 1988

74 Canada, Department of Finance, *The Budget Speech*, 10 February 1988, 7–10

75 Consultation with Treasury Board officials, Ottawa, various dates

76 See Canada, Agriculture Canada, *Program Fact Sheet and Summary of Initiatives*, Ottawa, various dates. See also Canada, 'Final Supplementary Estimates for 1987–88 Tabled,' news release, Ottawa, 2 March 1988.

77 Canada, Department of Finance, *The Budget Speech*, 23 May 1985, 18–19, and *The Fiscal Plan*, 10 February 1988, 85–103; see also 'Ottawa Spends More, but Higher Taxes Help Slow the Rise in the Federal Deficit,' *Globe and Mail*, 3 September 1987, 88.

CHAPTER 8 Ministers: Nothing succeeds like excess

1 Consultation with a former federal cabinet minister, Ottawa, 12 January 1988

2 Harold D. Clarke et al., *Absent Mandate* (Toronto: Gage Publishing 1984), 8

3 Ibid., 10

4 Ibid.
5 Ibid. The one exception is the 1988 general election campaign which saw at least two of the three political parties stake out a distinct policy position on the Canada-United States Free Trade Agreement.
6 Ibid., 110
7 Ibid., 130
8 See Jeffrey Simpson, *Discipline of Power* (Toronto: Personal Library 1980), chapter 1.
9 See *Canadian Annual Review of Politics and Public Affairs*, ed. John Saywell (Toronto: University of Toronto Press 1975), 23–5, and *Canadian News Facts* (Toronto: Marpep Publishing 1972), 878–2 and 895–2.
10 George Radwanski, *Trudeau* (Toronto: Macmillan 1978), 263
11 See, for example, Van Loon and Whittington, *Canadian Political System* (1981), part 5.
12 'Political Football ...,' *Toronto Star*, 5 December 1987, 2
13 See 'Dear Minister. A Letter to an Old Friend on Being a Successful Minister,' notes for remarks by Gordon Osbaldeston to the Association of Professional Executives of the Public Service of Canada, 22 January 1988, 11
14 Exceptions include George Hees who was able to shift Pierre Sicard out as deputy minister in Veterans Affairs, Marcel Masse who removed DeMontigny Marchand from Communications, and Lloyd Axworthy who saw to it that Doug Love would leave as deputy minister of CEIC. Some of these cases, particularly the Sicard one, were widely reported in the media.
15 Quoted in Donald J. Savoie, 'The Minister's Staff: The Need for Reform,' *Canadian Public Administration* 26, no 4 (1983): 523
16 See Osbaldeston, 'Dear Minister,' 22 January 1988, 3.
17 Ibid., 4
18 Ibid.
19 Henry Kissinger, quoted in Flora MacDonald, notes for remarks to annual meeting, Canadian Political Science Association, 3 June 1980, 11
20 P.M. Pitfield, 'Politics and Policy Making,' address to the Alma Mater Society, Queen's University, Kingston, Ontario, 10 February 1983, 5
21 Heclo and Wildavsky, *Private Government*, 130
22 Savoie, 'The Minister's Staff,' 521
23 Quoted in Timothy W. Plumptre, *Beyond the Bottom Line: Management in Government* (Halifax: Institute for Research on Public Policy 1988), 122
24 Quoted in Savoie, 'The Minister's Staff,' 523
25 There are many studies that look at the motivations of political leaders.

The terms 'status' and 'mission' participants and other such terms have also been employed elsewhere. See, among others, Oliver H. Woskinsky, *The French Deputy* (London: Lexington Books 1973), and James L. Payne, *Patterns of Conflict in Colombia* (New Haven: Yale University Press 1968).

26 Maurice Lamontagne, 'The Influence of the Politician,' *Canadian Public Administration* 11, no 3 (1968): 263

27 Consultation with a senior departmental official, Ottawa, 12 March 1988

28 Pitfield, 'Politics and Policy Making,' 5

29 Quoted in Plumptre, *Beyond the Bottom Line*, 130

30 See Donald Johnston, *Up the Hill* (Montreal: Optimum Publishing International 1986).

31 See, for example, Lloyd Axworthy, 'Control of Policy,' *Policy Options* 6, no 3 (1985): 17–19.

32 Consultation with a senior federal cabinet minister, Ottawa, 8 April 1988

33 Ibid.

34 Richard Simeon, 'Some Issues of Governance in Canada,' in *The Changing Shape of Government in the Asian–Pacific Region*, ed. John W. Langford and K. Larne Brownsey (Halifax: Institute for Research on Public Policy 1988), 275, 279

35 Quoted in George Peabody, Carolyn MacGregor, and Richard Thorne, *The Maritimes: Tradition, Challenge and Change* (Halifax: Maritext 1987), 167

36 Herman Bakvis, 'Regional Minister, National Policy and the Administrative State,' paper presented to the annual meeting of the Canadian Political Science Association, University of Manitoba, June 1986, 35

37 D.V. Smiley, *Canada in Question: Federalism in the Eighties* (Toronto: McGraw-Hill Ryerson 1980), 134

38 Consultation with a former federal cabinet minister, Ottawa, 7 March 1988

39 Bakvis, 'Regional Minister, National Policy and the Administrative State,' 2

40 Ibid., 21

41 See Donald J. Savoie, *Federal-Provincial Collaboration: The Canada-New Brunswick General Development Agreement* (Montreal: McGill-Queen's University Press 1981).

42 Peter Aucoin, 'Organization by Place, Regional Development and National Policy: The Case of the Atlantic Canada Opportunities Agency,' a paper presented to the annual meeting of the Canadian Political Science Association, University of Windsor, June 1988, 1

43 See Savoie, *Regional Economic Development*.

44 Consultations with a senior central agency official, Ottawa, 12 January 1988
45 Bakvis, 'Regional Minister, National Policy and the Administrative State,' 35
46 Ibid.
47 See Savoie, *Regional Economic Development*, chapter 5.
48 Consultation with a former federal cabinet minister, Ottawa, 7 March 1988
49 French, *How Ottawa Decides*
50 See Savoie, *Regional Economic Development*, appendix 1.
51 Douglas Fisher 'When Ministers Become Ex-Ministers,' *The Times-Transcript* (Moncton), 14 June 1986, 7
52 Consultation with a former federal cabinet minister, Ottawa, 7 March 1988
53 Ibid.
54 Consultation with a senior government official, Ottawa, various dates
55 Quoted in French, *How Ottawa Decides*, 77
56 Quoted in 'Turner Would Scrap Sub Plan,' *Chronicle-Herald* (Halifax), 3 June 1988
57 Consultation with a former federal cabinet minister, Ottawa, 11 December 1987
58 Consultation with an assistant to Gerald Merithew, Ottawa, 11 June 1988

CHAPTER 9 Departments: On the inside looking in

1 See G. Bruce Doern, 'Horizontal and Vertical Portfolios in Government,' in *Issues in Canadian Public Policy*, ed. G. Bruce Doern and V. Seymour Wilson (Toronto: Macmillan 1974), 310–19.
2 Consultation with a former senior federal government official, Ottawa, various dates
3 Richard Simeon, 'Studying Public Policy,' *Canadian Journal of Political Science* 9, no 4 (1976): 548–80
4 Sandford F. Borins, 'Mandarin Power,' *Saturday Night*, August 1982, 7
5 See 'Bureaucracy Unlike Soldiers, Won't Go Away,' *Globe and Mail*, 20 August 1987, 9
6 Canada, *Expenditure Plan – Part III*: Veterans Affairs Canada (Ottawa: Minister of Supply and Services 1988), 1988–9 estimates
7 Consultation with a Treasury Board Secretariat official, Ottawa, various dates
8 Canada, Public Service Commission, *Annual Report, 1984*, 14

9 Consultation with a former official of the Department of Supply and Services, Ottawa, 20 May 1988

10 Manion, 'New Challenges in Public Administration,' 18

11 'Canada's Threatened Civil Servants,' *Toronto Star*, 22 August 1987, 14

12 See Michael Hicks, 'The Treasury Board of Canada and Its Clients: Five Years of Change and Administrative Reform, 1966–1971,' *Canadian Public Administration* 16, no 2 (1973): 182–205.

13 Consultation with a senior official of the Canadian Employment and Immigration Commission, Ottawa, various dates

14 Consultation with a senior official, Ottawa, 11 February 1988

15 Quoted in *Quotes*, 15

16 Consultation with senior officials, Ottawa, various dates

17 Quoted in Donald J. Savoie, 'New Challenges in Studying Canadian Public Administration,' unpublished paper, August 1986, 8

18 Ibid., 9

19 Ibid.

20 Ibid., 10

21 Consultation with a former cabinet minister, Ottawa, various dates

22 Consultation with a Treasury Board secretariat official, Ottawa, various dates in May 1988

23 Lee Iacocca, 'The Fine Art of Compromise,' *Newsweek*, 23 December 1985, 1

24 Michael J. Prince and John A. Chenier, 'The Rise and Fall of Policy Planning and Research Units: An Organizational Perspective,' *Canadian Public Administration* 23, no 4 (1980): 540

25 H.L. Laframboise, 'The Future of Public Administration: Programs and Prospects,' *Canadian Public Administration* 25, no 4 (1982): 507

26 Prince and Chenier, 'Rise and Fall of Policy Planning and Research Units,' 541

27 Quoted in Savoie, 'New Challenges in Studying Canadian Public Administration,' 11

28 Canada, Department of Finance, *The Budget Speech*, 23 May 1985, 11

29 Laframboise, 'The Future of Public Administration,' 515

30 Quoted in *Quotes*, 15

31 Consultation with a senior federal cabinet minister, Ottawa, 17 June 1988

32 Ibid.

33 Consultation with a federal cabinet minister, Ottawa, various dates

34 Consultation with a federal cabinet minister, Ottawa, 26 January 1988

35 See Adie and Thomas, *Canadian Public Administration: Problematical Per-*

spectives, chapter 5; see also Sandford Borins, 'The Theory and Practice of Envelope Budgeting' (York University, Toronto, Faculty of Administration Studies January 1980), 3. He writes: 'Departments, which cannot be expected willingly to terminate their own programs, responded to early 'x' budgets with a devastatingly effective tactic. They proposed for elimination those programs which were major priorities of the Cabinet and Prime Minister. The classic was bilingualism.'

36 See Kenneth Kernaghan and David Siegel, *Public Administration in Canada* (Toronto: Methuen 1987), chapter 23.

37 See B. Guy Peters, *The Politics of Bureaucracy*, 2nd ed. (New York: Longman 1984), chapter 6, and *Better Value for the Tax Dollar: Improving Productivity in the Federal Public Service* (Ottawa: Canadian Chamber of Commerce February 1984), 13.

38 Van Loon and Whittington, *Canadian Political System*, 407

39 A. Paul Pross, *Group Politics and Public Policy* (Toronto: Oxford University Press 1986)

40 John Meisel, 'The Reformer and the Bureaucrat: A Remedial Dissonance?' Alan B. Plaunt Memorial Lecture, Carleton University, 8 April 1983, 12

41 Gerald Kaufman, *How To Be a Minister* (London: Sidgwick and Jackson 1980), 31

42 See, for example, 'Cultural Groups Get $75 Million Increase in Federal Assistance,' *Toronto Star*, 27 February 1986, A18. The minister's personal involvement in obtaining added funding from cabinet is highlighted in the article.

43 Lloyd Axworthy, 'Control of Policy,' *Policy Options* 6, no 3 (1986): 17

44 'Coalition Fears Cut in Annual Grant,' *Globe and Mail*, 26 May 1988, A4.

45 Manion, 'New Challenges in Public Administration,' 18

46 Canada, Privy Council Office, *The Office of Deputy Minister*, June 1984, 1

47 Plumptre, *Beyond the Bottom Line*, 150

48 Consultation with a senior deputy minister, Ottawa, various dates

49 Quoted in Canada, *Office of Deputy Minister*, 151

50 See Gordon Osbaldeston, 'Job Description for DMS,' *Policy Options* 9, no 1 (1988): 33–4.

51 Plumptre, *Beyond the Bottom Line*, 150

52 Quoted in Canada, *Office of Deputy Minister*, 33

53 Plumptre, *Beyond the Bottom Line*, 150

54 Ibid.

55 Quoted in *Quotes*, 11

56 Plumptre, *Beyond the Bottom Line*, chapter 5
57 The meeting of assistant deputy ministers now held regularly is labelled the 'ADM update.' It is attended by all ADM or ADM equivalents, and the most senior officials, including the clerk of the Privy Council and secretary of the cabinet, are invited to speak.
58 Quoted in Otto Brodtrick and Richard Paton, 'Public Sector Executives, Businessmen and Professors Talk about Managing in the Public Service,' Ottawa: Office of the Auditor General, January 1984, 14
59 See Donald J. Savoie, *Federal-Provincial Collaboration*.
60 Canada, Office of the Prime Minister, 'Reorganization for Economic Development,' news release, 12 January 1982
61 See 'Federal Officials Rally To Defend Job Training Programs,' *Citizen* (Ottawa), 29 March 1988, A13.
62 Meisel, 'The Reformer and the Bureaucrat,' 12
63 See Osbaldeston, 'Job Description for DMs,' 36–7.
64 Plumptre, *Beyond the Bottom Line*, 212
65 Otto Brodtrick, 'Constraints to Production Management in Public Sector Organizations,' notes for remarks to the Canadian Public Personnel Management Association, 5 June 1986, Ottawa, 21
66 Quoted in Brodtrick and Paton, 'Public Sector Executives,' 13
67 Ibid., 38
68 Canada, 'Constraints to Productive Management in the Public Service,' in *Report of the Auditor General of Canada to the House of Commons, Fiscal Year Ended 31 March 1983* (Ottawa: Minister of Supply and Services 1983), 61
69 Quoted in Canada, *Quotes*, 37
70 Quoted in Brodtrick and Paton, 'Public Sector Executives,' 18
71 Plumptre, *Beyond the Bottom Line*, 391
72 Canada, The Public Service Employment Act, 1966–7, c.71, s.1, 6094–5
73 See Douglas Hartle, *The Expenditure Budget Process of the Government of Canada: A Public Choice – Rent Seeking Perspective*, Canadian Tax Paper no 81, (Toronto: Canadian Tax Foundation 1988), 57.
74 Canada, Public Service Employment Act, 6094–5
75 See, among others, *Moonlighting for Public Servants* (Ottawa: Media Tapes and Transcripts Ltd. 29 December 1987).
76 Consultation with senior federal government officials, Ottawa, various dates
77 See Canada, Public Service Commission, *Annual Report*, 1988, and *Citizen*, a special report, 11 June 1988, B3–8.

78 See Hartle, *Expenditure Budget Process*, 57.
79 See Canada, Public Service Commission, *Annual Report*, 1988, and see also *Citizen*, 11 June 1988, B3–8.
80 Plumptre, *Beyond the Bottom Line*, 393
81 See Hartle, *Expenditure Budget Process*, 57.
82 Ibid., 59
83 Consultation with a senior official of the Privy Council Office, Ottawa, 8 March 1988
84 Otto Brodtrick, 'Constraints to Production Management in Public Sector Organizations,' notes for remarks to the Canadian Public Personnel Management Association, Ottawa, 5 June 1986, 6
85 See Osbaldeston, 'Job Description for DMs,' 35.
86 Ibid.
87 See *Citizen*, 11 June 1988, B6.
88 Consultation with a federal government official, Ottawa, 7 March 1988
89 See Manion, 'New Challenges in Public Administration,' 2.
90 Consultation with a federal government official, Ottawa, 25 February 1988
91 See *Citizen*, 11 June 1988, B6; see also David Zussman and Jak Jabes, *The Challenge of the Vertical Solitude in the Public Sector* (Halifax: Institute for Research on Public Policy, forthcoming).
92 Ibid.
93 Consultation with a federal government official, 16 May 1988, Ottawa
94 This message was communicated to all departments and agencies by the Treasury Board secretariat in March 1988.
95 See Canada, Public Works Canada, 'The Make-or-Buy Policy,' *Situation*, October 1987.
96 See 'Union Vows to Fight Transfer of Mapping Sector,' *Citizen*, 6 March 1987, 1.
97 'Montreal Company Says Mapping Deal Not Yet Concluded,' *Globe and Mail*, 10 March 1987, A5.
98 See Manion, 'New Challenges in Public Administration,' 2.
99 Ibid.
100 Quoted in 'Rhodes to Glory,' *Globe and Mail*, 27 February 1980, D5.
101 Consultation with a senior central agency official, Ottawa, various dates
102 Quoted in 'There Is a Malaise,' *Citizen*, 11 June 1988, B3
103 See Canada, Public Service Commission, *Annual Report*, 1988, and see also *Citizen*, 11 June 1988, B3–8.
104 Based on data provided by the Treasury Board secretariat, Ottawa, May 1988

CHAPTER 10 Crown corporations: Financing the jewels

1 Canada, *Minding the Public's Business* (Ottawa: Economic Council of Canada 1986), 1
2 Canada, *Crown Corporations* (Ottawa: Privy Council Office 1977), 7
3 Ibid.
4 See, among others, *On the Issues: Brian Mulroney and the Progressive Conservative Agenda*, 8–9.
5 Canada, Treasury Board, 'New Crown Corporations Bill Proclaimed,' news release, 31 August 1984
6 Canada, Royal Commission on Financial Management and Accountability, *Final Report*, chapter 17
7 Canada, *Crown Corporations*, 11
8 See Canada, *Report of the Auditor General of Canada to the House of Commons, Fiscal Year Ended 31 March 1982* (Ottawa: Minister of Supply and Services 1982), chapter 2.
9 Canada, *Crown Corporations*, 1
10 Canada, Financial Administration Act, Office Consolidation, Part VIII, March 1984, 30
11 Consultation with a senior official of the Treasury Board secretariat, Ottawa, various dates
12 Ibid.
13 See, among others, 'New Legislative Proposals for the Control and Accountability of Crown Corporations,' statement by Herb Gray, president of the Treasury Board, March 1984.
14 Ibid.
15 See Canada, *Air Canada Inquiry Report by the Honourable Willard Z. Estey* (Ottawa: Information Canada 1975), 1.
16 Canada, Treasury Board, Crown Corporations, Quarterly Report to Parliament, Fourth Quarter, 1987, Ottawa, 1988
17 See, among many others, Marsha Gordon, *Government in Business* (Montreal: C.D. Howe Institute 1981), and Walter Stewart, *Uneasy Lies the Head* (Toronto: Collins 1987).
18 Consultation with a senior official of the Treasury Board secretariat, Ottawa, various dates
19 Gordon, *Government in Business*, 87
20 Stewart, *Uneasy Lies the Head*, 160
21 See Canada, Treasury Board, *Employment Equity for Crown Corporations*, 1986.
22 Consultations with central agency officials, Ottawa, various dates

23 See, among many others, 'PM Seeks to Tie NDP's Name to Moncton Demonstration,' *Globe and Mail*, 9 May 1988, A1; see also 'Angry Crowd Demand Cochrane's Resignation,' *Times-Transcript*, 24 June 1986, 1.

24 Consultation with a private sector representative, Moncton, 16 January 1987

25 See 'CN Achieves Profit for '87 after '86 Loss,' *Globe and Mail*, 30 April 1988, B1, and Canada, Ministry of Transport, speech by Hon. John Crosbie on the 'Newfoundland Transportation Initiative,' Toward 2000, 20 June 1988, 1.

26 'Report of New Aircraft Job Losses Angers Manitoba's Doer,' *Globe and Mail*, 9 April 1988, A5

27 Consultation with a former senior official of the Ministry of Transport, Ottawa, 30 May 1988

28 See Canada, Receiver General for Canada, Public Accounts of Canada – 1987; Vol. III, Annual Report to Parliament on Crown Corporations and Other Corporate Interests of Canada, 1987, 8.

29 Consultation with a central agency official, Ottawa, various dates

30 See, among others, Canada, Public Accounts of Canada – 1987, Vol. III, 238.

31 'McKenna Says CBC Slights His Province,' *Globe and Mail*, 30 April 1988, A4

32 Jeanne Kirk Laux and Maureen Appel Molot, *State Capitalism: Public Enterprise in Canada* (Ithaca: Cornell University Press 1988), 191

33 Canada, Department of Finance, *The Budget Speech*, 23 May 1985, 10

34 G. Bruce Doern and John Athecton, 'The Tories and the Crowns: Restraining and Privatizing in a Political Minefield,' in *How Ottawa Spends: 1987–88 – Restraining the State*, ed. Michael J. Prince (Toronto: Methuen 1987), 131

35 Canada, Department of Finance, *A New Direction for Canada*, 8 November 1984, 63

36 See Canada, Department of Finance, *Securing Economics Renewal: Budget Papers*, 23 May 1985, 26–7.

37 Kirk Laux and Appel Molot, *State Capitalism*, 194

38 Quoted in ibid., 195

39 Stewart, *Uneasy Lies the Head*, 210

40 'Crown Self Decisions Harder to Get,' *Financial Post*, 28 December 1987, 4

41 Canada, Office of Privatization and Regulatory Affairs, 'Federal and Saskatchewan Governments to Merge Then Privatize Uranium Companies,' news release, 22 February 1988

42 'Derailing Tactic Provides Some Relief,' *Citizen*, 14 April 1988, A8

43 See 'Airline for Sale,' *Globe and Mail*, 14 April 1988, A6.
44 'Air Canada Sell-off Launched by Tories,' *Financial Post*, 13 April 1988
45 See 'Putting Airline on Block Rejuvenates Lagging Tory Privatization Program,' *Financial Post*, 13 April 1988, 20.
46 'Ottawa Seeks Control of Publisher,' *Toronto Star*, 12 March 1988, C1
47 See, among many others, Doern and Atherton, 'The Tories and the Crowns,' 164–5.
48 Consultation with a senior central agency official, Ottawa, various dates
49 Consultation with a cabinet minister in the Mulroney government, Ottawa, various dates
50 Consultation with a senior central agency official, Ottawa, various dates
51 Consultation with a senior official of the Treasury Board secretariat, Ottawa, 5 May 1988

CHAPTER 11 The provinces and the regions: A federal responsibility

1 Quoted in 'Regionalism Is Selfishness,' *Citizen*, 7 July 1981, 6
2 See Roger Gibbins, *Regionalism* (Toronto: Butterworth 1982), and Garth Stevenson, *Unfilfilled Union* (Toronto: Gage 1987).
3 See R. MacGregor Dawson, *The Government of Canada* (Toronto: University of Toronto Press 1957).
4 See Ontario, *Interprovincial Trade Flows, Employment and the Tariff in Canada* (Toronto: Treasury Department 1977); Canada, *Preliminary Observations on the Economic Accounts of Quebec* (Ottawa: Federal-Provincial Relations Office 1977); Quebec, *Presentation of the Economic Accounts of Quebec, 1961–1976* (Quebec 1977).
5 See J. Maxwell and C. Pestiau, *Economic Realities of Contemporary Confederation* (Montreal: C.D. Howe Research Institute 1980).
6 Allan Tupper, *Public Money in the Private Sector* (Kingston: Institute of Intergovernmental Relations, Queen's University 1982), 41
7 Canada, *Proceedings of the Standing Senate Committee on National Finance*, 4 December 1980, issue no 18
8 See, for example, Ontario, William Davis, 'Notes for Opening Statement to the Conference of the First Ministers on the Economy,' Ottawa, 27–9 November 1978.
9 Quoted in Peter Aucoin, 'Organization by Plan, Regional Development and National Policy: The Case of the Atlantic Canada Opportunities Agency,' a paper presented to the annual meeting of the Canadian Political Science Association, University of Windsor, June 1988, 2
10 Consultation with a senior federal official with the Department of Finance, Ottawa, various dates

11 Quoted in Newfoundland, 'Discussion Paper on Bilateral Issues: Canada-Newfoundland,' St John's 1981, 4
12 Annual Conference of First Ministers, *Report of the Federal-Provincial Task Force on Regional Development Assistance* (Toronto May 1987), 43
13 Harry Bruce, 'Roar from the Sea,' *Saturday Night*, July 1988, 53
14 Ernest R. Forbes, 'Consolidating Disparity: The Maritimes and the Industrialization of Canada during the Second World War,' *Acadiensis*, spring 1986, 3
15 Bruce, 'Roar from the Sea,' 53
16 Ibid. For a discussion of the federal government's equalization program, see Canada, *Fiscal Federalism, Report of the Parliamentary Task Force on Federal-Provincial Fiscal Arrangements* (Ottawa: Minister of Supply and Services 1981), chapter 7.
17 Tupper, *Public Money in the Private Sector*, 41
18 Council of Maritime Premiers, 'Communiqué – 51st Session of Council held on December 13, 1982,' Newcastle, NB, 2
19 See, among many others, 'Premiers Pushing for a BNA Summit before Court Rules,' *Globe and Mail*, 8 April 1981, 1.
20 See Stuart Mackinnon, 'First Ministers' Conference,' paper presented at the Fifth Conference on Public Policy and Administration Studies, University of Guelph, 22 April 1988, 21.
21 Ibid., 7–8
22 Ibid., 8
23 Ibid., 7
24 Ibid., 16
25 Bruce Little, 'The Message Is the Media,' Globe and Mail, *Report on Business Magazine*, November 1987, 20
26 Ibid.
27 Consultation with a senior official from the Federal-Provincial Relations Office, Ottawa, 7 December 1987
28 'Procurement Game Draws More Players,' *Financial Post*, 28 March 1988, 4
29 'Anglo Bureaucrats Blamed in Space Agency Backtrade,' *Toronto Star*, 13 March 1988, 1
30 'New Brunswick Big Winner on Frigate Contacts,' *Globe and Mail*, 19 December 1987, A3
31 Ibid.
32 Manion, 'New Challenges in Public Administration,' 24
33 'De Cotret n'accouche pas d'un maigre $35 millions,' *Le Devoir* (Montreal), 25 February 1988

34 David Kilgour, 'How to Diversify the West,' *Policy Options* 8, no 9 (November 1987): 12–16
35 'Have the Tories Written off Metro Toronto's 40 Seats?' *Globe and Mail*, 24 March 1988, A2
36 A.W. Johnson, 'Social Policy in Canada: The Past as It Conditions the Present,' Discussion Paper, Institute for Research on Public Policy, September 1987
37 Ibid., 16
38 Ibid., 28
39 Consultation with a central agency official, Ottawa, various dates
40 See Savoie, *Regional Economic Development*, appendix A.
41 Savoie, *Federal-Provincial Collaboration*, 87
42 See Savoie, *Regional Economic Development*, chapter 7.
43 Savoie, *Federal-Provincial Collaboration*, chapter 8
44 'McMillan Quits Part of Portfolio Connected to PEI Fixed Crossing,' *Globe and Mail*, 22 January 1988, 4
45 Alan Cairns, 'The Governments and Societies of Canadian Federation,' *Canadian Journal of Political Science* 10, no 4 (1977): 700
46 Ontario, Ministry of Treasury and Economics, *1988 Ontario Budget*, 20 April 1988, and Canada, *Federal-Provincial Programs and Activities*, Federal-Provincial Relations Office, 1986–7, 115
47 Ontario, Ministry of Treasury and Economics, *Budget Statement*, 1981
48 Allan M. Maslove et al., *Federal and Provincial Budgeting*, Royal Commission on the Economic Union and Development Prospects for Canada, Research Studies vol. 41 (Toronto: University of Toronto Press 1986), 233
49 Quoted in 'Premiers – Atlantic,' Canadian Press Wire Service, 27 August 1987
50 Canada, Public Works Canada, *History of the Municipal Grants Program*, Ottawa 1982, 2
51 Ibid., 4
52 Ibid.; see also Canada, Public Works Canada, *Municipal Grants in Lieu of Property Taxes*, undated. Also consultation with an official of Public Works Canada, Ottawa, 15 July 1988.
53 See Canada, 'Speaking Notes for the Hon. Robert R. De Cotret on the Occasion of the Meeting of Provincial Ministers of Municipal Affairs,' Treasury Board secretariat, 15 August 1987.
54 Consultation with officials with the Federation of Canadian municipalities, Ottawa, various dates

55 Canada, Department of Finance, and Statistics Canada
56 'Experts Say Spending Clause a Puzzler,' *Citizen*, 4 June 1987, 2
57 J.A. Corry, 'Constitutional Trends in Federalism,' in *Canadian Federalism: Myth or Reality*, ed. J. Peter Meekeson, (Toronto: Methuen 1968), 62
58 See Thomas J. Courchene, 'Meech Lake and Federalism: Accord or Discord?' Research Centre for Canadian Studies, York University, 1987.

CHAPTER 12 The private sector: Grabbing with both hands

1 See, among others, Savoie, *Regional Economic Development*.
2 'The Public Purse,' *Canadian Business* (Toronto), April 1980, 65
3 See Savoie, *Regional Economic Development*, chapter 8.
4 See J.L. Granatstein, *Canada's War: The Politics of the Mackenzie King Government, 1939–1945* (Toronto: Oxford University Press 1975).
5 Gordon, *Government in Business*, chapter 6
6 Michael Bliss, 'Forcing the Pace: A Reappraisal of Business-Government Relations in Canadian History,' in *Theories of Business-Government Relations*, ed. V.V. Murray (Toronto: York University, The Max Bell Business-Government Studies Programme 1985), 113
7 Ibid.
8 Canada, *Report of the Royal Commission on Canada's Economic Prospects*, 1957, 404
9 See Anthony Careless, *Initiative and Response: The Adaptation of Canadian Federalism to Regional Economic Development* (Montreal: McGill-Queen's University Press 1977), 39–88.
10 Frank Walton, 'Canada's Atlantic Region: Recent Policy for Economic Development,' *Canadian Journal of Regional Science* 1, no 2 (autumn 1978): 35–52
11 Quoted in Savoie, *Regional Economic Development*, 24
12 See Thomas N. Brewer, 'Regional Development in Canada in Historical Perspective,' in *Regional Economic Policy: The Canadian Experience*, ed. N.H. Lithwick (Toronto: McGraw-Hill Ryerson 1978), 215–29.
13 Canada, Department of Regional Economic Expansion, *Annual Report 1969–70*, 12–16
14 Walton, 'Canada's Atlantic Region,' 44
15 See Careless, *Initiative and Response*, 91–108.
16 Quoted in Richard W. Phidd and G. Bruce Doern, *The Politics and Management of Canadian Economic Policy* (Toronto, Macmillan 1978), 324

17 See Robert S. Woodward, 'The Effectiveness of DREE's New Location Subsidies,' in *Regional Economic Policy: The Canadian Experience*, ed. N.H. Lithwick (Toronto: McGraw-Hill Ryerson 1978), 244–51.
18 See Savoie, *Regional Economic Development*, 39–43.
19 Ibid., 41
20 Ibid., 59–60
21 Canada, Department of Regional Economic Expansion, *Montreal Special Area*, undated
22 This commitment led to a new special economic development effort for eastern Ontario. See Canada, Department of Regional Economic Expansion, Canada-Ontario Subsidary Agreement – Eastern Ontario, 20 December 1939.
23 See Savoie, *Regional Economic Development*, chapter 9.
24 Canada, Department of Regional Industrial Expansion, 'Speaking Notes – The Honourable Ed Lumley to the House of Commons on the Industries and Regional Development Programs,' 27 June 1983, 1–2
25 Annual Conference of First Ministers, Report of the Federal-Provincial Task Force on Regional Development Assessment, Toronto, 26–7 November 1986, 21
26 See Savoie, *Regional Economic Development*, appendix A.
27 Canada, Departments of Industry, Trade and Commerce and Regional Economic Expansion, 'Background to Community-Based Industrial Adjustment,' news release, undated
28 Canada, Office of the Prime Minister, 'Formation of the Canadian Industrial Renewal Board,' news release, 26 October 1981
29 See Savoie, *Regional Economic Development*, chapter 8.
30 Bliss, 'Forcing the Pace,' 116
31 Canada, *Economic Growth – Services and Subsidies to Business*, A Study Team Report to the Task Force on Program Review (Ottawa: Minister of Supply and Services 1986), 1
32 Ibid., 15
33 Ibid., 116–19
34 See Canada, *A Perspective on the Regional Incidence of Federal Expenditures and Revenues, 1972–73 to 1975–76* (Ottawa: Department of Regional Economic Expansion 1977).
35 See, among many others, 'Ottawa Offers Enticements for Tire Makers,' *Globe and Mail, Report on Business*, 8 January 1988, 31.
36 See Tupper, *Public Money in the Private Sector*.
37 See Canada, *Living Together: A Study of Regional Disparities* (Ottawa: Economic Council of Canada 1977), 160, 215.
38 See David Springate, *Regional Incentives and Private Investment* (Montreal:

C.D. Howe Institute 1973), and Carleton L. Dudley, 'Summary of a Theoretical Financial Analysis of the Long-Term Subsidy Value of the Regional Development Incentives Program in Canada: 1969–1972' (Ottawa: University of Ottawa, Department of Geography April 1974).

39 D. Usher, 'Some Questions about the Regional Developments Incentives Act,' *Canadian Public Policy* 1, no 3 (fall 1975): 557–75

40 Harold Crookell, 'The Impact of Government Intervention on the Major Appliance Industry in Canada,' in Donald G. McFetridge, research coordinator, *Canadian Industrial Policy in Action*, Royal Commission on the Economic Union and Development Prospects for Canada, Research Studies vol. 4 (Toronto: University of Toronto Press 1985), 73

41 Canada, *Economic Growth – Services and Subsidies to Business*, 1

42 Neil Brooks, 'Making Rich People Richer,' *Saturday Night*, July 1981, 30–5; see also Richard A. Musgrave, Peggy B. Musgrave, and Richard M. Bird, *Public Finance in Theory and Practice* (Toronto: McGraw-Hill Ryerson 1987), and Richard M. Bird, *Tax Incentive for Investment: The State of the Art*, Tax Paper no 64, (Toronto: Canadian Tax Foundation 1980).

43 See Savoie, *Regional Economic Development*, chapter 8.

44 See Donald J. Savoie, 'Establishing the Atlantic Canada Opportunities Agency, A report prepared for the Prime Minister,' Ottawa: Office of the Prime Minister, May 1987, 18.

45 See 'The Real Risks in the Subsidizing of Ste-Thérèse,' *Globe and Mail*, 2 April 1987, B3; see also Michael Trebilcock et al., *The Political Economy of Business Bailouts* (Toronto: Ontario Economic Council 1985), vol. 2.

46 Michael Bliss, 'The Battle That Business Lost,' *Canadian Business*, November 1982, 48

47 See, for example, 'Our Economy Is Improving. Let's Make It Stronger,' a newspaper advertisement that appeared in the *Globe and Mail*, 6 April 1988, A9.

48 See 'The BCNI – How Big Corporations Are Calling the Shots,' guest column by Eric Kierans in the *Citizen*, 10 May 1988, B1.

49 See 'Regional Disparity – The Light at the End of the Tunnel?' guest editorial by Rino Volpé, president of Conseil économique du Nouveau-Brunswick, in *Atlantic Chamber of Commerce* 1, no 10 (March 1988): 2.

50 Conference Board of Canada, *Annual Report, 1987*, Ottawa, 2

51 See Canada, *1988–89 Estimates: Part II* (Ottawa: Minister of Supply and Services 1988), 28.4.

52 See Public Policy Forum, *The Forum Salutes Four Great Canadians*, Toronto, 14 April 1988.

53 See André Blais et al. 'L'Aide financière directe du gouvernement fédéral

à l'industrie canadienne, 1960–80,' Notes de recherche 12 (Montréal: Université de Montréal, Département de science politique 1983).

54 Ibid.

55 See, among others, Brooks, 'Making Rich People Richer,' 30–5; see also Canada, Department of Finance, *The Fiscal Plan*, Ottawa, 10 February 1988, 90.

56 Bliss, 'Forcing the Pace,' 113

57 See, among others, Donald J. Savoie, 'Cash Incentives versus Tax Incentives for Regional Development: Issues and Considerations,' *Canadian Journal of Regional Science* VIII, no 1 (1985) 9.

58 Consultation with a senior business executive with a major Canadian firm, Montreal, 22 June 1988

59 Consultation with a business person from Moncton, New Brunswick, various dates

60 Consultation with a business person from Ontario, Ottawa, 19 July 1988

61 Consultation with a business person from Ontario, Toronto, 6 June 1988

62 Canada, Department of Finance, 'Economic and Fiscal Statement,' delivered in the House of Commons by Michael H. Wilson, 8 November 1984, 8

63 See 'Tory Government Brings a Change of Style But Not of Substance,' *Globe and Mail*, 18 July 1988, A2.

64 Ibid.

65 Canada, *1988–89 Main Estimates – Part II* (Ottawa: Minister of Supply and Services 1988), 1-22, 1-30

66 'Rethinking Industrial Development Strategy,' *Financial Times* (Toronto), 11 January 1988, 7

67 ' "Hibernia" Means Dignity for Newfoundland, P.M. Says as Oil-drilling Deal Signed,' *Citizen*, 18 July 1988, A2

68 See, among others, 'Hibernia Oil Scheme Nearly Came Unstuck over Firm's Demands,' *Globe and Mail*, 19 July 1980, A1, A2.

69 'Tory Government Brings a Change of Style But Not of Substance,' *Globe and Mail*, 18 July 1988, A2

CHAPTER 13 The ghost of spending past: Revisiting the guardians and spenders

1 See Edward A. Carmichael and Katie Macmillan, *Focus on Follow-through* (Scarborough: Prentice Hall Canada for C.D. Howe Institute 1988); Paul G. Thomas, 'Public Administration and Expenditure Management,' *Canadian Public Administration* 25, no 4 (1982): 692; and Robert Plamon-

don, 'Debt, Deficits and Dangerous Complacency,' *Citizen*, 30 January 1988, C3.

2 Peter Aucoin, 'The Mulroney Government, 1984–88: Priorities, Positional Policy and Power,' a conference paper prepared for 'Beyond 1984: Political Management and Public Policy in the Mulroney Era,' Montreal, 1 May 1988, 11

3 Ibid., 10

4 Hartle, *Expenditure Budget Process*, 270

5 See, for example, Canada, *1988–89 Estimates: Part 1* (Ottawa: Minister of Supply and Services 1988).

6 Quoted in David A. Wolfe, 'Politics of the Deficit,' in G. Bruce Doern, Research Coordinator, *The Politics of Economic Policy*, Royal Commission on the Economic Union and Development Prospects for Canada, Research Studies vol. 40 (Toronto: University of Toronto Press 1985), 113

7 Canada, Department of Finance, *The Federal Deficit in Perspective*, April 1983, 5

8 See, among many others, David A. Wolfe, 'Politics of the Deficit,' 111–56.

9 Canada, Department of Finance, *The Federal Deficit in Perspective*, April 1983, 8

10 Consultation with central agency officials, Ottawa, various dates

11 Canada, Department of Finance, Budget Papers, *The Fiscal Plan*, February 1986, 63

12 G. Bruce Doern, 'Tax Expenditures and Tory Times: More or Less Policy Discretion,' in *How Ottawa Spends*, ed. Katherine A. Graham (Ottawa: Carleton University Press forthcoming)

13 Ibid.

14 A comparative study of government spending reveals that 'Canada ... experienced a larger increase in spending over the two previous decades than ... three nations: between the mid-1960s and the early 1980s, the share of GDP absorbed by government spending expanded by about 40 percent in Canada, compared to increases of 25 percent in the United States and France and 33 percent in Britain. However ... the Canadian public economy is considerably larger than that of the United States and those of southern Europe and the Pacific but somewhat smaller than those of Britain, France, West Germany and Italy ...' The reader should note that the author looked at total expenditures by all governments. See David R. Cameron, 'The Growth of Government Spending: The Canadian Experience in Comparative Perspective,' in

Keith Bouting, Research Coordinator, *State and Society: Canada in Comparative Perspective*, Royal Commission on the Economic Union and Development Prospects for Canada, Research Studies vol. 31 (Toronto: University of Toronto Press 1986), 26

15 Canada, Treasury Board secretariat, Expenditures and Program Review, November 1984

16 Canada, Department of Finance, Economic and Fiscal Statement, 8 November 1984

17 Canada, Department of Finance, *The Fiscal Plan*, 10 February 1988, especially 13–18, 37–46

18 See, among many others, 'Wilson Gambles on Good Times,' *Financial Post*, 15 February 1988, 1.

19 Quoted in ibid. It is also important to note that finance officials calculate that each percentage point change in economic growth has a $1.3 million (1988) impact on the deficit.

20 Canada, Department of Finance, *The Fiscal Plan*, 10 February 1988, especially 13–18, 37–46

21 Quoted in 'Interest Rate Level Key to Pre-election Spending or Deficit Cut,' *Globe and Mail*, 17 February 1988, A3

22 See, among others, Hyman Solomon, 'Wilson Had to Fight Hard to Do Little,' *Financial Post*, 15 February 1988; Carmichael and Macmillan, *Focus on Follow-through*, chapter 4; and Jack McArthur, 'It's a Pity All Those Deficit-Haters Accept Fiscal Immorality So Easily,' *Toronto Star*, 14 February 1988.

23 Quoted in William Watson, 'Other Views,' *Financial Post*, 19 February 1988

24 Paul G. Thomas, 'Public Administration and Expenditure Management,' *Canadian Public Administration* 25, no 4 (1982): 682

25 Ibid., 683

26 E.J. Benson, 'Budget Breakthrough: Adoption of PPB,' *Canadian Tax Journal* XVI (May-June 1968): 161–7

27 There is a wide body of literature on PPB. See, among many others, James Cutt, 'The Program Budgeting Approach of Public Expenditure: A Conceptual Review,' *Canadian Public Administration* 13, no 4 (1970): 396–426, and A.W. Johnson, 'Planning, Programming and Budgeting in Canada,' *Public Administration Review* 33, no 1 (January-February 1973): 23–30.

28 Adie and Thomas, *Canadian Public Administration* (1982), 172

29 See Sandford F. Borins, 'The Theory and Practice of Envelope Budget-

ing,' Faculty of Administration Studies, York University, January 1980, mimeo.

30 Simpson, *Discipline of Power*, 122

31 See, among many others, R. Van Loon, 'Stop the Music: The Current Policy and Expenditure Management System in Ottawa,' *Canadian Public Administration* 24, no 2 (1981).

32 See, Canada, Department of Finance, *Securing Economic Renewal: The Budget Speech*, 23 May 1985.

33 Jeffrey Simpson, 'Beyond the Headlines,' *Globe and Mail*, 7 April 1988, A6

34 Quoted in ibid.

35 French, *How Ottawa Decides*, 31

36 John K. Galbraith, *Economics in Perspective: A Critical History* (Boston: Thomas Allen & Son 1987)

37 Aaron Wildavsky, 'From Chaos Comes Opportunity: The Movement toward Spending Limits in American and Canadian Budgeting,' *Canadian Public Administration* 26, no 2 (1983): 170.

38 Rod Dobell, 'Pressing the Envelope: The Significance of the New, Top-Down System of Expenditure Management in Ottawa,' *Policy Options* 2, no 5 (November-December 1981): 17

39 Thomas, 'Public Administration and Expenditure Management,' 682

40 Adie and Thomas, *Canadian Public Administration*, 147

41 See Richard Johnson, *Public Opinion and Public Policy in Canada. Questions of Confidence*, Royal Commission on the Economic Union and Development Prospects for Canada, Research Studies vol. 35 (Toronto: University of Toronto Press 1985), 129.

42 Quoted in A. Selson, p. x of the preface to G. Tullock, *The Vote Motive* (London: Institute of Economic Affairs 1976)

43 Anthony Downs, *An Economic Theory of Democracy* (New York: Harper and Row 1957), 28

44 Niskanen, *Bureaucracy and Representative Government*, and *Bureaucracy: Servant or Master?*

45 Hartle, *Expenditure Budget Process*, 287

46 See Savoie, *Regional Economic Development*.

47 Consultation with a senior federal government official, Ottawa, various dates

48 Consultation with a cabinet minister, Ottawa, various dates

49 'Western Premiers Slam Fat Cat Ontario over Interest Rates and Federal Contracts,' *Gazette* (Montreal), 21 May 1988, B1

50 'The Politics of Hibernia,' *Globe and Mail*, 19 July 1988, A6
51 See Benjamin Higgins and Donald J. Savoie, 'Canadian Regional Development Planning at Home and Abroad: A Comparative Perspective,' *Canadian Journal of Development Studies* VIII, no 2 (1987): 227–50.
52 See, among many others, 'Atlantic Agency Fights to Establish Reputation,' *Globe and Mail*, 24 December 1987, A8.
53 Canada, Department of Finance, *Economic Development for Canada in the 1980s*, November 1981, 11
54 Bill Rompkey, MP, 'Signed, Sealed, Delivered!' House of Commons, undated
55 'Toronto Riding Got Contracts Valued at $1.3 Billion,' *Gazette*, 21 November 1987, A6
56 See, among many others, David Daubney, MP, 'Quarterly Report,' House of Commons, 'Householder,' June 1988, 3.
57 'Hewers No More,' *Globe and Mail*, 10 November 1987, A10
58 Ibid.
59 Ibid.
60 See, among others, 'Le Québec aura sa part des programmes spatiaux fédéraux,' *La Presse* (Montréal), 21 May 1988, A1.
61 See 'A Lot of Things Aren't Fair in Provincial Farm Subsidies,' *Globe and Mail*, 31 December 1987, B1, B2.
62 'Alberta Carries the Biggest Load, Study of Regional Transfers Show,' *Globe and Mail*, 28 December 1987, B5
63 'Manitoba Ex-minister Regrets Meech Signing,' *Globe and Mail*, 29 December 1988, A3
64 Quoted in 'Submarine Program Foundering over Fears about Cost,' *Globe and Mail*, 24 June 1988, A9
65 Consultations with federal government officials, Ottawa, various dates
66 Consultation with various central agency and Ministry of Transport officials, Ottawa, various dates
67 Consultations with federal government officials, Ottawa, various dates
68 See 'Less Is More,' *Report on Business Magazine*, June 1988, 90–101.
69 Niskanen, *Bureaucracy and Representative Government*, 159
70 See, among others, Guy B. Peters, *The Politics of Bureaucracy: A Comparative Perspective* (New York: Longman 1978), 175.
71 Niskanen, *Bureaucracy and Representative Government*, 40
72 André Blais and Stéphane Dion, 'Are Bureaucrats Budget Maximizers? The Niskanen Model and Its Critics,' Department of Political Science, Université de Montréal, August 1988, mimeo., 22
73 Ibid., 29–30

74 Ibid., 22
75 Ian Stewart, 'Consensus, Flexibility and Equity,' *Canadian Public Policy* 12, no 2 (1986): 312
76 Consultation with various central agency and Ministry of Transport officials, Ottawa, various dates
77 See, among others, 'The New-look Government: Set Up to Say No,' *Citizen*, 4 February 1989, B1.
78 See Canada, Privy Council Office, *Background Paper on the New Cabinet Decision-Making System*, undated.
79 Ibid., 1
80 'Mulroney to Crack Down on Government Spending,' *Gazette*, 31 January 1989, D1
81 See 'The New-look Government.'
82 Ibid.
83 'Inner Cabinet Will Centralize Control over Government Spending,' *Globe and Mail*, 31 January 1989, A3
84 Ibid.
85 See, among many others, 'Our Crushing Deficit,' *Citizen*, A Special Report-Section H, 8 April 1989, H1–12; 'The Debt: Where Does All the Money Go?' *Globe and Mail*, 8 April 1989, D1; 'Are We Sinking or Just Swimming in Debt?' *Gazette*, 18 February 1989, B1; 'Mathematics of Federal Debt Add Up to Necessity for Drastic Measures,' *Globe and Mail*, 24 April 1989, B1.
86 'Debt Needs Tougher Action, Wilson Says,' *Globe and Mail*, 11 April 1989, A1, A2
87 Ibid.
88 Quoted in 'The Budget: That Deficit Was Just Hiding,' *Citizen*, 7 May 1989, A10
89 Canada, Department of Finance, *The Budget Speech*, 27 April 1989, 5
90 Consultation with a senior central agency official, Ottawa, 20 February 1989
91 Canada, Department of Finance, *The Fiscal Plan: Controlling the Debt*, 27 April 1989, 30
92 Consultation with a cabinet minister, Ottawa, 22 March 1989
93 Canada, *The Budget Speech*, 1989
94 Canada, *The Fiscal Plan*, 35
95 Ibid., 34
96 Canada, Department of Finance, *Budget Papers*, 27 April 1989, 21
97 Ibid., 26
98 Ibid., 14

99 See Canada, Treasury Board, *Estimates 1989–1990 – Fact Sheet No. 2*, 28 April 1989.
100 Canada, *Budget Papers*, 25
101 Ibid., 24
102 'Navy Has Alternatives to Subs, Admiral Says,' *Globe and Mail*, 2 May 1989, A4
103 'Residents of PEI Cite Liberal Vote for Ottawa's Move,' *Globe and Mail*, 2 May 1989, A4
104 Ibid.
105 Consultation with three cabinet ministers, Ottawa, various dates in March, April, and May 1989
106 The minister of defence made this observation on CTV's 'Sunday Edition,' 14 May 1989. Surely what the minister of defence meant was that the Department of Defence was asked to identify x amount of spending cuts. The minister of defence and the minister of finance accepted the proposed cuts. It goes without saying that the minister of finance, in consultation with the prime minister, has the final say in what goes into his budget speech.
107 Canada, *Budget Papers*, 13
108 Ibid., 35